The Great Southwest Railroad Strike and Free Labor

NUMBER THREE:
Red River Valley Books, sponsored by
Texas A&M University–Texarkana
Doris Davis, General Editor

Cartoon by Thomas Nast appearing in *Harper's Weekly*, April 17, 1886, p. 253.

WILLFUL SLAVERY MAKES WOEFUL SUFFERING

COLORED LABOR TO WHITE LABOR: "No sooner am I really set free than you enslave yourselves, and at the expense of your families, too."

Cartoonist Thomas Nast echoed railroad officials in casting the Southwest strikers as foes of the free labor system, caught in the ideological "grip" of Missouri union leader Martin Irons and the voluntary "slavery" of unionism. In the drawing, the choices exercised by white labor baffle a freedman. Nast's depiction ignored the widespread participation in the strike by both black and white railroaders and the popular support on Gould's roads for the union strike order. Harper's Weekly, *April 17, 1886.*

THE GREAT SOUTHWEST RAILROAD STRIKE AND FREE LABOR

Theresa A. Case

Texas A&M University Press
College Station

First edition

This paper meets the requirements of ANSI/NISO Z39.48-1992 (Permanence of Paper).
Binding materials have been chosen for durability.

Frontispiece illustration, "Willful Slavery Makes Woeful Suffering," *Harper's Weekly*, April 17, 1886.

Library of Congress Cataloging-in-Publication Data

Case, Theresa Ann, 1965–
The Great Southwest Railroad Strike and free labor / Theresa A. Case.—1st ed.
p. cm.—(Red River Valley books ; no. 3)
Based on: Thesis (PhD)—University of Texas at Austin, 2002, entitled: Free labor on the Southwestern railroads : the 1885–1886 Gould system strikes.
Includes bibliographical references and index.
ISBN-13: 978-1-60344-170-4 (cloth : alk. paper)
ISBN-10: 1-60344-170-0 (cloth : alk. paper) 1. Strikes and lockouts—Railroads—Southwestern States—History—19th century. 2. Railroads—Employees—Labor unions—Southwestern States—History—19th century. 3. Gould, Jay, 1836–92. 4. Knights of Labor—History. I. Title. II. Series: Red River Valley books ; no. 3.
HD5325.R121886 S683 2010
331.892'81385097909034—dc22

2009028569

For Francine Cardillo Case and William Edward Case

Contents

Acknowledgments

It wasn't quite nostalgia for nineteenth-century "boomer" railroaders or old-time locomotive engines that drew me to the subject of the "Great Southwest Strike," although the monograph that first concentrated my mind on the pursuit of historical research and writing was Marcus Rediker's *Between the Devil and the Deep Blue Sea: Merchant Seamen, Pirates, and the Anglo-American Maritime World, 1700–1750*, a social and cultural history of an earlier era's peripatetic, daring, purportedly happy-go-lucky waged laborers. Nor did personal experience with unions or industrial work send me into the archives, even if a dozen or so years waiting tables taught me something about occupational identity.

Instead, it probably began with a small puzzle, one that I could not solve as a young person and that for complicated reasons I came to care about: How was it that my grandfather, a self-reliant and decent man, actively participated in his postal workers' union in El Paso, even though nothing in my upbringing in a Texas suburb in the 1980s otherwise associated unions with anything self-reliant or decent—that is, when unions received mention at all?

I cannot conceive of this book's fruition without the aid of Kevin Kenny and James Sidbury, who shepherded me through the academic world, both at the University of Texas at Austin and beyond. Their integrity as teachers and historians and the moments that I had with them in which I accepted the confidence that they had in me made all the difference in the world. The generous and perceptive feedback from Jim and Kevin at numerous points in this project, and also from Eric Arnesen, Melvyn Dubofsky, George Green, and especially Alan Lessoff, crystallized my understanding of crucial issues and events, emboldened me to take controversial positions, and provoked fresh questions for me. It almost goes without saying that I am wholly responsible for the outcome.

I am indebted to my professors at the University of Texas at Austin—Howard Miller, George Forgie, Shelley Fisher Fishkin, Harry Cleaver, and Milton Jamail—for the vital intellectual energy that they brought to the classroom, and to my companions in graduate school: Patricia Martinez, Ramona Houston, Adriana Ayala, and Lilia Rosas. I still remember warmly our dinners together. I am similarly fortunate to have known over the years David Ryden, Jo Bailey, Jane Creighton, Robin Davidson, Melinda Kanner, and Kris Anderson, my colleagues at the University of Houston–Downtown, each of whom, in his or her own way, has helped me to juggle less clumsily, and more efficiently and enjoyably, service to the university, teaching, scholarship, and parenthood. Special thanks go to David Ryden, who always gives me terrific advice and is never cross when I stubbornly refuse to take it.

The University of Houston–Downtown has afforded this project critical aid in the form of research grants and a semester-long sabbatical. I have benefited greatly as well from the skill, persistence, attention, and good cheer of the university's inter-library loan librarians, Anita Garza and Alice Lewis, and from the assistance of the staff at the Missouri Historical Society and the Center for American History at the University of Texas at Austin. Two editorial internships at the Texas State Historical Association thrust me out of graduate school and into the wider world of academic publishing, training me to approach my own writing with a more judicious eye. I am particularly obliged to George Ward for his willingness to entrust me with challenging work. For the map of strike towns, a word of gratitude to Richard Jensen for permission to use his digitized version of the historical Missouri Pacific map, and to my partner in life, Christopher Pharis, who expertly transformed this for me into an illustration of the strike's scope and intensity.

My mother and father, Francine and William Case, and my sisters Shannon and Angie, by their own example, have imbued in me a keen urge to do all I can to get it right, especially the gray areas. I cannot think of how to thank them enough. Mary and David Pharis, my parents-in-law, permitted me long breaks to write during family visits and reassured me often that I would finish. My final thoughts on the completion of this book turn to my three-year old, Josephine, my six-year old, Elijah, and to Chris. I marvel at their embrace of our rather jumbled existence over the past few years. To a certain extent, a natural exuberance about life explains their enthusiasm, but it also demonstrates broadmindedness about me. For that, and for the countless other ways that they sustain me, I offer my deepest appreciation.

The Great Southwest Railroad Strike and Free Labor

Introduction

There are all along the [Southwest system] roads out there a great many men who have no regard for organization or law, men of hardy spirit, energy and daring. Such men as have... taken up their homes out in the wild country... will not submit as quietly as the men they have left behind in the east.

—Terence Powderly, April 11, 1886

In every well-ordered institution a code of regulations, properly understood, and truly conducted, is desirable for the good order and the success of that institution, whether it be the simple domestic family of home or the more extensive family of the railroad.

—A Texas Knights of Labor Committee to railway receivers J. C. Brown and Lionel A. Sheldon, February 2, 1886

IN APRIL 1886, national union leader Terence Powderly was in a state of utter exhaustion. The preceding weeks of labor tumult, he confided to an associate, had added "a hundred years to my life. All over... they are showering work on me just as if I had nine lives... I have had ten committees to see me to day, from everywhere." He felt "unstrung," as though he would "never be the same again." Surveying the social landscape in 1886, many Americans would have understood Powderly's emotional disarray. The events of that year seemed to many to portend social collapse. Labor protest reached a crescendo, with 610,000 workers participating in at least 1,400 strikes, more than double the scale of unrest in 1885. Intense violence marked a number of these confrontations, from the coalmines of southern

Pennsylvania, to the streetcar yards of New York City, to the McCormick Reaper Works and Haymarket Square in Chicago. High tide came on May 1, when 350,000 of the nation's inhabitants joined a general walkout, demanding shorter hours. Historians call 1886 the year of "the Great Upheaval."[1] To one contemporary of the upheaval, the influential Harvard economist F. W. Taussig, one strike in particular stood out as having "the widest effects and the greatest significance." The 1886 Southwest Strike was "an extreme case—extreme in its magnitude, extreme in its methods and the temper of the strikers."[2]

The "Great Southwest Strike" effectively buried a historic labor agreement between the notorious, powerful financier Jay Gould and the nation's first mass industrial union, the Knights of Labor. It involved one of the greatest sympathy strikes in U.S. history, a cross-racial alliance in an era of Jim Crow, scenes of anguish, resentment, and bloodshed on the streets of cities and towns across five states, and an unprecedented use of state power against striking workers. Historians looking back several generations later have, like Taussig, seen the strike as a seminal episode. Observes Leon Fink, it "shook the entire social order of the trans-Mississippi West," galvanizing a "fierce debate over the very definition of progress and the question of whose interest it would serve." James Green ascribes to the strike "epic significance because it raised an essential question about American freedom: When a wage earner freely contracted with an employer, did the employee agree to sacrifice his liberty in return for compensation?" The walkout's defeat, William Forbath tells us, "turned the tide against labor" and helped to set in place "the main elements that composed" the federal courts' repressive role in the 1894 Pullman strike.[3]

Although the "Great Southwest Strike" is commonly referenced in historical monographs and syntheses, this book is the first in more than sixty years to sift through the mass of evidence left behind and offer a new interpretation of its causes, trajectory, and meaning. How can it be that this conflict has no recent historian, when no shortage of scholarly attention has been spent on the Knights of Labor, the union associated with the walkout, or the other crucial railway strikes of the Gilded Age and Progressive Era—the 1877 strike, the 1888 Burlington strike, the 1894 Pullman strike, and the 1922 railway shopmen's strike?[4]

The dearth of in-depth treatments is curious given the outdated and romantic character of the last book-length study of the strike, authored by

Ruth Allen. While Allen offered keen insights and amassed an indispensable collection of firsthand accounts, ultimately she tells the story in mythic terms as a battle between the forces of good and evil. Allen conceived of the Southwest system strikers, many of whom were organized by District Assembly 101 (DA 101) of the Knights of Labor, as "frontiersmen" who drew upon the democratic and egalitarian spirit of the West to confront the encroaching "corporate machine system" in the figure of the ruthless monopolist Jay Gould, and to defy national Knights leaders such as Terence Powderly, whose eastern character encouraged a more conservative approach to labor conflict. The rashness that Powderly feared Allen found "virile, courageous, and hopeful"—the western Knights' resolute, simple, and even revolutionary answer to "the industrial struggle" stemmed from their "pioneer" character, which, she regretted, is foreign to those who have accommodated to "the institutional framework of settled life." DA 101 leader Martin Irons, who received much of the blame for the strike's defeat, was for Allen, as well as for celebrated labor organizers "Mother" Jones and Eugene Debs, a shining martyr to the cause of labor, not the dictatorial, loathsome figure depicted by hostile observers.[5]

With two exceptions, subsequent historians have delivered a top-down narrative of the titanic clash between union leaders and Gould, the most infamous tycoon of the era.[6] Their debates mostly centered on whether the Knights' national leaders, particularly Powderly, or leaders of the Knights' DA 101, notably Irons, could have averted the conflict's disastrous end and, by extension, the decline of nineteenth-century reform unionism generally. To the extent that Southwest system strikers came to life at all in these histories, they are portrayed as an impulsive, aggressive, and undisciplined lot, goading an overwhelmed Knights leadership into a confrontation that it did not want and could not win.[7]

The only study that examines actors and events on the local level during the 1886 walkout draws a sharp line between the Knights leadership on the Southwest system and the rank and file. It echoes the judgment of contemporary accounts in the wake of the defeat of the 1886 strike, including those of some railroad and state labor officials, in casting strikers not as belligerent, reckless dreamers but as innocents at best, or, at worst, the pawns of more powerful, warring factions. These sources locate the causes of the unrest elsewhere, outside of workplace issues—in the drive for power by regional Knights officials, who misled, cajoled, and intimidated railroaders into accepting the strike order—or, strangely enough, according to strike leader Martin Irons, with a shadowy gunman who compelled him to call thousands of men out to wage a doomed labor battle. None of these interpretations accords railroaders and railroading much more than a bit part in the story.[8]

Surprisingly, historians who, beginning in the 1960s, embraced history from the "bottom-up" did not undertake a new investigation of the strike. Perhaps this was because the Knights' fight for recognition on the Southwest system already seemed to fit snugly into the thesis that gradually gained dominance, which, in general terms, holds that nineteenth-century American labor activists understood their world in terms of their republican political heritage, so that the survival of a Republic in their eyes relied on the moral and intellectual development of an independent citizenry, the defense of the common good against unbounded individualism, and the centrality of labor to society's measure of a "dignified life." These ideas stood in pronounced contrast to the ones that industrialists emphasized, that also were rooted in republican political ideology—the limitless pursuit of wealth and power and the sanctity of private property as a means of safeguarding the Republic from the mob and economic decline. For this generation of historians, "labor republicanism" represented a common language uniting diverse and often divided workers against their employers. As an industrial union that promised to organize and actively recruit regardless of skill, and across racial, ethnic, religious, and gender lines, the Knights provided a powerful symbol for such a common identity.[9]

One might think that the ascendance of "labor republicanism" as the prism through which historians observed nineteenth-century labor protest would have inevitably brought new attention to these pivotal walkouts, but they remained largely unexamined, perhaps because the standard accounts' emphasis on Gould's motivations satisfies a deep, abiding interest in powerful, ruthless people, especially ones who personify a society's worst excesses. Aside from two flattering biographies of Gould, historical treatments of the 1886 conflict invariably cast him as a sinister, power-mad figure who intentionally and methodically lured DA 101 leaders into a confrontation that would allow him to destroy the Knights on his railroads. The tendency to highlight Gould's motives and machinations has made it difficult to imagine reframing the story from the angle of railroad workers and their communities.[10] Also, while scholars have plumbed the depths of populism and twentieth-century labor movements among timber, waterfront, oil, and agricultural workers in the region affected by the Southwest strikes, Gilded Age industries and labor protest in much of this geographical area have received far less notice.[11] Hence, we do not usually associate nineteenth-century industrial labor struggle with Arkansas, Kansas, or Texas, states that were sites of fierce conflict in 1886 but whose histories are today popularly associated with cattle, cotton, and foodstuffs. Those potent images of an agricultural society clash with the fact that the walkouts on the Gould system made union recognition the issue of the day in strike centers such as Marshall, Dallas, Fort Worth, Palestine, Big Springs, Denison, and Sherman, Texas; Little Rock and Texarkana, Arkansas; and Parsons, Kansas City, and Atchison, Kansas.

A fresh look at the "Great Southwest Strike" bolsters the notion that, even in regard to the relatively socially mobile United States, class is not necessarily a dull, clunky concept "imposed upon the evidence." Borrowing E. P. Thompson's formulation, this study conceives of class as "something which in fact happens (and can be shown to have happened)" when human beings, as "a result of common experiences (inherited or shared)" in productive relations, "feel and articulate the identity of their interests as between themselves, and as against other[s] whose interests are different from (and usually opposed to) theirs." At the heart of this book, however, is a concern not so much with how workers related to their employers but how they related to one other and to a complex of ideas about "free labor" that they had inherited from the pre–Civil War era. What is needed is an understanding of railroaders on the Southwest system as historical actors and thinkers; their regional context; the social, cultural, and economic transformations brought to life and work on the western railways during the "boom" years of the post–Civil War period; the internal pressures and tensions within strike towns and cities; and especially the intricate relationship between race, gender, skill, and labor among the thousands of men along the system's far-flung lines who stopped their work in unison in shops, roundhouses, and yards at the blow of a whistle in early March 1886. This volume, then, offers a social and cultural history, not a business history, a study of union leadership, or an examination of community and leisure.[12]

One source on the 1886 walkout that beckons one away from a narrative about the national test of wills between Gould and Powderly, and toward the largely untold but equally compelling regional drama, is the transcript of testimony before a congressional committee that investigated the conflict.

In the wake of the 1886 defeat, the Curtin committee traveled to each major site of activity and interviewed a wide variety of participants and observers—trackmen, shopmen, brakemen, engineers, railroad company officials and foremen, farmers, merchants, boardinghouse keepers, local factory owners and Knights leaders, and city and county authorities. The record of witness testimony runs over one thousand pages and brings forth a fine-grain picture of the communities affected by the work stoppage. A tension is built into this source that is enormously interesting and revealing: on the one hand, one sees a grand democratic pageantry of citizens—especially railroad laborers, who otherwise left few documents behind—elaborating on their positions and relating in their own words detailed descriptions of both their ordinary lives and the extraordinary circumstances of the 1886 walkout. On the other, one confronts a war of words aimed at persuading rather than informing, obfuscating rather than illuminating. The transcript allows a reconstruction of some of the social relationships involved and also the arguments, beliefs, and prejudices of the participants.

Discontent first exploded on Jay Gould's Southwestern railway empire in March 1885, when a series of wage cuts moved workers, representing a spectrum of occupations and skill levels, to combine in a mass walkout. Smarting from the depth of strike sympathy in railroad towns and the standstill in freight traffic, railway officials agreed to most of the strikers' demands. In the wake of this David-and-Goliath-like stand-off, the Knights of Labor organized at a dizzying speed along the lines of the Southwest system and across the United States. When later that year the national Knights forced the financier-entrepreneur Gould to the negotiating table and exacted from him a promise to end, among other things, job discrimination against Knights members on his railways, the organization experienced another explosive wave of growth, reaching more than seven hundred thousand members from one hundred thousand only a year before, and its inclusive strategy and philosophy attracted to its ranks women and men, blacks and whites, immigrants and native-born, Catholics and Protestants. Because system managers routinely violated the 1885 agreements, a more massive walkout by black and white workers under DA 101 ensued in March 1886, beginning in Texas and spreading to four other states. This time the key demand was union recognition and the tactics were more militant. Strikers could not sustain the level of unity and support expressed the previous year. The courts enjoined Knights from engaging in even peaceable strike activity, skilled trainmen refused to leave their trains, and law-and-order leagues formed in town after town to protect railway property and reinstate freight traffic. Some Knights turned to the use or threat of force as a means of enforcing the walkout, and bloody altercations broke out between pro-strike crowds and company-hired deputies in Fort Worth, East St. Louis, and elsewhere. By mid-April 1886, the walkout was effectively over, leaving the Knights greatly weakened, the bulk of strikers unemployed, jailed, or blacklisted, and railroaders deeply and bitterly divided over the meaning of the crisis.

Three related sets of questions are central to the project of this book. The first concerns the relationship between race and labor. Why did a broad cross-section of black and white railroaders on the Southwest system ally against their managers and railway officials in the mid-1880s? What was the nature and significance of this cross-racial alliance? Answers do not come easily because accounts of both walkouts on the Gould system do not dwell on the issue of race. The strikes never devolved into "race strikes," nor did the railroads or the local press make much mention or use of race until late into the 1886 conflict. Before this point, much of what is documented was said in passing, despite the fact that the racially inclusive Knights organized in a region and era in which racial strife, racial separation, and racial violence were endemic. Moreover, although southern Knights typically organized locally on a biracial rather than interracial basis, meaning that black members sought an equal or improved position in the workplace but joined separate assemblies from whites, this instance of biracial unionism occurred in an otherwise intensely segregated industry. From this, another question arises: why did near silence on the issue of black-white relations, instead of controversy over the specter of "social equality," greet Knights' efforts for most of the upheaval?[13]

The story of cross-racial organizing on Gould's Southwest system points to the complexity and ambiguity of biracial associations and their unpredictable and potentially far-reaching outcomes. The strikes were rooted in the experiences of "boomer" railroaders, who migrated from job to job during the years of expansive railroad growth. By the early 1880s "boomers" found deteriorating conditions and declining wages on the western railways instead of the economic and social mobility that they had anticipated. The difficulties these men faced in affirming their notions of the connection between railroading and manhood led many to conceive of labor organizing in new, more inclusive terms. In 1885, when inhabitants of railway towns and cities embraced the cause of strikers as a rallying point in a larger, regional antimonopoly struggle, the inclusion of black residents in the communities' protest against powerful outsiders received little notice. In the aftermath of the 1885 gains, a number embraced the Knights' push to organize across lines of sex, skill, ethnicity, and race. While the hierarchy of race in the industry, along with the particular hostilities that free itinerant workers felt toward convict and Chinese laborers, undercut the universalizing ideology of the Knights, strikers succeeded in making common cause across racial lines. By the height of the 1886 unrest, black and white strikers claimed that they were "producers" confronting an emergent system of "wage slavery" bent on crushing "free labor." Their alliance was sturdy enough to inspire a wave of organizing, particularly among black laborers. These cooperative efforts spilled over beyond the railroads into the urban politics and cotton fields of Texas and Arkansas, and represent a kind of prehistory of populism in these two states. It was at this point, when the strike was lost and railway towns were in disarray, that the Knights' biracialism drew public fire.[14]

By the strike's end in 1886 a cross-racial coalition of Southwest system railroaders had come to see themselves, albeit uncomfortably and awkwardly, as a class with interests "different from and opposed to" to their employers, as a force preserving freedom in the face of a new form of bondage. A second set of questions flows from this: How did these western railroaders, and the Knights among them, relate to the Gilded Age's reigning "free labor" ideology and to the changing legal and cultural notions of workers' rights in this critical period? Finally, tied inextricably to these issues is a third question as to whether, or to what extent, "labor republicanism" captures the belief system of the Southwest system Knights.

A fuller explanation of "free labor" ideology is in order. A simple, static definition will not do, because the Southwest system strikers drew on older and newer aspects of the concept. We must gain a sense of the long view as to how ideas about "free labor" shifted between the pre- and post–Civil War periods. By the 1880s, both the popular and legal meanings of this set of ideas were in flux, but the general trend was toward a narrower definition than what had prevailed during the antebellum era.

Antebellum free labor ideology evolved out of, first, the Revolution's republican political ideas, and second, national debates over the merits of slavery as an economic system. The American revolutionaries' equation of the imposition of parliamentary control by imperial Britain with slavery and degradation led a significant segment of the revolutionary generation to question the systems of slavery and servitude that had served as bases for the colonial economies. The effects of this were slowly felt in the North, which had less invested in either system by the early nineteenth century. The gradual emancipation of northern slaves typically involved moving enslaved youths and children into indentured servitude or selling them south, but the courts there, under the logic that free will is essential to a society that champions self-government, eventually overturned even agreements freely entered into that held a laborer in servitude. By mid-century, a consensus had emerged against the notion of freedom as "a matter of degree." American workers and employers entered labor agreements "at will." This was the "core legality underpinning a conception of free labor that imagined American labor relations as a universe of independent and equal individuals."[15]

As slavery expanded and sank even deeper roots in the South, and as abolitionist agitation gained momentum nationally, pro-slavery advocates charged that freedom in the North was merely an illusion. It cloaked a Hobbesian nightmare, they held, in which employers were under no obligation to look after their employees' well-being. They could freely exploit their labor source, in contrast to paternalistic southern masters, who, these defenders of slavery supposed, protected enslaved people from the vicissitude of an impersonal market. Critics of slavery fashioned an elaborate attack on this line of reasoning. First, slavery chained the South to a backwards, wasteful economy, because the enslaved could not rise, and so had no incentive to work hard or well, while the ability of individuals, on a broad basis, to pursue their self-interest and to better their position powered a dynamic, progressive, materially bountiful society in the free states. Second, a free laborer's self-ownership, lifetime of noble toil, and self-discipline had an essential political value as well, in that he (at this point, only he and not she) therefore had the opportunity to gain the economic autonomy and the political virtue that nineteenth-century Americans considered central to the survival of a republic. A land dominated by idle masters and populated by a large dependent class lacked the qualities of independence and virtue necessary to safeguard liberty.[16]

Northern workers prior to the Civil War embraced "free labor" ideology to a point. By the 1830s, white men possessed the right to vote, and celebrated and exercised their political liberties. Any waged laborer could quit at will and move about in search of better circumstances, and the emphasis on the dignity of labor appealed across a wide variety of occupations that demanded great physical exertion or hard-won expertise, or both. At the same time, the cry against "wage slavery" in the North reverberated with many antebellum workers as advances in technology and the introduction of new, more efficient ways to organize work threatened the workplace leverage and social mobility of skilled workers. A cycle of boom and bust as well as large-scale immigration tightened competition among laborers in urban areas so that the ideal of marketplace freedom seemed for many to conceal a harsh reality of economic coercion and a growing gulf between rich and poor. The threat of wage slavery was perhaps greatest for black workers in the North, as they were subject to bans on skilled employment, other forms of jobs discrimination, and prohibitions against their migration to new U.S. territories in the West. Artisans, who possessed status and leverage, were able to use the precepts of "free labor" for their own purposes. They focused less on the goal of moving up and out of waged labor altogether, which was less and less possible, and more on the project of maximizing control over their property, which now chiefly took the form of their skilled labor power.[17]

There was more than an economic component to earlier, popular notions of "free labor," however. It was often linked to equal rights (the equality of employers and workers before the law), citizenship (the ability of workers to intellectually improve themselves and to participate in and influence public life), and the dignity of labor (the idea that honest, manual work is honorable and deserving of a basic competence), so that laborers of all kinds claimed themselves "producers," the chief contributors toward the nation's wealth and progress. This claim enjoyed some public recognition, as it was not uncommon for communities to "turn out" on behalf of aggrieved workers and place public pressure on the targeted employer to come to a "fair" settlement, with some success. In this context, as one historian observed, the "criminalization of trade unions clearly would not do, not in republican America, with its citizen workers and enshrined rights of assembly." The era's landmark ruling on trade unions, *Commonwealth v. Hunt* (1842), recognized the legality of trade unions and their right to use lawful methods to advance their members' position.[18] This ruling rested on a "rough compromise" between two competing principles—the right to individual freedom and the right to association. For Lemuel Shaw, the chief justice of Massachusetts who wrote the opinion in *Hunt,* such a truce was possible because free laborers have the right, Shaw held, to freely associate in forming a union and to "induce" by lawful means "all those engaged in the same occupation to become members of it," just as any other association does. The trade union's goal of pursuing a better, larger piece of the economic pie at the expense of the employer represented to Shaw not criminal conspiracy but just another legitimate attempt to compete in the marketplace.[19]

The legal power of unions to act was severely circumscribed in the post–Civil War period, as labor unrest intensified. It was in this period that the courts, and many influential Americans, came to associate "free labor" almost exclusively with freedom of contract. The rise of giant corporations and the great leaps in productivity and managerial and technical innovation undermined the older "producer" ideal and the "close link between freedom and equality." Economic freedom seemed paramount in this context, so that any intervention by government or other forces in the decisions of free agents in the market, employers or employees, came under fire. By 1867, judges saw even nonviolent aspects of strikes, such as mass gatherings of strikers, circulars that "contain appeals to the passions or are otherwise inflammatory," and a general "attitude of intimidation," as "dangerous" and unlawful "interference with an employer's business."[20] Senator Henry Teller articulated well the new, pared down understanding of "free labor" that emerged in the aftermath of emancipation: "No laboring man for a moment should surrender [the right of free contract], either to the State, to his fellow-workman, or to capital... Any interference... is an invasion of his right... The difference between a slave and a freeman consists mainly in the fact that the freeman may freely dispose of his labor... on terms fixed by himself."[21] In defending the economic rights of freemen to make their own choices regarding employment, judges were aware that the rise of national corporations and monopoly power rendered the playing field vastly unequal. However, they tended to see a more immediate threat in the large-scale combinations of workers and members of working-class communities that organized in response to corporate control and that engaged in boycotts, sympathy strikes, and strikes for union recognition. The courts worried that labor was a "rival law-making authority" that challenged the dominant version of "free labor" ideology with a "competing language of rights," which "enjoyed substantial sympathy or at least toleration among elected officials in industrial towns and cities."[22]

Judicial fear of strikes was especially strong in regard to the railway industry, the lifeblood of the national economy. It experienced wave after wave of labor unrest in the late nineteenth century. In 1877, when massive walkouts paralyzed much of the nation's railways, crowds clashed with militiamen, and city and state leaders and everyday citizens in the Midwest identified against the railways, federal judges intervened to seize control over events. They enjoined strikers and their supporters, who disrupted bankrupt roads under federal management or who prevented the movement of the mail, to desist or be charged with contempt of court. Federal troops and federally deputized forces moved in to restore the railways' ability to do business.[23] The injunction thereafter emerged as the courts' favored means of acting quickly and decisively against labor protest on not only federally managed roads but, in the 1886 Southwest system strike, also on financially solvent ones, and by the mid-1890s against a wide range of trade union action in non-railway strikes, such as "picketing, boycotting, organizing, and closed-shop strikes."[24]

Southwest system railroaders, then, confronted a situation in which the courts and the broader culture held up the ideal that employers and workers were free agents on the economic playing field, each possessing a form of property to exchange, unencumbered by outside forces. But, increasingly, employers combined, and their property, defined broadly by judges as the health of the entire business enterprise, was under protection from even nonviolent forms of labor protest. Discontented western railroaders lived in an era in which *Commonwealth v. Hunt,* the case that had carved out a legal place for unions to exist and operate, "came undone."[25] Their responses to this state of affairs can best be understood as attempts, sometimes confident and sometimes despairing, to grope toward reestablishing a workable, just balance of power between railroad officials and railroad workers. In this they drew not only on traditional and modern ideas about what constitutes "free labor" but also their experiences at work on the western railways. The failure of their efforts to secure a resolution had less to do with dissension in the ranks of Knights and more to do with external pressure in the form of blanket injunctions, backed by military force, against a wide range of strike activities, and the enormous strains placed on cross-class alliances in railway cities and towns. Still, the collapse of the 1886 walkout brought to the fore deep ambivalence and disagreement among Southwest system railroaders about the utility and nobility of postbellum "free labor" principles. This was to such a degree that, while one can still say that "labor republicanism" loosely describes the ideas and visions of this Gilded Age labor movement, to focus on railroaders' unifying moments obscures the powerful centrifugal forces pulling them apart, ideologically and culturally, particularly in times of crisis.[26] It was a profound sense of crisis, in the midst of the tumultuous "Great Upheaval" of 1886, which exacerbated the divisions among Southwest system railroaders and often sent them down colliding paths in their answers to the question of the proper balance between the individual and the collective. These disorienting circumstances are an essential backdrop to the drastic actions taken by DA 101 leader Martin Irons and other Knights on the verge of the defeat of the 1886 strike.

In this book, the term "Southwest" refers to the region through which Jay Gould's Southwest system passed and in which the 1886 strike was mostly intensely experienced—the states of Texas, Arkansas, Kansas, Missouri and southwestern Illinois. This may initially confuse readers, who likely associate Arizona and New Mexico with the American Southwest, and who see Illinois, for good reason, as a northern state, but from an eastern nineteenth-century American's standpoint, the conflicts wracking Gould's system were apparently in the Southwest. Their references to "the strike in the Southwest" permit me a less convoluted, if imperfect, discussion of the area as a whole and of the vast transformations that it saw in the late nineteenth century.[27]

The narrative is organized as follows. Chapter 1 traces the social, political, and economic transformations engulfing Southwest system towns and cities in the post–Civil War years, including the expansion of railways, massive migration, and urban growth. Black and white railroaders entered a region that was advertised as a departure from the competitive East and from the nation's recent past of racial and sectional friction and war. Anti-monopoly ideas flourished in response to the domination of powerful outsiders but also as a means of papering over divisions and antagonisms that threatened migrants' vision of the region as a new beginning. This common vision provided a basis for the community-wide backing of strikers in 1885, but its emphasis on cross-class unity did not anticipate or sanction the Southwest system Knights' class-based means, especially means that jeopardized their local communities' economic well-being and social order.

Chapters 2 and 3 explore the cultural significance of railroad work and the hierarchies of race, skill, and status that divided workers in the industry. The labor kinship widely felt and experienced at work on the western roads acted as a cultural bridge among workers and a foundation for collective action when management and non-railroaders placed stress on the mass of railroaders or conveyed their social and cultural distance from them. At the same time, a chain of command, organized principally around race but also according to skill, cut sharply against the odds of a common identity and egalitarian organization emerging and holding among railroaders. The distinct culture and material interests of brotherhood men, particularly, would pull them away from a broad coalition of railroaders in 1886, while the alliance of black and white railroaders would rest on a fragile base that turned in part on a long-held, shared hostility to bonded labor—Chinese and convict workers.

Chapter 4 outlines the conditions that western railroaders met with in the 1880s, the national Knights of Labor's successful negotiation of the 1885 conflicts, and the role of the Knights' "producer" ideology in inspiring a broad, formally organized coalition on Gould's southwestern roads. Over the course of the conflict, less skilled railroaders, whom their skilled coworkers and middle- and upper-class neighbors had traditionally ignored or denigrated, occupied center stage in a broad-based effort to protect local workers from the same distant, centralized, malevolent forces of monopoly that troubled small farmers, local merchants, and town officials.

Chapter 5 details the rise of the Knights of Labor on the Southwest system, worsening labor relations on Gould's Wabash, St. Louis & Pacific in August 1885, and the historic September 1885 agreement between Gould and national Knights leader Terence Powderly. In the midst of the tension, and due to the failure of the national Knights and the earlier community-wide alliance to shield them from management violations of the 1885 accords, railroaders departed from their local communities' anti-monopoly ideas and from their tendency to look to the national office for solutions. They instead embraced internal mechanisms, backed by the threat of mass action, for resolving labor conflict. These mechanisms, in the form of a regional Knights body, DA 101, depended not on the intervention of the national Knights or public officials but on the power of railway workers themselves to immobilize freight traffic. That power turned on the Knights' ability to attract members across lines of skill, race, and even sex, without disturbing in any obvious way white supremacy or the masculine sphere of railway work and unionism.

Chapter 6 explains the reasons for the 1886 walkout on first the Texas & Pacific (T&P), an insolvent road under federal management, and then the rash of sympathy strikes on the Missouri Pacific and other solvent Gould roads. The 1886 labor trouble was not a product of reckless decisions on the part of DA 101, or, as Martin Irons later alleged, the illicit maneuvers of a mysterious, armed man. DA 101 leaders responded to real and serious circumstances on the ground facing the Knights on the system. The defeat of the walkout was due chiefly to the unprecedented use of injunctive power by federal courts rather than to internal friction over race, strategy, or philosophy. Nevertheless, the reverses that strikers met laid bare deep fissures among railroaders over the lengths to which they should go in defending the Knights' cause.

Chapter 7 describes the divisive effects of violence on the strike, the fate of the Knights' biracial strategy, the legal precedents established with the Gould system strikes, and the punishing public attacks on Martin Irons in the aftermath of the strike and the Haymarket bombing. An examination of the strike's bloody height reveals that, in issuing anti-labor injunctions, judges did not wholly impose postbellum notions of "free labor" upon workers, as many historians have held; instead, such ideas resonated with a number of Southwest system railroaders—the belief that, while neither workers nor employers had the right to harm the public or community interest, the exercise of freedom of contract was sacred. While a significant body of Knights acted according to a set of values that accepted pro-strike assaults upon persons and property, the fragmenting effects of union violence on the Knights' movement and the words of strikers themselves suggest that the individualist emphasis of Gilded Age "free labor" ideology appealed to the hearts and minds of many others. In effect, the Southwest system strikers stood caught between contradictory systems of thought on the relationship between individual liberty and freedom of association.

The story of the "Great Southwest Strike" defies the boundaries of what we think we know or might expect of the history of Gilded Age America. Intense struggles over the terms of work shook not just the manufacturing centers of the Northeast and Midwest but also small and large railway towns throughout the vast intersection of the South and West, a locale that in the twenty-first century has virtually no public memory of any connection to industrial strife. We see the railroad industry itself at a junction, between a freewheeling, expansive, confident age and a more closed, anxious, and volatile one. Within that context, in the space of little more than a year, radical events radicalized a broad collection of western railroaders, who moved from the edges of their communities' awareness to the center of a powerful anti-monopoly movement in the region, and then from a guarded hope for a negotiated harmony of interests between employers and organized employees, to a realization that the ground had shifted beneath their feet; "free labor" in this new context meant no longer a "rough compromise" between individual freedom and the right of association but merely the freedom to hire on and the freedom to quit. As that realization set in, we see desperate scuffles between strikers and former strikers, and brutal encounters between Knights and the private and public armies of railways. The question of whether an uncompromising commitment to ideals in the face of mammoth setbacks is heroic or foolish, forward or backward thinking, life-affirming or life-denying, selfish or altruistic was at the crux of the Knights' dilemma in the strike's concluding phase. Finally, in the sweep of these events, we catch glimpses of optimism among a number of black southerners about the prospect for change, at work, in their communities, and at the polls. Many energetically take up the Knights as a new form of self-help and self-organization, and as a new chance for biracial coalition in the wake of Reconstruction's overthrow, reminding us that these actors did not know what was coming in the late 1890s—the defeat of urban and rural populism, the virtual snuffing out of a black political voice, the overpowering terror of racial violence, a nearly all-encompassing system of separate and unequal, and the dominance of the racially exclusive, craft-based American Federation of Labor. Nor did they, or their white allies in 1886, foresee that by the early twentieth century, the language of the republic would yield wholly to the language of the market, and the national alarm over social class, if not the realities of class and industrial violence, would give way to an emphasis on the transcendence of class through social reform and reconciliation.

CHAPTER 1

Constructing a New Southwest

THE RAILWAY STRIKES OF 1885–1886 galvanized men and women in towns and cities along the lines of the Gould system, in places as distinct as Marshall, a small town in rural East Texas with deep roots in cotton and slavery; St. Louis, a booming industrial metropolis with a large European immigrant population and a more ambiguous relationship to the Old South; and Fort Worth, a long-time center of the cattle trade and symbol of the western frontier. It involved locales heavily dependent upon railroads but also those with mixed economies, in which railroads occupied an important but not dominant place. What characteristics did these otherwise starkly different areas share? What historical background and issues might help to explain why people from such discrete settings would respond to the mid-1880s labor discontent on the region's railways in remarkably similar ways—with a spirited community-wide defense of railroad workers in 1885, and in 1886 with a bitterly divided response that ran the gamut from militant opposition to militant support of strikers' tactics and goals?

The most obvious and crucial tie between these towns and cities was the Gould railway system itself, a network of roads that laced the region and linked it to the West, Midwest, and East by 1884. Railroads fueled a whole host of changes to towns and cities, large and small, along the lines of the Southwest system: massive migration, explosive urban and industrial growth, and volatile economic prospects. These transformations came to a region already experiencing turmoil in the wake of civil war, Reconstruction, and what many white southern Democrats deemed "redemption." Inhabitants' overriding ideological response to this maelstrom was to latch onto the notion that prosperity and progress would surely cool the sectional and racial hostilities that had so troubled Americans during the previous decades. Their optimism was a bit forced. Haunting southwestern communities was a deep undercurrent of foreboding about the influence of eastern financiers and capitalists, the industrial protests of the skilled and unskilled laborers whom railroads and commerce had helped to attract, and the relationship between black and white migrants, who competed fiercely over resources and the very meaning of freedom. Those anxieties found common expression in the language of anti-monopoly, which, in casting outsiders as the chief source of the region's tribulations, permitted a broad audience, which was otherwise intensely divided, the illusion that the New Southwest was free of the dislocations and weighty controversies that had threatened the nation's past and continued to loom in its present.

Railroad Expansion and Migration

During the 1870s and 1880s the United States saw a tremendous boom in railroad growth: over forty thousand miles of new track in the first decade of mass expansion and a doubling in total mileage between 1878 and 1890. Most of this new construction took place in new, sparsely populated areas in the West, but a sizeable percentage affected locales already accessible by rail. Building crews, working at a fevered pace, crisscrossed the states that the Southwest strikes later engulfed. Two decades of railroad building in Arkansas brought the state's total track from roughly seven hundred miles to 2,373 miles. The density of roads in Kansas and Texas tripled. By 1890, Kansas, Illinois, and Texas topped the other states in total mileage.[1]

Railroads often preceded significant U.S. immigration to the West. Wherever companies laid their track, settlers flooded into the region. The influx of new people must have been both exhilarating and disorienting. Towns expanded with astonishing speed, averaging a growth rate of 75–100 percent in Texas in the 1870s.[2] During the 1880s the population of St. Louis grew by nearly one-third, to well over four hundred thousand people, and the much smaller Missouri community of Moberly, dubbed "Magic City," swelled from six thousand to ten thousand in only five years after it acquired the machine and repair shop of a major railway. Parsons, Kansas, was a "well-settled town of some three thousand" enjoying a "comfortable existence" by the mid 1870s, despite the deep, extended downturn in the nation's economy. Like Denison, Texas, it was an "oasis in a desert of poverty" due to its enviable position as a "gateway for new Indian Territory trade." To the north, Kansas City, Kansas, was the "young, western giant" that one hundred thirty thousand people called home in 1890, its rapid expansion based in good part on cattle, meatpacking, smelting, and refining.[3]

In terms of the scale and impact of these changes, the experience of Texas is a case in point. The first railroad came to Texas from Sedalia, Missouri, and Junction City, Kansas. The Missouri, Kansas & Texas Railway followed the old Texas Trail and ended at Colbert's Ferry on the Red River in 1872, its major aim to link cattle trails with markets in the East.[4] When Democrats regained power in Texas in 1873, the party continued the Republican Party's practice of luring railroad companies to the state with enormous land subsidies—over thirty-two million acres for about three thousand miles of track. Local governments and landowners also got into the act. In 1875, Texas had only 1,650 miles of railroad track, almost all of which was in East and North Texas. Over the next few years, several thousand more miles of track knit towns and cities together, paving the way for explosive growth in commercial agriculture, the lumbering industry in East Texas, and manufacturing. By 1873, over six thousand miles of track reached Houston, Austin, Waco, Dallas, Palestine, Longview, Marshall, and Denison.[5]

The effect was to integrate the state more securely into an interregional, national, and even international economy. Fort Worth's railroads, for instance, opened it to trade with the West, primarily southwestern Oklahoma, Colorado, and New Mexico. Marshall, Texas, in Harrison County, was one small town that, according to the *Galveston News,* owed "its growth to the railroad." The T&P linked Marshall to Texarkana, on the Arkansas and Texas border, where traffic flowed north to St. Louis and west to Sherman, Texas. Its access to both the east-west line and to northeast Texas and the Midwest made East Texas a center for cotton marketing, and pushed cattle drives west. The Southern Pacific linked the state to California and eventually to markets on the Atlantic coast and in Europe through the port city of Galveston.[6]

St. Louis's nineteenth-century course illustrates well the transformations that the expansion of railroads unleashed. Once a major port for the Mississippi River trade, St. Louis eventually came to dominate the cotton trade of East Texas rather than the region's traditional seaport, New Orleans. Change came fitfully and painfully. The city's long-prosperous trade route to Philadelphia met with fierce competition from the northern railways that connected Chicago and New York, so that Chicago rather than St. Louis became the powerhouse of the Midwest. Then, as southerners recovered from the Civil War, and as the Cotton Belt moved west into Arkansas, Texas, and Oklahoma, St. Louis faced intense competition from the Gulf ports for the cotton trade of the Southwest, since it was expensive to ship bulky cotton bales by rail.[7] The cotton compressor and the Eads Bridge helped turn the tide. By squeezing cotton into much smaller bales, the compressor drastically cut the costs of shipping by rail and thus generated a much higher volume of regional trade. The Eads Bridge, completed in 1874, sealed this transformation in the city's status in that it provided a cheaper, quicker route across the Mississippi than the Wiggins Ferry, which had for years held a monopoly over the achingly slow cross-river trade. When the bridge formally opened, thousands came to celebrate the values it symbolized—national unity between the eastern and western sections of the country, scientific progress, architectural beauty, and economic growth. By 1880, St. Louis was the third largest cotton market in the United States.[8]

The Age of Steam did not wholly assimilate the Southwest into the national economy. Industry remained concentrated in the Northeast and major cities of the Midwest and West, such as Chicago, Detroit, and San Francisco. Texas mainly supplied raw materials to the industrialized sectors of the United States and imported its manufactured products. Large factories or a single industry did not dominate even St. Louis's economy, which instead revolved around small shops. Farming remained the most common occupation in the region. Arkansas built a respectable grid of railways that ran to large cities such as St. Louis, Kansas City, and Galveston, and saw growth in its timber, lumber, tourist, and mining industries; yet only somewhere between one-fifth and one-fourth of Arkansas workers made their living in nonagricultural occupations. Moreover, rural inhabitants in the Southwest were often not as connected to the commercial economy as urban ones. Those in the outlying areas often produced their own clothing, furniture, tools, food, and medicines.[9]

That said, railroad development hastened considerable industrial development. The history of Dallas serves as one example. In some ways, Dallas was an overgrown, somewhat unsettled cow town during the 1870s, but the arrival of two railroads in 1872 and 1873 lured manufacturing establishments to the city, as well as waves of tens of thousands of migrants. By the mid 1880s, many of these migrants worked in Dallas's factories, which included twenty-seven boot and shoe manufacturers, six blank book printers, forty-nine dressmakers, several brick plants and breweries, and manufacturers of cotton gins, cottonseed oil, and cotton presses. Signs of modernization appeared as well, including telegraph lines, electric lighting, and paved downtown streets.[10] Like Dallas, St. Louis enjoyed a boom as a major processing center. Its factories and shops turned goods such as lumber, grain, cattle, leather, and tobacco into products such as furniture, chewing tobacco, and shoes that consumers in the West purchased. The city hosted nearly thirty beer breweries, manufacturers of porcelain-glazed cookware, and lead paint pigment factories, as well as cotton compressing plants. While many of these enterprises were small indeed, St. Louis ranked fourth in the nation in the gross value of its manufactured products. During the 1880s, the number of its industrial establishments roughly doubled, from 2,984 to 6,148, as did the number of "hands" employed in industry, from almost 42,000 to nearly 83,000 workers.[11]

An element that many smaller communities along the Gould railway lines held in common with the sprawling industrial city of St. Louis was the presence of industrial workers, particularly railway workers. Railroad companies were organized into divisions, each of which might encompass two hundred to three hundred miles of track. In division towns or cities, companies established operating, switching, maintenance, and repair facilities, and also allowed changeovers of train and engine crews. Railroad operations in Marshall, Texas, were significant enough that railroad workers comprised about one-third of the town's population. In places as different as St. Louis and Marshall, then, a noticeable number of skilled, semiskilled, and unskilled workers labored for wages, according to strict schedules, and under factory-like conditions. Crews of shopmen, engine men, trainmen, and track repairmen lived amid populations large and small along the region's railroad lines.[12]

Migrant Dreams and Realities

The city directories, immigrant guides, and tourist handbooks are replete with boosters' claims about the region's opportunities and attractions. Although booster literature is by definition exaggerated—these are advertisements meant to attract migrants, by hook or by crook, after all—arguably they reflect to some degree the yearnings of their audience, or railroad advertising departments and industry-minded city leaders would not have invested so heavily in them. If these tracts are any indication, newcomers entered the bustling, rough-and-tumble, sometimes chaotic environment of the Gilded Age Southwest with ambitious ideas about their futures.

The literature, for example, abounds with descriptions of the abundant land and minerals that awaited exploitation, its special targets being skilled and unskilled laborers, farmers, and miners, whether immigrant or native-born. Dallas leaders boasted, "What a field is opened in this vast fertile and healthy region of Texas, to the toiling people of the older states, who own little or no lands." Denison's guide to immigrants called for skilled and unskilled laborers to help build the railroads, promising "plenty of work, at good wages," and living expenses far cheaper than in the North. To prospective farmers, it related, "The poor man who has been raised up amid the dense population of the old states... where competition in everything is very great, and where he has toiled all his life to get a start, and yet finds himself just about where he commenced, only older, grayer and more rheumatic, is fairly bewildered [by Texas]."[13] Kansas, too, took up this theme. Its boosters announced an "abundance of land for the poor man." In the spirit of appealing to ideals of thriftiness and hard work, the literature invited "any nationality of immigrant." "We only look to his personal habits to determine whether he is worthy," a Dallas directory insisted, while an immigration agency committed to "securing for the emigrant every possible facility for easy and rapid transit to her borders and rendering to everybody without regard to politics, nationality, or religion, all possible assistance in securing cheap homes and reduced rates of fare from all parts of the country and Europe."[14]

In the tradition of "manifest destiny" ideology, booster literature tempted readers to explore the Southwest, with stories of the "indomitable courage, restless ambition, and great moral and physical strength" of European explorers such as La Salle. One guidebook gave a twelve-page historical sketch of the Texas Revolution and the Mexican War, retelling this history as a story of "daring deeds and brave achievements won by our forefathers in gaining their independence, suppressing tyrannical rule, and wrestling from Mexico the greatest country in America."[15] Quoting Alexis de Tocqueville, it linked this history to the immigration of the 1870s and 1880s, infusing that migration with nationalist and racial purposes as well as economic ones: "It is not to be imagined that the impulse of the Anglo-American race can be arrested. Their solemn progress toward the Rocky Mountains has the solemnity of a providential event. Tyrannical government and subsequent hostilities may retard this impulse but cannot prevent it from ultimately fulfilling the destiny to which the race is reserved. No power upon earth can close upon the emigrant the fertile wilderness, which offers resources to all industry and a refuge from want."[16] Promoters of the Southwest urged potential migrants to identify with the heroic image of past settlers, those "earnest and determined pioneers" who were unafraid to exert "either fingers or brain" in carving out a new world for themselves. As one featured poem stated, "The rudiments of empire here, are plastic yet and warm; / the chaos of a mighty world is rounding into form."[17]

At the same time that the literature invoked the courage of pioneers, it stressed the degree to which Americans had already "civilized" the region. A migrant could enjoy a sense of daring and adventure along with the comfort and security of knowing that familiar institutions, cultures, and peoples awaited them. In *American Sylvan Scenes,* the reader is taken on a tour of this "undiscovered country," as if aboard a train themselves, passing through Missouri, Kansas, Indian Territory, and Texas. The traveler beholds an attractive landscape in which "not a moment passes that something interesting is presented to view... rolling hills and dales, lakes, seas, and rivers, mountains, valley, fields, woods, charming landscapes, picturesque and sublime, just as the creator had fashioned the elements." This is also a conquered region, one with "immense ranches," "thriving cities," "evidence of wealth and enterprise," "cultivated prairies," and "well regulated farms of corn, cotton, and tobacco." Readers are told that in Indian Territory, immigrants may view "aboriginals," now sequestered on reservations. Similarly, promoters emphasized that Kansas City was the home of "a merchants' exchange, manufacturing, a live stock exchange, hotels, and an opera house."[18] One pamphlet made a concerted effort to dispel potential migrants' impression that Texas was a land of "excessive heat, flying snakes, death from sunstroke, lawless men and mob rule." Another asserted: "The Savage Indian, the cruel Spaniard, the wild animal, the herds of buffalo and wild horses are numbered with the past. Civilization under a republican form of government has changed the scene."[19]

These tracts described a region free of sectional conflict. Migrants to Kansas need not fear migrating to Lawrence, for example, where pro-slavery factions and supporters of free soil murdered one another in 1856. The guidebook reassures that the town, once "shrouded in misfortunes," had entered an era of peace and prosperity." "If the Texan people make bitter enemies in times of war," one promoter held, "they are the warmest and truest friends in time of peace." The Southwest was a "heritage of riches available to the industry of present and future populations and by their culture all losses by war or illegitimate adventure may be made good," another asserted.[20]

Such appeals attracted black and white migrants who had seen the turmoil and violence of Reconstruction and its overthrow, but as one Dallas directory made abundantly clear, the Southwest was not a land of racial equals. Texas was "emphatically a white man's country." The city's promoters went on to explain that certainly "reckless men and adventurers" had dominated Texas's political life after the war, but since whites now comprised the majority of the population, there was "no material for misguided men . . . to work upon." The racial order, in other words, was intact and undisturbed. Public schools were not only free, but "allowed to separate by color." Racial upheaval lay in the region's past. According to this view, white domination faced few significant challenges from black inhabitants of the region.[21]

Advertisements reveal desire more than reality, of course. While the booster literature of most towns and railroads conveyed an image of the Southwest as unfettered, redeemed or unspoiled, bountiful, and stable, migrants found that in addition to opportunity and energy, the region was home to rampant racial, sectional, and economic tensions. Black aspirations, especially, ran headlong into the rigid racial hierarchy that white migrants brought with them and expected.

Much post–Civil War black migration occurred locally within the Deep South states but as William Cohen writes, the "dominant migration was from southeast to southwest." Labor agents brought groups of black migrants but many also came without agents by rail. At least fifty-six thousand arrived during the 1880s to the labor-poor state of Arkansas, especially from Tennessee, South Carolina, and North Carolina, while others journeyed from Louisiana and Mississippi to Texas. In 1880, over one quarter (114,000) of Texas's black population (395,000) had been born in other states.[22] Kansas was the most famous and popular destination. Open to homesteading, the state offered the opportunity for land ownership. During the 1870s, black migrants settled in Dodge City, Parsons, Leavenworth, Topeka, Atchison, and in all-black settlements such as Nicodemus, more than doubling the black population in Kansas. Most originated in the bordering states of Tennessee, Missouri, and Kentucky, with a smaller number arriving from

Louisiana and Texas. Still, the economic factors that drew blacks to Kansas also lured whites, especially from Indiana, Ohio, and Illinois. Although the black population rose dramatically, blacks represented a decreasing portion of Kansas's general population.[23]

While the hope for prosperity motivated many of these migrants, a crucial "push" factor in the decision of thousands to leave familiar surroundings for Kansas was blacks' crushing economic and social existence in the South. In an eloquent address to an 1879 New Orleans convention in support of migration, George T. Ruby, a key Republican leader in Reconstruction Texas, argued that black Texans felt that they had no choice but to flee: "The... ever present fear which haunts the minds of these our people in the turbulent parishes of the State, that slavery in the horrid form of peonage is approaching; that the avowed disposition of the men now in power is to reduce the laborer and his interests to the minimum of advantages as freemen, and to absolutely none as citizens, has produced so absolute a fear that in many cases it has become a panic. It is flight from present sufferings, and the wrongs to come."[24] As another black Texan put it, "Our old masters will ever regard us as legal property stolen and forcibly taken from them, and if they cant [sic] get our labor for nothing in one way, they will invent some other plan by which they can."[25] Kansas, on the other hand, was not of the Old South. Its status as a free state had contributed to the outbreak of Civil War. Kansas symbolized the possibility of a new beginning.[26]

The most dramatic episode of black migration to Kansas was termed "Africa's Exodus" or "Kansas Fever" by contemporaries. In 1879 a mass of black southerners landed on the banks of the Mississippi River, where many hoped the federal government would fulfill a promise to fund freed people's transportation to Kansas and to allocate free land and supplies.[27] St. Louis, which was the main departing point for Mississippi valley blacks bound for Kansas, saw a large influx of migrants. Much of the city's black population and leadership offered food, clothing, and shelter to the refugees, many of whom were desperately poor and had spent their last few dollars on the steamboat up the Mississippi River. But St. Louis's mayor feared that feeding the starving migrants would "set up the precedent... that would encourage others to come and depend upon the charity of the city," although, he admitted, "they would sooner die than go down South again." To reporters and those who gave them aid, the "Exodusters" related their stories of the "store" system and also of "cruelties and murders for political opinions."[28]

Like this mayor, Kansas whites tended to greet the arrival of black migrants with trepidation and hostility. Six years after the 1879 exodus, the state's Bureau of Labor and Industrial Statistics sponsored a report on the progress of black migrants in Wyandotte. The report recalled that townspeople had "prayed to be relieved from the incubus." It cited one Kansas City paper's expectation that, in place of free land, mules, bacon, and corn, black migrants would find only "a cold reception, actual information that they are not wanted," and "a people bent on looking out for number one." Comparing the "utterly destitute" migrants to a swarm of "Egyptian locusts," the report begrudgingly went on to note that "many of the original company have, by their own efforts, found and profited from the opportunities offered in Kansas."[29]

Whites in Anderson County, Texas, typically held similar enmity toward black migrants and embraced political leaders' call to attract white laborers and to repel black ones. The Citizens' Club, an independent party that came to power in the county in 1878 with the argument that only racial peace would bring economic prosperity, one year later called the Exodusters' migration the "most fortunate movement for the South socially and politically," one that it urged the county's black population to join. White citizens had long resented black political power in the county, where blacks were a majority. With the hope of ridding themselves of black laborers, voters, and fellow citizens, Harrison County whites widely embraced the notion that white labor was more industrious, intelligent, and enterprising and so should supplant black labor in the county.[30]

An article carried in both the *St. Louis Republican* and the *Marshall Tri-Weekly Herald* reveals strong racial tensions over access to basic resources such as land. The piece charged that "the Negro" dominates the rich, flat, cotton-growing land and "leaves . . . to his white brother" the rugged, high, thin-soiled areas. "We see the same general law in Missouri, for here, too, the Negroes are thickest—in Lafayette, Howard, Pettis, Boone, Hooper, Marion, and Monroe [counties]." In a strange denial of masters' authority to force slaves' migration rather than the other way round, the article explains why slaves were most populous in rich areas: blacks are "heaviest and most inert" and "drift to soil that yields the largest return for the smallest amount of work." Now, the article observed, blacks "crowd their white superiors out and force them to seek homes elsewhere."[31]

The above example points to the intensely competitive environment that both blacks and whites found in the Southwest. The economic strains for black migrants are clearly evident in the 1886 state report on the progress of Exodusters outside of Kansas City. Even among those interviewees who had advanced financially enough to live in a neighborhood with "neat little cottage houses, the lots well [e]nclosed, and the surroundings pleasant," several reported a lack of "steady employment," which made it difficult to "accumulate." A laborer, who owned a decent house, worried, "I am afraid my condition will soon be as bad as it was in my old home." A washerwoman noted that while she "would rather be in Kansas than in Mississippi... I am harder worked by the white folks here than I was in the South, and they are more grudging in their pay." "During the winter we suffer greatly from cold and exposure," a minister told the official. A number acknowledged the greater social freedoms that black people enjoyed in Kansas but thought that economically they would be as well off or better in the South "if colored men's rights were as much respected there as they are here."[32]

In contrast, then, to many middle-class black leaders, who emphasized the ability of black migrants to progress in the Southwest through self-help, self-improvement, and assimilation, residents in this community of Exodusters cited considerable material obstacles in Kansas. Those obstacles at times overwhelmed white as well as black inhabitants. St. Louis's poor neighborhoods, such as "Wildcat Chute," "Clabber Alley," and "Kerry Patch," were infamous for their "stark poverty." One area of alleys and tenements bore the name "Castle Thunder," after a Confederate prison where Union captives had suffered starvation. Immigrants and migrants crowded into downtown areas, driving up rents and transforming single-family residences into multi-family tenements and boarding houses. New immigrants and most of the city's black population lived in the downtown slums, or in "seamy little pockets scattered through the older sections of the city." When the famous English socialist William Morris visited St. Louis in the 1870s, he described its "stinking slums," where one could find "women and children... as squalid and dirty as you would find... in the back slums of an English city."[33] In 1880, only about one in ten St. Louis families could afford what contemporaries considered a respectable middle-class home. For the unskilled or an impoverished widow, homelessness was a constant threat. These conditions stood in stark contrast to the city's fashionable neighborhoods, such as Vandeventer Place, a "grand address" by the 1880s where wealthy residents lived in mansions along a "tree-lined parkway filled with pools and fountains" and protected by fortress-like iron gates.[34]

In part because of this gulf between rich and poor, labor unrest rocked St. Louis during the 1880s, when an average of one hundred workers struck every working day. In 1881 alone, the street railroad employees, brickyard men, brewers, ship carpenters, stone masons, boilermakers, and chain makers called strikes. Most of these conflicts, in 1881 and in the following year, were over wages. This is unsurprising considering that, according to Missouri's Bureau of Labor Statistics, "the expenses of two-thirds of the laboring class [in the state] exceeded earnings" during the period 1875 to 1880. The bureau went on to conclude that, since the previous five years were even worse economically, the majority of "the laboring population began the year 1881 with the accumulated debts of ten years hanging over their heads—in fact, bankrupt."[35]

The Face of Monopoly

Southwestern communities shared firsthand experience with the daunting power wielded by railroad companies after the Civil War. Before U.S. settlers even arrived in the trans-Mississippi West, railroads influenced where they would alight. The federal government granted railroads large tracts of land in the Midwest and West, land the companies could hold and sell. The power of railroads over federal land translated into enormous influence over where new towns west of the Mississippi were built, and therefore which towns gained economically and demographically from connection to the roads. Equipped with information on future town sites, railroad officials engaged in land speculation, reaping huge profits.[36]

After building roads throughout the West, railroad companies continued to exercise considerable control over the towns and cities that lined their tracks. The local elite often depended upon railroad companies for land donations to benefit municipal development and decisions concerning the location of shops and offices, for example. Smaller division towns were especially vulnerable to the decisions of railroad companies, because they owed either all or most of their existence and welfare to the railroad. Contemporaries deemed such towns "magic cities." Either the "direct or indirect agency of the railroad themselves" created railroad towns, which otherwise lacked "commercial or industrial advantages." On the state level, railroads lobbied hard to prevent regulation of rates or taxation of company land, bestowing small favors (such as free passes) and large (such as financial backing or incentives) on those politicians sympathetic to their interests.[37]

Resentment of the railroad companies, especially over rates and land prices, ran deep among many southern and western farmers, many of whom suffered under or feared falling into debt under the crop lien system. Due to the South's inadequate banking system and lack of hard cash, southern states passed laws that allowed farmers to obtain loans from country stores, using unplanted crops as collateral. The lien system worked well in the first years after the Civil War, since the price of cotton rose in response to world demand. Country stores, which received credit from wholesalers, made large profits by lending money to farmers and tenants, and marketing crops, especially cotton. Cotton guaranteed credit, which farmers with little capital desperately needed, and it also was easier to grow than grain or vegetables. Overproduction of cotton, however, soon reversed the promise of prosperity. Throughout the late nineteenth century, the price of cotton fell, and in a context of rising debt, crop failures, and high taxes. Yeomen farmers clung to their farms, but tenancy and sharecropping became the lot of one-third of white farmers in cotton states by 1880.[38] "Settlin' time" almost always left the tenant or cropper in debt to the merchant or landlord for the next year. Additional obstacles confronted black sharecroppers. The threat of economic and violent retaliation discouraged many from questioning or disputing planters' record books.[39]

To a broad base of people in the region, Jay Gould's Southwest system elicited mixed feelings. On the one hand, clearly the era of record railroad building meant new opportunities for businesspeople as well as laborers and farmers. Its corporate organization created professional or white-collar positions, contributing to the growth of the middle class. Like most corporations during the late nineteenth century, railroad headquarters were mainly based in the Northeast, with important exceptions such as St. Louis and Chicago, where industrialization had its greatest effects. There a manufacturing boom dramatically increased the nation's output after the Civil War, by 75 percent in only eight years. Railroads themselves drove much of this growth by transporting raw materials from the West to the East and stimulating investment in other industries, such as coal and steel. Because railroad construction required enormous capital expenditures, the banking system also underwent reorganization. On the other hand, one price of the more efficient, technologically advanced, and productive economy that railroads helped to build was that railways, like other major corporations, relied on a massive workforce of permanent wage earners, many of them less skilled. Skilled workers, who had previously exercised considerable control over the speed and quality of production and the length of their working day, increasingly met with challenges from labor competition, rationalization of their work process, and new machinery. In addition, the construction of railroads encouraged high-stakes speculation and the concentration of capital in Wall Street. Also, the tendency of the industry to centralize had its industrial counterparts, namely in the iron and steel industries, where large-scale factories were organized on a corporate basis and with national reach. Rather than compete for traffic with various roads at each major point on the line, companies expanded their domain. Finally, railroads' command of great economic and political power risked the movement toward a largely nominal democracy. Charles Francis Adams Jr. voiced this fear when he lamented, "Our great corporations are fast emancipating themselves from the State, or rather subjecting the State to their own control."[40]

Gould was a self-made man, born to a farmer, who worked his way up first from mapmaking to partial ownership of a tannery firm. He made his fortune as a Wall Street speculator during the 1860s by inflating, or "watering," the stock of the Erie Railway, which he controlled along with Daniel Drew and James Fisk. In 1869 Gould and Fisk scandalized the financial world by attempting to corner the gold market, touching off a major panic. During the hard times of the 1870s, many recalled these maneuvers with great bitterness. As his biographer Maury Klein writes, in the eyes of much of the public, Gould was seen as the "sly, clever, treacherous, enigmatic, elusive villain of Erie and Gold Corner days." This reputation dogged him, even as he turned to the more visionary and creative effort of building an enterprise, a "self-sustaining" railway system protected from the instabilities of cutthroat competition.[41]

By the early 1880s, Gould had gained control of the southwestern system of roads. After buying the Texas & Pacific (T&P) in 1881, he engaged in a series of consolidations that led to his command over the Missouri Pacific; the International & Great Northern; the Wabash, St. Louis & Pacific; the St. Louis & Iron Mountain; and the Missouri, Kansas & Texas. This network linked Texas with the East and North. It consisted of one east-west line and three north-south lines. The T&P linked El Paso to Texarkana in

Northeast Texas and intersected all three north-south roads. The New Orleans & Pacific and the Iron Mountain ran north and south, tying New Orleans and St. Louis; the International and Great Northern connected Longview to Laredo in South Texas and also included Galveston on the Gulf Coast; and the Katy stretched across the Mississippi valley from Kansas to Hannibal, Missouri. With the focal point of his network in St. Louis, he "controlled nearly all the railroads entering from the West."[42]

Gould's empire allowed him to avoid rate wars with other railroads, maximize profits, and expand roads into new areas. Competition from other railway companies posed some problems, but these were largely resolved. When the Southern Pacific threatened Gould's dominance in 1882 by connecting the Gulf and the West Coast, he agreed to divide the state's business with Collis P. Huntington, the owner of the Southern Pacific. They formed a pool in 1885 that allowed Gould to monopolize traffic north and east of Fort Worth while Huntington dominated much of the territory west of Fort Worth. Even with this huge concession, Gould had created a system that at its height encompassed fifteen thousand miles of track spanning the vast area from Ohio to the Pacific Coast. Newspapers crowned Gould the new "railroad king" who controlled the "largest combination of roads... of any one individual or corporation in the world."[43]

Gould's ascent to the status of "railroad king" only reinforced his notoriety. His financial strategies magnified public fears of his growing political and economic power and willingness to use that power for purely selfish ends at public expense. Reduced competition meant an absence of rate wars, which benefited Gould's railway system but hurt smaller shippers such as struggling farmers, who had to pay higher rates for freight. Gould also invested his resources in maintaining control of his empire rather than repairs when in 1883 industrialists such as Cornelius Vanderbilt sought to undermine him. Consequently, the roads and equipment of the Wabash deteriorated, creating numerous problems for shippers, passengers, and workers. Dilapidated equipment along the International & Great Northern and the Missouri, Kansas & Texas lines endangered freight and lives. Then after leasing the latter road to the Missouri Pacific, Gould sold his own shares and proceeded to neglect maintenance of those lines. Actions such as these garnered considerable media attention and led a number of communities to regard railroad companies, and Gould's system in particular, as irresponsible and unlawful.[44] In the case of East St. Louis, Illinois, the city's mayor charged that Gould's company owed East St. Louis $50,000 in badly needed funds. He protested, "Our city is continually called upon by corporations to afford them aid and assistance, yet they, or some of them, notably the Saint Louis Bridge and Tunnel Company, leased by Jay Gould, will not pay one cent of their taxes without litigation." Such policies reinforced Gould's malignant image in the eyes of the public.[45]

Two particular moves further confirmed this image of Gould on a national level: his purchase of the *New York World* and his control of the Western Union telegraph system. Gould in fact gained a virtual monopoly of Western Union, since its lines were strung along the tracks of his southwestern railroad system. As a result, Gould's reputation during the 1870s as an irresponsible Wall Street speculator was replaced in the 1880s by a more menacing image of a magnate who had under his command "not only a transportation empire, but a communications monopoly." His possession of economic kingdoms, many feared, "enabled him to rig the market, confound business adversaries, promote his enterprises, tear down rivals, and punish his opponents" while his "wealth and power earned him the deference of presidents, congressmen, cabinet members, governors, legislators, and, or course, judges."[46]

The 1877 Railway Strike and the Rise of Anti-Monopoly

As indicated by the East St. Louis mayor's charges, the power of railroads, other large corporations, and Wall Street did not go unopposed in the Southwest. During the two decades following the Civil War, and especially after 1877, an anti-monopoly movement gathered force. One catalyst for this turn of events was a railway strike unprecedented in its scope, size, and character.

The 1877 strike's roots lay in part in the Panic of 1873, "the first great crisis of industrial capitalism." The dislocations it unleashed called into question a crucial assumption of a major segment of the labor movement as to the relationship between laborers and employers. Prior to the economic catastrophe of the mid-1870s, strikes had been frequent, but trade unionists had more often than not subscribed to "free labor" ideology, which, in its earlier, antebellum incarnation, celebrated not only the economic freedom of employees and employers to contract with one another in an open market but also the equality of Americans regardless of social class before the law, and the opportunity to rise and to participate politically. As long as mobility was still within reach, craftsmen could identify with Henry Teller's famous defense of an unregulated labor market—"To-day an employee, to-morrow an employer"—and therefore hold out hope for cooperation between capital and labor. This vision hearkened back to a time when "workingmen" might well labor under an employer who was on-site and dependent upon his employees' skills. Despite the growing threat to this rough balance of power, unionists in the 1860s and 1870s continued to avoid the language of class conflict and instead sought to restore by other means the independence that skill and social mobility had once bestowed. Movements established projects such as worker-owned cooperatives aimed at helping laborers obtain capital. Activists also agitated for legislation that would impose an eight-hour day. The broader purpose of these remedies was to restore virtue to the republic by reducing dependency and allowing workers more time to participate in politics and social life.[47] But in the wake of the Panic, labor activists more often spoke of "the reality of conflict between employer and employee."[48]

The 1877 conflagration came in the wake of railroad companies' efforts to stay afloat by minimizing labor costs. Managers cut train crews to dangerously low numbers, neglected equipment and roads, and slashed the wages of its workers. These wage cuts came at a time when as many as three million were unemployed and more than four-fifths of those employed were underemployed. On July 16, 1877, railroad workers struck en masse. By July 22 nearly one million had walked off their jobs without any organization from existing craft unions. Within a week, the strike spread from Martinsburg, West Virginia, to Pittsburgh, Reading, Columbus, Chicago, Terre Haute, Kansas City, and San Francisco. The *New York Herald* remarked, "Not since the dark and threatening hours of 1861...has the nation been called upon to confront such a grave condition as exists in five states." In Baltimore, St. Louis, Philadelphia, and other cities and towns, discontented non-railroaders and the unemployed joined the strikers. In many urban areas, large crowds destroyed railroad property and attacked militia units ordered to crush the strike. According to contemporary estimates, more than eighty thousand railroad workers and over five hundred thousand sympathetic citizens joined in the unrest at its height.[49]

Thus, eight years before the 1885 strike on Jay Gould's system, St. Louis workers succeeded in organizing a general strike, the first in U.S. history. Beginning in East St. Louis on July 22, and then the next day in St. Louis, workers took over railroad property and successfully blockaded freight traffic. While the Workingmen's Party took the lead, at the heart of the effort were the thousands of unemployed and non-railroad workers who joined the railroad strikers. The *Missouri-Republican* remarked, "It is wrong to call this a strike; it is a labor revolution." Coopers, newsboys, engineers, molders, and mechanics walked out in support. About five hundred mostly black workers marched to the levee and agitated for others to join them. Many had demands of their own for higher wages and shorter working hours, such as employees of a beef cannery, who struck for more than double their wages. Nearly ten thousand marched to Lucas Market for a mass meeting, and gave thunderous applause to speaker A. Barker's statement, "They simply want their rights, and a share of that which they have produced." After adopting resolutions calling for an eight-hour day and child-labor laws, the strikers proceeded to shut down about sixty of the city's factories. David Roediger's research on the available data on strikers confirms the popular nature of the protest. While often strike leaders were skilled workers or non-working class, the majority of rank-and-file strikers were unskilled. In the end, six hundred "citizen militia" quickly defeated the largely unarmed strikers, who had grown uncertain as to their next step.[50]

No serious violence occurred in St. Louis, and in various places local militia troops were by and large unwilling to repress the strikers and their sympathizers with violence, but rioting and bloody confrontations broke out in cities large and small. In Philadelphia, crowds set fire to railroad property after militia shot into an angry crowd. The fire spread and was not extinguished until the following day, leaving thirty-nine railroad buildings, over one hundred engines, forty-five passenger cars, and more than twelve hundred freight cars in its path of destruction. Similarly, in Pittsburgh, crowds took over the city in response to militia attacks, looting stores and freight cars. Street fights broke out between strikers and police in Chicago, resulting in the deaths of forty to fifty people, and in East St. Louis, police shot into a crowd of strike sympathizers, killing eleven. Ultimately, over one hundred mostly innocent onlookers died in clashes with militia, police, and federal troops. This was in fact the first time that federal troops had intervened on a national scale to crush labor unrest. A total of nine governors called upon President Rutherford B. Hayes for troops to put down the "insurrection," although the troops mainly played the role of strikebreaker rather than peacekeeper.[51]

The community-wide character of many of the protests against the railroads went beyond the shared economic grievances and anxieties of railroad workers and their working-class and unemployed neighbors. In his study of events in Buffalo, Albany, and Syracuse, David O. Stowell argues that the large number of non-railroad workers peopling many of the crowds—mostly working-class but some middle-class—behaved in ways that suggested deep discontent with the railroads' repeated "invasion of scarce urban space." A variety of workers and nonworkers, including women, children, and boys or young men, directed their energy not at closing down workplaces but at attempting to block "grade level railroad crossings," where the frequent passage of steam locomotives and their cars threatened the lives, limbs and well-being of neighborhood residents on a daily basis. These crossings, and the streets that railroads used, had long represented "contested terrain." Stowell finds a record of protest by citizens, before their city governments and the courts, petitioning the railroads to end disruption of small businesses and the danger to the laboring poor, especially playing or scavenging children, workers en route to factories and mills, and women on errand to market, peddling wares, or interacting with their neighbors in dense tenement neighborhoods. While the question as to whether similar issues involving urban space galvanized St. Louis and East St. Louis crowds remains to be answered, sympathy for the strike was strong enough in East St. Louis (and one section of St. Louis) that city officials endowed strikers with police powers, to help protect factories and ensure continued mail and passenger service.[52]

The general nature of the protests "confounded the crucial distinction between riotous workers and law-abiding ones" that had dominated elite understandings of crowd action. Prior to 1877, editorialists and commentators mainly had associated mob action with immigrant groups and communists, urging "the real workingmen" to "separate themselves distinctly from the dangerous fools" who had confronted police. The national press had blamed the "vile" Irish for the New York Draft Riots of 1863 and European communists for the demonstrations of the unemployed at Tompkins Square in 1871. With the 1877 strikes, however, skilled railroad strikers had reportedly mixed with "outlaws" and "gangs of roughs" so that "the riots seemed to spill across divisions of occupation, ethnicity, geography, and even gender, expressing resentments widely shared in the working class." Newspaper editors had difficulty explaining away the conflagration as the work of those traditionally identified as the "rabble"—immigrants, the unemployed, and communists. The two main St. Louis papers vacillated, deeming the unrest the work of "tramps," "loafers," and "rattlebrained visionaries" on some occasions, and on others acknowledging the role of the "better class of workingmen" in street parades.[53]

Even more troubling to mainstream commentators was that the riots were not entirely chaotic. Instead, strikers and their supporters appeared to exhibit "rational sentiments of sympathy and solidarity." Discipline characterized the parades of thousands through the streets of Philadelphia and St. Louis. The organization and self-control on the part of workers created confusion in the minds of elite and middle-class onlookers, who wondered aloud if the American economic system had not created a tiger. Were the dispossessed on the verge of a bloody, class-based revolution, of which the 1877 strikes offered merely a glimpse? If so, then strikes themselves posed a terrible danger, because they appeared to have unleashed the tiger. Influential observers laid responsibility for the violence, social disarray, and widespread evidence of class resentment at the feet of railway strikers. Their actions had inspired "lawlessness" and "aroused a spirit which, unless curbed and quelled," shook "the very fundamental root of the liberty and life of this country." In line with this thinking, much of the national press during the conflict bitterly attacked those companies that had capitulated to their workers' demands.[54]

The *Galveston Daily News,* like many papers, linked the 1877 strike's violence and organized resistance to trade unions, which, it claimed, "were themselves infiltrated by Communists." For a time, dominant opinion solidified against independent working-class organization and strikes in particular.[55] This shift in the mainstream press's view of strikes and unions as inherently revolutionary brought about several developments that played a role in the Southwest system strikes less than a decade later. First, the national press largely supported an expanded regular army, the purpose of which was to prevent future outbreaks of labor discontent. Even in St. Louis, where little violence had unfolded, the city augmented the police force and built a National Guard armory only a year after the conflict took place. Second, the government response to the 1877 strike produced major legal setbacks for labor movements. In the midst of the 1877 unrest, U.S. District Judge Walter Q. Gresham maintained that workers who struck a road in receivership were automatically guilty of contempt of court and did not have the right to a jury trial. He then called upon federal troops to enforce his decision, which President Hayes granted. Prior to this ruling, the government had only called upon troops to guard federal property. Over time Gresham's decision enabled the federal government to suppress future strikes "not only for the benefit of receivers, but for all other businessmen as well." Furthermore, the federal government held strikers legally responsible for disrupting the delivery of the mail. Even though railroad companies had made a concerted effort to obstruct mail trains in order to force the arrest of strikers for contempt of court, the courts targeted strikers, not railroad officials.[56]

However, trade unions and labor movements did not face a wall of unmitigated public and judicial hostility. Many judges appeared to have heeded the warning of several labor leaders, one of whom predicted, "Any vindictive prosecution which may aim to inspire alarm, will not only fail of the mark, but will leave a dangerous remembrance." Most of those convicted of participating in the trouble received relatively lenient punishments from judges, despite the strong urgings of district attorneys and railroad officials to make examples of those convicted under Gresham's ruling. Those who faced the severest sentences spent three months or less in jail, although several were forced to pay heavy fines in order to secure their release. Juries similarly dispensed fairly light punishments. The majority of the hundreds arrested in Pittsburgh never went to trial, and only a few served in the workhouse and only for a short period, and in St. Louis, a jury refused to convict members of the executive committee of the Workingmen's Party on charges of inciting a riot. Nor was support for an expanded regular army universal among newspaper editors. The *Philadelphia Commonwealth, New York Sun, Pittsburgh Post,* and *Cincinnati Enquirer* featured editorials condemning the "cry for a large army" as "nothing less than a radical revolution of our whole republican system of government," as one put it. Although the fear of strikes overwhelmed the fear of a standing army among most mainstream commentators, a number of those who favored a stronger military also began to recognize the need for social reform as a "preventative cure" against future strikes.[57]

A variety of labor leaders took the opportunity to discuss the class character of the 1877 strikes as a means of agitating for reform. John Swinton, who published a popular working-class newspaper in the 1880s, warned Americans that such unbearable conditions had to be changed, or else the tiger might again become unchained. In his fiery 1883 analysis of working-class mob action, Swinton thundered: "The tiger is not mankind, though he may lurk in the heart of the community. He was bred there by Wrong; raised to life by it, and stirred to action; he would have no being but for it...don't let us have a tiger among us that needs to be chained; let us have neither tiger nor chains; away with the Wrongs by which he is generated."[58] In the same year, Samuel Gompers similarly pointed to the prevalence of mob action to support his own remedy for industrial conflict. In contrast to Swinton, who urged a radical restructuring of society, Gompers emphasized the need for organization among skilled workers. The future leader of the American Federation of Labor condemned workers' lack of organization as the chief cause of strikes and social disorder in general. Without the discipline of a trade union, he maintained, workers tended to act "upon illy-considered [*sic*] plans, hastily adopted" and "upon passion." Unlike Swinton and like many liberal reformers, Gompers distinguished between respectable elements of the working class and the disreputable and dangerous "rabble," which he identified with anarchism. Trade unions, he contended, would act as "conservators of the public peace" and "check the more radical elements in society."[59]

Indeed, labor unions gained new life in the aftermath of the 1877 upheaval. Although blacklists and dismissals almost destroyed the railroad brotherhoods, these trade unions and others, particularly the cigar makers' unions, attracted a host of new members in St. Louis and elsewhere. The labor organization that made the greatest strides in the decade following 1877 was not limited to particular craft workers but was instead industrial in character. Called the Knights of Labor, this organization had its start in a number of secret societies formed among Philadelphia artisans following the Civil War. Despite the threat of blacklists and dismissals, a growing number joined the Knights after 1878, when the order rejected secrecy and began to openly organize on a national scale. Rather than limit membership to skilled white male workers, as labor unions had done in the past, the Knights admitted and actively recruited a far broader range of people: blacks and whites, native-born and immigrant, skilled and unskilled workers, sympathetic shopkeepers and business owners, and, beginning in 1881, women. While excluding the Chinese, the order represented by the mid-1880s "the first mass organization of the American working class."[60]

The Knights did not emerge in force in the Southwest until the mid-1880s. Prior to this, new political parties organized in the region and made proposals aimed at alleviating conditions for discontented workers and farmers. Many of these experiments with reform, to varying degrees and in different ways, embraced anti-monopoly ideology, which saw several dangers to the political democracy in the changes that engulfed the nation after the Civil War. Industrial magnates, they charged, had accumulated vast amounts of wealth with little regard for the public good. The unlimited pursuit of economic liberty had generated tremendous prosperity for some but had also unleashed economic and social chaos. Equally explosive busts, they noted, followed economic booms, and high unemployment or underemployment dogged workers even in good times. Furthermore, wealth carries with it political and economic influence, anti-monopolists argued. What good is representative government if the rich and powerful can buy votes and court rulings with money and flattery, especially when many previously independent citizens find themselves slipping into a state of economic dependency? Since the American Revolution, republican political thought had held that the bulwark against immorality and corruption was a self-sufficient populace, but after the Civil War, bankruptcy threw many southern and western farmers into what seemed to be perpetual tenancy or sharecropping. Larger and more powerful employers undermined the leverage and autonomy of skilled workers with new and cheaper technologies and an industrial organization, which broke production down into a series of small steps performed by more plentiful and dependent unskilled laborers. The degradation of unskilled laborers posed further dangers to the republic. Poverty, economic instability, and long working hours combined with an intense pace of work hindered self-improvement and social mobility, creating in America a permanent class of the dispossessed alongside a class of the rich and well-born. Social conflict, born of misery and bitterness, would inevitably flow from such circumstances, anti-monopolists concluded.[61]

Anti-monopolist farmers proposed a number of solutions to the problems of industrial society. One of the first was the Patrons of Husbandry, better known as "the Grange." Primarily a southern white phenomenon, the Grange won support from farmers, many of whom suffered debt and declining prices. Over one hundred eighty thousand had joined the Grange by 1875 to fight the "money system," merchants, and railroad officials, and to help organize for farmers' mutual benefit. In order to combat debt peonage, Grangers supported cooperative solutions, such as the establishment of Grange stores, gins, warehouses, and brickyards. During the early 1880s, an offshoot of the Grange in Arkansas, called the Agricultural Wheel, organized several successful cooperative stores and used the combined buying power of its members to obtain farming tools more cheaply. Grange leaders encouraged the creation of agricultural colleges and crop diversification to allow farmers to improve farming techniques and more efficiently organize production.[62]

The Grange's call for "Greenbackism" drew thousands to the anti-monopoly cause. Greenbackers demanded the expansion of the money supply in order to combat falling agricultural prices in the West and South. By releasing the nation from the gold standard and pumping hard cash into the economy, their plan sought to relieve overburdened farmers and other debtors and to rescue the nation's financial world from the hold of what Greenback supporters called "the money power," "Wall Street sharks," and "bloated bondholders." The Farmers' Alliance, founded in 1877, championed a similar platform. Like the Grange, the Alliance stressed cooperative strategies for farmers and attacked the "monopolistic railroads, greedy bankers, and a punitive credit system . . . that kept Southern farmers poor." In the early and mid 1880s, traveling lecturers spread the message of the Alliance and Greenbackism to towns and farming communities throughout Texas and the Midwest with much success.[63]

In the late 1870s and early 1880s, labor activists in the Southwest allied with various farmers' groups to support independent parties in the hopes of forcing the political system to address the "people's" concerns. Texas independents drew an impressive number of voters away from the Democratic Party on the heels of the 1877 strike. In these states, nearly one-third to one-half of voters supported independent congressional candidates between 1880 and 1884. Economic divisions within the Democratic Party—between landless tillers of the soil and landowners, railroad supporters and railroad men, urban and rural dwellers, for example—provided independents a political opening. A state convention of Greenbackers in Waco in 1878 promised that the National Greenback Labor Party would "save business men from bankruptcy, the working classes from starvation, the whole country from revolution, and the Nation from repudiation." To broaden its base, it championed railroad regulation, frontier protection, low taxes, and public schools. This rhetoric attracted voters from both of the major parties. Surely the successes elsewhere of independent tickets such as the Greenback-Labor Party, the Labor Reform Party, and the Workingmen's Party, in southern states such as Alabama, Arkansas, Florida, Georgia, and Mississippi, and in major cities such as Chicago, Cincinnati, and Milwaukee, buoyed independents' aspirations.[64]

Yet Greenback supporters never became strong enough to topple the reigning Democratic Party. While they practiced fusion with Republican Party members in order to amass the numbers necessary to overthrow Democratic rule, this strategy proved unworkable. In the 1870s, the Republican Party represented only about one-third of Texas voters; most of its supporters were black voters reluctant to leave the party of emancipation and Reconstruction, whatever its flaws. White Texans, including many members of the Farmers' Alliance, remained solidly Democrat.[65] Nor did the Greenbackers achieve the passage of meaningful reform legislation. The popular call for state regulation of railroads pushed the Democratic Party to place a cap on rates and to establish a board to review railroad companies' annual public meetings and records. These efforts were also unsuccessful. The laws were poorly enforced, and the railroad industry's business allies blocked the Grange and the Greenback Party's petitions for more effective action. Western railroads were especially resistant to regulation, since they found it easier to control larger areas than eastern companies did. Eastern companies tended to favor some type of regulation in order to avoid costly rate wars, a problem that plagued western roads far less. When a number of legislators pushed for the establishment of a railroad commission, Jay Gould exerted his enormous financial pressure. He suggested that legislation would mean an end to the much sought after expansion of the Missouri, Kansas & Texas Railway in the state. Railroad lobbyists used similar tactics in blocking other attempts at regulation, despite the support lent to the cause of regulation by not only the Farmers' Alliance and the Knights but also business groups hurt by rate discrimination.[66]

Despite these failures, independent parties had forced the reigning parties to adopt the rhetoric, if not the mechanisms, of reform. The mainstream press, too, took up the banner of anti-monopoly. In 1882 Fort Worth's major paper published a poem entitled "All We Want Is to Be Left Alone," which asked why "a few corporations or railway rings / should hold in this country greater power than kings?" In its editorial "Jay Gould's Royal Train," the *Dallas Morning News* revealed, with unconcealed disgust, the size of Gould's estate (eight hundred acres), his seventy servants, and the $200 per month paid to his French chef. As president of Western Union Telegraph Company,

Gould earned $10,000 a year, compared to his messenger boy who could only earn that sum with forty-nine years of labor.[67] The *St. Louis Post-Dispatch* in turn bewailed Gould's influence on both the Democratic and Republican parties in Missouri, and lent its support to an upcoming anti-monopoly convention with this argument: "We would like to see a Legislature in Missouri throwing its lasso over the head of a man who has 42,000 employees at his beck and call. Go to California if you wish to see how beautifully a ring of capitalists can take possession of the transportation, the press, and the law-making power of the state... Such gentlemen are able to make judges and control courts. They are above the law to a considerable extent."[68] In Texas, Arkansas, and Missouri, all prior slave states where Democrats held the reigns of state power, anti-monopoly, anti-eastern, and anti-Republican sentiments fused and found a common foe in Gould. In 1884 the *St. Louis Post-Dispatch* commented on Gould's Republican sympathies: "Mr. Gould and the men of his class are doubtless satisfied with the favors they have received, and are not inclined to turn out of power the party whose favor has enabled them to accumulate such colossal fortunes at the expense of the toilers and producers of the country." In casting Gould as an enemy of "the people," his critics played not only on the region's considerable anti-monopoly sentiment but also on its antipathy to Republican Party supporters, whom most southern whites deemed meddling outsiders or traitors to the South and to their race. This sectional pride was explicit in an 1883 editorial that attacked the "ignorance of Eastern capitalists" whose "prejudices" led them to invest in established monopolies of the East rather than manufacturing interests in the West. Men like Gould, the editor perceived, stood in the way of the Southwest's progress, prosperity, and autonomy—in short, of a New Southwest.[69]

In many ways, however, mainstream attacks on monopoly and defense of "the people" remained within traditional boundaries of race and class. Anti-Gould sentiment, even abhorrence of Gould's labor practices, did not commit anti-monopolists to a deep sympathy for labor. One illustration of this is the *St. Louis-Dispatch*'s quick retreat from its attacks on Gould during a strike in 1883 of Western Union's telegraphers. It contended that a "private squabble" over money and hours should not "clog the wheels of the commerce of the country." While reform efforts had dampened the fears of class revolt that the 1877 strike had inflamed, the overriding mainstream view of strikes and labor protest remained tentative and suspicious. The press stood ready first to defend local communities from the likes of Gould, not class-based movements.[70] Similarly, the close ties between white anti-monopolists and the Democratic Party highlighted the racial as well as economic character of blacks' predicament in the South and in large portions of the Southwest. Exodusters interviewed by Kansas's Bureau of Labor and Industrial Statistics in 1886 protested, for example, the monopoly over political and economic life exercised not by railroad officials but by southern whites. One laborer complained of white men who, with the legal sanction of the state, made "a business of robbing the poor ignorant black man." A grocery keeper and ex-Union soldier spoke of how Louisiana whites had refused to allow them to vote in some areas and "in others only when they would vote a designated ticket." As Lawrence Goodwyn, a historian of populism, notes, "It was the *whiteness* of corporate monopoly—and the *whiteness* of those who wanted to trim the power of monopolists—that worried Negroes," because "both sets of white antagonists lived by the values of the American caste system."[71]

This is not to say that black southwesterners rejected anti-monopoly politics or that whites denied them participation. In the late 1870s and the early 1880s, a number of black political organizers and actors in Texas pursued "fusion" with independent parties such as the Greenbacks or factions of the Democrats. There were at least seventy black Greenback organizations in the state in 1878. In the same year black defectors from the Republican Party joined various "workingmen's" clubs and farmers' groups to attend the Independent Greenback convention in Austin, Texas, which attracted white farmers and mechanics but also blacks. When an independent party again challenged the Democrats in 1882, a meeting of four hundred Republicans, about half of them black, supported the ticket.[72] One Exoduster laborer and minister blamed the "legislators" who "are too willing to obey the demands of capitalists." An 1882 mass meeting of black men agreed that "a large proportion of the present colored residents of Southern Kansas . . . do not possess the requisite teams, farming implements, etc., to properly engage in [farming]." A reverend told the meeting of farmers that he had met over two hundred farmers who faced "high rents on farms, lack of farm houses for rent, and unfavorable terms." For this he condemned the government, which had "given the right of way and a bonus of every alternate section" of land to a "rich railroad corporation" but failed to lend aid to "its true friends and supporters."[73]

While most black Texans remained within the Republican camp, significant black participation in white-supremacist-dominated independent political movements illustrates the pliable, flexible nature of anti-monopoly politics. On one level it reflects what historian Maury Klein calls the "folklore of reform," in which anti-monopolists attacked the "railroad kings" and robber barons in defense of "the people," though "the people," he observed, "were a collage of individuals and groups seeking advantage" themselves. While Klein underestimates the integrity of reformers' critiques, there is some truth in his observation. Beneath the banner of "anti-monopoly" were people with wildly opposing visions of a New Southwest, however much anxiety they shared about the imagined machinations of Gould. Many black migrants saw the region as a land, potentially, of racial equality, or at the very least, a place less constraining and violent than the South, while whites generally sought a "white man's country." Middle-class inhabitants hoped for a region free of social and class warfare at the same time that working-class people realized that these conflicts could not be wished away. Migrants' contradictory impulses and the strife that characterized the region stand at odds with the Southwest that economist Ruth Allen described in her 1942 book on the 1886 "Great Southwest Strike." She drew on the language of anti-monopoly, depicting the region as liberated and harmonious until the eastern corporation extended its grasp, and the Southwest strikers as representative of a unified "people" innocent of power.

The language of reform brought together disparate groups—native-born Americans and immigrants; whites and blacks; merchants, shop owners, newspaper editors, city officials, railway workers, tenants, and manufacturers—because the economic, political, and social issues that railroads and industrialism introduced and antagonized were troubling ones. In identifying a common foe, anti-monopoly adherents tended to paper over their colliding visions of a New Southwest. Understanding the ways in which these ideas worked to contain tension within communities in the New Southwest is crucial to explaining the widespread local endorsement of the 1885 walkout, as well as the rapid disintegration of that support in 1886. Those elements of railroad work that pulled railroaders, especially "boomers," away from the cross-class identity that was at the core of anti-monopoly thought, and toward a feeling of labor kinship, is the subject of the next chapter.

CHAPTER 2

Labor Kinship

LABOR UPHEAVAL on the Gould system in the mid-1880s was unusual in that it brought together an array of railroad employees whose working worlds varied dramatically according to their occupation, age, race, skill, and stability. To illustrate, during the nineteenth century and well into the twentieth century, a white engineer would have likely designated himself and any other white, skilled, or semiskilled, full-time railroad employee a "railroader" or "railroad man" but would have denied that claim to an unskilled laborer or to an irregular, semiskilled worker, and almost certainly to a black employee, whatever his skill and experience. Beyond issues of skill and racial caste, many workers were from entirely different departments or were on the move and so came into contact with one another on merely a passing basis. What experiences, assumptions, worries, and hopes did railroaders share, despite the gulfs that often separated them? How did ideas about gender, combined with the experience of a virtually all-male industry, give rise to collective cultural understandings of the meaning of railroad labor?

The historical record does not yield easy answers to such questions. While railroaders' stories, songs, and reminiscences reveal the heartfelt sentiments which they and others attached to their work, these sources tend to romanticize. Also, only a few limited public sources specific to nineteenth-century employees of the Missouri Pacific and Texas & Pacific railways are available for study.[1] For these reasons, but also because railroaders themselves often wandered extensively in search of work, finding employ with a number of roads over the course of their lives, one must cast the net widely and consider sources relating to nineteenth-century railroading generally in order to understand the circumstances of black and white Southwest system strikers.

While a number of Chinese and Mexican men labored on construction and section crews in West and South Texas during the 1880s, and both Texas and Arkansas leased convicts to work at railway construction sites during the 1870s and 1880s, these men were far removed from the scene of the 1885–1886 strikes. They are part of this story but are not at its center.[2]

The central point that arises from key primary texts such as railway worker reminiscences and autobiographies and from the principal studies of railroad workers is that, while to a large degree railroad work simply represented a means to earn a living, it also held a rich and complex cultural significance, whether one ran the engines or maintained the tracks. It offered men the chance to establish and affirm their common notions of manhood by associating them with the nation's chief engine of commerce and symbol of technological and cultural dominance, testing their physical strength and resolve, and requiring many to leave familiar surroundings in search of work as a part of their jobs and to find their place within an overwhelmingly male working and living environment.[3] Such commonalities among railroaders help to explain how a significant portion of this heavily itinerant workforce, though divided along multiple lines, under certain pressures came to identify with one another and to embrace a broad-based labor coalition and labor militancy.[4]

Occupations and Hazards

Because a single railway company commanded such a huge expanse of track, officials organized a company into a number of different divisions. Each division represented between two hundred and four hundred miles of track, with the division headquarters and repair shop situated at the center. A departmental structure was in place in addition to the geographic one. The locomotive and transportation department was composed of enginemen (engineers and firemen) and shopmen (machinists, boilermakers, blacksmiths, carpenters, car inspectors, painters, hostlers, wipers, and roundhouse laborers). Conductors, brakemen, flagmen, yardmen, car cleaners, porters, and switchmen made up the train and yard service department. The station service department included station agents, clerks, telegraph operators, and baggage-men, and the road service department, track labor and section labor. A railroad official managed each major sector. Engine crews reported to a road foreman, and shopmen to a master mechanic.

The division superintendent commanded all of the departments in a division. Above him was a system-wide hierarchy of managers, including the general superintendent.[5]

The duties of a conductor did not involve much in the way of manual labor. Conductors held general authority over the trains they worked and interacted closely with their crew. They received the train's orders, directed the engineer to stop and start, kept track of the train's time, inspected the cars, and directly supervised brakemen. Freight conductors were responsible for the content of cars and calculating the timetables that kept them safely out of the way of passenger trains. Passenger conductors sold and collected tickets and dealt with travelers, and thus had to be diplomatic as well as authoritative. Their job also necessitated adeptness with numbers, since they kept track of accounts and handled money in the fast-paced world of railroad travel.[6]

Locomotive engineers ran the engines. The engineer checked the train before departure, was responsible for "making time," supervised the fireman, and watched for signals and dangers. This latter duty involved looking out for obstructions on the track, flags warning of washed-out bridges, and misplaced switches (which ran a train off track). Engineers were also to run the engine efficiently through the careful control of the locomotive's steam pressure. An engineer's ability to do this well depended upon his knowledge of and expertise in working steam engines and handling heavy machinery. To execute these tasks, an engineer required considerable technical expertise, common sense, strength, alertness, and good eyesight.[7]

Conductors, engineers, brakemen, and firemen made up the "running trades." While conductors and engineers engaged in highly skilled work, brakemen and firemen were less skilled and were often recruited from the ranks of the unskilled. Firemen were usually hired out of railroad shops, while brakemen often had little to no prior experience on the railroad. Fireman and brakeman positions were potential stepping-stones to engineering and conducting, respectively, although promotions to these well-paid positions were usually few and far between.[8]

A fireman shoveled about five tons of coal per day into the box that fed the engine. If he did his job well, he supplied the firebox with just enough coal and set the coals in the box in such a way to evenly fuel the fire. The fireman also cleaned the fire by forcing water into the boiler to avoid an explosion. He ensured that the engine was ready for departure and helped the engineer to check the rails while en route. Many companies expected firemen to clean the engine and empty the locomotive ashes at the end of the day. In sum, although a good fireman exhibited some skill in keeping the engine hot, in essence, his job called for more brawn than brains.[9] During his first ride in the cab, railroader Charles Brown witnessed the intense physical toll involved: "[The fireman] shoveled scoopful after scoopful of coal into the roaring hot firebox, and the glare from the fire would reflect on his hot, red face, and the heat from the open door would start the smoke curling up off his overalls, and after closing the door he would step to the gangway between the tank [tender] and the engine-cab to one side, and lean out to get a breath of fresh air and also to let the draft that sucked through the gangway cool his heated body for a few moments, and then he would grab the chain again and swing open the heavy door and put in another fire."[10] Brakemen were responsible to the conductor for checking over the train's car doors, wheel bearings, and couplings before departure. Their main task, however, was to move along the top of the train cars to set and release the hand brakes upon the engineer's signals. The head brakeman served as the engine's flagman. He opened and closed switches, coupled and uncoupled cars, and relayed signals from the back of the train to the engineer. The rear brakeman or flagman signaled approaching trains from the rear once the train stopped. Also, from his perch on top of the train or on the caboose, he made sure the train held together. Experienced brakemen could prevent a "break-in-two" by listening carefully to the engine's exhaust as the train traveled. A change in exhaust signaled that slack had run forward, which made the accidental uncoupling of a section much more likely.[11]

Switchmen were relatively immobile compared to men in the "running trades," although they often moved from yard to yard in large cities such as St. Louis and Dallas. These men watched the switches in the railroad yards, keeping them in a safe position so as to avoid throwing an engine or car off track. They also navigated a jumble of cars onto the same track and helped the brakeman to couple and uncouple them in order to make up trains. While the switchman's job required quickness and adroitness, men with no experience were regularly employed after only a few days of training to do this work. They had little opportunity for advancement and were poorly paid. Few switchmen were promoted to the position of yardmaster or brakeman, and yard foremen were not paid much more than regular switchmen.[12]

Shopmen were comprised of a mix of occupations and a wide range of skill levels. Their work differed greatly from men in the running trades in that they worked in a particular location and under factory-like conditions. At the division headquarters shop, men were responsible for the repair of the engines and rolling stock. Roundhouse shopmen provided daily maintenance and preparation for the locomotives. In other company shops, men engaged in new construction. This, as well as repair work, forced shopmen of various craft traditions to be creative in applying their skills. The craft of machinists, David Montgomery tells us, was founded not only on "experience and manual dexterity but also abstract reasoning." At any of these sites, supervisors held direct authority over shopmen, although the degree to which this power was exercised varied from shop to shop. A strict hierarchy of skill governed relationships between shop workers.[13]

Trackmen maintained sections of track on a division to make the road safe for travel, reinforcing weak roadbeds, tapping down loose pins, replacing worn ties, and cleaning the tracks. These men were on the road a good deal of the time, traveling to different points to do their work. Although track work demanded no special skills, experience made a difference in the care and precision with which laborers cared for the track. As one historian points out, a section boss had to understand "the scientific principle of easements, or runoffs, the gradual reduction of the elevation of a curve, which causes a car to regain equilibrium after rounding it." Still, the trackman's prospect of advancement was slim.[14]

Except in the cases of shopmen and of senior railroaders able to secure regular runs, for most railroaders the rhythm of work on the railroads was quite irregular. Weather, the economy, and seasonal demands affected service. Between April and October, railroads typically hired large numbers of trackmen to maintain the roads during the heavy traffic produced by the spring cattle rush, fall harvest, and summer vacationers. But the number of trackmen regularly employed dwindled from November to March, when freight and passenger traffic dropped precipitously. Because they were at the company's beck and call, railroaders often lived within earshot of railroad roundhouses, shops, and yards. During rushes, most worked long hours, up to twenty hours a day for those in train service, but saw their working hours severely cut back during slack months.[15]

Compounding the irregularity of many railroaders' work schedule was the frequent practice by financially taxed roads of withholding payment to employees. Railroad companies did not pay workers regularly in currency on a weekly or biweekly basis until the 1890s. Prior to this, when a company was unable to meet its monthly payroll obligations, it could resort to delay or payment in kind or in post-dated company notes. Or it might withhold any payment whatsoever for long periods. This practice entailed risks of course, primarily the risk that workers would protest with strikes or sabotage, as they did, for example, in 1875 on the Toledo, Wabash, & Western Railway when the company neglected to pay most of its employees for four months. Protesters attempted to derail trains in response. In 1884, about 500 employees of the Wabash, St. Louis & Pacific Railway in Moberly, Missouri, pledged to withdraw their labor "until last month's wages are paid." A Missouri paper reported that some of the town's businesses had extended credit to the strikers but were about to refuse more to "men who have not a dollar to pay these bills." Two years earlier the paper reported on the same problem on the Wabash and commented, "The [Wabash men] cannot go elsewhere to work. They are caught and held in a mesh of debt and distress."[16]

Railroaders could and often did supplement their income in various legal (but not officially sanctioned) and nonlegal ways, such as stealing freight and coal, pocketing fares, transporting messages and packages for a fee, or buying goods at one location and selling them along the line. Some railroads offered bonuses and premiums to men for outstanding or special service or provided free passes to "cultivate among . . . employees . . . a feeling of sympathy" with the road. After mid-century, however, "turning an honest penny," as conductor Charles George called it, became more difficult. Railroad companies objected to providing the extra room on freight cars that railroaders' private business ventures demanded and to losing shipping profits to their employees. Although certainly these activities continued behind the backs of railroad managers, by the 1870s a major source of employees' extra income was extra work, for which they were typically paid the same rate as their regular wage.[17]

Railroad work involved danger and discomfort, whether one laid track, set the brakes on a train, or commanded a locomotive engine. Trackmen's use of heavy tools and materials to repair the tracks, especially on bridges and steep inclines or during rough weather, posed the constant threat of injury. In the railroad shops, accidents involving heavy, hot machinery or stray pieces of flying metal threatened. Trainmen's work was especially hazardous. Locomotive engines could explode without proper maintenance, and companies often understaffed the track department, which meant trains might travel on weak bridges and eroded beds, increasing the risk of a wreck. Engineers and firemen had to remain vigilant in order to avoid various obstructions—horses, cattle, or a stray freight car.[18] At times, accidents were freakish in nature, an inevitable product of working with steam and massive equipment. Within the space of a year, for example, engineer J. J. Thomas witnessed his conductor's instantaneous death in a collision, contracted frostbite while helping with a winter wreck, mashed his hand working in the shops, and was badly scalded when an engine turned over on him in the yards.[19]

Thomas's meetings with disaster were not unusual. They were part of a long history of "carnage" on American railways, as historian Mark Aldrich describes in his study of railroad safety. In 1890, the Interstate Commerce Commission tabulated that during that year 2,451 railroad men were killed on the job and 22,396 met with serious injury. In Kansas in 1885 alone, one in twelve railroad employees was injured or killed. What these statistics fail to convey is that most injuries were far worse than simply a cut or bruise or even a bone break. Railway accidents more often resulted in the loss or mangling of a limb or limbs. Charles Brown, whose father died after he "got knocked off the top of this train by a low bridge while setting up the handbrakes," lost both his feet when his "clothes caught on the brake rigging" and he was "rolled in under the train."[20]

Brakemen and switchmen were the most susceptible to death or serious injury. Switchmen ran the risk of accidentally falling or making a wrong, spur-of-the-moment movement around heavy, running freight cars, engines, and wagons in the yards, often with little room to maneuver. Hand braking required that a brakeman climb on top of cars to set brakes, no matter the weather or train's speed. A momentary loss of balance could send a man tumbling to his death, as it did with Missourian Harry Taylor, who fell off the train while setting the brakes in the spring of 1884. His remains were found "scattered along the track for some distance." The fall alone may have been fatal. As Aldrich calculated, "A man falling from a 14-foot car going 10 miles per hour would hit the ground at about 23 miles per hour—easily enough to kill him."[21] Both switchmen and brakemen coupled and uncoupled cars, often while cars were still in motion. As "boomer" railroader Harry French related, the job required "skill and perfect coordination of mind and muscle." "In order to make...a coupling the link was first fastened with a pin in one car. Then a pin was 'cocked' at a slight angle in the other car to be coupled. As the two cars came together, the trainman guided the link into its slot...If the pin did not shake down, the trainman stepped in between the cars and pounded it down. Wary feet, an alert mind, and chilled nerve were needed every instant." French obtained a job switching in the Missouri yards during the 1880s. He somehow escaped injury, even to his fingers and toes, which was unusual among switchmen. Breaking pins and links often resulted in crushed fingers or hands, marking men for life as railroaders. French's friend was not so lucky. Despite his long experience and skill switching, a simple slip of the foot left him caught and crushed to death between two cars. In March 1885 fireman George Fish died under similar conditions while working for the St. Louis and San Francisco railroad in Pacific, Missouri. His skull was smashed when he became trapped between a flat car and a caboose he was trying to couple.[22] Stories like Fish's abound in late nineteenth-century newspapers.

Despite these dangers, few railroad men sued their companies for losses due to work-related injuries. They feared being fired and blacklisted, and usually lacked the finances to pay for legal expenses. Railroad companies usually compensated injured passengers but were not legally liable for the physical harms that their workers suffered on the job. Companies sometimes elected to pay a worker or his family a significant sum, but this voluntary assistance was on average low, "provided little security for workers," and reflected not only humanitarian concerns but also managerial and legal ones. On October 20, 1884, an Illinois switchman's wife sought the company's aid in caring for her two children and herself after her husband's death on the railway. Officials agreed to aid her only if she signed papers acknowledging that payment in no way indicated culpability. Similarly, William Rockwell, who worked on the Southwest system in Wyandotte, Kansas, testified before a congressional committee in May 1886 that he had signed a paper with the Missouri Pacific Railway after his thumb was crushed coupling cars. The paper offered him $1—less than half of his normal day's wages—in return for the promise of continued employment. Rockwell explained the outcome: "I knew very well it would be a mighty poor policy for a poor man to fight a railroad company. I didn't have no money to fight them with. I thought it would be better to take the job and go along about my business than to kick up any stink." His case was not unusual.[23] Given these circumstances and the fact that private insurance groups considered railroaders high risks, charging them high rates or denying them coverage completely, mutual aid helped to support families affected by a railroader's injury or death. Some railroaders belonged to multi-class protective organizations, such as the Ancient Order of United Workingmen, which provided for the family of Fort Worth car repairer Thomas Kenniford when he died in an 1882 railway accident. Lodges of the railroad brotherhoods, however, proved the most reliable source of help. These unions organized better skilled and relatively well-paid workers, and therefore had greater resources at their disposal. Most of the major railroad brotherhoods offered death and disability insurance plans at a substantially lower cost than commercial insurance firms.[24]

For men who did not or could not belong to a brotherhood, help was more difficult to obtain, but the dangers of railroad work encouraged collective action and fraternal protection. Passing the hat for a well-liked man, directly after payday or especially during economic upturns, often met with success. Harry French took up a collection for the widow of his friend, a car repairer, from men working on the Hannibal & St. Joseph, the Kansas City, Fort Scott & Gulf, and the Kansas Belt Line. He obtained generous contributions from the train crew, yard crew, and office employees—basically "anyone who would listen." French recalled the relatively small amount switchmen donated. As he explained, this was due to the much more frequent collections they took up amongst themselves to benefit the families of switchmen killed or injured on the job. Few refused to donate some amount, since "one never knew when [the hat] would be going around for him or his widow."[25]

Officials who discounted safety in order to "make time" or to pare down the company's operating budget inspired the bitter resentment of railroaders, who argued that management's refusal to heed the maxim "Safety first" posed a direct threat to their lives and the lives of passengers. After a head-on collision between a sleeper car and a freight train on the Chicago & Alton road, the conductor involved in the wreck blamed the company. It had failed to employ "competent freight brakemen" and allowed "the freights to so closely follow passenger trains." Rescuers pulled passengers from one of the burning cars, the conductor's hip was crushed, and the doctor predicted the brakeman's injuries to be fatal.[26] "Drew the Wrong Lever," a popular Scottish poem reprinted in the Knights of Labor's *Journal of United Labor,* expressed popular indignation over railroads' violation of safety measures. Its tragic hero is an overworked switchman whose disabling fatigue leads him to mistakenly divert two trains to the same track, causing a terrible crash with great loss of life.[27]

The safety issue cut both ways. Although drinking on the job was prohibited, and the railroad brotherhoods had long preached temperance, the problem was rampant. Nearly 30 percent of the workers whom the Chicago, Burlington & Quincy Railroad fired between 1877 and 1892 had lost their jobs for imbibing during their work hours. During their off-hours, many trainmen and engine men patronized saloons, which in some areas were the only places available to them to wait, rest, and refuel. There alcohol beckoned, especially to men in the running trades, who might be laid over for some time without any sense as to when they would be called to duty. The Atchison, Topeka & Santa Fe attempted to end off-duty drinking but with little success.[28] Railroad workers often responded that drink was a just reward for their hard labor and the trials that separation from home involved. Some believed drink sharpened their senses and reinvigorated rather than weakened them. Officials tolerated moderate drinking and often drank themselves, even along with the employees.[29]

The Meaning of Risk

Even when railroad work was unnecessarily hazardous, one major aspect of railroaders' response was to celebrate risk. The very definition of a "rail" among nineteenth-century railroaders was a man who displayed a willingness and ability to work with others, strength, skill, attention to safety measures, and alertness. Railroaders' reminiscences as well as the stories published by brotherhood journals tended to depict railroad labor as, in one historian's words, a "heroic, manly confrontation with 'the task.'" The task involved performing one's job well, knowing when and when not to conform to workplace rules, and doing everything possible to avert disaster. Railroad workers of various professions boasted of their ability to cope with or to tough out even the worst conditions. As long-time conductor Charles B. George wrote in his autobiography: "Knowing that amid the darkness of night, the storms of winter, and the war of the elements, hundreds of human beings are to be kept in safety, carries with it a peculiar dignity and sense of responsibility that is felt all along the line, from the man at the switch, the man on the locomotive, the man who controls the train, up through all the various ranks."[30] That sense of dignity and responsibility was deeply embedded in nineteenth-century notions of manliness. Physical and psychological endurance, technical knowledge, inductive and deductive reasoning, and resourcefulness were traits understood to be naturally masculine. A railroader's manhood, in the eyes of others and himself, often hinged upon how well he responded to a crisis, the proficiency with which he executed his job, his reliability or "steadfastness," or simply his tenacity in facing the elements. When Harry French witnessed the gruesome death of a brakeman as a boy, the sight did not convince him to abandon his dreams of railroading. Instead, the danger of such work enticed him, confirming his own ample self-confidence. He was certain he "would never get killed in such a foolish manner." He remarked, "From that time on, everything pertaining to the farm was too tame for my active interest." Indeed, an element of bravado runs through the stories and music produced by and about railroaders. As a railroad worker reminds his quarrelsome lover in one such song, "I'm out on this new railroad... ristin [*sic*] my life for you."[31]

Called the "hero of the rail" by contemporaries, the engineer in particular was the subject of romantic tales in which traits traditionally associated with masculinity are enlisted to prevent a horrifying disaster.[32] Published in union journals and mainstream papers, these tales typically involve an engineer who must act quickly and decisively to preserve the lives of passengers and crewmen. In "Saved By a Scratch," for example, an ex-fireman tells the story of an engineer he worked under, Silas Markley, who had to obey the order he received via telegraph from the controller. Markley knew that following the order would result in a collision between the express train and his own train. He could not disobey the order without risking collision with other trains, the schedules and routes of which only the controller knew. After quickly "calculating chances," Markley realized in horror that he had to pull his train onto the siding before the express train's arrival. It was his "coolness and nerve" that allowed him to make a difficult decision, command his mutinous fireman, and control the train as it hurtled down the track at sixty miles an hour, thereby narrowly missing a wreck and saving a "hundred lives." Another story's narrator likewise observed, "The preservation of the lives of the passengers was due to the fact that the engineer was well balanced, quick to act... not excitable," and "unerring" in his judgment.[33]

All of this is not to say, of course, that railroaders embraced wholeheartedly the "romanticism of the rail" as put forth in story and song. Notwithstanding their popularity in railroad brotherhood journals, these sources' depiction of a very complicated and often harrowing existence in simple, melodramatic terms may have struck a number of railroad workers as overly sentimental. For some, a personal encounter with danger shattered whatever romantic hold railroading had on them. After barely escaping two wrecks in the span of less than a month, locomotive fireman Steve Brown left railroading altogether. He later explained, "I sez to myself… 'If youse want to live, go on de farm,' an' thar am whar Ise go." Even Harry French, who sprinkled a number of thrilling stories throughout his narrative and claimed to have become "calloused to danger," was sobered by the death of a fellow switchman. He quit his job switching shortly afterwards.[34]

French's experience seems to indicate that railroad men came to see danger as simply a part of their jobs. In explaining his decision to give up switching, he refers to a common "superstition" among nineteenth-century railroaders about "working after you have decided to quit." "To do that," he comments, "was regarded as the acme of bad luck." While expressing disdain for "superstition," he agreed in spirit: "There is no room for any other thought than the particular job that is being performed. If a man has decided to leave the service, if he has another job, or is studying where such a job could be secured, such thoughts or plans are certain to lower his safety efficiency both to himself and to his co-workers." In other words, in order to continue railroading, one had to, in a sense, surrender to it. Although quite young, French had already in large part done this. He had come to identify himself as a "railroad man" and railroading as his life's work. Yet French did not view danger fatalistically. Instead, by ending his switching career and moving into the relatively safer employ of brakeman, he attempted to exert control over the degree of risk he faced.[35]

French's response to one accident later in his career, a particularly troubling incident because he blamed himself for its occurrence, suggests that his adventure stories, and thus the various yarns railroaders told generally, served as a way for him to steel himself against inner doubts and fears. Upon the death of a young brakeman under his charge, he became "pretty well broken up," so much so that he started drinking heavily again. "There were weeks," he admitted, "that I never drew a sober breath." Especially for those in the more perilous railroad occupations, many appear to have made a virtue of necessity. This probably explains why railroaders like French gathered at local restaurants and saloons to "swap lies" about their railroading exploits, insulted the lives of non-railroading men as dull and undesirable, and created nicknames for each other, such as "Crazy Horse" Williamson and "Black Jack" Leonard.[36] To nineteenth-century American ears, these names connoted "wildness," courage, and virility. These were characteristics many railroad men hoped to emulate, in part because such qualities were the stuff of heroes and legends, and also because the occupation required considerable nerve, especially from those who clung to railroad work purely out of economic necessity. Themes of anxiety and dread often accompanied expressions of occupational pride in railway songs, as the popular late nineteenth-century railroad ballad "The Wreck on the C. & O." attests, "Many a man has been murdered by the railroad / And laid in his lonesome grave."[37]

That railroaders sought to reach outside of themselves for inspiration, confirmation, or assistance in confronting workplace dangers did not necessarily undermine their identification of risk with manhood. As the above example suggests, it was not uncommon to express fear or dread, and doing so probably nurtured or reinforced the fraternal bonds that railroaders created amongst themselves.[38] But the inner struggles railroaders experienced in regard to their own ability to measure up to the task and to live to tell an exciting tale of near disaster means that the dangers involved in railroading also posed dilemmas for railroaders' sense of themselves as men.

"Steeling" oneself, then, prepared one not only to face danger but also to meet the high expectations of railroad officials and coworkers. As the tale of engineer Silas Markley suggests, one measure of manliness among railroad men involved how an individual dealt with company rules, particularly in a time of crisis. The company rulebook governed how railroad workers of various occupations were to perform their duties. A violation of the rules meant dismissal or suspension. However, given the myriad problems of operating a far-flung bureaucracy, supervisors oftentimes allowed for, and in a sense depended upon, a railroader's common sense interpretation. As brakeman Horace Herr observed, "When you take a chance and get away with it, you're a good railroad man," while "the fellow who never violates one of those rules is the guy who is always looking for a job." Applying the rules appropriately and bending them without openly breaking them required the ability to solve problems, take control, and act independently. These same qualities were often stressed in the stories and anecdotes passed among railroad men in their union journals and popular with the public.[39]

Coming of Age

The opportunity for adventure that railroading offered seems to have impressed many young men and boys more than its dangers. Charles Maier was the young son of a farmer in Kansas when the first passenger train rolled into his county station. When interviewed over half a century later, he recalled the excitement with which he and other townspeople greeted the train's arrival in Allen County. Like "other young fellows there too," he wrote, his feet were sore from the "pinch of new store shoes," bought for such special occasions. Despite the pain in his feet, he noticed the "girls. . . decked out in gay colored calicoes and ribbons," flirting with "the boys." Maier saw railroading as an escape from the dreariness of farm life and the watchful eye of his parents. As a boy, he watched for trains from his lookout point on a nearby hilltop. When he could not be on the lookout, he listened for the train's whistle, having memorized its schedule of arrivals and departures at the nearby town of Colony. Maier established acquaintances with the conductors and brakemen who passed through the area and visited the railroad shops while in town. Despite his mother's fervent objections, he entered railroad work, first in the roundhouse and later in train service as a fireman.[40]

Harry French, J. J. Thomas, and Charles B. George shared Maier's youthful enthusiasm for railroad work. An orphan at age seven, French was bound out to a farmer in Illinois, but he "hated the farm." At age twelve, he "thrilled" at the sight of a train in Kansas City and decided at that moment to become a "railroad man." George was seventeen when his parents died, leaving him "thrown upon" his "own resources." He, like Thomas, lacked a taste for farming and jumped at a career in railroading.[41]

The chance to travel and to earn cash wages attracted many young men from small towns and farms to the occupation in the same way sailing fired the imaginations and ambitions of young men of the clipper-ship era. When economic times were good, a young man could easily move from place to place to find work. For members of railway brotherhoods this was particularly true. Union "traveling cards" facilitated the movement of brotherhood members from one place to another in search of work. Henry George calculated proudly that in his forty years as an engineer, he had traveled nearly two and one-half million miles, or "nearly one hundred times around the globe." French's story illustrates the potential economic benefits of railroad work. Despite his youth, French landed a job as a telegraph operator in St. Charles, Missouri, in the mid-1870s. The salary and position signified a major transformation in French's status. No longer was he a "hungry kid in a hickory shirt and jeans pants." Instead, he was a "well-dressed young man" and "very popular with the younger generation."[42] For French and others, railroading offered a way to "come of age" and begin an independent life.

As a young black man in an intensely segregated and discriminatory industry, Thomas Cole had in many ways a profoundly different railroading experience from Thomas, Maier, French, and George, all of whom were white. However, all enjoyed earning the relatively high wages offered by the railroads and the opportunities those wages afforded a young man entering manhood. After escaping slavery during the Civil War and serving as a spy and soldier in the Union army, Cole found work on the railroad in Stevenson, Alabama, and later, Chattanooga, Tennessee. In Chattanooga, he laid new track, switched spurs, and installed turntables in the railroad yards. He celebrated his first payday by dressing up and "walkin bout town at night wid some of de other boys." He also worked up the nerve to ask the girl next door, Nancy, to a dance. Cole remembered well the social wages of railroad employment: "We all went ter de dance and danced nearly all de night, dis dance was a cullered mans in dat part of town and it was one of dem ole fashioned kind... I buys dem anything dey wants as I had jest got paid and had more money den any one at de dance." Nancy's uncle soon urged his niece to marry Cole, because he was a "railroad man" and could therefore "make her a good livin."[43]

For anyone poor living in the rural areas of Arkansas and East Texas, where hard money was scarce, the lure of cash wages was likely considerable.[44] Poor black men may have viewed railroading as particularly attractive, because few opportunities existed for them to work in town, and laborers could usually earn more working in factories, mills, public works, and on railroads than on farms. Those able to secure positions as porters, baggage handlers, or waiters earned tips in addition to a low base wage, which allowed them to enjoy a middle-class life and status within black communities. Although the waged work available tended to require migration to distant locations, the poverty of many black southerners pushed a significant number to risk leaving familiar surroundings for relatively higher wages elsewhere, even if that work proved temporary. For this reason, Eli Coleman moved to Texas from Kentucky in the late 1860s. He had heard, "They was building the first railroad down across Texas and that they hired lots of negroes." He was paid sixty cents a day, which was "lots of money in them days."[45]

Railroad labor agents, too, understood the appeal of cash wages. In 1883, for example, the National Labor Agency ran a large advertisement in the *St. Louis Post-Dispatch* announcing five hundred openings for men, including one hundred "colored men," for railroad work in Kansas. One white agent, R. A. "Peg-Leg" Williams, claimed to have recruited eighty thousand black men from the South Atlantic states to migrate to Mississippi and Texas.[46]

Upon employment in railroad shops, depots, yards, and construction and repair points, young men such as Cole, French, and George entered a virtually all-male world. Outside of a few positions as clerks, telegraph operators, and "Harvey Girl" waitresses, women did not engage in railroad work.[47] For many, the all-male environment often extended beyond the regular workday to living accommodations. Engineers, firemen, brakemen, and conductors regularly stayed together overnight at boardinghouses in small division towns along their routes, as did section men when they traveled to various points on the road to maintain the tracks. The 1880 census for Marshall, Texas, for example, recorded eleven young section men—black and white, immigrant and native-born—boarding at the home of their foreman. A number of other railroaders lodged at various homes and hotels, usually eight or nine men per establishment.[48]

Although shopmen and switchmen were far less mobile in their work, those young and unmarried often boarded with other railroaders, a fact also reflected in the Marshall census. Some of these men apparently migrated ahead of their families in search of work, and paid room and board until they could establish themselves or find work elsewhere. Their occupations ran the gamut, from trades that generally required travel to less mobile jobs, such as boilermaker, machinist, and engine wiper. Out of about two hundred black and white railroad men in Marshall in 1880, more than half lived in boardinghouses or hotels, generally with other railroaders. Of those who boarded, about one-third worked in the shops or yards. Thus, railroad men in Marshall often found themselves living as well as working with fellow co-workers, far away from the constraints of family and community.[49]

While a virtually all-male workforce was not unusual in the industrial world, railroading offered an especially raucous environment in which to "come of age." Separation from home and community tempted young men and old to cross social boundaries to gamble, brawl, drink, and spend their pay at houses of prostitution. Saloons offered warmth and shelter in small division towns, and call boys for the railroad often looked for men in their favorite drinking spots rather than at home. Henry French first saw the inside of a saloon at the age of fifteen when he began work on the railroad in St. Charles, Missouri, and pit stops along his route provided him with fresh opportunities to win at the gaming table.[50] Railroaders regularly celebrated payday in Kansas towns during the 1880s by roaming the streets in drunken revelry, occasionally starting fights with passersby. Construction crews even at times received a portion of their pay in alcohol. When Harrison Boyd undertook railroad construction in East Texas during the 1870s, the company paid him $1.50 a day plus three shots of whiskey.[51]

The use of alcohol tended to encourage brawling. A St. Louis newspaper reported one evening's events at several saloons located near the railroad tracks: two men stabbed, a fight that ended with a man's scalp split by a coal-oil lamp, and another bloody encounter in which a man's jaw was broken by a cue-wielding opponent.[52] But alcohol could also act to smooth over or repress disagreements and differences. In the railroad brotherhoods, drinking was a socializing ritual that "took on an oppositional tone" to management and "intensified the bonds of work-group solidarity." This apparently extended to non-brotherhood men as well. Harry French began drinking immediately upon entering railroad work. He recalled that he drank because he liked it, but also because "all railroadmen drank."[53]

J. J. Thomas had not consumed a drop of alcohol when he gave a "thrashing" to his master mechanic, who had a habit of cursing the men. Like a number of his coworkers, Thomas prided himself on his "wrestling powers," boasting that he once threw a challenger to the floor so hard that the crash "could have been heard a quarter of a mile." His autobiography lauds sheer brawn, an independent spirit, and self-defense.[54] Perhaps in a similar spirit, railroad employees referred to groups of railroaders whom they knew and worked with as "the boys." On occasion, "the boys" described men who differed in age, race, occupation, skill, and marital status. When Thomas Cole used the phrase, he may have included his white coworkers. He remembered that upon becoming a father for the first time, he "hads ter set it up ter dem all, and dese railroad boys sho don't care bout your pocket book." The *Switchman's Journal, Railroad Brakeman's Journal,* and the *Locomotive Fireman's Magazine,* all union publications that sought to convey an image of maturity and respectability, frequently called fellow railroaders "the boys," despite the playfulness and youthfulness the word implies.[55] The expression suggests camaraderie and familiarity and also railroaders' self-image as men who felt themselves a bit freer from the responsibilities constraining non-railroaders.

Boomers

Not all railroad workers drifted in search of work, traveled as part of their jobs, or participated in a bawdy, rough-and-tumble lifestyle. Switchmen and shopmen generally remained in town to work, and thus were well within the control or influence of community and family. Although in 1880 more than half of the railroaders in Marshall, Texas, boarded, almost half lived with their families or had families of their own, and, despite the drifting and traveling their jobs often required of them, a number of railroaders aspired to be—and over time became—respected, conservative members of their communities.[56] Yet many of the men who worked on the Southwest system of roads during the 1870s and 1880s were "boomers," transients who "worked for first one road, and then another," and comprised "a significant portion of the generation of workers that built and operated the railroads during the expansive years of the late nineteenth century." The extension of railroad lines west created not only a frontier area of U.S. settlers and native inhabitants but also introduced a "frontier of labor scarcity." Railroaders found their services most needed in those areas only recently linked to the rest of the country by rail, since "railroads had to maintain a basic level of service even in territories that were generating relatively little business, and providing that service required a full complement of railroad trades."[57]

In order to attract workers to areas sparsely populated by Americans, railways typically offered higher wages than they did in established places. An added, obvious incentive was the greater chance of gaining promotion in a locale where labor, especially skilled labor, was relatively scarce. Although railroaders frequently migrated in search of work or a better position, companies found it necessary to offer them incentives to do so. The cost of living was often more expensive in newly settled railroad boom towns, and many railroaders found it difficult to leave a place to which they had formed some attachment, particularly those who owned their homes.[58] But a significant number realized, as Harry French did during the early 1880s, that "the railroads of the East were settled railroads—a new man had to work for a considerable period of time to get seniority to hold a regular job."[59]

"Boomers" perceived another benefit to migration. Many identified their jobs on the nation's expanding railroads with national and technological progress. Railroaders, especially shop workers, expressed tremendous interest in inventing and patenting technological improvements. Granville T. Woods, a fireman-engineer on the Iron Mountain in Missouri during the early 1870s, went on to invent the automatic air brake, for example.[60] The names that members of the Brotherhood of Railroad Brakemen gave to their western lodges—Prairie Queen (Sedalia, Missouri), Southwestern (Trenton, Missouri), Gate City (Denison, Texas), Magic City (Moberly, Missouri), Lone Star (Marshall, Texas), Big Rock (Little Rock, Arkansas), and Future Great (St. Louis, Missouri)—reveal that these workers celebrated their contribution to the booming, expanding economy of the late nineteenth century. As did engineer Sam Hobart, who reportedly loved the regularity of trains, seeing them "loaded up, the hurrying of passengers, the rolling of the baggage, the start, and best of all, the race."[61] Charles Maier's autobiographical account demonstrates that pride in national progress, and in the expansion of railroads specifically, likely grew out of personal experience. Maier remembered cutting and loading ties for the construction of a road from trees that grew on his parent's farm. The railroad, he noted, allowed his father to transport crops much more quickly and easily than before, when he had hauled his produce to market "a hundred miles" overland.[62]

Although unskilled black laborers experienced far less compensation, recognition, and occupational mobility than Charles Maier, who was a white fireman and later an engineer, a number exhibited a similar pride in their contribution to the growth of railroads. More than a half-century after the industry spread to Texas, ex-slave Litt Young recalled that he had "cut three cords a day, helping to clear all the land where Texarkana, Texas is located" for the incoming road. Likewise, freedman Harrison Boyd recounted how he had worked to "cut the right-of-way for the T&P Railroad from Marshall to Longview," and Josh Miles related that he had "worked for the IG&N, helping to build it from Houston, Texas, into Waco." Arguably, Young, Boyd, and Miles's expressions of pride may more accurately represent their sentiments as old men, far-removed from the experience of railroad work and presumably steeped in the lore of expansion and progress, than as young, unskilled men engaged in back-breaking labor. This may well have been the case; unskilled laborers certainly felt bored, frustrated, and alienated by their work. Yet pride and frustration often existed simultaneously and in mutually reinforcing ways, as the fleeting evidence on one strike suggests. When black construction workers on the Austin & Northwestern railroad struck in February 1882 for $2.50 per day, they underlined that the road needed them to complete its work.[63] Probably many unskilled black railroaders shared in the excitement with which communities greeted railroad expansion at the same time that they held deep misgivings about the nature of the industry and their relationship to it.

While "boomers" often romanticized the "freedom" of transitory employment, they did not necessarily see themselves as free of manly responsibilities. The typical drifting or mobile railroad worker may or may not have assigned much importance to marital fidelity, but still would have embraced the ideal of domesticity, which held that a man should provide for his wife and family. Marriage represented a new stage of manhood, one that required a family wage. When J. J. Thomas married, he decided to ask his boss in the shops for a raise in wages, since he was "feeling like a man." Economic concerns and not simply culture or ideology inspired Thomas's request. Marriage necessitated an income that would support two or more people, and men generally earned far more than women did. However, the ideal of the male breadwinner was clearly central to the identities of railroaders, as it was to most nineteenth- and twentieth-century people. Hence, the image of Sam Hobart, who "looking the 'workingman' with his cap and overalls," always found his wife waiting by the window for him to come home from work.[64]

When the wife of a railroader worked for wages, the common assumption was that it was only temporary. As many southern planters noted following the Civil War, black men and women tended to prefer that wives spend time working in the household rather than in the homes of whites or in the fields.[65] Although this proved to be economically impossible for a number of black families, especially in growing towns, where women had a better chance of gaining employment, the hope persisted. As a young boy growing up in East Texas during the early 1890s, Charley White imagined that in heaven, "everybody's mama didn't have nothing to do but stay home all day and cook corn cakes and fatback and turnip greens." He waited impatiently for the day when he could go to work to support his mother, who worked most of her life as a servant and washerwoman.[66] A fictional account of a romance published in the *Switchman's Journal* further illustrates the potency of the ideal of domesticity among railroaders. "The Telegraphic Signal" tells the story of a romance between an engineer and a telegraph operator who, in the process of disobeying company policy, managed to prevent a train wreck. The railroad directors fire them both for their transgressions, but reward the engineer with a supervisory position in the repair shops, work that will presumably support them both and thus restore them to gender roles more acceptable to their contemporaries.[67]

At the same time that the relatively high wages paid railroaders allowed them an opportunity to fulfill their role as family provider, major aspects of their work threatened to undermine or undo these gains. Families paid a price for railroaders' itinerancy in that migration opened up new and troubling possibilities. As Edward Ayers observes, the father "might enjoy the new freedom and high wages too much to return; he or his wife might meet someone else; perhaps illness or death would incapacitate one parent or another."[68] The dangers associated with railroad labor and the raucous lifestyle many itinerants led or encountered made this latter possibility one of particular concern.

Certainly the loneliness itinerants experienced undercut and at times overwhelmed the excitement that travel and freedom from family and community restraints aroused. The poem "The Passing Signal" empathizes with the "toil-worn" and "travel-stained" engineer, whose family lovingly greets him upon his return home from "journeys drear." It ends with the wish that "everyone of the iron horse" may "meet with such a hearty welcome." In one song popular among black southerners, a railroader pledges to "find me a woman and roam no more," while in another the singer laments, "If I had wings like Noah's Dove . . . I would fly away to the one I love."[69] Orra Langhorne, a white visitor to late nineteenth-century Harrisonburg, Virginia, captured the depths of itinerant laborers' loneliness well. She relates the apprehension evident among five hundred "able-bodied colored men" who had assembled at the local railroad station to depart for coal-mining work in southern Iowa. While there were shouts and hurrahs, Langhorne believed "this hilarious parting between them and their friends covered the heart-ache of separation."[70]

On the one hand, the fraternal cultures that railroaders built provided some solace. As Gunther Peck points out, drinking, gambling and fighting disrupted ties among itinerants but also "created a medium of risk taking and danger necessary for the performance of manhood and creation of fraternal bonds among sojourners."[71] On the other hand, establishing and negotiating one's relationship with male coworkers did not always come easily or in some cases at all, notwithstanding boomers' common experiences and socializing rituals. Some never quite fit into the rowdy culture of drifting or mobile male workers.

Although Charley White worked with an East Texas section crew two decades after the Southwest strikes, his recollections tell us something of the pressures felt by those with little taste for bawdiness and rough behavior or its possible consequences. After White's coworkers repeatedly taunted him for refusing to accompany them to the local red-light district, he eventually yielded and began going out with the men on Saturday evenings. One evening, after a game of craps, he witnessed a fight in which several men were "cut up pretty bad." There was "too much going on" in the red-light house, he remembered, "Killing folks, and beating up, and slashing with knives." White found himself enjoying, however, a visit to "the quarter," where the men visited prostitutes—"some old, some young, some half-naked, some dressed nice—just any type you wanted." He would have gone with a particularly insistent woman to her room had he not thought about some of his coworkers who had the "clap." One man was "half eat up," with sores all over his body. Rather than risk such a fate, White returned to his bunkhouse with a bottle of whiskey. He soon left railroading to pursue work in a sawmill, so that he would have more time to spend with his wife-to-be.[72]

White's status as outsider and the concerted efforts of "the boys" to win him over to their world is suggestive, not just about the rowdy, bawdy lifestyle that he rejected but about the fraternal cultures built by railroaders generally. First, fraternal culture was strong enough to drive outsiders such as White away from railroad work. One can also see this, for example, in the letter of one El Paso railroad brakeman to the *Railroad Brakemen's Journal.* In it he reported in great detail on the health and whereabouts of a host of his brakemen brothers, many of them scattered across the country.[73] Second, that White's coworkers felt it necessary to pressure him to join them socially indicates that those who embraced fraternal cultures on the railroads felt themselves to be somewhat vulnerable to criticism or rejection, from both within and without. Probably this was so because within that culture there were men who, like White, had misgivings about the rituals they engaged in and their relationship to fraternalism itself. Fraternal culture defended against internal discord and the external threat posed by the wider public's criticism of railroaders or indifference to them.

Railroaders' relationships with non-railroaders, especially the middle-class and wealthy, were strained. Community leaders at times vigorously defended railroad employees against company policies that deprived them of a living wage. When Jay Gould's Wabash, St. Louis & Pacific Railway failed to pay laborers their monthly wages, the *St. Louis Post-Dispatch* loudly condemned this policy and the general condition of the road's employees. It indignantly reported, "Many were met whose average income was $30.00 a month and who, on this pitiful pittance, were expected to keep life in a wife and from two to five children." Local papers often reported in a familiar and friendly manner on the doings of railroad men. The *Fort Worth Gazette* was not atypical in referring to the Texas & Pacific men as "the boys." It and other newspapers frequently included brief announcements about conductors' and engineers' social lives, and, as mentioned previously, ran stories that celebrated their brave deeds.[74] Yet the public did not always appreciate the significance of their work or the dangers they faced. The *Railroad Brakemen's Journal* printed the poem "A Railroad Man," for instance, that asked the public to think about the "poor brave railroad man, forced to do his duty in the cold wind and the storm," while others sit at home by their fireside. It urged non-railroaders to "say a kind word" to "cheer the heart of this lone wanderer." The journal also published two editorials on a subject that was a very sore point for railroad men. The pieces scolded the public's habit of ignoring their sacrifices, noting that the daily papers' long descriptions of train accidents often ended, without any further detail, "Only a trainman killed." The editor called it an act of cruelty for the press to carefully investigate accidents involving passengers but to make no such effort when railroad men were killed or injured on the job. These were not isolated examples. They confirmed railroaders' more general sense of horror at how callously the non-railroaders regarded them, as one biting poem drives home:

Wooden coaches were battered,
  Train was torn in two
  And yet no passenger injured
  Nobody killed but the crew.
None but the men in the engine
  Hogger and fireman, too:
  Didn't we get off lucky?
  Nobody killed but the crew.[75]

Class resentment coalesced around that sense of horror. Even the renowned "heroes of the rail" felt a distance between themselves and the larger public. In 1885 the *Locomotive Engineer's Monthly Magazine* lamented that "few people understand and appreciate the duties of this class of railroad man," though engineers stand "at their posts in the face of death." The author predicted that "the time will come when labor will occupy its proper position and the engineer will fill no second rate niche." One fireman, writing to his brotherhood's journal, revealed this when he wrote that because there was a "general waking up of the people," he expected that it would soon be as "respectable to be a mechanic as a dude clerk in a dry good store." The editor of the engineers' journal suggested the depths of railroaders' frustration with this prejudice when he urged brotherhood members to "take advantage of our opportunities for spreading kind words": "There are lives thirsting for a word, a look; starving for a kindly smile...The indifferent or repellent glance of good breeding and high standing stabs with a poisonous blade, makes a wound that never heals, but the grasp of a friendly hand, and the sound of a friendly voice, thrills the despairing brain and...awakens it afresh with the determination to deserve the friendship so unselfishly given."[76]

If skilled and semiskilled men detected strong disdain for them on the part of white-collar workers, the middle class, and people "of good breeding," then surely the unskilled experienced this contempt much more intensely. Few heroic stories of trackmen or shop laborers emerged in the mainstream press. The lives of the unskilled usually only attracted notice, and brief notice at that, when tragic incidents occurred, such as the drowning of a delirious section hand and the attempted suicide of a despondent car driver.[77] The "poisoning blade" of prejudice contributed to railroaders' sense of themselves as outsiders, as a class apart.

Given the workforce's high rates of geographic mobility, one might reasonably assume that little existed in the experiences of the industry's workers to help them to develop a feeling of labor kinship. Historians, notably Stephen Thernstrom, have compiled a mass of data that points to the fragmenting effects of American restlessness on class consciousness. However, reading the autobiography of "boomer" Charles Brown, one wonders why Brown, who rarely stayed in one railroad town for long, and who was apparently uninterested in social questions or involving himself in collective forms of labor protest, would so fiercely decry strikebreakers and identify with unionism. Although he characterizes himself as a "boomer, who is a happy-go-lucky, not caring-a-hang sort of cuss, here today and there tomorrow," everywhere this seemingly pure individualist went, to every railroad yard, boardinghouse, and freight train, he easily established ties with other workers and evinced a strong ethic of mutuality. The following explanation makes sense of such contradictory evidence: "If class consciousness does imply some sense of mutualism, it may not be bounded by time and place... Seasoned industrial workers, either from their own experience or as their inheritance from a previous generation of workers, require little time to define themselves in relation to their fellow workers. Their perception of class is facilitated by the ease with which they move from community to community... and find a place for themselves."[78] Brown's tendency to quit a position and move elsewhere in search of work when he had a grievance was itself a form of labor protest. His individual freedom, which he was able to take full advantage of since he was single and unattached, at once encouraged his individual solution (migration) and reinforced the communal bonds that he felt with other railroaders.

Men like Charles Brown, who came from various circumstances and backgrounds, found a place for themselves in the expanding world of railroad work. They shared in its promises and its costs, and in the process drew upon common notions of manhood to create a wide array of fraternal attachments. Railroad men relied upon these bonds in facing their work's hazardous conditions, securing financial help for themselves or their families in case of injury or death, easing the loneliness many felt when on the road or in search of work, and negotiating their relationships to coworkers, their "social betters," and the wider world. Labor kinship on the railways was not without internal tension. The ritual of drinking suggests that community did not necessarily arise spontaneously from railroaders' work experiences; social pressure was brought to bear in nurturing and maintaining occupational ties. Hierarchies of race and skill also framed railroaders' awareness of their social place and infused their labor kinship with particular and often clashing meanings.

CHAPTER 3

Hierarchy and Conflict

IN 1883 STEVE BROWN found a job as a section man on the Missouri, Kansas & Texas. He learned how to fire an engine and worked as a fireman between 1887 and 1895. While in Mississippi on a passenger run, Brown was nearly involved in a terrible wreck. The train was running late. As Brown told it to an interviewer in the 1930s, the engineer ordered, "Boy, bear down on dat shovel," in the hopes of beating the express train. "He don't have to tell dis nigger to bear down on de shovel, 'cause Ise know weuns have to make de lake sidin' or Ise a gone nigger," Brown recalled. However, the engineer inexplicably pulled the throttle "wide open an' leves it thar," placing the burden upon Brown to "make de steam to get de speed." He had to deposit the coal more carefully than usual so as to maximize its use by the engine. The speed of the train and the low areas in the track led Brown to fear that the train would jump the track, and the rocking of the train across low spots made it difficult to feed the coal. Despite the train's high speed, the engineer never pushed in the throttle. Just as they pulled onto the sidetrack and cleared and closed the switch, the express train "thundered by." Brown's achievement went unrecognized by the company. The engineer was discharged for bypassing a stop, and Brown was given a thirty-day layoff.[1]

Brown's narrative reveals some aspects of railroad work. It dramatizes that the commonalities among railroad workers were also part of a context in which black and white, skilled and less skilled, occupied vastly unequal positions of power. What Brown's story does not convey is that whites' association between blackness and subordination did not wholly conform to reality: the unskilled labor force, which labored at the bottom of and under the supervision of an immense occupational hierarchy on the Gould system, was of mixed ancestry. In 1880 in Little Rock, Arkansas, for example, it was not unusual for both whites and blacks to work as porters, car cleaners, trackmen, and laborers. Forty percent of all laborers in Dallas, Texas, in 1886 were white, and although native-born whites "avoided section work at all costs," a number of white laborers, both native and foreign-born, worked in railroad construction crews and as section hands.[2] These men, and the semiskilled men they labored with on a daily basis, indeed the mass of railroaders, stood outside of the railway trade unions. How did non-brotherhood men relate to one another? How deeply were racial and ethnic identities felt, what forms did they take, and under what circumstances did they ebb and flow? In other words, how did these railroaders, who came from varying traditions, regard themselves?[3]

Divisions of race and skill were reflected in the distinct fraternal cultures that railroaders created and nurtured. The most significant and unyielding hierarchy involved race, which white railroaders, whatever their skill or background, accepted and in most cases embraced. Black men's racial consciousness is more difficult to document, but many seemed to have seen railroad work as a means of escaping or at least mitigating the limitations that whites imposed. Much more permeable than the color line, but still significant, was the barrier between railroad brotherhood and non-brotherhood men. Brotherhood men mainly drew and guarded this line, but some semiskilled and unskilled railroaders rejected the brotherhood credo and posited their own conception of the relationship between labor and manhood. Outside of these experiences and identities stood bonded laborers—Chinese and convict workers—whose presence helped to inspire resentment and anxiety over the fate of free laborers in the post–Civil War era.[4]

Inside and Outside the Brotherhoods

Railroaders who belonged to the major trade union brotherhoods—the Order of Railway Conductors (ORC), the Brotherhood of Locomotive Firemen (BLF), and the Brotherhood of Locomotive Engineers (BLE)—in many ways stood apart from those who did not. This was largely due to the course charted by these unions during the late 1870s and early 1880s. Following the great railway strike of 1877, the ORC, BLE, and BLF struggled to attain legitimacy in the eyes of the public and railway officials by distancing their organizations from labor conflict almost entirely. They sought to provide railroad companies with, in one BLE leader's words, "good, reliable, trustworthy men," and in return gain for their members job stability, social respectability, and recognition for the critical role they played in railroads' operation and growth. With trade unions' legal obstacles and the state's demonstration of its power in 1877 in mind, leaders of the railway brotherhoods proceeded cautiously. Their speeches and union literature emphasized an acceptance of powerful railroad corporations, acknowledgment of employer authority, and rejection of strikes as a means of resolving labor conflicts. Peter M. Arthur of the BLE proclaimed in 1883, for example, "There is no occasion for this constant warfare between capital and labor... Their interests are identical."[5]

Arthur's philosophy attracted members due in large part to the success railway trade unions had enjoyed in negotiating work rules and wages during the early 1880s. Railway officials, still reeling from the social crisis of 1877 and in need of manpower, generally cooperated with the brotherhoods, signing a number of contracts with the BLE.[6] By January 1886, Eugene Debs, editor of the *Locomotive Firemen's Magazine*, could boast that some railroad companies had allowed delegates free transportation to the BLE convention, saving the order approximately $24,000. Union journals confidently claimed that management had come to value the expertise and dependability of union members, and to trust the peaceable overtures of union leaders. Debs remarked in 1884, well before the Pullman strike radicalized him, "We take it for granted that when [sober, industrious, faithful] men are employed, railroad officials will pay them all they can afford."[7]

For evidence of the benefits of seeking conciliation, brotherhood loyalists had only to look to the experience of the Order of Railway Conductors. Between 1868 and 1890, the ORC renounced the use of strikes, carefully cultivated its relationship with management, and sought to uplift members through self-help. In contrast to the BLE and BLF, both of which were split and nearly destroyed by members' participation in the 1877 strikes, members of the ORC avoided involvement in that conflict almost entirely. The order therefore did not face the uphill battle that the BLE and BLF did to regain legitimacy in the eyes of railroad officials and middle-class Americans.[8]

Brotherhood leaders realized that their bargaining power and influence depended upon more than a conciliatory stance. Craft exclusivity was crucial to their strategy. Both the ORC and the BLE, for example, banned firemen from membership, and the BLE required engineers to work for one year before applying for membership.[9] However, the brotherhood activists also had faith that they might foster cooperation between railroad companies and employees, and contribute to the society's moral and economic advancement, by exhibiting "manly virtues." These virtues were defined by active citizenship, industriousness, and attention to duty and responsibility. BLF delegates greeted with enthusiastic applause a lawyer for the railroad industry who emphasized this theme in his speech before an 1882 BLF convention. Bayless W. Hanna addressed the firemen not as "employees" but as "representatives" of the railroad industry, the "animating spirit of the entire universe." He linked those qualities understood to be "manly"—"a sober, steady, strong hand"—to the development of the railroads and thus the nation, concluding, "You are a part, and a necessary part, of our entire railroad system. How important, how vast, how essential that system has become, I need not tell you."[10]

Whether members of the BLF, the ORC or the BLE, skilled railroaders were steeped in a fraternal culture. Brotherhood fraternalism emerged due to strategic, social, psychological, and ideological impulses. Secrecy served the pragmatic purpose of protecting members from employer retaliation and public attack, especially in the early years of the brotherhoods, while complex rituals bound participants to one another. Brotherhood membership provided insurance benefits in case of death or injury, a travel system to help unionists find work, and protection against newcomers undercutting wages. At the same time, the appeal of moral uplift, the pull of occupational identities, and desire for respectability played significant roles in inspiring fraternalism.[11] A particularly attractive feature of the brotherhoods was the refuge they offered to railroaders from an unstable world—the uncertainty and dislocation that accompanied not only railroad work but also industrial society. One brotherhood member explained, "Here the world is shut out. You are now separated from its cares and distinctions, from its dissension and vices. Here friendship asserts its mild dominion, while unity and true brotherly love combine to bless the mind with peace and soften the heart with justice."[12] This is not to say that railway workers neatly divided between skilled brotherhood members and unskilled or less skilled nonunion men. First, a significant number of firemen and engineers who outwardly embraced the unions' moral and social codes either found it impossible to live up to them or were rejected for political or personal reasons. The names of these men appear in the long lists of expulsions published in union journals.

Second, the apprentice-like quality of work arrangements among trainmen to some extent blurred the line between brotherhood and non-brotherhood men. Frequently engineers and conductors expected certain brakemen and firemen to eventually acquire the skills necessary for promotion and brotherhood membership. Engineers and conductors were typically older men who supervised younger men, a situation that encouraged a sort of parental relationship in the running trades. It was not altogether uncommon, for instance, for a brakeman to refer to the conductor as "chief," "dad," or "old man," or for the conductor to call a brakeman "nipper" or "brakie."[13] Finally, at times the brotherhoods were in the forefront of successful labor protests that benefited railway workers more broadly. In Texas, for example, the 1877 strike played out peacefully, and, under the brotherhoods' leadership, workers saw pay cuts restored. Under these circumstances, the less skilled likely felt some camaraderie with their skilled counterparts.[14]

While these nicknames communicated affection and signified the opportunity for occupational mobility, they also underlined the considerable authority that engineers and conductors held over less skilled railroaders. Brotherhood members tended to view the source of this authority as both moral and technical in nature. One contributor to the BLE journal asserted that firemen who hoped to become engineers needed to be of "good moral character and temperate habits," intimating that those firemen who failed to gain promotion lacked such qualities. Seeking to carry the banner of "respectability" that other railroaders were to follow, brotherhood members attempted to set themselves apart from those below them on the occupational ladder and from non-brotherhood men in general, as the magnificent pageantry and formality of brotherhood conventions illustrate.[15]

The extent to which the unskilled or less skilled resented the brotherhoods' condescension and exclusiveness is difficult to determine, because on the one hand, the brotherhoods' approach to the "labor question" was increasingly influential during the early 1880s among a number of less-skilled railroaders. Brakemen formed a benevolent society in New York in 1883 and switchmen organized the Switchmen's Mutual Aid Association, which by 1885 had spread to a number of midwestern and western towns and cities, including locales along the lines of Jay Gould's southwestern roads. Both organizations were based on the brotherhoods' model. The stated purpose of the switchmen's union was "mutual advancement, mutual protection, and mutual good, which is necessary due to the hazardous employment" of its members.[16] On the other hand, the brakemen and switchmen brotherhoods were far weaker than the BLF, BLE, or ORC. While approximately four out of five engineers and firemen belonged to the BLE and BLF, respectively, few railroaders outside of these occupations received any kind of union protection, and skilled shopmen's unions had suffered in the aftermath of the 1877 strikes.[17]

Certainly the dearth of engineers, conductors, and firemen proved important to the strength of their trade union movements, in contrast to machinists, who were overcome by the entry of semiskilled men. Presumably a number of brakemen and switchmen expected to win promotion and thus forewent membership in brakemen's or switchmen's brotherhoods. Beyond these economic factors, however, one must consider that many railroaders came away from the 1877 strikes with a far different set of lessons than the brotherhood leadership did. Some renounced unionism altogether and committed themselves to individual solutions to the "labor question." Others, who had participated in the 1877 strikes and supported industrial organizations involved in the strikes, such as the Brakemen's Brotherhood and Machinists and Blacksmiths Union, continued to harbor sympathy for a cooperative strategy, despite the collapse of these unions in the strike's aftermath. In the late 1870s, machinists such as Terence Powderly left the Machinists and Blacksmiths Union to join the Knights of Labor, an industrial union, and an unknown number of 1880s-era migrants carried their support of federation and distrust of craft unionism with them to the West and Southwest.[18]

Moreover, a significant number of switchmen and brakemen developed identities rooted in the nature of their work, identities that directly challenged the brotherhoods' exclusive creed. Rather than look to the brotherhoods for guidance, switchmen traditionally acted as a "natural bridge between workers employed on different roads." Their inclination to engage in sympathy strikes was in large part a result of their frequent contact with men in the running trades as well as men in other industries, such as meatpacking and freight handling, and men working in the yards of other railroads. Finally, however much conductors, engineers, and firemen looked askance at them, brakemen and switchmen took deep pride in their considerable skill and distinct occupational culture. Conductors might refer to brakemen as "clowns" and the caboose where brakemen spent much of their time as the "zoo" or "ape wagon," but brakemen tended to revel in their reputation as footloose, rowdy risk takers whose precision and nerve helped to make railroad operation possible.[19]

As the conflicting identities of conductors and brakemen indicate, skilled and less skilled railroaders articulated different and often competing conceptions of manhood. Brakemen, along with switchmen and engineers, were more inclined to view the mobility, physical deftness, and danger that characterized their work as evidence of virility. The relative absence of manual labor, the confrontation with the elements, and the direct mastery over technology in the conductor's work led engineers to call them "posturing dandies in kid gloves," "brass buttons," and "silk gloves." Conductors returned this contempt and so expressed their own particular ideas about what qualities best define an honorable man. They nicknamed engineers "hogs" and "grunts," emphasizing conductors' distance from the operation of trains and identification as junior railroad officials.[20]

Aside from these tensions, social factors such as age, itinerancy, and marital status often bridged the gap between the identities of the semiskilled and skilled. For Harry French, for example, the allure of migrating from one exciting western town to another receded with time. After several moves, he had tired of roving and finally settled in a place satisfactory to both he and his wife, Molly. He "hated the thought of selling" his home and even sought a demotion from conductor to fireman in order to avoid discharge by a hostile trainmaster and the loss of his hard-won, more sedentary existence. Thus began the slow transition in French's self-image from rambunctious "boomer" to community-minded "old-timer." The latter group tended to regard itself as quite different from and superior to the former. A similar process occurred for many brakemen, firemen, and switchmen, who came to seek the stability and respectability they had once rejected as younger, more geographically mobile men.[21]

Race and Ethnicity

In his history of race and turn-of-the-twentieth-century railroad brotherhoods, Eric Arnesen notes, "Brotherhood men set themselves apart from new immigrants and African Americans through a process of self-definition in which their notions of American nationality were linked explicitly to beliefs about character and behavior and implicitly to notions of racial difference." Brotherhood members were white, usually native-born men who generally saw the unskilled as degraded, dependent, and unmanly, in part because they associated common labor with blacks, Mexicans, European immigrants, and the Chinese.[22] Like many nineteenth-century whites, they generally believed blacks and Mexicans to be devoid of "mental and moral attributes" and Chinese and European immigrants to be ignorant and more committed to Old World ways than to the United States and its democratic institutions. Brotherhood leaders drew upon republican political theory to argue that the republic would fall without white workingmen like themselves, since civic virtue depended upon personal autonomy, economic independence, and manhood, characteristics, in their view, that only native-born white Americans possessed. The major brotherhoods made whiteness a requirement for membership. The BLF's 1885 constitution, for example, directed locals to admit only those who were "white born, of good moral character, sober and industrious, sound in body and limb, and not less than eighteen years of age, and able to read and write the English language."[23]

In the newly conquered region of the Southwest, race took on a particular significance to skilled white railroaders' understandings of the meaning of their work. The journals of railroad brotherhoods regularly published tales of frontier life meant to thrill readers with accounts of Indian wars, famous scouts, and "savage" customs. These stories suggest considerable identification with the expansionist fervor of the period. This was expressed for example in New Mexico's *Silver City Chronicle*, which proclaimed the arrival of the Missouri, Kansas & Texas Railway as the dawning of a new era in which "the red inhabitants could no longer bar the doors against his pale face brothers" and concluded, "Enterprise backed with push is following in the wake of the Great Bonanza Civilizer."[24] Engineer Sam Hobart made a direct association between race, skill, manhood, and Anglo domination of the West. After lauding the engineer as a key figure in the nation's commerce and the "Anglo-Saxon races" for their role in "opening up the western lands," he asserted: "The man who labors with his hands and does not work his brain must forever live from hand to mouth. It is brainwork attended by hand work that makes Titans of men."[25] If placed within the broader context of the brotherhoods' pattern of racial exclusion, one frequent theme in the literature of skilled railroaders further evinces the link many made between race, manhood, and skill. The struggle for dominance between technology and man, in the form of the locomotive and the engineer, was commonplace in the stories, poems, and articles published by the *Locomotive*

Engineer's Monthly Magazine. These sources echo engineer Sam Hobart's metaphor of the locomotive as a "fiery steed," its "great breast . . . a furnace of burning coals," its "lymphatic blood . . . boiling in his veins." It is an "iron horse" that the engineer must master, despite "storm and snow," "slush and mire," and other assorted hardships. In the brotherhoods' view, however, only whites were capable of possessing the qualities necessary to avert disaster, qualities such as wise judgment, presence of mind, and supreme control.[26]

The brotherhoods' hostility stemmed not only from racial beliefs but also economic anxieties. Over the late nineteenth century, their leaders increasingly expressed the fear that the "aristocracy of wealth," with the help of "cheap negro labor and cheap foreign labor," would reduce white workingmen to slavery, misery, and squalor. Racial and economic fears intertwined in the minds of J. J. Thomas and his fellow southern engineers, for instance, who during the 1870s threatened to "quit to a man" if blacks were hired for hostler work. They argued that while blacks had won political rights, "they could not run engines." A hostler's work merely involved wiping the engine clean and running it in and out of the roundhouse, but the position was a stepping-stone from which one might be promoted to fireman and then engineer, thus the ferocity of the engineers' protest. Thomas and his cohorts probably feared that black hostlers would not only eventually compete with them for runs and depress their wages but also that the presence of black hostlers would jeopardize the psychological benefits that Thomas and many other whites derived from racially exclusive rules.[27]

Certainly whites' cumulative experience on the roads, and in society at large, encouraged them to equate black men and women with work that seemed to them the antithesis of industrialism or with work considered undesirable in general. Their popular slang reveals this: "nigger locals" were short runs with frequent stops, while "nigger track" referred to seldom used track in a remote area. These assumptions also guided the decisions of government and railroad officials, reinforcing the notion that whites were at the forefront of industrial progress and therefore should be its principal beneficiaries. In 1867, George Mortimer Pullman fortified the traditional association whites made between servility and black people when he accepted only blacks as Pullman porters on his luxurious "hotels on wheels."[28] The engraving on a silver soup tureen, given in 1880 to James Paramore, the owner of St. Louis's first cotton press, conveys a similar message. On one side of the tureen a modern cotton press is pictured, and the tureen's lid handle is shaped to resemble a freight car filled with flattened cotton bales. On the other side are black sharecroppers working in a field. Though in reality crucial actors in the industrial process celebrated by the tureen, black working people were ideologically relegated to the most elemental role within that process.[29]

The racial code etched onto Paromore's tureen largely governed the working relationships among black and white railroaders. Until the late 1960s and early 1970s, across the United States, the most desirable positions of locomotive engineer and train conductor were reserved for whites only, and in shops and roundhouses throughout the South whites relegated blacks to the lowest occupational rungs. Exclusion of black men from the running trades may have been even stricter in the 1870s and 1880s than in the heyday of Jim Crow. Eric Arnesen describes the white backlash to black workers in firing and braking positions on southern railroads at the turn of the twentieth century, but in 1880 few African Americans engaged in this kind of work in Dallas, Texarkana, Marshall, or Little Rock, four major sites of labor unrest on the Gould system. Odds are that those who managed to enter semiskilled work enjoyed less pay, performed extra duties, and were never promoted to conductor.[30]

The racial and ethnic fault lines between railroad workers shifted according to time and place. In the antebellum North and Midwest, construction and track crews were often Irish or German. Few blacks worked on northern railroads before the war, but in the South, an estimated twenty thousand enslaved people worked as firemen, skilled shopmen, brakemen, and yardmen on the eve of the Civil War. During the war, both the Confederacy and the Union relied upon black laborers to build, repair, and maintain roads essential to the war effort. At the war's end, southern blacks and whites increasingly competed over unskilled or lesser-skilled railroad jobs. Mainly Chinese, Irish, and Japanese workers constructed and maintained the roads in the Far West, while chiefly Chinese laborers but also native-born whites, blacks, Mexicans, Indians, and European immigrants graded, laid, and maintained track in remote areas along the lines of the Southern Pacific and Atchison, Topeka & Santa Fe.[31]

The fault lines between white railroaders of different origins were complex, as an examination of two Texas strike towns illustrates. In Texarkana and Marshall, white railroaders came from many different sections of the country—from northern and midwestern states such as Pennsylvania, New

York, Illinois, Indiana, and Maine, and from southern states such as Georgia, South Carolina, Tennessee, Alabama, and Arkansas—with no one region dominating. Presumably a number of men may have fought in the Civil War on opposing sides or may have been the sons of those who did. Besides Irish and English immigrants, there was in Texarkana a switchman from Denmark, a carpenter from Canada, and a brakeman from Sweden. In Marshall, white railroaders also hailed from Germany and Scotland. Germans, Italians, and native-born whites, along with Mexicans, Chinese, and blacks, built the southern transcontinental road through Texas in the early 1880s. Although the lines of separation were evident, many worked and lived near one another. Julia Grimes Jones Ocklbary, for example, remembers cooking for Irish, Mexican, and black section hands, and serving them at separate tables at a boardinghouse in Austin during the late nineteenth century.[32]

The presence of laborers from varying traditions and backgrounds did not necessarily fracture white racial identity. Walter Licht notes that "between 1830 and 1880, the [railroading] trade expanded rapidly and genuine and growing employment and promotion opportunities materialized for both native and foreign-born Americans, with one great proviso: that one's skin color was white." While the available evidence on the Gould system relates more to exterior circumstances than to railroaders' interior sense of identity, the 1880 census data for Marshall and Texarkana bears this statement out, at least in regard to northern European immigrants. In both Marshall and Texarkana, Irish immigrants, and to a lesser extent English immigrants, frequently held skilled positions as engineers, boilermakers, firemen, machinists, and blacksmiths. That a Scottish-born machinist named Martin Irons could readily find railroad employment, serve in several multi-class and multiethnic protective organizations in Kentucky and Missouri, and lead the 1886 Southwest Strike further demonstrates that the line between immigrant and native-born was less important in railroad work that it once had been.[33]

Combined with a relatively cohesive white racial identity, social mobility limited the extent to which the unskilled identified with one another across racial lines. Especially on the expanding southwestern roads, where skilled positions were scarcer than in the East, white "boomers" could reasonably expect to climb to a more skilled position. They tended to associate their own dreams of social mobility with control over black labor. Harry French, for example, did not reveal any fear in his biography that he would remain a switchman; he seemed to expect a steady rise up the ladder. Upon meeting a conductor for the first time when he was twelve years old in East St. Louis, French admired the man's immaculate clothes, his self-assurance, and his ability to pay a black man to shine his shoes and "negro waiters in spotless white garments" to serve him dinner. Had French journeyed to Marshall or Texarkana, he almost certainly would have been impressed with the large number of conductors and engineers who hired black cooks, washerwomen, and nurses for their families and that boardinghouses frequently employed black servants to wait on white railroaders.[34]

Certain conditions cut against racial identities. Unskilled blacks and whites lived in a particular working world, for example. They labored in close proximity to one another, often in remote locations, were more vulnerable to the arbitrary rule of foremen and the vagaries of the labor market, and, despite the risks of their work, suffered social stigma, unlike the engineer, whom the public celebrated in story and song as a "hero of the rails" and a pillar of the community. Moreover, the distinctive work cultures of non-brotherhood men made cross-skill and even cross-racial organizing imaginable. Not coincidentally, these workers played a leading role in the 1885–1886 strikes and identified strongly with the more inclusive Knights, in contrast to conductors, engineers, and firemen, who ultimately remained loyal to the craft-based, racially exclusive, conservative brotherhoods.

However, outside of a context of immediate crisis, unskilled whites likely sought to emphasize the differences that they perceived between themselves and black workers. Whites generally shunned section work, probably because such work was poorly paid, dangerous, physically demanding, and less likely to result in promotion, but also because they associated common labor with nonwhites, as the brotherhoods did. Racial hierarchies among whites and blacks working and living near one another were not as flexible as one might suppose, even in the western cattle industry, where black cowboys' skills and courage otherwise won them the respect and admiration of white coworkers.[35] The influx of northern white or European immigrant railroaders into the Southwest probably reinforced Jim Crow on the roads, as Irish and Irish American men and women in the Northeast had long come into conflict with blacks over mainly unskilled work.[36] Furthermore, in the experience of most northern white railroaders, blacks were largely excluded from railroad work. Many of these men may well have expected to find the same level of racial exclusion on the southwestern railroads. Finally, black and white laborers often worked in segregated gangs, and boarded and ate separately. Even among convict laborers on the railroad, the color line dictated that white prisoners cut three-quarters of a cord of wood per day while blacks were to cut one full cord.[37]

The narratives of twenty-nine ex-slaves interviewed in Texas during the 1930s offer some insights into both the aspirations and dilemmas of black railroaders. Most were men who worked for the railroads, while a few were women who had known railroaders or were married to them during that period.[38] A number were employed in the railroad industry for a substantial length of time but most remained at the bottom of the occupational ladder. Robert Wilson, for example, worked for the railroads in Marshall for nearly thirty years between 1873 and 1900 but never moved beyond the position of helper in the railroad shops. Others worked for a short period of time or on a seasonal basis as laborers, section hands, tie cutters, and construction crewmen, mainly during the 1870s when companies built roads through Texas.[39]

One theme that emerges from the narratives is the strong desire not to work as a "rail" but to farm. For many black men and women this occupation remained the best hope for an independent life relatively free of the obstacles that hindered black advancement in industry. Andy McAdams explained, "If we did other work we did not get fair wages for it" and "they were so low that we could not feed ourself, so we farmed." He added that farming allowed his family to grow "near about all that we ate." When Exodusters turned out for a mass meeting in Parsons, Kansas, in 1882, they agreed that most of "the present colored residents of Southern Kansas . . . have been cultivators of the soil before coming here and still prefer that occupation." For many the path to land ownership, or at least to the financial solvency necessary for land ownership, was waged labor on the railroads. Smith Wilson saved his money while working for the railways for eight years, and bought a farm in Rusk County. Many white railroaders also eventually farmed as a sole means of sustenance, but the discrimination in hiring, pay, and promotion probably led black railroaders to view railroad work as temporary work that would allow them to pursue an ultimate goal of land ownership.[40]

For Henry Baker, railroading represented an opportunity to travel and sow his wild oats while earning the cash wages necessary to establish a farm and family. Baker worked on an extra gang for a railroad in Palestine for three months in the early 1880s, but this job was just one of many he held on farms and at hotels as a young man. In seeking work, he moved from Hempstead to Austin and then to Palestine. But he was "jus' foolin' 'round in Palestine" and soon "tired of runin' 'round," so he used the money he had saved to rent a farm in Robertson County. He married and had two sons. Similarly, Anthony Christopher left his father's farm to work in San Antonio and then on the railroad, laying track to Devil's River, where he took up gambling. After working for the Santa Fe Railway near Brenham, Texas, he married and began farming.[41]

Baker's and Christopher's travels demonstrate the role the railroad industry played in swelling and broadening black migration throughout the South, thwarting the web of labor controls planters had implemented to control black labor since the end of the Civil War. During the 1870s, thousands of freedmen working in the fields found employment on railroad construction projects. Planters complained that they increasingly competed for laborers with other planters, new enterprises such as the railroads, and in Texas, also the cattle and lumber industries. Upon their return to the farms at the end of their terms on railroad construction gangs, black laborers "brought with them a new sense of independence" and willingness to challenge planters' authority.[42]

By the 1880s, railroads crisscrossed the northern and eastern parts of Texas, and extended into the western, northern, and southern portions of the country, allowing black men a greater opportunity to work on railroads, and in saloons, lumber mills, and hotels throughout the South and Southwest. Although blacks saw these prospects dwindle following Reconstruction, itinerant workers, porters, and waiters who returned home to farm or to visit family and friends in rural areas brought with them knowledge of the wider world. Others never returned to their rural hometowns. Migrants, especially young men, who moved to fast-growing towns and cities, often remained there or moved on to "look out for new opportunities, resist indignities, and join new organizations."[43]

Jiles Joplin, the father of Scott Joplin, the famed composer of ragtime piano songs, ballets, and operas, managed to secure a stable position as a laborer for the Texas & Pacific in Texarkana, Texas, during the 1880s. He saw it as "a step up from the uncertainty and isolated drudgery of farm labor." He made clear his belief in the advantages of railroading when he recommended it to his son as a responsible and stable career. Jiles Joplin's railroad work also made it possible for his children to attend public schools, an advantage more readily available in bustling towns such as Texarkana than in rural farm areas. Furthermore, as Susan Curtis puts it, "the coming and going of trains gave Texarkanans—both black and white—a sense of movement and opportunity and brought them into contact with people, goods, ideas, and sounds from all parts of the country."[44]

Geographic mobility offered space for better wages, excitement, fraternal bonding, and new beginnings that might affirm manhood, but separation was often hard on families. While in isolated rural areas black men had great difficulty finding work, black women could usually earn money laundering, ironing, cooking, and cleaning in white homes. The migration of male members of the family represented a chance for the family to escape abject poverty and even to gain wages sufficient to support the family, but, in contrast to a white itinerant, a black itinerant had less reason to hope for promotion, job stability, and the wages necessary to support wife and children, and to eventually move them to his new place of employment. Even those black families in which a man worked regularly as a railroad laborer needed other members to supplement the family income. Although Jiles Joplin remained a steady employee of the Texas & Pacific, as a laborer he received the lowest wages paid to railroad employees. One of his sons worked as a porter while a daughter labored as a laundress in order to meet the family's needs.[45]

Ex-slave Thomas Cole's story illustrates the precarious position that black railroaders occupied in a region deeply marked by the conflicts of Civil War and Reconstruction. While enslaved in Alabama, Cole ran away and joined the Union Army and fought in battles at Lookout Mountain, Orchard Knob, and Chattanooga. He was horrified at the war's human toll, but he apparently held high hopes for his future following the war. He recalled that during the late 1860s his hard work on the railroads won him the trainmaster's recommendation and a promotion to a yardman's position in Chattanooga. There he spent a portion of his wages on a new set of clothes and a dance in the black section of town. He married, eventually bought a house, a cow, some chickens, and a brood sow, and apparently got along well enough with his white coworkers to occasionally share a drink. Probably in the late 1860s or early 1870s, Cole got a job as a switchman, which he held for seven years. His stable world crumbled, however, when the white men he worked with at the railroad yards "found out dat I had runs off from de south and jined de north" during the war. Some of the brakemen tried to have him fired, so he had to watch his step, paying extra attention to signposts and train rules. He finally quit when another brakeman attempted to sabotage his job by opening a switch Cole had just closed. Cole then moved his family to Illinois, where he applied for railroad work without success.

Cole's position on the railroad was not necessarily doomed because he was black. Had his wartime activities remained a secret, he might have continued switching without serious challenge from white railroaders. The fact that his white coworkers resorted to sabotage in order to have him fired indicates that Cole's supervisor, for whatever reason, did not find service in the U.S. Colored Troops sufficient cause for dismissal. But his fellow railroaders considered Cole to have violated a racial code that demanded from him at the very least a neutral stance in regard to the issues the war raised. He had participated in a military force that many southern whites equated with insurrection, northern treachery, the humiliation of defeat and occupation, and "outrages" against white manhood and womanhood. Given the level of Klan terror following the war, it is surprising that Cole lost his job and not his life.[46]

Black railway workers, then, faced a stark contradiction. At the same time that the occupation provided a chance to affirm their manhood—to provide for a family, gain some measure of self-sufficiency, and move about—it required black men to conceal these independent and worldly traits from whites. The cultural resources of black workers express frustration with this dilemma. Songs dedicated to the black steel driver John Henry, for example, found widespread appeal among black laborers of all kinds, whose work was otherwise uncelebrated and denigrated by whites and many middle-class black leaders. What Robin G. Kelley might call a "hidden transcript of resistance" is revealed in less epic tales as well, such as Steve Brown's oral history to the WPA about his near-wreck. Brown was an ordinary man forced to draw upon all of his skill and courage, the same "manly virtues" white railroaders claimed only for themselves, in avoiding a disaster not of his own making. His story offered a black "hero of the rails," a fireman who had to think and act quickly in a battle against not only technology but also an incompetent white engineer, thereby inverting the famous picture presented on the cover of an 1873 issue of *Harper's Magazine* of a brave white engineer, "sticking to his post," with his faithful black helper at his side.[47]

Black railroaders faced another dilemma: their experiences did not meet the expectations that a number of mainly middle-class black leaders held of them. Major black newspapers in the Southwest focused their protests on mob violence and civil rights discrimination on railway passenger cars and in organizations such as churches, schools, and fraternal societies. The editor of the *Arkansas Weekly Mansion* of Little Rock was less critical, however, of the obstacles black men faced in employment, emphasizing instead, as many black leaders in Arkansas did by 1880, self-help, self-improvement, and assimilation rather than protest. Of Arkansas he urged, "You are as free here as in Canada... Come on, boys." Black men should "do like white men, serve first awhile as a porter, then as clerk, then for themselves and in this way we will become able to fill all the positions in life, filled by any other race." While acknowledging there was still room for complaint, this editor pronounced, "the colored people have more privileges here than in any other northern state."[48]

Certainly some fluidity existed in black migrants' social status. Little Rock was the home of a small but growing middle-class black community composed of dentists, ministers, landowners, editors, businessmen, and steadily employed railroad brakemen, porters, and mail clerks.[49] Black editors issued reminders to laborers of the presence of this middle class and of the necessity of remaining "sober and industrious" in order to enter it. This likely troubled men who were employed as itinerant laborers in track and section work or resistant to affecting servility, a requirement for gaining steady work among white railroaders. Failure to join the middle class appeared as a moral failing, not only an individual failing but also a failing as a representative of one's race. In "A Word to Our Young Men," the *Kansas Herald* warned that the "future of the race" rested upon their shoulders. If young men did not attain refinement, respectability, and intelligence, they "will be culpable" when the race "still stands accursed, bearing slavery's footprints." An 1882 letter to the *Colored Patriot* sent a similar message. While decrying the racial bars that prevented "our educated young men" from entering accounting houses or trades, the writer urged, "Our boys and girls must be trained to be more ambitious and aspiring and self-dependent. We must be menials and pariahs no longer."[50]

While unskilled blacks labored in the shadow of slavery to establish themselves as free men, the railroads exploited two forms of bonded labor, convict and contract labor. As had been the case since colonial times, when free men and women, Jack Tars, apprentices, indentured servants, and slaves worked under varying conditions and compulsions, different degrees of freedom and bondage existed among workers on the post–Civil War railways.[51]

Free and Bonded Labor

The first large gang of Chinese laborers came to Texas in 1870 under contract with the Houston & Texas Central Railroad. The laborers, numbering around three hundred, helped to construct the company's road from Calvert to Corsicana and then on to Dallas. When financial duress forced the company to renounce its contract, and a suit by the laborers against the company failed to regain them employment, many of the migrants settled where they were, in Robertson County, and worked as field hands and sharecroppers there until at least the early 1880s. In 1874 J. H. Hanna, a cotton farmer, replenished his work force with fifty-nine farm laborers brought directly from China and perhaps Cuba through the port of Galveston. A much larger contingent of Chinese, many from California, entered Texas in 1881 when the Southern Pacific employed mainly Chinese laborers to maintain the track from Los Angeles to El Paso and to construct a road 460 miles eastward from El Paso to the Pecos River. By the time the Southern Pacific reached the Pecos, where it became the nation's second transcontinental railroad line upon linking up with the Galveston, Harrisburg & San Antonio, about twenty-six hundred of the three thousand laborers in the area were Chinese.[52]

Contract laborers were immigrants who agreed to work for a specified period of time (usually one year or more) in order to eradicate the debts they had incurred migrating and boarding in the United States, and to save money that was usually put toward establishing a more secure life in their home country. They could be physically coerced under the law. In May 1867, for example, Chinese workers on the Union Pacific Railroad struck in protest of both low wages and "the right of the overseers of the company to either whip them or restrain them from leaving the road when they desire to seek other employment."[53] J. H. Strobridge, who oversaw the Chinese laborers' construction of the Central Pacific in the Sierra Nevada Mountains, supervised Chinese gangs as they built the Southern Pacific Railroad through Texas during the early 1880s. Under his authority, it was reported, "The

Chinese are treated more like slaves than anything else, they are drove [*sic*] round and sometimes used severely, if they don't work to suit the bosses."[54]

Such coercion developed primarily among supervisors of unskilled laborers who possessed little knowledge of the English language, worked in isolated areas, and suffered public antipathy. Where this was not the case, contract labor was generally not a viable option for companies seeking to attract a steady and reliable source of labor, because immigrants often either refused to sign a contract due to the long length of service, or signed and then abandoned their jobs and thus their debts. For a large number of Chinese immigrants the situation was quite different. About one hundred eighty thousand migrated to the United States under the supervision of a few major Chinese merchants, most to work in remote western locations for railroad and mining companies. They agreed to a credit-ticket system, which required that laborers sign contracts upon their arrival in the United States (rather than in their home country) after they had already amassed debts to their Chinese agents for passage and board.[55]

Upon the railroad's completion, many Chinese laborers left the state, but several hundred remained. Their communities came to include Chinese laborers fleeing the virulent anti-Chinese movements in Oregon, California, and Washington, so that over seven hundred Chinese lived in Texas by 1890. Most lived in railroad towns in East, West, and Central Texas. El Paso especially possessed a flourishing Chinese population. A number there owned almost all of the city's laundry businesses in 1886. Chinese migrants also established laundries in other major Texas cities such as Galveston, and in small towns like Corsicana, Denison, San Angelo, and Amarillo. In addition to Chinese-run laundries, Chinese-run restaurants were, according to historian Edward J. M. Rhoads, a "familiar feature of... Texas cities" and were "usually located near the railroad station," where they catered to passengers as well as railway men.[56]

Nineteenth-century Chinese migrants in Texas, as elsewhere in the United States, were overwhelmingly male. A "society of bachelors" developed in small towns and cities where the Chinese resided, in large part because many were "sojourners" whose chief aim was to return to China with savings, and possibly even riches, earned in the United States. The Exclusion Act of 1882, which barred Chinese migrants (except for teachers, merchants, students, and travelers) from entry into the United States, reinforced the male character of the immigrant population, since wives could not migrate to join their husbands. Women in fact comprised only two percent of Chinese migrants to the United States during the 1880s. Due to prevailing racial codes, intermarriage was rare, which further contributed to the continuance of a society of "bachelors." In Robertson County, only four of the seventy-two Chinese railroaders remaining there in 1880 married.[57]

In Robertson County and in El Paso, two major areas that the Chinese settled in Texas, they "pursued their own way of life, separated from the rest of the population." "They consulted their herbalist doctors and celebrated their distinctive festivals," and their celebration of the Lunar New Year "never [failed] to attract the attention of the city's newspapers." Chinese laborers living in isolated railroad camps along the Southern Pacific lines also lived a separate life. Archaeological research conducted at a number of labor campsites in West Texas demonstrates that imported items allowed them to continue their cultural practices, at least as far as diet and medicine were concerned.[58]

Segregation was also imposed by non-Chinese railroaders and by the surrounding community. This was felt in various ways, but two chief ways in which the Chinese were set apart were by the wages they received on the railroads and by railroad policies regarding laborers' camps. The Southern Pacific Railroad paid the Chinese about half of what was paid other workers, for example. Moreover, the living area for Chinese construction workers on the Southern Pacific was located a considerable distance from the track, far away from the area designated for white laborers, and troops were stationed nearby the Chinese camp. The troops were probably present not only so as to prevent the Chinese from escaping their contracts but also to protect them from their non-Chinese coworkers.[59]

Concern on the part of railroad officials and the state about attacks was certainly warranted. Hostility against the Chinese ran deep. In 1870, 150 Irishmen quit work on the Houston & Texas Central road rather than work beside the "pig-tailed Chinese," continuing a tradition of conflict between Irish and Chinese laborers that had also occurred, with violent, tragic consequences, during the building of the Central Pacific Railroad.[60] In the rugged, barren country of West Texas, Chinese railroaders suffered attacks by Mexican section hands and Irish laborers. Townspeople bolstered anti-Chinese feeling on the railroads with actions of their own. In Toyah, a town on the Southern Pacific line in West Texas, Charles A. Siringo remembered that a crowd that had gathered for the New Year's ball at the Alvarado House celebrated by running all the Chinese men out of town. The *Fort Worth Gazette* singled Chinese residents out for public ridicule, and in 1885 white labor activists in Austin urged a boycott of Chinese businesses and laborers.[61]

While youths "without distinction of race or color" delighted in the Lunar New Year parade of Chinese inhabitants of Calvert, Texas, racial and economic fears overtook cultural curiosity in the minds of many non-Chinese. These economic fears were not wholly unjustified. During the late 1860s, one Union Pacific leader commented that the road's employment of the Chinese had "kept the Irishmen quiet" about wages and working conditions.[62] In an 1874 coal miners' strike, Jay Gould famously had filled the mines with Chinese, who accepted $32.50 per month rather than the $52 paid white men. In addition, those railroading families that depended in part upon the wages of female members earned by laundering also resented the Chinese monopoly over this work. Such resentment surfaced in El Paso during 1880s, when a movement grew to boycott Chinese laundries because they competed with white washerwomen. Black women and their families also felt this competition keenly. The unrest in Galveston associated with the 1877 railway strike included black laundresses' pledge to drive Chinese laundries out of town.[63]

Perhaps the presence of Chinese laborers appeared as a special threat to black sharecroppers and workers since white southerners had once advertised widely the intent to replace black labor with Chinese labor. Such a proposal enjoyed considerable favor at an 1869 convention in Memphis. Though some newspapers, such as the *Dallas Herald*, bemoaned the prospect of "filling our fields and work shops and railroad lines with the offal of China and other idolatrous lands beyond the western ocean," other Texas editors embraced the idea. They reasoned that the Chinese were the "best, cheapest, and most reliable laborers ever known" and pointed out that competition with the Chinese would force emancipated slaves to "work or starve." This idea had tangible effects. It inspired the Houston & Texas Central to import Chinese laborers to Texas and farmers in Robertson County to hire the discharged men and to import more Chinese through the port at Galveston.[64]

Indeed, fearing competition from "cheap labor," skilled and unskilled laborers across the country had rallied against the migration of Chinese labor since the 1850s, and nativist labor movements supplied critical support for the passage of the 1882 Exclusion Act. The Knights of Labor, whose membership requirements were otherwise far more inclusive than those of previous unions, was at the forefront of this movement. Knights participated in and led numerous organizing campaigns against the Chinese, as well as acts of large-scale violence and intimidation, and barred Chinese workers entirely from membership.[65] The mainstream of the labor movement drew upon widespread and long-held ideas that portrayed Chinese people as servile, dirty, corrupt, and backward. Whites commonly complained, for example, about the use of opium among Chinese laborers and the establishment of opium dens and gambling halls in Chinese communities, although, as one historian noted, "Such establishments were characteristic of all Chinatowns, inhabited as they were by unattached males with time on their hands... Probably it was because they were patronized by many non-Chinese as well as Chinese that they drew the wrath of the press and clergy."[66]

Racial beliefs and economic factors proved mutually reinforcing. The unskilled positions the Chinese filled, because this is what they were relegated to, inspired ridicule. Non-Chinese applied the term "coolie," meaning unskilled labor, almost universally to them, which further strengthened the widespread association between the "degraded" Chinese and menial work.[67] Similarly, the participation of the Chinese in the service industry affirmed the view of Chinese men as feminine creatures. As Stephen E. Ambrose notes: "White men despised the Chinese even as they used them. They constantly compared the Chinese to another subordinate group, white women: The Chinese were small, with delicate hands and hairless faces and long, braided hair. One editor called them 'half-made men,' which fit nicely with their two most common jobs, laundrymen and domestic servants."[68] Laundries proved popular among the Chinese because they could be established with only a small investment. Also, since there was little danger of the Chinese competing with white males, this was one area of work from which the Chinese were not barred. But laundering was viewed as women's work, so Chinese men's participation in this field conformed to a number of stereotypes of the Chinese as weak and submissive beings. These stereotypes prevailed even as some could not help but recognize the role of these purportedly "half-made men" in building the nation's most important railroads over inhospitable and dangerous terrain.[69]

The often-exaggerated transience of Chinese immigrants also troubled many non-Chinese. Transience among nonwhites was traditionally seen as a sign of their cultural impoverishment and unmanliness. Writing of immigrant workers, whose relationship to whiteness many mid-nineteenth-century Americans viewed as suspect, Gunther Peck comments, "Devoid of the domestic attachments that in crucial respects defined middle-class manhood and respectability, these 'birds of passage' were seen as beyond the redemption of familial and paternal care."[70] The image of the Chinese as unstable sojourners persisted even where the Chinese set up more permanent residence, such as in El Paso. The instability of their virtually all-male communities convinced their non-Chinese neighbors of their debased character.

If native-born Americans often condemned Chinese immigrants and other immigrants for their perceived lack of attachment—to family and to a fixed geographic location, how secure was the position of those black and white railroaders who moved about in search of work without any apparent evidence of connections to or support for family? The labor mobility of white skilled railroaders does not appear to have greatly tarnished their claim to citizenship. Surely this was because so many inhabitants were new to the region themselves and placed no small amount of faith in skilled white labor's ability to lead the unskilled in building a "New Southwest" free of labor, racial, sectional, and economic conflicts. Certainly, during the 1870s, whites could generally expect to find employment and promotion on the railroads in this labor-scarce area, but by the 1880s unskilled and semiskilled white railroaders who wandered the Southwest in search of work presumably noticed newspapers' worried reports of "tramps" or "vagrants" arriving in town. As long as itinerant white railroaders could find work easily, they probably avoided the label of "tramp" and the complications it posed for their status as citizens.[71] In other words, white railroaders' increasingly vitriolic attacks on the Chinese during the 1880s were likely rooted in part in the concern that in economic hard times they too might find themselves tramping for work, with all of the cultural as well as economic uncertainties this implied.

The social dangers of labor mobility held far different implications for black and white railroaders, however. The arrival of a young black man in a small town, without any identifiable link to family or to a person who could vouch for his character, unsettled many whites. One white Southerner observed, "In nearly all communities there are Negroes of whom none knows the coming, or the going, or even the real names. The Negro is restive, the white apprehensive, and both are growing more and more suspicious."[72] White apprehension quickly turned murderous against black strangers who violated "some invisible and shifting line of permissible behavior," especially in areas of low rural population density and rapid black population growth. One such area was the cotton uplands that spread across central Mississippi, northern Louisiana, southern and central Arkansas, and eastern Texas; this region had the second highest rates of lynching during the late nineteenth and early twentieth centuries.[73]

As they did in regard to Chinese laborers, union activists and local community organizations combined during the 1870s and 1880s to abolish the use of convict laborers. In both Texas and Arkansas, convict leasing received a great deal of bad press and was generally considered barbaric, corrupt, and antagonistic to the interests of free laborers, who argued that the system drove down their wages and limited their opportunities. Anti-leasing petitions signed by citizens of Longview, Harrison County, and Bowie County poured into the Texas governors' office against the use of convict labor. More than three hundred Longview residents urged the governor to end the system and thereby "stay the advancing hand of the monopolist." Reports of the horrific conditions under which prisoners worked and the large number of successful escapes made by leased convicts intensified this opposition.[74]

In Texas, Arkansas, and a number of other southern states, convict leasing grew out of efforts in the 1860s to maintain and control prisoners without rebuilding dilapidated prisons. The practice also opened up possibilities for corruption to both Republican and Democratic politicians. Despite public protest, the system persisted, in part because it provided states with needed public funds and major employers with a cheap, although controversial, source of labor. As historian Michael Mancini concludes, most of all, convict leasing allowed state officials a way of managing convicts, whom they otherwise did not know, or could not imagine, how to occupy.[75]

Texas leased prisoners to plantations and, to a much lesser extent, woodcutters and railroads. Race typically determined where one worked. Between 1878 and 1883, the bulk of convict laborers worked on "Sugarland," a sugar plantation on the Brazos River, known also as the "Hell-Hole of the Brazos." Black convicts, who made up about half of the state's prison population, mostly worked in the sugar fields. In 1882, for example, 710 convicts at Sugarland were white, 128 Mexican, and 812 black. Because prison officials believed blacks were "better adapted in field labors," they were almost always leased to farms or plantations. The railroads generally hired a much smaller number of convicts. In 1880, for instance, only 156 men worked on the railroads but 1,045 on farms. As a general rule, railroads hired from the pool of white prisoners not assigned to plantation labor.[76]

Harrowing reports frequently surfaced on the conditions of convict laborers. The first major lease in Texas, to A. J. Ward and E. C. Dewey, ended in 1876. Their haphazard approach to managing a large population of prisoners had resulted in high rates of death, disease, and escape. Although legislators attempted to resolve this problem by pledging to only do business with "good" lessees, this stance appeared less defensible in 1879 when complaints by citizens of Mineola inspired an investigation of a convict camp near town. There the mostly white workforce was found to be suffering such mistreatment that eighteen had died within four months. Similarly, in 1880 death from typhoid and pneumonia befell one-fifth of the prisoners engaged in railroad construction under the management of one particularly negligent and cruel Arkansas lessee.[77]

Arkansas ran one of the worst leasing systems, as the horror story of Coal Hill on the Arkansas River indicates. Convicts employed in the mines near town in 1888 died in droves of scurvy, malaria, overwork, and outright murder by a particularly sadistic warden, J. A. Gafford, who beat and whipped prisoners, forced them to fight each other to the death, and set dogs upon captured escapees. The corpse of one whipped man had no flesh on the back, and the autopsy of another killed in a forced fight revealed that he had a "broken spinal cord, crushed genitals, and eyes hanging out of his sockets." Significantly, the inspector appointed to oversee the system's reform argued that there was "no reason that working [convicts] in the mines should be condemned," since "they have been just as badly abused out on farms, railroad construction, and other places under this system as at Coal Hill."[78]

Like many antebellum white northerners who abhorred the "slave power" but also slaves, those who called upon the state and employers to end the use of convict and Chinese labor held little sympathy for either Chinese people or prisoners. For black and white railroad workers, the central question that the employment of Chinese and convict laborers raised was: "How free is free?" The Civil War had abolished chattel slavery, but the insecurities, inequalities, and dependence many free railroaders experienced, especially the unskilled, existed uneasily alongside the claims of "free labor" ideology, which promised to the thrifty, industrious man social mobility, an income adequate to support a family, and the absence of coercion. As one historian puts it, "For the unskilled, transient worker, the right to earn wages was as much a gamble as a promise, a chance to earn a livelihood but also the right to starve if one failed or was injured on the job."[79]

Although modern historians do well to caution against conflating slavery and contract or convict labor, the gulf between these often appears clearer to twentieth-century observers than it did to post–Civil War Americans. David Brion Davis comments in regard to black southerners, "If one has been working on a plantation or in a penal camp for most of one's life, it probably makes little difference whether one got there by the legal fiction of sale as a piece of property or as the result of some alleged civil or political crime." That the lives and well-being of Chinese and convict laborers were of so little value to employers beyond their productive capacity likely reminded free laborers of how uncertain and ill-defined the relationship was between free and slave labor.[80] This was particularly true for employees of large corporations such as the railroads, which enacted oppressive labor policies conceived in distant places. Reports of "the degraded Chinese" and the brutal conditions of convict labor camps heightened free laborers' anxieties about the stakes involved in the "gamble" of the labor market and hardened their determination to guard their chances.

While Steve Brown's harrowing experience as a fireman on a speeding train reminds us of the dangers that railroad men knew and thus the labor kinship that they shared, hierarchy and conflict was the crucial theme in his story. The power of white workers and railroad officials intertwined to form a taut knot holding Brown and other black workers in place at the bottom of the railroads' social and economic ladder, binding black to black and white to white. Another bond pulled brotherhood men in one direction and skilled shopmen, the unskilled, and semi-skilled in another. The conditions that western railroaders met with in the 1880s and the Knights' "producer" ideology slackened these knots, allowing a broad coalition to gather against Jay Gould's railroad empire. This alliance was in part based on widespread opposition to the employment of Chinese and convict workers—whose presence helped to inspire resentment and anxiety over the future of free laborers' liberty and power.

CHAPTER 4

Southwestern Railroaders and the Receding "Frontier of Labor Scarcity"

FOR "BOOMER" RAILROADERS, migration west held out the hope of both tangible and intangible benefits in the form of higher wages, a less competitive occupational ladder for whites, some social recognition for and cultural identification with work that contributed to the nation's economic lifeblood, and a path to manhood. "Boomers" sought the freedom to seek out someplace better, freedom from debt and unnecessary risk, and freedom to offer one another mutual economic and psychological support. In the 1880s, when broad forces diminished their prospects for realizing these freedoms in the Southwest, many turned to their workplace ties, as well as the region's powerful anti-monopoly traditions, in initiating and winning the first system-wide general strike on Jay Gould's southwestern railways. In response to a wage cut in the shops, the strike began on the Wabash in Illinois and Indiana in late February 1885, and by early March had spread across Missouri, Kansas, and Texas along the Missouri Pacific. In mid-March, at a conference with Kansas and Missouri state officials, the Missouri Pacific entered into a settlement that strikers and local citizens came to view as a sacred compact. In the process, the walkout transformed railroaders' relationships to their communities and to one another, and brought to the fore an interpretation of "free labor" ideology at odds with the mainstream emphasis on freedom of contract.

Western Railroading in the 1880s

During the 1880s, the railroad industry experienced growing financial instability. Despite the numerous sources funding railroad expansion, such as public land grants, foreign countries, local and state subsidies, private investment funds, and rates charged for carrying passengers and freight, solvency still eluded many companies. This was in part due to increased competition among roads in overbuilt areas, which forced railroads to reduce their rates. Although many railways responded to the drop in rates by cooperating to set fares, depression and then competitive transcontinental system building doomed these associations by the early 1880s. Added to this financial strain was the high fixed cost of railroad operation, which included not only the cost of the physical construction of the roads but also maintenance, servicing, and debt finance. Maintenance included labor costs. A shortage of skilled trainmen kept wages high, and railroad operation in general demanded a vast workforce. Because railroad companies' non-wage costs were so high, wage payments often came directly out of earnings. Falling rates for freight and passenger service, especially in the context of economic depression, squeezed earnings and brought a wave of bankruptcies.[1]

Railroad companies did not simply succumb to the vagaries of the marketplace. Railways represented enormous capital investments, the economic livelihood of many communities, and the nation's main arteries of commerce and travel. Judges ordered not dismantlement of insolvent roads but their reorganization, which entailed refinancing a company's debts and curtailing its operating costs with the hope of rehabilitating it. Because judges lacked expertise in maintaining and managing railroads, they had traditionally appointed managers of the road or "company insiders" as receivers.[2]

Financial problems were especially acute for expanding western roads, because for several years companies provided service to remote areas that generated little revenue. Offering service entailed hiring all of the requisite trades, and maintaining repair facilities, bridges, and roads. For the brief time that a company dominated an area, it could charge higher rates, which it used to fund the high costs of operation in the West. But as more roads were built, competition quickly whittled rates down, leading railroad managers to look elsewhere to cut expenses. It was under this condition of labor scarcity that "western railroad employees were offered, or won, wage rates that were high relative to those railroad employees in other parts of the country." In addition to higher wages, western railroaders, especially skilled workers, negotiated favorable work rules and schedules, and gained recognition for their unions. These victories inspired railroaders in other areas to seek similar gains.[3]

The Receding "Frontier of Labor Scarcity"

In the 1880s, western railroads enacted a number of policies with the goal of creating a ready pool of available labor that would allow companies to deal better with business fluctuations and to diminish their employees' power to resist wage cuts and other measures. To attract workers, managers established recruitment offices and hired labor agencies in the East that touted the benefits of western employment—higher wages and the chance of rapid promotion. Western railroads' efforts to expand their labor supply gradually had an effect. While the number of railroad workers more than doubled nationally between 1880 and 1905, western railroaders' numbers increased sevenfold. The massive influx of railroaders into states west of the Mississippi did not completely end railroad companies' labor supply problems, to be sure. Agriculture drew laborers away from railroad work, leaving managers to face seasonal shortages. Serious shortages also arose due to periodic increases in railroad freight and passenger traffic. During the 1880s and into the 1890s, however, western railroad managers felt confident enough in the supply of labor available to them to push for reductions in operating costs, which entailed cutting the least "fixed" portion of railroads' expenses, namely labor costs. Management therefore sought to attack wages, resist extra payment for overtime and special conditions, get by with smaller crews, gain full control over hiring and firing, and, in regard to the running trades, impose work rules that would grant railroads greater flexibility vis-à-vis its skilled employees.[4]

Three examples of this last measure are relevant to an understanding of Gilded Age labor struggles on the railroads in general and the Southwest strikes in particular. The first involves the dramatic increase in irregular service and the number of "extras" hired during the 1880s. Prior to this period, most engine crews worked regular shifts during which they maintained their engines and received payment by the day. This system made less sense to managers as freight traffic increased in western areas, since engines required continuous upkeep and railroads' business frequently and unpredictably expanded and contracted. Railroads responded by hiring more and more men as "extras" to work freight and passenger runs on rotation. While regular runs continued, most enginemen experienced a fragmented and erratic work life and difficulty in gaining compensation for the innumerable extra duties demanded of them. A second example of managerial policies initiated during the 1880s to control work rules was "promotion from within," a policy whereby a railroad company sought to "make" or promote existing employees into skilled positions rather than to hire skilled men from the outside. This policy served multiple and related purposes. It wrested control over hiring away from the brotherhoods and increased the number of men available to work during peak as well as slack times, thereby heightening management's ability to impose wages cuts upon relatively well-paid skilled workers. During times of labor scarcity, this policy tended to benefit employees, since it offered a greater chance of promotion. However, as the supply of labor increased, companies frequently advanced men from regular to irregular service (from a regular firing position to an irregular position as engineer). Those promoted to irregular service experienced a "starvation period" rather than greater security and higher incomes. The similarities between various railroad occupations and the mobility of railroad workers facilitated managers' use of promotion from within. Although many types of railroad work required special skills, usually men were on hand who possessed at least the minimal experience necessary to perform these jobs, even the more skilled vocations of conductor or locomotive engineer. As historian James Ducker observes: "The clearest incentive to perform on the job was the knowledge that no railroader was indispensable. Even a skilled engineer had only to look at his fireman to see someone eager for his position. After all, there was nothing in the engineer's job that put it beyond the capacity of a normally intelligent youth with enough nerve and a little experience in a cab."[5] Technical innovation represented a third option in railroad companies' cache of strategies for reducing operating expenses. New technologies posed little threat to skilled men of the running trades during the 1880s. The situation for journeymen in the shops, particularly in the West, was much different. Between 1880 and 1905, railroads introduced standardized parts and new machinery into western shops; this undermined the power of machinists' trade unions especially, because railroad companies had less need for the wide-ranging skills of journeyman machinists and could replace them with specialists responsible for one machine or operation.[6]

The history of the Gould system fits into the general pattern of explosive railroad construction, cutthroat competition, and retrenchment. Between 1884 and 1887, Jay Gould threw himself into a war of expansion against his economic antagonists. As a result, the total track of the Missouri Pacific–Iron Mountain system more than doubled, from 1,960 to 4,150 miles. Gould's control of the Missouri, Kansas & Texas (MK&T), the Texas &

Pacific, the International & Great Northern, and the Central Branch of the Missouri Pacific added another 4,311 miles to his empire, not counting the Wabash. As Gould's biographer Maury Klein writes, "In less than a decade Jay had transformed the Missouri Pacific from a road between St. Louis and Kansas City to one of the largest systems west of Chicago." But he "had made it prosperous and powerful . . . not secure." Gould struggled to maintain his advantage against the attempts of other western railroad presidents, including Charles E. Perkins of the Chicago, Burlington & Quincy, and William B. Strong of the Atchison, Topeka & Santa Fe, to capture his market. A period of rate cutting ensued, as newly constructed roads fought for traffic.[7] Gould saw the Missouri Pacific as the linchpin of his empire, which he hoped would extend far beyond Kansas and Nebraska to Colorado and the Pacific. According to Klein, his purpose in furiously constructing new roads was to further his ambition of creating a transcontinental system. He needed the Texas & Pacific and the Wabash because both of these roads allowed the Missouri Pacific road its east-west connections. The trouble was that both the Wabash and Texas & Pacific were in deep financial trouble. In 1884 the former went into receivership and the latter was well on its way to the same fate.[8] When and where they could, Southwest system officials began to place pressure on employees to absorb some of the costs of expansion.

It is difficult to identify exactly when and where the "frontier of labor scarcity" shifted, or, in other words, when and where the transition occurred between relative labor shortage, which afforded workers greater leverage, and relative labor surplus, which afforded them less power. Both railroad managers and railroaders were aware of the significance of this shift, but did not always correctly gauge its advent. Clearly, railroad men and their families on the southwestern roads felt the effects of cost-cutting measures during the mid-1880s.[9]

The most direct measure, and the one most widely experienced, was reduction in wages, which various major roads in the region—the Union Pacific, the Denver & Rio Grande, the Missouri, Kansas & Texas, and the Wabash, St. Louis & Pacific Railway—attempted to impose in 1884, 1885, and 1886.[10] Indirect management strategies also depressed wages. In some shops, for example, workers continued to receive apprentice wages long after they had acquired a journeyman's skills. Local managers at times fired old men and hired new ones at lower wages, for the same positions. In addition, switchmen, roundhouse employees, and brakemen often could not obtain payment for overtime work and time spent in the yards waiting for their assigned run, while painters and bridge men had to travel long distances without pay to and from work sites along the road.[11]

Beyond the issue of wages, Gould system railroaders pointed to deteriorating conditions during the 1880s. By 1885 many Missouri Pacific engineers viewed the company's assignment of men as "extras" as excessive and thus a threat to their ability to enjoy decent, stable living and working situations.[12] Specifically, officials pushed for fewer men to do the work of many. One railroad song attests to the dizzying speed of work in the late nineteenth- and early twentieth-centuries on the railroads that ran through Texas, New Mexico, and Kansas:

> Lemee tell you what de engineer done
> He lef' de station at a quarter to one
> De engineer said to me
> We're goin' to make time wid de Santa Fe
> De Santa Fe does fairly shout
> Trying' to make time with the Central route...
> GH & H runs all night
> Tryin' to keep time wid de ol red light[13]

M. J. Reed, a St. Louis trackman, testified in 1886 that his hours repairing track were cut to only a few days per week, despite the dangers associated with understaffed maintenance crews: "There was work enough for a hundred right along, let alone the six men that was on. They could work twice as many men and have just as much as they could do... because there was breaking down every day, and the track was... in bad repair, and there wasn't men enough to do it in the few minutes they was on; they couldn't do it."[14] Similarly, switchman Richard Berry of the Indianapolis & St. Louis Railroad related that he and other yard employees typically labored fourteen hours a day (rather than the usual ten to eleven).[15]

The recollections of Charles Maier offer another firsthand view of these changes. Having escaped farm work to pursue railroading, Maier found his dream of freedom and independence in some ways fulfilled. He was able to move up the occupational hierarchy fairly quickly. After working in the shops and the roundhouse in Parsons, Kansas, he became a locomotive fireman in 1883 when illness called the regular fireman away. However, he quickly came to understand that the world he had entered was an unstable one. Due to railroad officials' attempts to more profitably reorganize the railway, he and about one hundred other carmen and employees at the Parsons shops were fired "without an hour's warning." As a fireman, he remembers having "no fixed hours for work or rest." When business was high, "we had to double out at either end of the road without regard to hours." "Men," he continued, "would often be out for three to four days without rest except what they could snatch while the train was at a standstill for a short time off the track."[16]

On a different occasion, when Maier worked on a section gang, overgrown grass and weeds along the tracks threatened the trains' operation. His foreman wired the supervisor that he had only three shovels and five section hands, but the official responded, "Fire two men and you'll have shovels enough." The details remained clear to Maier fifty years later of an instance in which a leaking engine had produced a number of delays on the trip of Maier's train. He had no rest or sleep and only a little food on the forty-two hour journey. Although the company expected firemen to scour and polish engines after a run without pay, he decided that after such a long workday, his job was complete, and went home to bed. His master mechanic fired him, then relented and ordered him to clean the engine and start yet another run. Maier recalled his humiliation. He contrasted his own situation to the hired man on his family farm. He had "enjoyed every comfort that the family had." Maier felt "confused and troubled to find that what had promised so much to me... had placed me in the position of a man without a chance to preserve his self-respect and at the same time provide bread for himself and his family."[17]

For "boomers" such as Maier, the cost-cutting policies western railroads introduced during the 1880s threatened to undermine the cultural significance of their work and to disrupt the fraternal bonds that made it more tolerable and survivable. The frantic pace placed an enormous strain on men in an already dangerous occupation and also on the pride and sense of duty with which they often approached their jobs. Slashed and depressed wages made it more difficult to roam in search of a better situation, to contribute to mutual associations or collections taken up for injured men, and to accumulate savings for a farm or shop. Men both young and old increasingly found themselves caught in unstable unskilled or semiskilled work rather than rapidly promoted and engaged in regular service. Certainly the long hours also frayed relations in the boardinghouses and barracks of itinerant men. In short, railroaders increasingly faced the limitations and impositions that many had attempted to leave behind in the East.

Cost-saving policies of railroads affected railroaders' sense of themselves and their relationship to their households. Certainly the lives of railroaders' family members had never been easy. As Paul Michel Taillon has noted, "The chaotic work rhythms of train crews set railroaders and their wives apart from other working class women and men." Families experienced little free time together, frequent migration, and separation. The separation might last a few days, or months, if, for example, a married man migrated to and boarded in a new location with the aim of sending for wife and children once settled. Even when a family unit shared the same residence, railroaders' wives were often on their own. Men absented themselves to the saloon or roadhouse, leaving wives at home to resolve domestic problems on their own. Women who married or lived with railroaders had to juggle their usual domestic routine in order to accommodate railroaders' ever-changing work schedules and sleeping patterns.[18] And the relatives of railroaders commonly worried about the occupation's dangerous aspects. When Harry French gained a job switching in Missouri during the 1880s, his older sister expected the worst. Throughout his employment, "she kept one clean sheet for the express purpose of wrapping up my mangled remains." The young Eugene Debs abandoned employment as a fireman in order to dispel his mother's fears of his potential involvement in an accident.[19]

Policies that slashed wages and otherwise intensified the pressures of an already burdensome occupation threatened to further upset the precarious balance of relationships and responsibilities between railroaders and their families. The prevailing vision of a proper family life, in which men provided for and headed their families while women managed the household, contrasted sharply with reality for many railroading families. In 1884 the Illinois Bureau of Labor Statistics found that about one-fourth of trainmen relied upon their wives to supplement the household income by laundering clothes; selling eggs, chickens, and home-grown vegetables; or taking in boarders (often other railroad men).[20] Of 337 reports on working and living conditions collected by the Kansas Bureau of Labor Statistics from working people across the state, about one-third of the seventy-one railway laborers, switchmen, and brakemen who responded had family members besides themselves working outside the home. A railroader's reduced wages, unemployment, or underemployment might push female family members to work in a factory or as domestic servants or washerwomen. Black women, who often became domestic servants or laundresses to help to meet families' financial needs, had fewer options. Most manufacturing establishments did not hire black women, and the wages for domestic service and washing work were extremely low. One Exoduster in Wyandotte, Kansas, reported that she made fifty cents a day as a washerwoman, which, she told an interviewer, "does not furnish me enough to eat and wear."[21]

These pressures on family life and gender roles occurred within a context of general discomfort about the fate of family and gender in the industrializing Southwest. Newspapers regularly published stories that both reflected and fed this unease, such as the September 1884 report about the "despondent car driver" in Little Rock who attempted suicide when his wife threatened to leave him during economic hard times. The breakdown in family ties appeared to cross boundaries of class and status, confounding wage laborers' hopes for the stability that skilled work presumably brought. Sensationalized accounts—about a middle-class married woman in Kansas City who inexplicably hanged herself in 1883 and a wealthy Illinois landowner who, upon returning from the insane asylum, killed his wife, two children, and himself, for example—seemed to underline the fragile nature of family life in an era of tremendous dislocation and turmoil.[22]

Railroaders faced a number of common obstacles to protesting their workplace conditions. First, it was often unclear whether certain policies emanated from a railroad's general office, or its division or local managers. Central bodies within railroad companies ordered the major wage reductions of 1884 and 1885, and pushed for local managers to achieve the highest levels of production at the lowest expense, but specific cost-cutting policies, such as continuing to pay apprenticeship wages to a man who had obtained a journeyman's skills, or banning wage increases at a division's shops, may well have originated with a particular master mechanic. Although railroads were corporations, local management traditionally wielded a great deal of power over employees and continued to do so well into the 1890s. Master mechanics could be quite arbitrary in their exercise of power, and favoritism and nepotism often governed local officials' hiring and firing decisions. As railroads expanded west, companies merely added divisions rather than changing the industry's existing structure of authority.[23]

A second impediment to labor protest on the railways was the outlook of the federal courts. Increasingly after the Civil War, judges held that workers who struck had effectively resigned their jobs and that this act of withdrawing their labor basically ended their right to protest collectively. Even peaceful labor actions, in this view, threatened "free labor" by interfering with the right of a free person to decide for whom he or she would work, for how many hours, and for what price. However, free citizens' right simply to quit en masse had its limits. The critical function that the railroads played as the nation's economic artery encouraged the conclusion that railroad workers had a special obligation to refrain from striking. Judge David Brewer's comments in the 1885 receivership case, *Frank v. Denver & the Rio Grande Railway Company*, reflect this dominant vein of thought on the courts: "I do not know of any large organization of business, any aggregation of labor, where there is more imperative demand for almost military law and discipline... You must have corps of employés who are loyal to the road, who are looking after its interests ungrudgingly and without any divided allegiance." This held true particularly for roads in receivership. The courts cast workers who struck bankrupt roads under government reorganization as a danger to the public welfare. "In the perspective of labor governance," Karen Orren tells us, "the receivership was continuous with the older tradition of judicial discipline of workers in conditions of economic emergency."[24]

In addition to legal obstacles to labor protest, aggrieved railroaders confronted the blacklist. During the 1880s, railroad companies commonly drew up lists of the names of discharged employees, which were then circulated to other points on the company's system. Between 1877 and 1892, for example, the Chicago, Burlington & Quincy added over eight thousand men to its list. It was policy on the Illinois Central, the New York Central, and, apparently on Gould's Missouri Pacific. A lawyer for a blacklisted man submitted a Missouri Pacific pamphlet to the congressional committee that investigated the 1886 strike. It listed detailed information about men fired for cause in 1883. One manager claimed that the practice had only ended recently. As one sympathizer with the 1886 strike pointed out, consolidation rendered the blacklist even more damaging to strike organizers and participants, because it forced them to search for work outside of the large system of roads owned by one company.[25]

Social movements often emerge due to a clash between rising expectations on the one hand and declining conditions and diminishing possibilities on the other. Many southwestern railroaders held high hopes for their future as "boomers" on the frontier of labor scarcity. Despite the legal, economic, and structural obstacles they faced, a number sought to defend the freedoms and opportunities that western railroading had traditionally offered. Although railroaders surely were aware of examples of crushed and defeated strikes, the 1883 telegraphers' strike against Jay Gould's Western Union being one example, by March 1885 railroaders could point to two major labor victories on the region's railroads less than a year before, both on the Union Pacific.[26]

The 1884 Union Pacific Strikes

On May 4, 1884, Union Pacific supervisors posted notices in shops and yards announcing that wages were to be reduced by 10 to 25 percent, depending upon the scale of wages received. Only engineers and firemen remained untouched. A body of machinists in Denver quickly protested the order, and within half an hour about five hundred men and boys had quit work in the city's shops. Despite the fact that "not a shop on the system was organized," within less than two days of the railroad's announcement, Union Pacific shops "from Omaha [Nebraska], to Ogden [Utah], and on all branch lines" had joined the walkout. A movement began among strikers in Ellis, Kansas, to urge the Denver's strike committee to assume responsibility for negotiating with the company. By May 6 this was unnecessary, as the company had rescinded the order.[27]

In the aftermath of this victory, railroaders quietly organized Knights of Labor assemblies in shop towns along the Union Pacific road. When railroad officials abandoned their previous policy of wholesale system-wide wage cuts in favor of disciplining a small number of shop workers, they were met with widespread, coordinated resistance. In August 1884 the company reduced the wages of Ellis machinists by 10 percent and dismissed twenty Denver shopmen, most of whom had played a prominent role in the May strike. After a flurry of communication between the Denver committee and officers of various local Knights assemblies, the district assembly's executive board ordered the men to quit work until the railroad agreed to revoke the new orders, renounce discrimination against members of the Knights, and reduce hours rather than wages when it became necessary to curtail labor costs. The editor of Denver's *Labor Enquirer*, Joseph Buchanan, who had supported the May strike and organized numerous Knights assemblies on the road, stepped in at the request of the executive board to negotiate on strikers' behalf. Buchanan refused to abandon the discharged men in order to gain settlement of the other issues, lest he send a message that the Knights were unwilling to defend their organization from employer attacks. Although the brotherhoods had not joined the strikers, the Union Pacific apparently heeded Buchanan's warning that "it takes more than train crews to get trains over the road." The road's roundhouses and repair shops were emptied of men whose job it was to give the engines proper maintenance. Faced with a decline in freight service, intent on improving the railroad's image, and busy with challenges from Congress and Gould's growing system, the Union Pacific's new president, Charles Francis Adams Jr., capitulated to all of the strikers' demands on August 18, 1884.[28]

The Union Pacific must have impressed southwestern railroaders. It demonstrated that a massive yet orderly walkout, across lines of skill and occupation and miles of track, was not only possible, it could be enormously effective, especially if strikers held the element of surprise. The events of that summer also made evident that the integrity of a strike's victory had to be vigorously defended against companies' efforts to punish strike leaders and members of the Knights of Labor.

The March 1885 Wabash Strike

On the afternoon of March 7, 1885, some four hundred employees of the Missouri Pacific and Missouri, Kansas, & Texas shops in Sedalia, Missouri, left work en masse at the sound of the whistle. They joined, along with hundreds of Wabash shopmen at Parsons and Moberly, Missouri, a strike involving nearly one thousand Texas & Pacific employees, who, over the previous two days had immobilized the Gould system at Fort Worth, Denison, Marshall, Palestine, and Longview, Texas.[29] The next day 135 Kansas City employees of the Wabash and Missouri Pacific also left their jobs in protest. By March 11, the strike had spread to shops and yards along the Missouri Pacific and other Gould lines in Dallas, Galveston, Atchison, and Hannibal, as well as to points in Illinois and Indiana. All told the walkout involved at least forty-five hundred railroaders. Everywhere that the Missouri Pacific crossed the lines of the MK&T or Wabash, Missouri Pacific men struck.[30]

The immediate cause of the walkout was a wage reduction on the Wabash in late February 1885. Shopmen saw their wages cut by 10 percent, and engine wipers and laborers by 20 percent. The Wabash also imposed a ten-hour workday on shopmen. With the accompanying pay cut, this amounted to more work for nearly the same paycheck at the end of the month, or ten hours work in order to make the same income previously earned in nine hours. The new policy on the Wabash came on the heels of a general assault on labor costs by the Missouri Pacific. In September 1884 and again in October of that year, the Missouri Pacific had imposed wage cuts on the same class of workers. The railroad in some areas reduced employees' hours, allowing some to work nine hours per day only three to five days per week. At other locales, such as Palestine and Denison, Missouri Pacific shopmen, like Wabash shopmen, were to work longer hours at a diminished rate of pay. Charles Maier, a fireman for the MK&T at the time, remembered that the news came to shop employees in midwinter, when "actual privations stared them and their families in the face."[31]

A feeling prevailed among discontented railroaders that they were being made to suffer for Gould system officials' financial mistakes, or worse, maneuvering. "They have got to do more work but at the same time they have got to economize, because they are in the hands of a receiver," one striker began, but, "Who put the Wabash in the hands of a receiver? Was it them who worked for it or the man who owned it?" It was Jay Gould's "watering of the stock," that had plunged the road into economic turmoil, he concluded. While his most recent biographer has called Gould a "creative financier" and "businessman who thrived on the challenge of working with unformed clay," asserting that Gould deserves admiration because he "risked and planted his millions in developing a new country," one Gould striker voiced a starkly opposing view. Labor had a right to "honest treatment," he insisted, because "that difference between what I earned and what I got is in those cars somewhere" and "that's just as much of a right in proportion as the man who puts up the money and bought the lumber." Other strikers more pointedly accused Gould and Missouri Pacific vice president H. M. Hoxie of treachery. Missouri's labor commissioner reported that once the strike was underway, "the feeling of dissatisfaction was intensified by the publication of the financial statement of the Missouri Pacific Railway Company... showing a large earning for the road." The statement neglected to show, he added, "the deficiencies in the earnings of its leased and other lines operated by it." At a meeting in Sedalia, speakers demanded Hoxie's removal, charging that he garnered a "commission of 10 percent on all reductions made on us." They asked for the appointment of a man in his place "with a soul, in one little corner of which will, at least, flash one spark of suffering humanity."[32]

An obvious element of strikers' appeals, and the one that gained them most public sympathy, was that the railroads' policies imposed severe economic hardships. "Labor is already at starvation prices," protested Sedalia strikers. This economic argument was not at the heart of their grievances, which emphasized more a fear of the dependence that economic woe brought. In Big Springs, Texas, for example, the local assembly promised that "the boys" would "prevent capital from robbing labor of all its dignity" and forcing "us to the walls of subjection where we can lay hold of nothing but the bare necessities of life, where we cannot provide for our families in anything kindred to refinement or even decency."[33] In Dallas, one "intelligent-looking" strike leader, and presumably an unskilled railroader, "made a marked impression on the spectators by his simple and quiet" justification for the walkout: "At $1 per day, taking off Sundays and averaging two rainy days per month we will earn $24. Board costs $15. You see we have only $9 to keep ourselves in clothing, tobacco, pay wash-bills and other expenses during the month, to say nothing of sickness. For pity's sake, gentlemen, considering we are honest peace-loving citizens in this free and enlightened country, tell me the difference between us in this condition and the most menial slaves?"[34]

The dread of dependence was also implicit in the grievances listed in the circular distributed by Wabash men at Moberly. The circular decried the Wabash's practice of paying employees only by the entire hour, with no fractional portion of an hour paid. To strikers this practice not only robbed railroaders economically of earned income and socially of their time, it signified the growing power of western officials to impose such a requirement, and on men already burdened by a demanding and dangerous occupation. Kansas City strikers maintained that the system had paid them "little enough" in October 1884, "taking into consideration the work assigned us." Now "patience has ceased to be a virtue."[35]

The walkout beyond the Wabash began quietly and gained momentum slowly on the MK&T and Missouri Pacific. The earliest evidence of the movement to protest the railroads' policies surfaced in Springfield, Illinois, where two hundred Wabash men met late in the evening on February 25, 1885, and, after a long discussion, voted to walk out. Fellow shopmen in Moberly, Fort Wayne, Chicago, and Decatur sent word of their support for a strike via telegraph.[36] Two days later, 350 Wabash machine-shop employees in Galveston joined the strike, and on March 1, T&P shopmen agreed to quit work, and sent an appeal to employees along the lines of the Gould system to make the action general. But Missouri Pacific and MK&T men remained at work throughout most of the Southwest until March 7, over a week later.[37]

Missouri Pacific and MK&T railroaders had good reason to feel ambivalent about joining the protest. The long meeting held in Springfield suggests that Wabash shopmen were also somewhat hesitant. First, as Sedalia shopmen for the Missouri Pacific and MK&T pointed out, the Wabash strike was on some level a separate struggle from theirs, since the Wabash was in receivership and therefore in a uniquely worse position vis-à-vis other parts of the Gould system.[38] A second factor that certainly gave railroaders pause was the power of the Gould system itself. The Missouri Pacific had broken strikes before, including a strike waged by shopmen in Sedalia and St. Louis just five years earlier. That the economies of many southwestern communities depended on the Gould railways also meant that a mass walkout would test the endurance of local citizens, who would surely grow to oppose an extended or violent conflict. Finally, no organization was in place to coordinate activities among different strikers, negotiate with railroad managers, or diffuse or resolve disagreements over strategy and goals. Migration had sundered the ties most railroad shopmen had held to the old Machinists and Blacksmiths Union, and benevolent organizations such as the Ancient Order of United Workmen, which emphasized class reconciliation over labor militancy, was not inclined to lead strikes.[39]

One major factor that surely inspired the spread of the walkout was early encouragement from the local press and public. On March 3, the *Marshall Tri-Weekly Herald* printed a letter from a striker in Big Springs, Texas, who reported that the protest had the "sympathy of all the [town's] citizens" and that "all persons who do not favor the strike keep their mouths shut. Of this class there are only three or four." A striking employee of the Wabash coach shops in Moberly reported on March 6 that local boardinghouses were refusing to house strikebreakers, and that the few men who had come to town for work "take the first or second train out." Palestine and Denison shopmen received sympathetic coverage from the *Galveston Daily News*, and on March 6, the paper commented on the popularity that Palestine strikers enjoyed among engineers and citizens generally. Although the *Missouri Republican* editor feared the potential social and economic disruptions of such a massive labor protest, he warned "railroad managers and the business public of the larger cities" of the "intensity" of anti-railroad feeling prevailing "in sections of the country where agriculture is the principal business." The paper urged officials to "concede to the great silent majority."[40]

Of particular importance to many of those railroaders who had not yet taken action was whether engineers and firemen respected the walkout. As western labor leader Joseph Buchanan later wrote, "A strike that doesn't stop the trains—or a considerable proportion of them—on a road against which it is aimed, doesn't get ahead very fast." Without the support of "runners," or trainmen, striking shopmen and others knew that they would have to prepare psychologically and financially for a "long siege." Their choices would be, at best, to exert pressure on the company by preventing necessary maintenance of the roads, and, at worst, to do so by physically driving trainmen from their posts, a strategy that would risk public opposition. No doubt the March 6 edition of the *Missouri Republican* encouraged wavering railroaders. It reported that engineers had cooperated with T&P strikers in a number of Texas towns, leaving freight traffic in those areas at a "standstill."[41]

Once Missouri Pacific and MK&T employees quit work en masse beginning on March 7, 1885, whatever hesitancy had existed largely evaporated. Strikers demonstrated extraordinary discipline and unity of purpose. To retain the public's support and to avoid legal prosecution, most committed themselves to moral suasion rather than intimidation or violence in keeping trainmen from their engines. They focused their blockade on freight traffic rather than extending it to passenger traffic and mail delivery. In Sedalia, Parsons, Moberly, and elsewhere, strikers pledged themselves to temperance for the duration of the conflict. Accordingly, the bars remained empty and the men "sober" and "orderly."[42] A pattern of action emerged in Sedalia and other strike towns that further dramatized strikers' organizational discipline. In Sedalia, they established their own guard unit to protect railroad property, and a crowd of strikers met each freight train attempting to leave town. Each time officials ordered the crowd off company property, at which point strikers moved to a public crossing where they blocked the tracks and stopped the train. Fred Page, a twenty-eight-year-old leader of the crowd, typically addressed the engineer with this carefully worded appeal: "If you insist on doing so [taking out the train] we will not prevent you, but as a favor to your striking co-laborers we request you not to do so." The engineer almost always acquiesced and returned the engine to the yard amidst the cheers of the surrounding crowd.[43] These interactions between strikers and engineers often took on the character of a ritual. Engineers generally did not claim that they feared the crowd; instead many clearly identified with the strikers' cause. Oftentimes it required only one request from the crowd's leader for an engineer, in defiance of repeated orders from his superiors, to reverse his train. The primary reason that engineers did not refuse entirely to take out trains is that their brotherhood had not endorsed the fight and had pledged not to join in any labor alliances.[44]

In some ways the interaction left strikers vulnerable to trainmen. The request might be refused (and some were). In the main, however, it represented a show of strikers' power, not simply their physical power to block freight traffic but also the moral power of their argument, which engineers recognized and legitimated when they refused to run their trains. When confronted with the plea, "For the sake of your family and ours, don't take out that engine," most engineers could not deny men whom they had the worked with or commanded.[45] That the protest involved skilled shop and roundhouse men no doubt lessened the apprehension these skilled brotherhood men felt in regard to the protest. More to the point, a rumor reported in the *Missouri Republican* that the Gould system was to reduce its force of engineers, firemen, and laborers surely hardened engineers' resolve, and engineers had grievances of their own against the company, such as the growth in the assignment of "extra" engineers.[46]

Declarations of sympathy and promises of aid galvanized strikers' hopes for a settlement. Local labor organizations such as the Telegraphers' Protective Union of Dallas wired, "Gould's slaves of the wire extend sympathy and aid to Gould's slaves of the rail." From three hundred Houston railroad employees came "stirring resolutions" promising to brand any strikebreakers "scabs on society" who rob "honest men of the means of supporting their families." Employees of one railway company in San Antonio resolved almost unanimously to assist if requested to do so.[47] Most impressive by far was the offer of Union Pacific Knights of Labor, who sent Joseph Buchanan to the scene of the Gould strike to organize and to offer $30,000 in aid.[48]

The strike extended beyond skilled shop and roundhouse men to both yardmen and the unskilled. Coal-chute and freight-house operators, though unaffected by the February wage cut, struck in order to restore their wages to $1.50 per day from a lowly $1.15.[49] In Hannibal, Missouri Pacific hostlers, wipers, and coal heavers also quit and demanded a restoration of wages. The strike spread to T&P trackmen and section men, who, having seen their wages reduced from $1.25 to $1 per day, left the tracks in an "unprotected condition" from Dallas to Fort Worth. In Sedalia brakemen and helpers joined the strike, as did yardmen in Leavenworth, Kansas, and Joplin and Kansas City, Missouri.[50]

When Buchanan arrived in Missouri on March 13 with his promise of massive material support and a brief but successful history of leading western railway strikes behind him, he organized Knights of Labor assemblies wherever he went, in Armourdale, Kansas City, Sedalia, Moberly, Hannibal, and St. Louis. He later recalled that a majority of strikers joined in and around Kansas City. At a mass meeting in Sedalia, he and other Denver delegates were "heartily welcomed," and 150 of the attendees formed a Knights assembly directly afterwards.[51] While the creation of these locals greatly augmented the order's presence among southwestern railroaders, the Knights of Labor was not the animating, organizing force behind the strike. The rise of the Knights in the region was a consequence, not a cause. Although the order proved influential early on, Michael J. Cassity points out that strikers were generally "free of institutionalized pressures and procedures" and "relied on a sense of spontaneity and a clear sense of purpose to establish discipline and secure victory." "The absence of permanent institutions," he observed, "proved to be the strikers' single most important advantage." In Sedalia, the town that Cassity studied, strikers created an executive committee that included a chairman, a secretary, and a "yard manager" to direct the crowd's attempts to stop traffic. Committee members played a key role, in dealing with the public, for example, but it was the daily mass meetings that made the final judgments on major issues.[52] Local committees and organizations also formed in other strike towns, such as Jefferson City, Marshall, and Palestine.[53]

According to Missouri's labor commissioner Oscar Kochtitzky, strikers maintained a "perfect police system" that "fully protected" railroad property and private individuals. This was not entirely the case. On occasion strikers took command of railroad property and threatened violence when peaceful appeals did not stop freight traffic. Perhaps because trainmen's acquiescence was not assured in Atchison and Hannibal, strikers in these towns bypassed engineers and firemen, and marched to railroad yards and roundhouses in an "orderly" but "determined" manner to take direct possession of switch engines.[54] Dallas men seized and "tied up" a gravel train's engine and two yard engines, despite the engineer's protests that this would ruin the locomotive's boiler. Angered that a train had managed to leave even while under the watch of "hundreds of men standing about the yards and depots," Sedalia strikers threatened an engineer who attempted to run his engine. He backed down after much resistance, and the committee gave him until 8:15 that evening to leave the town. Thus, the strikers' entreaties to engineers were outwardly peaceful but potentially rested upon the use of force. Ordered by the superintendent to man his train, Engineer Pace desisted after a striker announced, "Mr. Pace, I ask and request you for the good of your family and our own to run your engine back to the house." Pace complied because he feared for his physical safety, reasoning, "I can find another job but not another head." A letter to the city's marshal from "Three Hundred Strikers" made the threat of violent retribution explicit. It informed him that if he directed trains out of the yard for the company, he should "bring a box along to be buried in" or he would "be buried without a box."[55]

The walkout faltered at various times and places. In Marshall some railroaders reportedly desired to return to work and were only kept from doing so by strikers, and at Parsons strikers could not persuade engineers, conductors, and brakemen to join them. The strategy of moral suasion broke down completely in Hannibal. U.S. marshals arrived there with a strong force of deputies to protect the road, and arrested two men attempting to block freight traffic. While the engineers refused at first to run the trains without the strikers' permission, a policeman who was also a half-time engineer convinced regular engineers to resume work when he successfully ran his engine under troop protection. The Wabash walkout was especially vulnerable to collapse. Early on in the conflict the *Missouri Republican* reported that the company was "steadily filling [the strikers'] places with new men." By March 11, the shops in Springfield were working at full capacity, and the master mechanic had refused to employ those who had quit in protest. The fact that the Wabash was in the hands of the U.S. courts made it a risky affair for strikers to interfere with freight traffic, as they could be charged with contempt of court.[56]

Despite this, the Wabash men were confident. They could point to the expansion of their protest across thousands of miles of road and to the near total absence of skilled men attempting to move trains. Some also believed that the Knights of Labor would back their protest with a general railroad strike if necessary.[57] They may have also pointed to the many examples of continuing local support for the walkout. In Dallas, two hundred met at city hall to show their sympathy, and on March 9 the *Marshall Tri-Weekly Herald* claimed that "all classes of citizens" in Marshall sided with the strikers. The *Missouri Republican* reported that Sedalia citizens were "naturally with the strikers and this was manifested by offers of credit on the part of merchants in the city." As a show of compassion, churches in East Sedalia, where railroaders mostly lived, did not collect contributions from strikers' children in Sunday school. Charles Maier later recalled that, because citizens generally sided with the strikers, few men attempted to fill positions in the shops, roundhouses, and yards.[58]

Local opposition to the Gould system's labor policies exhibited a decidedly anti-monopolist strain. The Southwest had hosted anti-monopoly movements for some time, and sentiment against the railroads, as articulated by the Greenbackers and some Democrats and Republicans, had long played a role in both local and state politics. Local press editors and community leaders drew upon this well of suspicion and hostility in their response to the conflict, because, as Cassity observes, "the workers" seemed to stand "in the same relationship with the railroad that was so familiar to merchants [and, he could have added, farmers and railroad-town residents], a position in which the railroad flagrantly abused those who depended on it for the sake of higher profits."[59]

Unsurprisingly, numerous newspaper editors blamed the railroad entirely for the conflict, and attributed to the Gould system sinister, conspiratorial motives. The *St. Louis Globe-Democrat* wondered whether railroad officials, in devising the wage cuts, had "proposed allowing the evil to work out its own remedy in the starving of the men and the inconvenience of merchants." After calling the Wabash's policy of paying men in March the wages they earned in January "practicing upon the weakness of the poor," the editor of the *St. Louis Post-Dispatch* asserted that if the Wabash paid its laborers rather than built stock, it could avoid labor unrest. The *Kansas City Journal* went further and argued that manipulators of the Wabash and Missouri Pacific roads had pressed labor in order to keep watered stock afloat.[60]

Critical reports on Jay Gould's railroad empire in local newspapers in the month prior to the strike probably helped to fan the flames of this resentment. On February 3, 1885, the editor of the *Marshall Tri-Weekly Herald* urged the passage of railroad legislation that would force companies to comply with the state's constitution. This legislation required a company to keep a public office in the state, hold one directors' meeting annually in the state, report on its doings, and refrain from consolidating parallel or competing roads. These requirements, he charged, were "openly, flagrantly and defiantly violated by most of the railroad companies of the State, and especially by those that are now under the management, by sale or lease, of the Gould and Huntington systems." The Texas Constitution was being "ruthlessly overrun by corporations and money monopolists." In a similar vein, and at about the same time, the *Missouri Republican* reported that Missouri's attorney general had initiated legal proceedings against the Missouri Pacific, the Wabash, St. Louis & Pacific, the MK&T, the St. Louis, Iron Mountain & Southern, and the Pacific Express. The suit named Jay Gould and H. M. Hoxie among the defendants, and charged them with "being officers of Parallel and competing lines of railway," in violation of Missouri's laws and constitution." The article outlined a web of ownership and control in the case of several officers, including Jay Gould, who, it noted, was president of the Missouri Pacific, the Iron Mountain, and the MK&T railway companies.[61]

However, the reasons behind public support for the strike were complex, and cannot be explained merely by referencing the region's deep-rooted anti-monopoly sentiment.[62] Little public criticism of strikers' takeover of railroad property and intimidation of potential strikebreakers surfaced. The *Missouri Republican* did not comment editorially against Parsons men who kept "tramps" away from the shops, nor did the *Dallas Daily Herald* when it reported that strikers had taken the water and fire out of ("killed") captured engines and spiked the switches at Mineola, Texas. The *Marshall Tri-Weekly Herald* editor commended strikers on their "manly" abstention from violence during the strike, but a separate article on the same day reported that they had run a master mechanic out of town. The *St. Louis Republican* cast the Dallas men who occupied shops and roundhouses as soldiers engaged in a just battle. When strikers at Hannibal and Atchison took command of a railroad switch engine, the *Missouri Republican* affirmed that though the men were "determined," "good order prevails."[63]

In Sedalia, city officials clearly favored strikers and were willing to look the other way when infractions of the law occurred. As soon as the strike commenced, Superintendent A. M. Hagan insisted that Sedalia's police force ensure the movement of trains as scheduled. The mayor agreed to this demand, but, to Hagan's displeasure, he hired about fifty to sixty extra policemen, mostly men idled by the strike and even some strikers. The police refused to verify Hagan's charges against individual strikers and even arrested him when he loudly and profanely protested police favoritism. No public reaction was discernable against Sedalia strikers when they issued an ultimatum on March 10 that they would refrain from using force until March 14 if the governor and adjutant general would agree to mediate by that date.[64]

Given that many middle-class residents of these towns and cities were familiar with events of the 1877 railway strike only eight years earlier and had lived a bit uneasily along railroad employees, public acquiescence and even encouragement of these tactics is surprising. One might imagine that a crowd of two hundred to three hundred railroad workers blockading freight trains, taking over shops, roundhouses, and yards, driving their opponents out of town, and threatening the use of force would have created more alarm, less than eight years after the scenes of 1877. This mild public reaction only makes sense if one considers these communities' relationships to both the railroads and railroaders. Southwesterners had invested much land, money, and political capital in obtaining roads, and much effort and money in legal and political fights, mostly failed, to ensure that those roads charged area merchants and farmers affordable rates. In their criticism of the Gould system's wage cuts, some insisted that railroads had a public duty to pay men a decent wage, in the interest not only of justice but also of preventing labor unrest, especially of the kind that had so taxed cities and towns in 1877. The editor of the *Missouri Republican* voiced this sentiment in his vindication of the strikers. He drew a line between the private affairs of the railroad and its employees on the one hand and the railroad's public role on the other. The government, militia, and "all citizens when called on to enforce the law and preserve the peace" must uphold railroad companies' public role, he wrote. If the strikers could stop trains without large-scale violence, with the community's blessing, in other words, then the company should bear responsibility for the conflict and its resolution, he concluded.[65]

The notion that communities should defend local rights and concerns against unwanted outside forces also played a role in public support for the strike and tolerance for strikers' more aggressive tactics. In Sedalia, when Superintendent Hagan responded to police favoritism by demanding that the city deputize twenty Pinkerton agents, the mayor firmly refused, arguing that such action would likely lead to riots. He pointed to a state law that required one-year prior residency in the state of all public officials, including policemen. As Cassity comments, Hagan's demand that the trains move under hired police protection "confirmed prevailing suspicions that the company was an alien power, too little concerned with the needs of those people it was supposed to serve."[66]

The sentiment that railroad property was in large part public property and that action taken in defense of local concerns and rights was acceptable proved popular only so long as strikers did not unleash chaos and destruction on, or deepen divisions within, their communities. Hence, one detects a somewhat nervous, cautionary element to local citizens' support of strikers. At times this undercurrent of apprehension broke to the surface of public comment. Only one day after it attacked the Missouri Pacific's policies, the *St. Louis Globe-Democrat,* under the headline "A Riot Imminent," noted ominously that the city of Pittsburgh was still paying off the debt it had incurred during the 1877 riots. The editor went on to call the strikers' resolution to adopt "prompt and positive measures" to prevent strikebreaking "a strange idea of honor." Similarly, the *Labor Enquirer* reprinted a story from a major southwestern paper that reported "trouble feared" in Pleasant Hill, Missouri, where the "mob" had taken possession of the town's yards and shops.[67]

Mostly, however, the press and local citizens communicated their concerns in more subtle fashion. Early on in the strike, the *Marshall Tri-Weekly Herald*'s editor combined praise for strikers with his advice that they remain lawful in order to keep "the sympathy of the people." After strikers paraded through the streets of Parsons "carrying loaves of bread placed on the ends of sticks," the mayor and Judge David Kelso "counseled the boys" at a meeting "to continue in their present quiet and peaceful manner," and one newspaper reassured readers that they were unlikely to riot. Similarly, attendees of a March 15 meeting at Smith's Opera House in Sedalia urged sobriety and orderliness.[68]

That skilled shopmen led the walkout, and skilled trainmen participated, helps to explain why strikers' more aggressive tactics did not create a backlash against their cause in most southwestern communities. Skill connoted a measure of control not only over oneself but also over unskilled workers, whom most middle-class citizens did not trust to independently protest, organize, and assemble in large numbers. The public could identify with this important and highly visible element of strikers and their sympathizers for another reason. Among railroaders, shop workers were the most likely to be long-term residents and established homeowners, while engineers typically held the public's respect as "heroes of the rail." As the *Missouri Republican* noted of Sedalia, strikers there were "nearly all residents... and some of them possess homesteads, and this the citizens feel entitles the strikers to some consideration." Similarly, the *Marshall Tri-Weekly Herald* defended the "honest, peaceable citizens, residents and tax-payers of this city" who "refuse to submit to oppression and are not willing to work for starvation wages."[69]

Finally, if in the intervening years between 1877 and 1885 many town boosters had viewed the migration of respectable, skilled, sober white labor to the Southwest as the answer to the perceived "labor problems" of the post–Civil War era—the "fiendish" insurgents of 1877 in Missouri and the "lazy," "impudent" freedmen and freedwomen of Radical Reconstruction in Texas and Arkansas, then 1885 perhaps represented an opportunity to affirm that solution. While the strike also tested the remedy, which would in part account for citizens' cautionary statements, in the main communities appear to have placed their faith in its success. Segments of the public clearly felt caught between their fears of working-class violence and disorder on the one hand, and, on the other, retribution by railroads. Palestine's Board of Trade condemned the Missouri Pacific wage cuts and even offered strikers a small allotment during the walkout, but it also wished to avoid a "closing of the shops." The *Moberly Daily Monitor* tellingly entitled its first news story on the conflict "Sons of Toil" and expressed outrage at railroads' policies. But it soon feared the strike's possible consequences, including the chance that the railroad might move its shops from Moberly to St. Louis in the wake of the trouble.[70]

This is not to deny the public's general approval of the walkout. Strikers enjoyed substantial support and were encouraged by it. One can see this, for example, in the decision of Sedalia and Parsons strikers to participate in the mass meetings of citizens and city officials during the conflict, a marked change from the earlier practice of meeting in secret.[71] Though strikers likely met in secret so that their walkout would take railroad officials off guard and to protect the identity of those assembled from blacklisting, the shift to mass meetings suggests their willingness to work with middle-class people and non-railroaders in general.

Yet, if the alliance between strikers and their supporters rested solidly upon the common ground of anti-monopoly, defense of local authority and rights, the necessity for orderly strike activities, and the belief that employees had a right to a living wage, tensions nevertheless rumbled below the surface within the pro-strike camp and sometimes spilled out into the open. Public opposition to the protest emerged most notably in Fort Worth, perhaps due to the particular difficulty that town had in moving and obtaining goods. By March 7 no freight from the East and only one car from the North and West had arrived in the previous five days. By March 11, the town was forced to draw upon Dallas for beer, coal, and potatoes. While public sentiment still "probably preponderates in favor of the strikers," the *Missouri Republican* surmised, strikers and businessmen clashed over these issues, with strikers refusing to yield "a single point" and citizens fearing a "lawless outburst."[72]

Condemnation of strikers also came from more powerful quarters. The governors of Texas and Missouri were outspoken in their opposition to the strikers' tactics. Governor John S. Marmaduke of Missouri defended the right of "every man to refuse to work for unsatisfactory" wages and at the same time rejected "any interference with the business or property of his former employer." Texas governor John Ireland issued a similar proclamation: "If any class is wronged or oppressed the remedy should be sought through legislation and other peaceful methods," not by disrupting the employment of others. He pushed a bill in the Texas legislature that would require railroad companies to give thirty days notice before any wage reduction. The bill also would have directed courts to impose a maximum fine of $500 and six months of jail time on any person who obstructed train movement.[73]

The class cleavages that the conflict exposed and aggravated are best illustrated by two newspaper pieces, both of which appeared in the *Missouri*

Republican. The first was an editorial, published on March 11, 1885, at the height of the strike, entitled "Workingmen's Discontent." In it the editor defended the strikers as part of the "great army of American workingmen" who are "dissatisfied and ill-paid." He then argued that workingmen were regrettably "not poets, sculptors, [or] philosophers" and that "they have no genius, little imagination, and less talent in things where we are accustomed to admire talent." "Their clothes are frequently soiled" and "there is often grime on their faces, and often callous places on their hands"; yet, he continued, with an air of charitableness, "They are still a part of "our common humanity, moved by its necessities, sensitive to its wants and controlled by its weaknesses."[74]

A very different defense of strikers appeared on March 16, 1885, in "A Soldier Boy's Letter," perhaps in response to the class prejudices exhibited in the March 11 editorial. Whatever the true source, the letter clearly represents a pro-strike position and seeks to combat the disdain with which some elements of the public approached railroaders. Although the author characterized this prejudice as emanating solely from the strike's opponents—the militia and the "rich people in St. Louis," who "didn't care for poor people"—it could also be found among some major supporters, such as the editor of the *Missouri Republican*. Rather than see strikers as simpletons who deserve the sympathy of their betters, the "soldier boy" holds strikers up as integral members of the community who deserve not only a living wage but also the respect of communities and even positions of leadership in them. The newspaper introduces some doubt as to its authenticity: "The following letter was picked up on the street yesterday and is supposed to be a militiaman's letter to his mother about the Sedalia strike."[75] The letter communicates the militiaman's initial enthusiasm for the idea of suppressing "a lot of drunken strikers." However, when he is sent with a fellow soldier to Sedalia to "mix among the strikers" out of uniform in order to gain information on the cause of the conflict, he undergoes a dramatic shift in his view of railroaders and strikers in particular. He does not meet, as he expects, desperate-looking, "soiled," grimed, or alcohol-ridden strikers. Instead they are healthy, robust, and formidable: "The strikers are mostly big fellows, with square shoulders and big, strong arms." Moreover, he learns from a storekeeper that "the strikers were not ignorant men, by any means; that as a rule they had better sense and were better informed than the members of the general assembly of the state; that the business of railroading was very intricate and required the best talent obtainable... [and] that the road had hundreds of rules that everybody connected with the road had to know... so fully and thoroughly that they could perform all their duties even in the severest storms and the darkest nights." Chiding the militiaman for his naiveté, the storekeeper also characterized strikers as long-term employees of an industry that prohibited drunkenness and as stable residents of the community, family men, and honest patrons to whom he gladly extended credit to during the strike.[76]

The March 1885 Settlements

A major catalyst for the settlement of the March 1885 strike emerged in Sedalia, the "fountainhead of the uprising," according to Gov. Marmaduke. Less than a week after the conflict began there, seventy "killed" engines littered its railroad roundhouses and yards, and ten miles of loaded freight cars sat uselessly on the town's sidetracks. The Missouri Pacific vice president, H. M. Hoxie, demanded that Gov. Marmaduke call in the state's militia to force a resumption of freight traffic. Despite his personal opposition to the strike, the governor resisted, arguing that he preferred that local authorities handle the conflict, and, at any rate, the militia was in poor condition. Upon hearing that strikers' numbers had grown to nearly one thousand in Sedalia, he ordered the militia raised and sent to Centertown, a town forty-five miles from Sedalia. He dispatched Adjutant General John C. Jamison to Sedalia to evaluate the situation there.[77]

The city's businessmen and officials promised Adjutant General Jamison that law and order was in force and that there was no need for state troops to intervene. The strikers, for their part, agreed to greet the "citizen soldiers" with "customary hospitality." They also resolved to only request that engineers honor the walkout. Impressed, Jamison returned to Jefferson City to convince the governor to refrain from sending troops and to encourage settlement of the strike. Shortly thereafter, however, he arrived again in Sedalia, determined to move the trains himself with the help of Commissioner Kochtitzky.[78]

In this effort Jamison and Kochtitzky failed completely. Engineers again and again refused to obey their orders to disregard the crowds of strikers who called upon them to stop their trains. Superintendent Hagan even became exasperated and told Jamison that his exhortations pushed engineers too hard, that the trainmen did not want to violate the wishes of people with whom they lived and worked. He quickly came to this conclusion, as did Jamison and Kochtitzky: the presence of state militia would more likely incite than prevent a riot. Jamison hurried back to Jefferson City to urge the governor to demand that the railroads seek arbitration. Said Hagan, "we can't stir here without permission of the strikers," and Jamison later reported, "That the strikers had the sympathy and encouragement of almost the entire people of Sedalia was clearly manifest to the most careless observer...This sympathy was as widespread as the strike itself." On March 12, Sedalia's citizens and strikers met and resolved that the officers of the system should contract with its employees to hire them back without prejudice against strikers, begin paying them the wages they made in September 1884 on April 1, avoid reducing wages for one year, and pay one and one-half time for overtime work.[79]

Events in Sedalia alone did not pave the way to a settlement, although strikers there demonstrated to state and railroad officials the depth and breadth of their popular support. Trains also went unmoved at Marshall, Fort Worth, Palestine, Denison, Parsons, Atchison, and other small towns. Denison strikers demonstrated their dogged determination when the railroad posted discharge notices, and almost no one picked up their pay, so as to avoid legitimating the company's right to fire them. And on March 14 the Gould system faced new challenges: Missouri Pacific section men joined the walkout and engineers threatened to do the same if they were not compensated for time spent idled by the strike.[80]

Although some strikers expressed "little confidence in the effort to arrange matters," officers of the Missouri Pacific and Texas & Pacific railway companies met with state leaders in St. Louis on March 15, 1885, and accepted all of the demands of Sedalia's March 12 meeting except one. Railroad officials considered the demand that they pledge to not lower wages for one year "very obnoxious" and "dictatorial," and instead promised to give thirty days notice of any change in wage rates. In addition, "with a spirit of amity and harmony" toward employees, First Vice President R. S. Hayes immediately restored wages to the September 1884 levels. At 10:00 p.m. on March 16, 1885, the strikers' executive committee at Sedalia sent word out across the Southwest system that the strike was over. The contract was "regarded as a great victory for the men." Commissioner Kochtitzky remarked, "I hope the boys will go to work and behave themselves well." "Labor Omnia

Vinciti," declared the *Marshall Tri-Weekly Herald*, "Labor is the foundation and when combined with honesty, justice, right, and truth, will in the end triumph over tyranny and oppression." Strikers replied from Sedalia, reportedly, "Glory to God," and applauded the agreement and the help of executive committee members, citizens, civil authorities, engineers, and firemen in achieving it.[81]

A number of strikers worried about accepting the March 15 agreement because it did not include engineers on the Gould system. Those regrets soon dissipated as engineers won a separate contract with the Southwest system on March 24, 1885. It addressed a number of long-standing issues, including the companies' practice of hiring "extras," fining men for the loss or breakage of tools, or damage of freight, and requiring engineers to perform work traditionally done by hostlers. In a case where an engineer felt he was unjustly discharged or suspended, railroad managers agreed to abide by the mutual decision of both the master mechanic and an engineer of the same division, to be chosen by the aggrieved party. In regard to the assignment of "extras," system officials promised to govern the scheduling of regular engines or runs "by seniority and capacity in regular road service" and not to assign "any more extra engineers than are necessary to move the traffic with promptness and certainty." Those engineers who objected to the assignment of extras had the option to appeal their grievance. Overall, the agreement heightened the distinction between irregular and regular service, suggesting that in the Southwest the "frontier of labor scarcity" was fast receding for engineers. The 1885 agreement then represented an opportunity for imposing some measure of control on this development, leverage that many engineers were unwilling to jeopardize in 1886.[82]

The March 1885 settlement demonstrated the potential of resolving the "labor question" through arbitration, and bolstered local elites' less-than-abundant faith in railroaders' ability to protest and organize without descending into riot and chaos. The agreement also dramatized the power that local communities might wield against monopolists, even the seemingly omnipotent Jay Gould. Yet the strike appeared to most as a purely defensive measure against a debilitating wage cut. This emphasis diverted public attention from the host of other issues that "boomer" railroaders confronted as the frontier of labor scarcity receded during the 1880s.

For railroaders, the 1885 strikes and the March 1885 settlement offered different lessons, ones that grew out of the distance they had long felt between themselves and non-railroaders, particularly the middle and upper classes. The unskilled and semiskilled especially, who had joined shopmen in the walkout, had moved from the margins of their communities' consciousness to the center. The walkout impressed on many their capacity for shaping the terms and conditions of their work and the character of the debate over the "labor question" through a determined, orderly, sometimes illegal effort across lines of skill and race. They had adopted a leading role in their communities' anti-monopoly movement in the face of class condescension. Beyond these perceptions, those railroaders who looked to the 1884 Union Pacific strikes also came away from these experiences with the sense of how quickly managers could undermine gains and retaliate against strike participants. Finally, in defending their actions, strikers articulated a set of ideas that recalled the older strains of "free labor" ideology, strains that historians associate with "labor republicanism," or "producer ideology." Rather than limit their rights as employees to the purely economic one of contract, as most mainstream thinkers did by the mid-1880s, these men conceived of "free labor" as at once economic, cultural, and political—freedom meant dignity, stability, a fair return for labor, a producer's claim on the workplace itself, and the opportunity to provide for families and to be public actors as worker citizens. As they conceived it, this broad notion of worker freedom was potentially compatible with the interests and rights of employers, but their faith in cooperation between strikers and railway officials depended on the efficacy of the March settlement.

CHAPTER 5

Testing the Hierarchies

DESPITE LASTING ONLY a little more than a week, the March 1885 strike had a profound effect. It created a network of railroaders committed to protecting the 1885 contract and expanding it to take on the host of other pressures they felt at work. The spring walkout also sparked a movement among railroaders to join, along with thousands of working-class people, the Knights of Labor. That organization, with its emphasis on the struggle of "producers" against "capital" and "monopoly," provided a forum for encouraging the relationships and networks that had emerged in March and that had cut across lines of skill, occupation, and race. In taking up the cause of "producers," broadly defined, the Knights tested the material and ideological structures long dividing railway workers and offered a distinct alternative to the brotherhoods and other exclusionary nineteenth-century fraternal organizations. While the March 1885 Wabash strike had pulled railroaders and their local communities together against a common foe, linked railroaders to a national organization, and culminated in an agreement that seemed to strike a balance between railway officials and railroaders, the August 1885 Wabash strike had the opposite effect. It set Southwest system Knights on their own path vis-à-vis both their national organization and their local communities, and heightened their fears that railroad officials meant to undermine the March agreement and thus the tenuous hold that railroaders had on freedom itself.

The Rise of the Knights of Labor in the Southwest

The Knights of Labor were to be found in towns and cities along the Southwest system lines prior to the March 1885 Wabash strike. As elsewhere in the nation during the early 1880s, Knights had often allied with various farmers' groups and supported independent parties in the hope of forcing political and economic reform. St. Louis, with its large industrial base, hosted the greatest number of locals—a total of thirty-four formed between 1879 and 1884, many of these according to trade. In roughly the same period, supporters organized eight assemblies in Kansas City (Missouri), two in Dallas, and one in Fort Worth. In 1883 in several communities telegraph operators formed Knights assemblies, most likely as part of the national effort that year by operators to wage what was ultimately a failed strike against Jay Gould's Western Union. Smaller towns in Kansas, Missouri, and Texas tended to have one or two assemblies, usually mixed in terms of line of work or trade, and many, at least in Texas, attracted few members. In 1882, for example, Denison Knights numbered only twelve and Sherman Knights only fifteen. These numbers climbed in 1884 to 194 in Denison and 169 in Sherman, presumably as a result of the order's victories against the Union Pacific.[1]

During the months following the March 1885 strike, the order, according to Charles Maier, "sprung up overnight" and "took like wildfire." He recalled of Parsons, "The fever of joining seemed to be epidemic." In Sedalia nearly one thousand joined the town's five Knights assemblies within four months. Aspiring organizers and ambitious local assemblies from railroad towns such as Lawrence (Kansas), Palestine, Springfield, and Hannibal sought organizing commissions and advice from the order's national office. Palestine member P. A. McMeany promised that he could "do a great deal of good in this district."[2] If membership rolls in other areas of the state are a guide, his confidence was justified. Delegates sent to the statewide Knights convention in Fort Worth in July 1885 represented at least 200 members in Dallas, 350 in Fort Worth, 100 in Sherman, and 350 in Marshall.[3] In St. Clair County, Illinois, where East St. Louis is located, the order boasted over two thousand members. In addition, several pro-Knights labor newspapers circulated, although almost no issues survive in the archives: the *Labor Advocate* in Hannibal, the *Labor Union* in Sedalia, and the *Texas Artisan*. The Knights in San Antonio published the *Item* and in Houston, the *Echo*.[4] The Fourth of July celebration held in Marshall also demonstrated widespread public acceptance of the order. The Knights organized a picnic and barbecue that the *Marshall Tri-Weekly Herald* crowned a "success." The event drew visiting Knights from Palestine, Texarkana, Longview, and elsewhere to march in a parade that included an African American brass band, a procession of trade union members, and a triumphal car decorated with tricolors and national flags. Days before the celebration a local merchant announced the arrival of a collection of new fashionable hats for the occasion.[5]

The number of Knights members and supporters skyrocketed again in the fall of 1885 and the spring of 1886 after yet another success on the Wabash in late August. Railroaders in particular established assemblies at numerous points along the lines of the Southwest system of roads. One Sedalia organizer boasted to Terence Powderly, the chief national leader of the Knights, "About all of the Rail Road men on the Gould system are members of the Knights of Labor." In accord with the order's inclusive approach and in contrast to the brotherhoods, these organizations almost always represented a combination of men from various trades and skill levels. In 1885 such mixed assemblies appeared in East St. Louis, Springfield, St. Joseph, Kansas City (Missouri), De Soto, Hannibal, Sedalia, Moberly, St. Louis, Atchison, Hiawatha, Parsons, Leavenworth, Palestine, Dallas, Marshall, Fort Worth, and Kansas City, Kansas, and its neighboring towns. One local in St. Louis brought together engineers and firemen, while others combined firemen, car inspectors, and car repairers, and, in Marshall, shop workers. In St. Clair County, one local assembly's 540 members were drawn from twenty-four different occupations, and fourteen of the seventeen locals in the county had no less than five different occupations represented.[6]

The Knights' surge of popularity was not limited to railroad employees but extended across a spectrum of late nineteenth-century industrial production. Iron and steel workers in East St. Louis, plumbers and stonecutters in Kansas City, brick masons and carpenters in Dallas, and lathers, streetcar employees, and gashouse workers in St. Louis each formed their own assemblies according to their specific trade. There were also a large proportion of local assemblies that, like railroaders' locals, consisted of people of different trades and skills. Mixed assemblies organized in St. Joseph, Hannibal, Kansas City, Moberly, St. Louis, Atchison, Wynadotte, Parsons, Dallas, Denison, Sherman, Longview, and Marshall.[7]

Nor were the regions' organizers and members in 1885 restricted to white men. The information is scant because the most comprehensive study of the order's membership does not reveal the true extent of its members' racial, gender, or ethnic makeup. Only 5 percent of local assemblies reported such information to the national office, and the records that do exist "indicate that membership was composed preponderantly, not exclusively, of certain groups."[8] Still, the reports available document that mixed-skill assemblies, such as in Hannibal, Marshall, Weatherford, Harrisburg (Texas), and Houston, were popular among black Knights of Labor. Black members also organized by occupation. Railroad men in Sedalia and Longview established locals, for instance, as did black laborers in Palestine, Kansas City, Dallas, and Denton. Women, reportedly at least, only joined four assemblies. One in St. Louis was composed of female stocking knitters, while two mixed assemblies, one in St. Louis and the other in Parsons, included both female and male members. In Fort Worth, female "laborers," perhaps washerwomen or domestics, formed an assembly. Charles Maier indicated that the mixed assembly in Parsons was actually all women when he related that the town had four assemblies, "one for railroad men, one for the industrials, one for the colored population, and one for the women of the town."[9]

Although the Union Pacific Knights' generous offer of monetary aid and Joseph Buchanan's visit to the Southwest during the March strike proved the initial catalyst for the Knights' rise in the region, the order had already taken root among Wabash employees before the strike began. A March 5, 1885, letter from a Moberly striker in the Wabash coach shops told the *Marshall Tri-Weekly Herald*, "We are working with the Knights of Labor and our transactions are secret. Nobody knows what we do, nor how we do it until it is done." Strikers at Wabash shops at Fort Wayne (Indiana) and Moberly also belonged to the Order. Their numbers grew quickly. Less than a week into the strike in Sedalia, a leader of the walkout revealed that nearly all of the shopmen in the city held dual membership in their shop society and the Knights.[10]

Maier explained, it was the "desperate need of the railroad men that drove them to grab at the only available organization for relief." At base this desperate need was to protect the gains made during the March strike and with its settlement. Suspicions of the Missouri Pacific had run high among strikers during the conflict. In Sedalia they reportedly never trusted messages to the wire lest Gould exploit his control of Western Union Telegraph Company to spy on strikers' plans and ideas. When the committee agreed to the contract's terms, it wired out the number "13" to all strike points as the prearranged signal to begin work. Immediately following the announcement of the March agreement's terms, a number of strikers pushed for a written contract because they anticipated railroad officials' duplicity. These concerns were strong enough that Commissioner Kochtitzky addressed them before the strikers' executive committee: "The strikers are not a legally constituted body and the railroad cannot sign with each individual, can it? This order is entirely binding and has all the force of a legal contract." Even if the railroad were forced to sign a written agreement, he maintained, it could prolong any individual employee's suit in the courts for years. Railroaders surely took these words as confirmation that they should organize collectively.[11]

A Brotherhood of Producers

The Knights offered skilled railroaders new, common, fraternal ground upon which to organize across lines of skill and race for mutual benefit. A number of engineers and firemen, who had experienced increasing attacks on their craft control and the benefits of combination in the March strike, sought to move beyond the narrow bounds of trade unionism and joined the Knights. Like skilled workers across the country, many held dual membership in both the Knights and their brotherhood or society, and a movement arose, among firemen in particular, to push the brotherhood leadership towards a less conservative policy regarding strikes and labor alliances. In his speech before the firemen's 1885 convention, secretary-treasurer Eugene Debs appealed to these more cooperative sentiments by stressing the right of all producers to receive just recompense for their work. A "Plea for Federation," submitted to the BLE, BLF, and the Knights, also illustrates this new mood among skilled railroaders. In the summer of 1885, a Kansas Knights assembly composed of Union Pacific firemen and engineers pushed to "strengthen and unite in a firmer bond all employes" of the road due to the "necessity of continued and ever increasing vigilance upon the part of all persons engaged" in railroad service.[12]

For skilled shopmen, the semiskilled, and the unskilled, membership in the Knights surely represented an opportunity not only to secure better wages and working conditions but also to play an active and even leading role among their coworkers and in their communities. Skilled shopmen found in the order a forum and a mechanism for labor protest unknown since the 1877 strikes, which had severely weakened their trade union. Probably also because they tended to work in one place and among men of diverse skills and occupations, shopmen particularly identified with the Knights' industrial credo. Indeed, support for the Knights among railroaders across the country often centered in the shops. The semiskilled and unskilled, who were largely shut out of the brotherhoods, would play a significant role in workplace actions in the Southwest over the subsequent year. Among twenty-six Missouri strikers who testified before the congressional committee that investigated the 1886 conflict, for example, there was a switchman, an engine wiper, an engine cleaner, a blacksmith helper, and several trackmen.[13] Given the Knights' opposition to craft exclusiveness and the tensions between brotherhood and non-brotherhood men, their activism arguably represented in part a backlash against the elitism of the brotherhoods.

Many Southwest system railroaders identified with the order's "producer" ideology and scathing republican critique of "wage slavery." Industrial development, Knights charged, had created grave economic and political imbalances between the power of employers and employees. The order's leaders and editors contrasted the independent artisans of the early nineteenth century to their era's waged laborers, whom employers often treated merely as a factor of production, subject as any other factor to the vagaries of the marketplace. In order to prevent the "lords of labor," through their control of economic and political power, from imposing "wage slavery" upon free laborers, the Knights sought to promote arbitration between employers and employees. This was only possible, they argued, when employers and American society generally recognized the centrality of labor to economic wealth. "Capital" alone did not create prosperity, the Knights maintained, laborers were due a "proper share of the wealth they create." Workers were "producers" and their work "noble," in contrast to "idle" speculators and "monopolists."[14]

These ideas reverberated with striking railroaders, who had argued in March 1885 that the Gould system's policies threatened to impose on them a "life of slavery" not to be tolerated by any "civilized community." The Knights embrace of the rights and role of producers no doubt struck a special chord among railroaders, who viewed their work as central to the prosperity and progress of their local communities and the nation as a whole. Moreover, unskilled laborers of the roads responded to the order's recognition of them as fellow producers, as the union's publication of a poem entitled "Only a Dollar a Day" illustrates. It ends with the soul of the laborer's starved babe ascending to heaven while the soul of the rich man, who "gavest but a dollar a day," bears the "brand of Cain."[15]

The Knights' emphasis on the moral redemption of society attracted those seeking to make sense of their chaotic, unstable world. It also helped to reassure middle-class observers that strikers and other "workingmen" who joined the order were defenders rather than destroyers of the republic. Membership depended upon one's moral stature, as the Knights measured it, in the society at large. Employers who accepted the principle of arbitration could join the Knights, while lawyers, gamblers, and saloonkeepers could not because the order viewed these occupations as corrupt. The organization also embraced the cause of temperance, which won it friends among social reformers, women, and the middle class. The pledge to abstain confirmed the Knights' aim of protecting the family and individual from slavery of all kinds. The values necessary to uphold the pledge, self-improvement and self-discipline, held widespread appeal and were part and parcel of the Knights' goal of building a virtuous republican society.[16]

Redemption

A letter from a retired, New Hampshire-born railroader, J. B. Sawyer of Denton, Texas, to Powderly illustrates the ambiguities alive in the "producer" ideology's mutualism. Sawyer informed Powderly, "Our people are opposed to all kind of monopolies but they have been compelled to vote the Democratic ticket to free ourselves from the tyranny of the Republican party." "There is no ill feeling between the races and never would have been but for the damned carpet-baggers," he opined and then continued, "We are organizing the negroes so you can see we are carrying peace into Africa instead of war."[17] Did his reference to Republican Party "tyranny" condemn its support for black rights under Reconstruction, or its high taxes and generally anti-labor outlook? In other words, the Knights represented to Sawyer a salve for the region's Civil War and Reconstruction-era wounds, but does he have in mind an egalitarian, southern-based, cross-racial alliance or a white-ordered arrangement that, in exchange for some protection, required blacks' obedience and passivity?

The latter seems more in evidence in Marshall Knights' July 4, 1885, picnic and barbecue, which area Knights organized, and Palestine, Texarkana, and Longview Knights attended. The day belonged to the white members of the order. The *Marshall Tri-Weekly Herald* described the procession of the Marshall Knights as a "sturdy patriotic set of men" but ridiculed the "colored brass band" as "out of tune" despite its "airs." The orator of the day, Hon. Temple Houston, the son of Sam Houston, alluded to the late railroad strike when he bemoaned the consolidation of capital as the chief threat to the republic and approved the organization of labor for protection. An "old time barbecue" followed, the "first... spread in this place since ante bellum days." Anti-monopoly, then, served as a basis for another kind of unity among Marshall whites, one that drew upon the nostalgic image of prewar relationships as unsullied by outsiders, whether Republicans, the Union Army, or monopolizing railroads.[18]

Perhaps the procession of "sturdy patriotic" Knights that the Marshall paper referred to was comprised of blacks and whites, as a black assembly existed in the city in 1885. However, given the editor's deep hostility to black people and enthusiastic support for "labor," he surely equated "labor" with white control. On March 17, the editor held up "labor" as the "foundation," which, when combined with honesty, justice, and truth, would "in the end triumph over tyranny and oppression." Not long afterward he railed against "Radical and Negro" misrule, fraud, and swindling, which he charged had driven the city and county to bankruptcy. Rejecting the call for free elections for local offices, he argued that a free election would allow blacks to elect a "man of their choice—white or colored." "Do the people want to hold the city in the hands of honest white men, property holders and tax-payers," he asked, "or let it revert back to the control of ignorant negroes, or what is worse, to men who will seek preferment by negro vote?"[19]

The stance of state Knights leaders on the 1885 Galveston longshoremen's strike likewise sent strong signals that the order would not disturb white supremacy. The longshoreman's struggle against the Mallory Line essentially devolved into a race strike, though it began as a walkout in protest of a wage cut. Texas Republican leader and former slave Norris Wright Cuney, who had organized a company of about three hundred black screwmen to work on the lily-white docks in 1883 by underbidding white stevedores, enlisted about 120 of his men to fill striking white longshoremen's places in late October 1885. Cuney's men accepted strikers' offer to share the work equally on the Mallory wharf on the condition that the Mallory Line's agent also approve the agreement. When the agent insisted upon continuing with black laborers, white longshoremen made race a central issue of the strike and sought the aid of the Knights in winning their places. At first they charged that the company had fired them due to their Knights membership. The agent pointed out, correctly, that they had joined the order after their walkout, but denied, incorrectly, that the Mallory Line was "antagonistic to organized labor." The white longshoremen then launched a city-wide strike in early November that won the support of cotton pressmen, screwmen, barbers, and railroad men, and completely disrupted freight traffic on the Missouri Pacific and the Galveston, Colorado & Santa Fe railroads. The strike literature that Galveston's District Assembly 78 of the Knights of Labor distributed attempted to galvanize enthusiasm for the effort by invoking the cause of "Knights of Labor and other white labor" against the "Colored Rat and Scab Labor from other countries." No doubt in order to recruit a cross-racial coalition of railroaders into the order, the leadership of the Texas Knights sidestepped racial issues and claimed that the company's attempt to break the Knights of Labor had caused the strike. Their effort to recast the conflict as simply a fight between organized and unorganized labor disregarded these facts: two black dockworkers' unions existed at the time of the strike, and both the white screwmen's and longshoremen's unions had long refused black members and monopolized regular work on the docks.[20]

Neither the *Marshall Tri-Weekly Herald* editor nor most white Gould system Knights appeared to object to the admission of blacks to the order. Nor did the Knights' inclusive approach inspire in 1885 charges against white Knights that they were in consort with blacks, even though the order's chief national leaders, founder Uriah Stevens and Grand Master Workman Terence Powderly, had ties to abolitionism and carried egalitarian ideas about race with them into the labor movement. Powderly consistently urged white members to permit black assemblies, reasoning: "Does any man suppose that the universal Father will question our right to Heaven because of our color?" At times the Knights extended their support for inclusiveness to the political realm. In 1885, the General Assembly convention greeted Powderly with applause when he pledged to the only black delegate there "the service of the Order for his race to fulfill for them their complete enfranchisement in common with those whose faces were white."[21]

Perhaps whites along the Gould lines were unaware of the national leadership's racially egalitarian stances, or perhaps they simply did not take these seriously. After all, it was not until more than a year later, in October 1886, that Powderly and a number of New York–based white and black members garnered national press attention for challenging the color line at a national Knights convention in Richmond, Virginia.[22] Members joined the order so quickly in 1885 that few had time to acquaint themselves with its history, proceedings, or even its basic philosophy. As Powderly lamented to an Arkansas Knight, "Our organizers are pushing the work too rapidly and I know that they are not all doing it right from the letters that come to me." And those who did study the order's principles and Powderly's speeches would have found that the Knights more often justified racial inclusiveness as a practical strategy against the use of "cheap" black labor by employers. "Why," asked the *Journal of United Labor*, "should workingmen allow a foolish prejudice against color keep out of our organization any one who might be used as a tool to aid the employer in grinding down wages?" Similarly, in a letter to a white assembly that refused black membership, Powderly objected, "You cannot tell by looking at the finished piece of work whether it was a white man or a colored man who did it; capital makes no difference in oppressing labor whether it is white or black."[23]

While Powderly stood firmly against white members' requests to exclude blacks, for pragmatic reasons he advised blacks and whites to pursue a biracial rather than interracial strategy, meaning that black members might seek greater power in the workplace alongside whites and mix with whites in regional and national assemblies and meetings, but whites and blacks could form separate assemblies at the local level. This policy both accommodated to and reflected the realities of southern race relations. As Eric Arnesen reminds us, biracial unionism "barely required comment, much less debate" in the late nineteenth-century United States, given the pervasiveness of the color line. Separate assemblies allowed both black and white members, who adhered to the color line in social and cultural affairs, and most certainly in the highly segregated railway industry, to ally on an economic or antimonopoly basis without raising the much more controversial issue of "social equality." Separate assemblies no doubt prevailed in the Southwest. A least one white member in Larned, Kansas, wrote Powderly to ask whether "the assembly is compelled to take colored people where they [*sic*] are all whites."[24] In April 1885 the *Journal of United Labor* reported "colored" assemblies in Pine Bluff and Hot Springs, Arkansas, and the Knights' July convention in Texas specifically elected a "colored organizer," P. H. McMeans of Palestine.

Like black members in Alabama, Mississippi, and the Carolinas, a Texas member wrote Powderly seeking a commission to organize black communities. He explained, "Down in this country, the white people have set a decoy and fooled the colored people so much it is simply impossible for a white organizer to organize them to any good."[25]

Despite the predominance of segregated assemblies, 1885 black strikers found a space for themselves alongside whites as part of a local community under attack by a powerful and unpopular outsider. The exigencies of economic crisis relaxed the importance strikers attached to racial fraternalism in the same way that it later did for populists. Strikers' communities, whose residents had long seen themselves as victims of eastern capital, easily took up the call to defend the mutual self-interest of local blacks and whites against Gould.[26] Black participation in the March 1885 strike apparently made the notion of a shared status as producers more palatable to whites. The *Dallas Daily Herald*, for instance, reported in clearly approving terms a story about a black strikebreaker who had "returned to the rural district" after receiving "twelve stem-winders with a barrel stove" at the "hands of his own race."[27]

The racism of white members notwithstanding, the Knights represented a unique opening for black workers, who were often either dissatisfied with the traditional parties or demoralized by their declining fortunes in southern politics, or both. The Greenback cause had come and gone in Texas and Arkansas.[28] Of course, the opportunity that the Knights held out to address economic concerns played a large role, as poorly paid and black skilled and unskilled men had the most to lose from wage cuts and the greatest constraints on their social and occupational mobility. But more than this the order offered membership to an interracial organization with a considerable degree of social and political weight regionally and even nationally, one that, potentially at least, offered black working men the socially recognized status of "producers."[29] In a sense, state leaders' support of Galveston's white longshoremen may not have dissuaded black workers of this potential. The fact that Texas Knights distanced the order from the cause of a race strike, when many whites embraced one, indicated its commitment, at least rhetorically, to a producer ideology, which is not insignificant. To many black members it must have signaled an opportunity to turn the rhetoric of equality into action, to, in other words, institute a very different kind of redemption than that envisioned by white Knights.

Those in Kansas and elsewhere who sought membership in white assemblies took the order's egalitarian language seriously, as one white organizer in Indiana, Joe B. Kewley, complained to Powderly. In reference to the refusal of black Knights, at the behest of white members, to establish their own assembly rather than remain in a biracial one, he concluded, "This equality is what seems to be sticking in their craw." Kewley reported the argument made by one black member: "This is the only organization, in which we stand on an equal footing with the whites, and it is a big thing, and unless we can work here we will work nowhere." Indeed, a number of black newspapers across the country urged their readers to join or support the Knights and to participate in the only major biracial organization on the horizon willing to challenge the "color line." As one southern black member pointed out, "We are bond to join something what will led [*sic*] to better rights then we have."[30]

Placing the Knights' inclusive policy within the broader history of fraternal organizations in the United States helps to explain the varied responses black Knights had to segregated assemblies. While some viewed the order as a potentially redemptive force and wrote to Powderly strongly objecting to racial separation at the local level, others expressed a preference for separate locals and black organizers. "Racial exclusion was a hallmark of mainstream American fraternalism throughout its history," Mary Ann Clawson has noted. This forced blacks to form parallel organizations to the Freemasons, the Knights of Pythias, the Odd Fellows, and others. The Knights of Labor then was unique among fraternal organizations in expanding the boundaries of "brotherhood" to include both blacks and whites. However, blacks often formed wholly independent separate societies and associations. In Richmond, secret societies founded by enslaved and free blacks during the antebellum period emerged as an institution fundamental to the city's post-emancipation black community. Over four hundred societies flourished there, many of which attracted both male and female members, and which interlocked with black church life, neighborhoods, political activity, and the workplace. Such groupings continued black fraternal orders' long tradition of self-help and protection against white control and hostility.[31]

Black Knights who sought equality or at least greater leverage within the labor movement rather than the more controversial, difficult, and often undesired course of integration found in the Knights an appeal to a rough "stomach equality," not civil or political equality.[32] Gould system strikers made a similar appeal: the railroad had forced labor "to the wall of subjection" where they could "lay hold of nothing but the bare necessities of life."[33]

Women in a Masculine Sphere

In towns and cities across the country, the Knights expanded the bonds of fellowship to include women. This policy stood in sharp contrast to other major fraternal orders. During the last third of the century, women's auxiliaries to male fraternal orders emerged, but, Clawson notes, "Masculine opposition to the creation of women's auxiliaries was widespread, persistent, and often effective, and when women's orders were established, they were "defined by their connection to already-existing male organizations." The Knights, however, accepted women, whether they were wage-earners or the wives of working men, and often welcomed women's participation in the labor movement, so that approximately sixty thousand women belonged to the order at its peak during the 1880s. And unlike trade unions, many of its members and prominent leaders viewed domestic production as an important aspect of, rather than as divorced from, producers' contributions to society. Though many of the order's members did not endorse women's suffrage or equal pay, Powderly considered himself a "woman's rights man" and several times delivered speeches on the same stage as Susan B. Anthony and Elizabeth Cady Stanton.[34]

Beyond accepting women members and assemblies, southwestern Knights, too, demonstrated a degree of openness to the expansion of women's roles, in the labor movement and in society at large, not often found in the major male fraternal orders. One Kansas local, for example, urged the "advance of women" in politics because of their "refining and humanizing influence." In Fort Worth and Sedalia, at least three visiting Knights speakers made clear that they were "women's rights" men, including T. W. Low, who told one newspaper that the organization's goal was to "secure for both sexes equal pay for equal work," and Richard Trevellick, who proposed to a full house the radical notion that women should gain full political and economic equality alongside men.[35]

Knights in St. Louis took up the cause of striking female waged laborers in the city. In late February 1885, four hundred female hosiery knitters struck when their employer reduced their pay from twenty to seventeen cents per dozen pairs of stockings. One supporter pointed out that a hard-working "knitting girl" might make three dozen pairs of stockings per day. If she paid car fare to get to and from work, that left her with only fifty cents per day, so the wage cut attacked already very low wages. While several trade unions also supported the knitters, the Knights seemed to play a leading role, in that striking knitters held their meeting at St. Louis's Knights of Labor hall, many of the attendees were members of the order, and a Knights lodge made a donation to the strike. Elizabeth Meriwether, a well-to-do advocate of women's rights and the female strikers' cause, appealed to the order "to look into this matter and lend their influence to righting this great wrong done to their sisters." The strikers formed a Knights assembly and drew upon producer ideology in moving beyond the goal of a wage increase to seek full independence from their employers. On March 28 Joseph Buchanan's labor paper reported that the knitters were still on strike and seeking to use donations to establish "a stocking factory of their own."[36]

The knitters' cause was a popular one. The editor of the *Missouri Republican* wrote that their fight for a "living wage" had won broad sympathy, and a benefit held for them by the People's Theatre sold $50 worth of tickets. That the knitters were white and appeared to remain within nineteenth-century society's prescribed gender roles surely helped their cause. Meriwether described them as "young, fresh, innocent, good, cheerful, and some very pretty," and disassociated her fight for women's rights from the struggle of "young girls in such a deplorable plight." The article on the strikers' meeting at the Knights' hall did not mention any women speaking besides her. Instead, it noted the presence of a male leader, "Mr. Fuller," and described the debates that ensued between various male attendees over cooperatives and the treatment of a boss who had come to speak to the gathering. "Gentlemen" of the Knights of Labor reportedly organized the women, who apparently did not engage in violence or even any public protests. This evidence of male control and direction probably tempered the public's response to what otherwise might have been a controversial development, given that the widely accepted doctrine of separate spheres held that women were virtuous and compassionate beings who belonged in the home. Many evidently were coming to accept, tentatively, the presence of female waged workers, even striking ones, as long as they remained virtuous.

Evidently, one way that these women's virtue could be retained in the public's eye was if "gentlemen" Knights guided them.[37]

Southwestern Knights likely shared these sentiments, notwithstanding their dabbling in the ideas and arguments of the women's rights movement. Though at times swept up in the Knights' egalitarian and reformist spirit, most probably resembled members throughout the country in viewing women waged workers as victims of "capital" and as "sojourners in the labor movement awaiting freedom from non-domestic toil." The Knights were unique among fraternal orders in accepting women as full members and without regard for their relationship to male members, but the order had excluded women until 1881. In part this was due to male members' objection that women's habit of gossiping would undermine the secrecy and sacredness of its proceedings. Some historians believe that their resistance was also due to the value many men placed on fraternal orders in general as a masculine haven from feminized churches and homes. Clawson speculates that others saw in fraternalism an opportunity to heal sectional wounds and to re-create the male bonding that Civil War soldiers had so intensely experienced. The organization of the "Gray and Blue" illustrates the presence of this feeling among the Knights. In October 1885 Knights delegates representing ex-soldiers of the Union and Confederate armies, including regiments from Arkansas, Missouri, and Illinois, met in Ontario to "promote peace instead of war."[38]

The Knights' records indicate that Gould system railroad workers did not welcome women into their union halls. Not once did newspaper coverage of the March 1885 strike mention women's roles. While perhaps women's public activities went unnoticed because the press, like the strikers, cast the strikers' fight as a test of manhood, one would think that reporters and editors, in their more anxious moments about the possibility that strikers might riot, would have dwelled on women's participation if it existed, since women's battles with police during the 1877 strike had inspired the press to term them "Bohemians," "Amazons," and "unsexed... incendiaries."[39] Whatever the reason for the silence of the press in 1885, women's activism in the 1886 "Great Southwest Strike" did garner attention. Some evidence suggests that, while women engaged in a number of public protests and crowd actions, striking Knights' locals remained largely if not exclusively the province of men. Joseph Cramer, a painter in the Iron Mountain shops in De Soto, testified before a congressional committee that he learned of his expulsion from the Knights because "it was common street talk in the neighborhood, even the women in the neighborhood knew it the next morning." A number of witnesses to a separate Knights meeting during the strike related, for example, that there were "a great many men in the . . . hall" and that "they were evidently workingmen, all of them."[40]

That railroad work threw men together for long hours, often in distant places away from their families, and demanded of them those qualities deemed manly, namely physical strength and endurance, quick and rational thinking, and courage, contributed to striking railroaders' conception of their Knights of Labor locals as masculine spheres. This conception was probably greatly strengthened by the context of the Gould system railroad strikes themselves. As participants came to feel ever more intensely that their struggle was against slavery, and as they, during the 1886 strike, increasingly came to rely on workplace actions, secrecy, and certain forms of intimidation and violence to secure victory, they perceived their fight as one between men.

The August 1885 Wabash Strike

Yet another reason lay behind the rise of the Knights in the Southwest. Despite the March 1885 agreement, trouble quickly developed for employees of the Wabash, St. Louis & Pacific Railway. The road was under a receiver appointed by the U.S. district court and was entrusted to operate it under a safe financial plan. During a period of traffic disruption due to snow and washouts, its managers cut wages by 10 percent and continued to reduce the force of shopmen, mostly strike leaders in March 1885 and Knights of Labor members. Then, on June 16, the Wabash closed its shops in Decatur, Springfield, Moberly, Fort Wayne, and St. Louis and reopened them two days later using only nonunion men, effectively locking out sixteen hundred Knights. Though the company claimed economic motives in closing the shops, Wabash Knights of Labor charged that its sole purpose was to "crush out organized labor." One distraught employee wrote Powderly that upon closing the shops managers had sought to "get the men" to sign statements that "they belong to no labor organization."[41]

Powderly's response to the continuing assaults on the wages and working conditions of Wabash Knights was discouraging. Wabash Knights had formed in early June 1885, prior to the lockout, District Assembly 93. DA

93 leaders wrote Powderly urgent letters throughout June and July, requesting that he visit Moberly and Springfield, the focal points of the conflict, and that the order's General Executive Board (GEB) issue it strike funds and step in to arbitrate a settlement.[42] To the surprise and dismay of DA 93, the board decided against assisting the Wabash men with strike funds, and Powderly replied that he was "surrounded by complications" and could not visit immediately.[43] A few days after receiving this message, Moberly Knights received a second letter from Powderly that read: "My bare presence at the present time would do you no good, and I could not bring that most essential of all essentials in time of strike... funds. I could encourage your men by talking to them but talk at such times it seems to me is of little use. It appears to me that there is a national move among capital owners to destroy all labor organizations; my work for the last month has been in direction of heading off such things."[44] While Powderly promised to discuss the situation further, one can imagine the puzzlement and alarm his words inspired among members of DA 93. His seeming defeatism and disinterest bred suspicion to the point that rumors surfaced among the Wabash men that Powderly had met with the railroad's general manager and "told him that their lockout had nothing to do with the Knights of Labor." One Moberly Knight advised Powderly to write the men a letter denying the rumor and encouraging them in their battle against the Wabash.[45]

There was of course no conspiracy on the part of Powderly or the GEB. The general officers of the Knights were engaged on a number of fronts—against hostile trade unionists and also lockouts in New York, New Jersey, and Kentucky—when events on the Wabash unfolded. These activities prevented them from giving the Wabash trouble more attention, and Powderly could only satisfy a limited number of the multitude of requests he received from members desiring his immediate presence, intervention, advice, and judgment. The board's denial of DA 93's plea for strike funds stemmed from a similar set of problems. The DA 93 petition arrived behind those of fifty other locals and districts. What is more, the order did not have any funds to disburse, as each of its districts lacked the required $100 in their assistance funds to offer support to striking or locked-out members. Besides these obstacles, most DA 93 assemblies had not even existed long enough to be eligible for relief.[46]

Meanwhile, the Wabash men's situation became desperate. Although Knights in Moberly had reportedly enjoyed some success in convincing nonunion men to honor their protest of the lockout, about fifty others, armed with revolvers and brass "knucks," remained in the shops. And on July 16 Springfield Knights notified the national office, "Six of our men are in jail for no cause whatsoever." Three of the men were jailed for contempt of court and three arrested by U.S. marshals, presumably because they had interfered or were suspected of interfering with the traffic or property of a railroad under a U.S. district court's control. Powderly finally cleared his schedule and met with Wabash Knights in Springfield in late July 1885. When he sought to win an audience with A. A. Talmage, the Wabash's general manager, Talmage refused.[47]

At that same time, DA 93 leaders met with Knights representatives from across the Gould system on July 25 in Parsons. The delegates saw Talmage's rebuff of their national leader as yet one more reason to expand the Wabash strike to the Gould roads in general. Because the Wabash had "declared war on the Knights" and "weakened" its employees with "short hours and long lay-offs," the Missouri Pacific and Texas & Pacific delegates pledged, "as American citizens," to "stand firmly by the Wabash employés, sustaining them by our sympathy, money and *our lives*, if necessary." The meeting appealed to the states of Missouri, Kansas, Illinois, and Indiana to push the U.S. court to appoint a committee that would "treat with the arbitration committee of the Knights of Labor."[48]

DA 93 published the resolutions of the Parsons meeting alongside an address to Knights "everywhere." The language of the address was dramatic and unequivocal, more so than that of strikers' appeals in March 1885, suggesting their deepening frustration. It impugned the railroad for "arrogating the right to drive us as slaves, chain[ing] us in dungeons by the power of the U. S. court" and "violat[ing] with impunity every law that opposes their will." Indeed, the U. S. court came under special attack as a shield that protected corporations from justice. The assembly then declared that the "crisis is upon us; labor and capital have met in deadly conflict." It advised Knights to "be ready to obey the order of the general executive board. If railroads say that Knights of Labor shall not work, why may not Knights of Labor say that railroads may not work?"[49]

It was in large part Talmage's response to the July 25 meeting's repeated requests for arbitration that pushed the GEB to action. Talmage wired on August 15 that "he saw no reason why he should meet the Knights . . . for a discussion, friendly or otherwise," since he knew of no dissatisfaction among the company's employees nor of any prejudice against the Knights. If other railroad officers had "taken sides for or against the Knights," he asserted, "it was without my consent." The GEB received this message after it arrived in St. Louis on August 14 and had attempted, once again unsuccessfully, to meet with either Talmage of the Wabash or H. M. Hoxie, vice president of the Missouri Pacific.[50]

On August 18 the GEB countered Talmage's refusal to meet with an ambitious order. It not only called out on strike all Knights on the Wabash system, it commanded Knights on the Union Pacific, Gould's southwestern system, and on "any other railroad" to "refuse to repair or handle in any manner Wabash rolling stock" until further notice. If this order was "antagonized by the companies, through any of its officials," the GEB continued, then executive committees would call out all Knights on these roads. This move, labor historian John R. Commons held, threatened to paralyze "over 20,000 miles of railway and would have equaled the dimensions of the great railway strike of 1877." In addition, the GEB, in combination with the executive committees of the Wabash and the Missouri Pacific system, attacked the Wabash, St. Louis & Pacific Railway for causing them to be "arrested at the muzzle of a revolver" and "manacled like felons." They also again targeted the U.S. court, demanding that the states of Missouri and Illinois "prepare articles of impeachment" against U.S. court justices for "malfeasance in office and for high treason."[51]

Initially Southwestern Knights did not widely respect the August 18 order. This was probably in part because of the risks involved. A number feared that they too might be locked out, and Peter Arthur's order to members of his Brotherhood of Locomotive Engineers to drop dual membership in the Knights and to not cooperate with the strike and boycott probably further discouraged them. Another factor was the sense of mistrust reigning among many of the region's members toward the national office. At the St. Louis meeting, some Missouri Pacific and MK&T shopmen had pushed for a second strike, so the decision of the GEB to order a boycott probably appeared to a number as a less than manly course of action, and the board's reasoning that pro-strike shopmen did not have support outside the shops as somewhat irksome, given local assemblies' broad membership.[52] More to the point, members of the GEB had appeared aloof and indifferent at the July 25 meeting, according to Joseph Buchanan, who was a member of the board. Buchanan later complained, "Turner simply kept records of the meeting; Hayes looked on and said nothing; Bailey put in most of the time at the window." Exhaustion and overwork probably explain this behavior, but to the delegates, who regarded events on the Wabash as pivotal, it was no doubt frustrating and disappointing. Finally, Powderly's absence during the mid-August meetings, due to a serious illness that forced him to his sickbed, rekindled earlier misgivings among Moberly men about his loyalty. A St. Louis member alerted Powderly to the men's belief that not health problems but "political aspirations" explained his neglect of the Wabash strikers. That Wabash and other Gould system men waited for their local and district assemblies to confirm the GEB's order is telling in terms of their confidence in local institutions rather than the national body.[53]

Once the order was obeyed it had an almost immediate effect. The strike of Wabash shopmen and the boycott of Wabash cars by the Union Pacific and Missouri Pacific shopmen disrupted Wabash traffic noticeably, as engines and rolling stock required routine cleaning and maintenance. More importantly, Missouri Pacific railroad officials feared igniting a second and potentially general railroad strike. Vice President Hoxie complied with the demand of St. Louis Knights that the railroad's shops discontinue work on Wabash cars. Hoxie explained to the railroad's superintendent that "he did not want to bring about any disturbance." Gould agreed to meet Powderly and other members of the GEB in New York on August 26.[54]

At the New York meeting, Gould pressured Talmage to reinstate the Knights discharged on June 16. When Talmage continued to resist despite several conferences with Knights leaders, Powderly wrote to Gould on August 29. He began by informing him that he had suspended the Missouri Pacific boycott of Wabash freight until their conferences ended. Powderly then appealed to Gould's managerial instincts and desire for stability: "If... the suspended Knights of Labor shall be reinstated it will establish a precedent which will refer all future cases to the management of our General Executive Board, [and] this in itself is a guarantee that no hasty action will be taken in any event." Then, in reference to Talmage but also with Gould himself in mind, he argued, "Neither pride nor a wish to screen [a] subordinate should come into the controversy so long as the interest of the company... and the peace and the welfare of society are at stake."[55]

Powderly's proposals were the substance of the agreement made by Knights and Wabash officials in St. Louis on September 3, 1885. The Wabash promised to rehire the men locked out on June 16 and to reinstate strikers by October 1. Talmage also agreed to a nondiscrimination clause, while Powderly committed to hold a conference with railroad officials before calling another strike. The men were to be rehired according to their marital status and residency: first, home owners who had families; second, town residents who had families; third, young single men and also married "floating machinists and mechanics."[56]

The agreement brought the order to national prominence and ushered in yet another period of remarkable growth in Knights of Labor membership along Gould's southwestern railway lines. Jay Gould, the railway "king" and longtime symbol of moneyed tyranny, had negotiated with a national labor organization on an equal footing. "No such victory has ever been secured in this or any other country," trumpeted the *St. Louis Chronicle.* In the four months following the Knights' victory, over 650 local assemblies formed across the country, and the order's official numbers shot up from seventy-four thousand in 1884 to one hundred ten thousand in 1885 and to almost seven hundred thirty thousand by the spring of 1886.[57] From Texarkana one enthused organizer reported, "The cause is growing rapidly in this section." By mid-1886 District Assembly 93 claimed over eleven hundred members, and the state assembly in Arkansas nearly three thousand. Reports from St. Louis and Dallas claimed similar surges in the popularity of the Knights.[58] In a grand show of the order's impressive strength and wide public support in North Central Texas, over five thousand people attended local Knights' grand trades' procession and barbecue in Denison in October 1885. Although rain "threatened," onlookers assembled in the streets "long before the procession was to start." The parade marshal, a "handsome banner" of the order, and a band preceded one thousand marching Knights, who were followed by a series of floats, one "representing the Goddess of Liberty," another "with forty little girls, with banner 'We are Knights of Labor,'" and others celebrating the work of various tradesmen—carpenters, masons, mechanics, shoemakers, bakers, and butchers. The friendly connections between the order and non-working-class residents was clearly evident in the predominance of floats advertising businesses such as Bettes Furniture Company, J. M. Hill's "tailors' goods and sewing machines," two beer manufacturers, Excelsior Bed Spring Manufacturing Company, and others. The only reported participation of black citizenry involved six men, "dressed in white coats, black pants, and black hats," carrying a "large satin banner."[59]

Following the Wabash settlement, Powderly and the other national Knights of Labor officers turned to the job of processing the mountain of paperwork created by the order's growth, containing serious internal conflicts, and managing the upsurge in boycotts, strikes, anti-Chinese violence, and protests waged by local members emboldened by the Knights' victory. The work, stress, and anxiety at times nearly overwhelmed Powderly and the General Secretary Frederick Turner, both physically and psychologically. While the successful arbitration of the Wabash strike and the resulting influx of new members enlivened Powderly's hopes that the order might help to erect a more virtuous and democratic republic, he was also deeply troubled by the rawness and impulsiveness of many new members. "Our organizers are pushing the work too rapidly and I know that they are not all doing it right from the letters that come to me," he complained to one Arkansas Knights leader. If he could not "hold them steady," he feared, the press's exaggerations of the order's strength might spur them to "act as the setter when starting game for the first time—break and go too far; and get the buck shot in his own hide."[60]

In the aftermath of the Wabash victory, Southwestern Knights turned to confront a host of difficulties. Their approach to these problems in part grew out of their experiences with both railroad and national Knights officials over the preceding year. Wabash managers' apparent attempt to rid the railroad of the Knights, and Talmage's refusal to treat with employees or even to hear their grievances demonstrated, to a broad cross-section of railroaders, the need for an established structure to mediate disputes and to ensure that agreements were fulfilled. How else could they protect the gains made under the March 1885 settlements? Many also realized that they could not rely upon the national body for direction or organization. For some this realization was laced with anger, as one Knights organizer reportedly continued to denounce Powderly in Moberly. For others it merely recognized a fact that had to be faced.[61]

By the fall of 1885 a number of railroad men on the Gould system favored a forum and a mechanism above and beyond the scattered and largely autonomous local assemblies they had joined in the spring and summer. On September 27, 1885, five Sedalia assemblies of Knights employed by the Gould system followed in the footsteps of the Wabash men and established their own district assembly, District Assembly 101. By 1886, DA 101 had grown to represent about thirty assemblies and thirty-two hundred members, making it the region's second most populous district. Michael J. Cassity agrees that this represented a significant shift away from the decentralized character of the first Wabash strike toward a more centralized organizational approach.[62]

The impetus to consolidate came from various sources. The coordination among railroaders in Texas, Missouri, Kansas, Illinois, Indiana, and Arkansas during the first and second Wabash strikes laid the basis for system-wide organization, as did the railways themselves; trainmen and itinerant laborers carried rumors, orders, messages, and ideas along the lines, and delegates and speakers traveled to and from distant points by train. And, as Cassity observes, it was no coincidence that Knights formed DA 101 in Sedalia, the town that had emerged as a central site of the strike due to the importance of its shops and its near takeover by state militia. During the second Wabash strike, Knights on the Southwest system created a network and structure to carry out the boycott. When in August 1885 Colonel E. K. Sibley, superintendent of the Missouri Pacific and MK&T, asked for clarification of the Knights' expectations of the railroad in regard to the "Wabash business," he received instructions from R. W. Drew, who signed his letters to Sibley, "Chairman, Executive Board, Southwest System."[63]

Finally, the press cast the September settlement as proof that arbitration could solve the "labor question," but editorialists conceived of that process as one between two powerful bodies. The *Missouri Republican*, for example, called the agreement "one of the strongest acknowledgements yet made by monopoly of organized labor." The next step, it regretted, was the consolidation and legal recognition of "Labor" so that it might combat the legal consolidation of "Capital."[64] Martin Irons, who was elected first chairman of DA 101's executive committee, echoed this sentiment. What was needed, he believed, was a "broad and comprehensive union for labor on a basis that would counterbalance the power of aggregated and incorporated wealth."[65]

Knights along the Southwest system posited a new definition of "producers," one that moved beyond the brotherhood model to attract railroaders across lines of skill, occupation, race, and even, to a limited extent, sex. The new ties among railroaders to a degree relaxed the hierarchies that they had long known, allowing people with competing ideas, different backgrounds, and a history of deep division and resentment to cooperate on the question of railroad labor policies. These new alliances tested the boundaries of white racial dominance and masculine spheres but left those for the time essentially intact. Railroaders' experiences during the summer 1885 Wabash strike—with an overwhelmed national organization and with railroad officials' intransigence, inaccessibility, and discrimination against Knights—also led many to reconceive their relationship to the national Knights, their communities, and the railroads. The formation of District Assembly 101 signaled railroaders' loss of confidence in labor agreements that hinged on the intervention of outsiders, whether a concerned public or the widely respected national union leader Terence Powderly. By the spring of 1886, the interlocking freedoms that Knights on Gould's western railways claimed were under new assault.

CHAPTER 6

The Independent Path of District Assembly 101

THE 1886 "GREAT SOUTHWEST STRIKE" figures prominently in historical narratives of Gilded Age labor protest, yet debates over whom or what to blame for its collapse have eclipsed an explanation of its origins and course. Martin Irons, chief leader of DA 101, himself claimed that he was forced to sign at gunpoint what he believed at the time was an ill-fated strike order. Many historians and contemporary observers have attributed the strike's defeat to his alleged hot-headedness or, more broadly, to the rigid idealism of the Gould-system Knights. In her 1942 study, historian Ruth Allen cast that idealism in positive terms, as representative of the democratic and egalitarian spirit of the West, while national Knights leader Terence Powderly bemoaned it as a symptom of DA 101 impatience with and ignorance of the order's principles. Historian Craig Phelan has echoed previous scholars in claiming that Gould easily "maneuvered" the Knights "into calling the strike prematurely" because DA 101 "failed to understand the 'rules of the game.'"[1]

Considering the sequence of events more closely, the strike seems a logical, even inevitable outgrowth of railroaders' struggle to win a permanent voice with management. The 1886 strike cannot be placed at the feet of Martin Irons, nor, as he would have had it, in the hands of a mysterious gunslinger. It signified not the impulsiveness and inexperience of new members and local leaders, but western railroaders' sober realization that the involvement of even well-intentioned individuals on behalf of railroad workers had done little to change the terms and conditions of work on the Southwest system. Many if not most strikers joined the effort because they had come, over the previous year or more, to perceive their freedom as contingent upon recognition of their grievance committees. This sentiment was felt across lines of race and skill. Black and white strikers from a variety of occupations built on the biracial alliance that had emerged during the spring and summer of 1885. For most of the walkout, despite the active participation and leadership of black Knights, this cross-racial alliance remained uncontroversial in the public's eye, as it rested on symbols and mechanisms of white control and appeals to popular antipathies toward Chinese and convict laborers. The 1886 walkout fell apart due not to racial animosities or other internal pressures but to the Knights' weak support among brotherhood men, the growing distance between strikers and their communities over what was at stake, and, most crucially, the aggressive, unprecedented state intervention ordered by the courts against strikers on the Texas & Pacific and Missouri Pacific railroads.

Martin Irons

Little is known about Martin Irons beyond a few suggestive details. He was born on October 7, 1830, in Dundee, Scotland. His father was alternately a sailor and a sailmaker, and his mother may have been a milliner. Sail making may have been an occupational tradition in his extended family—several men with the last name Irons were employed in that occupation between the 1820s and the 1840s in Dundee.[2] The occupation was a common one, as shipbuilding and the production of coarse linen cloth dominated Dundee's rapidly growing economy in the early nineteenth century. By the 1830s, when Irons was a child, a new system of railways and improvements to the waterfront connected Dundee to markets in Europe and the Baltic. These trade links gave rise to a boom-and-bust cycle in the shipbuilding industry.[3] Perhaps the worry of supporting five children in times of economic uncertainty convinced Irons's family to send him and at least one sibling, a sister, to the United States in the mid-1840s. At any rate, Irons recalled that he was fourteen when he landed with a "guardian" in New York City and that he left the city six years later for a two-year stay in New Orleans.[4]

We know that Martin Irons married Mary Brown, also from Scotland, in 1852 in Fayette, Kentucky, when he was twenty-two years old. Mary Brown provided much of the information on his pre-strike life in an interview published in the *New York Times* after the 1886 strike. In the interview she describes how the couple wandered frequently, hopscotching first from

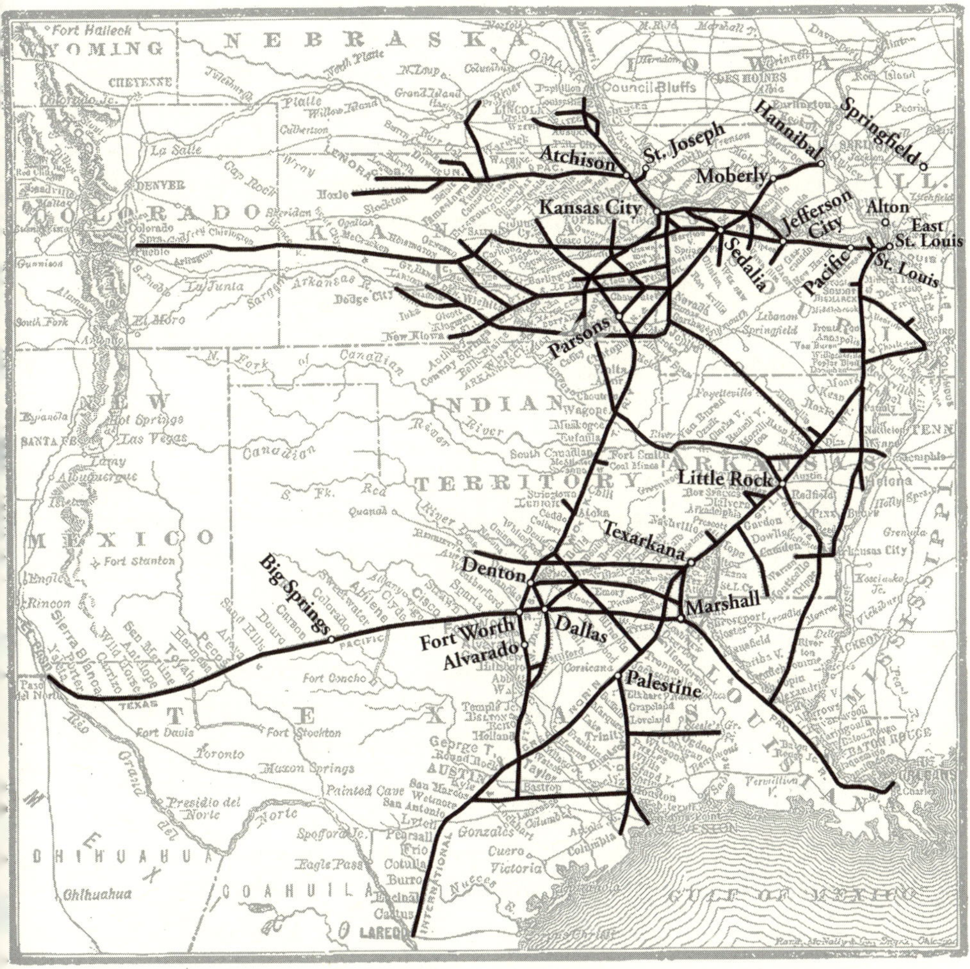

Major Strike Towns on the Missouri Pacific Railway System, 1886

Major strike towns on the Missouri Pacific Railway System, 1886. Courtesy Richard Jensen, http://tigger.uic.edu/~rjensen/railroad.htm.

Lexington, Kentucky, to Cincinnati, back to Lexington, then moving five times in five years to various Kentucky and Missouri locales, including St. Louis. During this erratic period, Irons worked as a machinist under his father-in-law, but he often met with unemployment.[5]

The Irons family settled down for a time, about six years, in Richmond, Missouri, where Martin advertised himself as a "Practical Machinist" and also tried his hand as an "Auctioneer and Appraiser."[6] When Irons left Richmond, Mary and their five children did not go with him. He again moved about—a year in Kansas City, Kansas, another in Joplin, Missouri, then back to the Kansas City area and on to Sedalia, Missouri, probably around 1880. Only a few shards of his pre-strike life in Sedalia emerge in the records. He married again, and there is cause to believe, based on the recollections of a fellow labor activist, that he began his strike involvement at least as early as 1884, when he reportedly met with a small group "almost every night in a cobbler's shop." The group "discussed among themselves the problems which then confronted labor." When the railroad company instituted a series of devastating wage cuts, "the shoemaker's shop became the center of activity" in Sedalia "for the now discontented toilers."[7]

The newspapers made no mention of Irons's role in the March 1885 walkout, but he did what many did in the wake of its victory—he joined the Knights of Labor. Several months later he was elected master workman and recording secretary of one of the local assemblies.[8] By September five local Knights assemblies had formed District Assembly 101, which by the following spring had grown to thirty assemblies representing between three thousand and five thousand employees. Martin Irons was their master workman and chair of DA 101's executive board.[9] How do we account for Irons's rapid rise to leadership? Little in the way of reliable evidence survives to tell us. His congressional testimony suggests that he was well spoken, and he did have previous experience in labor or fraternal groups such as the Grange, the Ancient Order of United Workmen, and the Odd Fellows. One possible source is his reputed autobiography, which *Lippincott's Magazine* published after the strike. It offers a sympathetic portrait of Irons as a spunky, resourceful fellow who at a young age "registered a vow to be among the first in coming years to help humanize men and debrutalize those that have power over the weak." However, the major factual errors in the piece, in regard to his birth date and the basic chronology of his life, raise serious questions about its authenticity.[10] In the absence of further evidence, we must look to the ways in which he articulated the purpose of the 1886 strike for clues that might explain his popular appeal.

"The settlement so far is no settlement at all"

Martin Irons and other strike leaders maintained that Gould and his top managers were intent on crushing the order and that railroaders' best defense against this was reliance not on the national Knights or public officials but on themselves.[11] In turning to self-reliance, DA 101 must have had the troubles on the Wabash in mind. Though the press heralded the September 3 agreement between Terence Powderly and Jay Gould as proof of the promise of arbitration, Wabash Knights who struck in late August did not find much relief in it. Members in Moberly wrote Powderly in late September 1885 to alert him, "The settlement so far is no settlement at all." The company had hired new men, setting to work only about 20 percent of the strikers, thus leaving the lockout intact. Powderly apparently attempted to resolve the matter with Gould, as Gould replied on October 11 that Wabash managers had assured him that the agreement was being carried out in all respects. Gould promised to correct any instance in which the agreement was violated.[12] But a confused and bitterly embarrassed Knight wrote Powderly on November 3: "We would like to know if the K of L Boys in this place and other Parts of the Wabash Road... [have]... any chance of getting... their Places again.... If this strike would Have Been settled that all the men could Have went Back in a Body the K of L would have prospered in this town. They all give us the Horse Laugh and say we were all dam fools for ever coming out and getting Left that way."[13]

Word of the Wabash debacle undoubtedly made its way south and west to men working on the Gould system, who had grievances accumulating of their own. Though railroad officials contended that their employees struck in 1886 in blind obedience of an order by dictatorial, power-hungry leaders of DA 101, railroaders before the congressional committee testified to grave troubles on the Southwest system in the months prior to the strike. By March 1886 it was clear to many of them that the Missouri Pacific and its associated lines were in various ways and at different points violating the March and September agreements, both in deed and in spirit.[14]

Though the March 1885 contract had called for the railroad company to "restore to its striking employés in Missouri and Kansas the same wages paid them in September, 1884," wages remained at pre-agreement rates at Big Springs, Fort Worth, and Chamois. Nor apparently were the wages of shop workers and laborers at Pacific, Missouri, restored, or among bridgemen and section men generally. James Barret, a St. Louis trackman, testified that in September 1884, "We got $1.50, and then we were cut down to $1.40, and from there to $1.30, and went on down to $1.25, and from that to $1.20," and despite the settlement "the rates kept on all the same."[15] Most alarming was company officials' argument to protesting bridge, section, and roundhouse men that the 1885 agreement applied only to shopmen. Knights leader E. F. Pagett railed, "Every disinterested person would understand, that that agreement included all those persons who were on a strike at that time, that they had not simply made a compromise with the shopmen."[16]

In addition, while the company agreed to compensate men time and a half for overtime, managers published a circular not long afterward stating that brakemen could only obtain overtime pay after twelve hours on the road. "If we went to work at 6:25 in the evening and didn't go out till 10 o'clock at night [which was common], we didn't get no overtime," D. H. Hartley explained. Brakemen were paid only by the full hour, so that "if you were on the road an hour and fifty minutes, you only got one hour extra time." Two St. Louis laborers reported a rule against overtime pay on Sundays, and an East St. Louis switchman, though he typically labored from 6:00 P.M. to 7:00 or 8:00 A.M. (thirteen to fourteen hours of hazardous work), received no overtime pay whatsoever. Missouri Pacific roundhouse and shop laborers in Kansas City and elsewhere testified that they regularly put in thirteen hours a day but were only credited for ten.[17]

Evidence also exists that, despite both the March and September agreements, Knights and those who had participated in the 1885 strike and boycott experienced discrimination. T. B. Duffy, a blacksmith helper, claimed that railroad representatives told unskilled men and apprentices in the De Soto shops that only those "loyal to the company" would receive the wage increase promised in March 1885. An Arkansas Knights leader maintained that a general foreman of the Little Rock shops had told him that he would not hire a well-recommended man because he was "one of the black-listed men."[18] One member of an extra gang related that when his section foreman "found out a man was a Knight of Labor he belly-ached around them and kicked all the time" and "kept [on] only two that I know of that belonged to the Knights of Labor." In a similar vein, another laborer offhandedly commented, "I know during the winter months here that our trackmen only worked three days a week. At least those that were Knights of Labor I know only worked three days a week."[19] Certainly these incidents deeply troubled Knights, especially in light of the Union Pacific and Wabash lockouts of strikers during the summers of 1884 and 1885.

Beyond the violations of the March 1885 contract, in the months preceding the 1886 strike, bridgemen, apprentices, and the unskilled sought satisfaction in regard to long-standing grievances. Although the Missouri Pacific paid bridgemen for day travel, they were not reimbursed for night travel, since, as one supervisor told bridge carpenter John Crow, he could "sleep reasonably well in his seat." Bridgemen were also responsible for acquiring their boarding on the road, a cause of great dissatisfaction among them. In addition, numerous young men objected to the railroad's frequent policy of continuing to pay them apprentice wages for journeymen's or "a man's" work. Finally, unskilled laborers, many of whom received only $1.15 a day in September 1885, sought a wage increase above and beyond the 1885 contract, to $1.50 per day. As Reverend Father C. F. O'Leary of De Soto told the congressional committee, railroad laborers, "especially the section-hands, do not get enough to support them decently." For trackman James Murphy, a wage increase also signified due respect for important and trying work: "We had to go out any hour of the night, when the weather was snowing and blowing away, at 12 and 1 o'clock, to repair the track, no matter how it blew, [we] was ready to help them through when they broke down or when rails broke."[20]

Over and over again railroaders expressed frustration with their inability to gain redress. When J. B. Deel of De Soto attempted to obtain pay owed him for five days work, he "could not get no account" of it. He emphasized, "That was one of our grievances—that no man can get redress of the company singly—and we wished to act in a body to force the company to recognize those rights." The company was likewise unresponsive to Patrick O'Brien of Kansas City, who had lost his arm in an 1873 railroad accident. He moved from flagging for $1 per day to switching in September 1885 with the understanding that he would receive $10 extra pay per month. Five months later O'Brien still had not received the extra pay, despite having informed his superiors of the problem, so, he told the committee, one of his sister's children "was taken from school at the age of twelve" to work for Western Union to help support the family.[21]

Both Deel and O'Brien reported their problems to their supervisors, but a number of railroaders undoubtedly followed William Hawkins's course.

Hawkins spoke only to his foreman about receiving single time for overtime work because, he told the committee, "I thought if it went any further they would discharge me." Others turned to their local grievance committees, the members of which were, according to DA 101 leader Martin Irons, "approached by men at all hours and times, by men bringing to them instances of a violation of this [the 1885] contract."[22]

Employees' charges that they had been cheated of a full day's wages or overtime pay, discriminated against for their Knights' membership, and poorly paid for grueling labor were leveled repeatedly at railway officials all along the system.[23] The statements before the committee of veteran railroader J. D. Knowlton, who was not a striker or a Knights member, lends further credence to strikers' testimony. The ex-conductor and section foreman explained that he was split in his loyalties while working for the Missouri Pacific. He wished to keep his job, and he felt that he should comply with the wishes of his superiors, but his supervisors pressured him to violate his conscience. A section foreman told him that he must require his men to deal at a certain store, at a certain place, to which he replied that he had not been used to doing business that way. At various locales he was instructed to make room for handpicked, incompetent men by firing men without cause. As a result, his track went to ruin, and so he was discharged, although he had been in the employ of the Missouri Pacific for a good many years and, he took care to mention, his father had been one of the first section foremen out of St. Louis.[24]

That railroad officials interpreted the March 1885 agreement as applicable only to shopmen explains much of the trouble in 1886. Probably some of these problems also grew out of the railroad industry's tangled bureaucracy, which evidently had grown more inaccessible to employees as a result of Gould's frenzied empire building. Some complaints involved traditional abuses of power by local managers, such as a Kansas City section foreman's discharge of family men who refused to board at his wife's boardinghouse or another's practice of selling section work to the highest bidder among underemployed laborers. But in a context in which railroad officials were violating or in various ways undermining the hard-won 1885 agreement, managers' transgressions and even their most innocent oversight heightened the feeling, as one local observer and strike sympathizer forcefully put it, that "the whole thing is a grievance... begotten in fraud [and] carried on by trickery... from Gould down to the lowest official."[25]

Part of the problem likely stemmed from many railroad managers' conception of their relationship to their employees, which tended to steer them away from investigating, discovering, and correcting even gross abuses by petty officers. Officials and supervisors typically looked upon their employees as a general does a soldier. Railroaders, to some degree, accepted this. As Knowlton commented, "A man generally, if he is considered anything of a railroad man, if he gets orders he obeys them, no matter where it comes from." It makes sense, then, that this top-down approach not only led managers to view their employees' demands as troublesome interference but also allowed petty officers to conceal their wrongdoings from higher-ups. As Irons explained: "If we bring the case before... [superintendent] Sibley, he sends his subordinate to investigate the matter. These grievances may occur on account of the one next in charge... [and] we having no person present when the testimony was taken, it was all one-sided."[26]

For the most part, railroad officials do not appear to have imposed a uniform set of cost-cutting policies throughout the Southwest system. Instead, the railroad's general office may have provided incentives for local managers to trim expenses, which would explain the wide array of different practices that emerged at various points on the roads. J. D. Knowlton related, "My experience has been, in about twenty odd years of railroading on the Missouri Pacific, that the officials generally are pretty fair with their men, but the cause of a great deal of trouble is from men that want to build themselves up in the estimates of their superiors." Probably general managers ordered a moratorium or severe limits on raising wages. When De Soto Knights leader Charles Laughlin sought to gain a promised pay boost, his foreman told him that he "could not do anything for him." Similarly, blacksmith John William Neely believed it was not in his bosses' power to raise his wages.[27]

Whatever the case, although dissatisfaction among Gould system employees was widespread in the year following the March 1885 strike, it was by no means felt everywhere. The Missouri Pacific generally lived up to its contract with engineers. Shopmen, for the most part, evidently either escaped the effects of the system's push to cut costs or over time negotiated some adjustment with their master mechanics. In addition, when Missouri Pacific Knights of Labor members walked off their jobs in March 1886, a large number related that they had no particular grievances. These locales included hotbeds of Knight activity, at Pacific, Parsons, Atchison, Cypress, St. Louis, and Sedalia.[28] Perhaps they truly had no grievances and obeyed the order because they expected a short strike or feared their fellow Knights would retaliate otherwise. Perhaps many feared reprisals from railway officials if they claimed their own grievances. More likely, given events during the first week of the walkout, a number simply followed the majority in obeying the strike order out of solidarity, a sentiment that officials and large segments of the public found incomprehensible.

As Texas Knights leader N. M. Lovin recalled, some violations were discussed, and policies adjusted at the behest of local boards of employees. Others were not. The difficulty that local and system-wide grievance committees had in obtaining an audience with railroad officials confirmed to some the company's malevolent motives. In August 1885 the executive board of the Knights of Labor obtained passes from H. M. Hoxie, vice president of the Missouri Pacific, to travel to speak with him in St. Louis about violations of the 1885 contract and assorted other issues. When board members arrived in St. Louis, however, Hoxie had already left for the East, so they left their list of grievances with his chief clerk. Hoxie later claimed that he had never received the list. Subsequent attempts by board member M. H. Palmer of St. Louis to see Hoxie met with no success, nor did similar efforts by local grievance committees to see officials at other points.[29] These events led Palmer and others Knights leaders to believe that Hoxie was "following the tactics of Mr. Talmage" in the August 1885 conflict: "couldn't learn where he was; didn't desire to see us."[30]

To railroaders on the ground, time seemed of the essence. The strategy of DA 101 was to take immediate action before its power to act eroded any further. E. F. Pagett, a De Soto Knights leader and chair of DA 101's grievance committee, told the congressional committee that investigated the walkout, "We made earnest and repeated efforts to get our grievances . . . before the officials of this road, and . . . we failed." He continued, "The longer it went the worse it was, and we saw very plainly that inside of another six months they would have the employés of the system back exactly where they were at the time that agreement was entered into," when the railroad introduced "the most notorious starvation cuts that ever wages the West received."[31]

Pagett's position clearly held sway at a DA 101 meeting in December 1885 in St. Louis, where delegates heard a long list of objections and complaints. Even so, Irons paid attention to process and made some effort to avoid the conflict. On February 1, 1886, he sent out letters to local assemblies requesting that they take a secret ballot on whether they would sustain the executive board if it demanded that railroad officials first recognize the board "as members of the Knights of Labor and not simply as railroad employees," and, second, pay unskilled labor on any part of the Gould system no less than $1.50 a day. In his letter Irons regretted railroad officials' claim that the 1885 contract only applied to shopmen, as it left "out in the cold a set of men who did, at least, as much as any of us to carry the strike at that time to a successful termination, and a set of men, who, from the smallness of their pay, need more protection than shop hands, namely, yard and section men." On the issue of recognition he reasoned, "If we don't do this to protect the class of men already named, we must demand a new contract, which will be attended by the same risks without having as great a beneficial result." All thirty of the district's local assemblies voted in favor of both propositions, with a large majority of members participating.[32]

According to J. L. Delay, an Arkansas delegate to DA 101, by "recognition" Irons meant that the railroad should identify the executive committee as employee representatives, not Powderley or the Knights GEB. The distinction was important to Delay as a railroader, and, given the experience of Gould system and Wabash Knights with the GEB during the August troubles, to members of DA 101 generally. It highlighted the degree to which many Southwest system railroaders had come to distrust the intervention of outside powers, whether the GEB or the governors, and to view the conflict with railroad officials as one that they must wage on their own. Delay explained, "An agreement made directly with the men would have a great deal more weight than an agreement made as the last one was, although the men respected the last agreement and carried it out." Local assemblies overwhelmingly voted for recognition, he claimed, "so that we could work direct with the railroad officials . . . I can place a grievance in a better light than either Governor Marmaduke or Governor Martin can. I can sometimes explain small points that they know nothing about unless they are railroad men themselves." In the statement of grievances and demands Irons prepared and published during the 1886 strike, he described the 1885 agreement as one in which railroaders had "had no voice" but which they still "accepted in good faith."[33]

In contrast to the portrayal of Irons as rash, vain, and uncompromising, the picture that emerges of him in the period leading up to the strike is of a relatively cautious labor leader. He told the congressional committee that he had wanted to "stave off" a strike because "we had just passed through a severe winter and many of the employees had no money ahead." While arguably his testimony was self-serving at this point, when the walkout had clearly failed, it appears plausible given his otherwise moderate vision for resolving the "labor question." As historian Michael Cassity put it, Irons's proposal for righting workplace wrongs on the railways was not meant "to alter alienating relationships" or to "break the power of railroad monopoly." Instead, he "put a premium on institutional power," specifically, a contract between railway system managers and workers over the terms of labor. Furthermore, although Irons became convinced that railway managers sought to break the Knights on the railroad, he paid attention to process and made an effort to avoid escalating the conflict. The shrillness that characterized many of his later pronouncements was largely absent in the exchanges that led up to the strike.[34]

The vote for recognition also came easily because the Knights had assumed an ascendant position at key points along the road, and a number of members, aggrieved shopmen particularly, were clearly feeling the order's power. While Missouri's labor commissioner, Oscar Kochtitzky, found in his travels all over the system many employees who were not members of the order, in numerous shops they were dominant. The Knights were in such control in the St. Louis shops that one master mechanic told three newly hired men, who were "importuned in the street... residences, and everywhere... to become Knights," to join so as to avoid trouble and annoyance to themselves, that the railroad would not hold it against them.[35] The same man recalled that after the March 1885 strike he saw a "growing insubordination": "We had men there that it made no difference with. There were some others that I thought took advantage of us; in fact I know it... I cannot consider it demoralization... I think it was aggressiveness. I think they felt they had the power which they could wield and showed it... Everything at that time of any moment was referred to the committee."[36]

In contrast, Marshall Knights sensed a real threat to their ability to shape the terms of work in the shops. When the Texas & Pacific was forced into receivership in December 1885, they likely thought of the Wabash Knights, who had not fared well under court supervision. The T&P came under the control of U.S. circuit court judge Don A. Pardee, who appointed as receivers governors John C. Brown of Texas and Lionel A. Sheldon of Louisiana. In December, a committee approached Governor Brown in the Marshall machine shops with the question of whether the receivers would recognize the 1885 agreement. Brown confirmed the committee's worry with his reply that the railroad's receivership status nullified all previous contracts but that employees would be treated fairly. Then in January 1886 he received a list of seven requests, with one involving the formation of an arbitration committee composed of three Knights and three company men. Brown rejected this set of proposals, "which the receivers believed would virtually relegate their authority to the Knights of Labor."[37]

Brown's reputation as Gould's "political whip for the Southwest" no doubt heightened concerns among T&P Knights that this rejection was part of a larger, sinister design to undermine them.[38] It was under these circumstances—rising fears that the 1885 contract did not offer sufficient protection and that the order's power was in jeopardy—that the discharge of C. A. Hall, a carpenter in Marshall's Texas & Pacific shop, touched off the T&P strike. This event, Martin Irons maintained, was the "culminating point or straw to break the camel's back." Hall's foreman had given him permission to attend a meeting of DA 101 delegates in Marshall on February 15, 1886. Two days later the foreman fired Hall for incompetence and neglect of duty. Hall quickly related his situation to an alarmed district meeting. Delegates perceived Hall's termination as "a direct thrust or insult offered by the railroad officials to the organization" and pushed for immediate action.[39] If the Knights could not protect one of its members from such a blatant act of discrimination, then its ability to shape the terms and conditions of work on the Gould system would be lost entirely. Irons and representatives from Marshall's four local grievance committees asked the foreman to reinstate Hall, citing two witnesses to Hall's request for a leave of absence to attend the meeting and previous supervisors' recommendations as to his competence, all to no avail. Irons also met with Judge Pardee and Governor Sheldon, and sent urgent telegrams to Brown and Colonel George Noble, a top T&P manager, but he could not convince any of them to journey to Marshall to investigate the incident.[40]

Nor could Irons entice to Marshall the busy William Kerrigan, general superintendent of the Missouri Pacific, in whom Irons had some confidence due to Kerrigan's willingness in January to adjust a matter involving a corrupt Kansas City foreman. Governor Sheldon's insistence upon offering travel passes to only two rather than all five members of DA 101's executive board, so that they could meet officials in Dallas, only confirmed their suspicions that the receivers did not take the Knights seriously. Irons later explained, "With the reluctance in giving passes and the manner of giving them, also that going to Dallas would cut me off from the books of the company, also all oral testimony, I thought it cost nothing for railroad officials to travel and that Marshall was the proper place to investigate, and I concluded that they had better come there and so telegraphed Governor Brown and Colonel Noble [the T&P receivers]." Noble did not reply. By then each of DA 101's local assemblies had received Irons's telegram, which asked, "Will you sustain your executive board in demanding the reinstatement of Bro. C. A. Hall?" According to one participant, local assemblies voted in the affirmative, and after one more failed attempt to contact Colonel Noble, Irons ordered a strike on the T&P on March 1, 1886, and on March 4, DA 101 requested Knights of Labor on the railroads to honor a boycott of all T&P rolling stock.[41]

A strike on the Missouri Pacific followed quickly thereafter, despite that railroad company's compliance with the Knights' boycott of the T&P Hoping to avoid trouble, General Superintendent Kerrigan had sent orders out across the Missouri Pacific system that no T&P cars were to be handled, though the T&P represented about 30 percent of the Southwest system's business. However, Kerrigan's response to Irons's request that he "use [his] influence in settling trouble" in Texas and "prevent calling out of the system" only sparked further distrust among Knights, including Irons. Kerrigan wrote that because the T&P was in the hands of receivers, he could not interfere without the receivers' permission. This made no sense to many Knights, who, like most anti-monopoly observers, believed the T&P to be only nominally separate from the Gould system and saw the trouble as involving all of the Gould roads.[42]

Irons later commented that Kerrigan's emphasis on the legalities of receivership suggested to him the idea that the T&P had been forced into receivership in order to protect it from labor difficulties, destroy the Knights' power, and, "by depreciating the stock of the Texas and Pacific, fill more rapidly the coffers of Jay Gould."[43] Given Gould's reputation, and the fact that as head of the Missouri Pacific he had successfully pressured the Wabash receivers to settle the August 1885 strike, this was not an unreasonable fear. Whatever the case, the decision to launch a broader struggle on the Gould system was of historic significance, as James Green testifies: "Unionists had been extremely effective in organizing boycotts to support fellow workers on strikes in various cities...but they had never engaged in a sympathetic strike like the one that Knights called against Gould's railroads in 1886, initiating a trend that disturbed employers for years to come."[44]

Two factors explain DA 101 leaders' expansion of the T&P strike to the Missouri Pacific. First and most importantly, an expanded strike offered the Knights the chance to settle a host of grievances on that road. Many Knights came to the conclusion that only a broader struggle could settle what were in actuality system-wide grievances. Second, they realized that Knights on the T&P could not carry their point alone. As Nathan Lovin, DA 101's master workman, reportedly told one official, the Knights "would make their fight on the Missouri, Kansas & Texas [which was part of the Gould system]," since the T&P was in the hands of a receiver and this placed severe limits on strikers' actions. By March 5 Judge Pardee had called upon U.S. marshals to intervene if strikers obstructed freight traffic, an order that had the effect of decreasing the number of "idle strikers" in the T&P yards. Although the strike had brought trains to a standstill at Fort Worth, Marshall, and Big Springs, in order to carry their point, T&P Knights would likely require the aid of Missouri Pacific railroaders.[45]

At the time that DA 101 called the 1886 walkout, the district was in debt $800 and had learned from experience that funds would likely not be forthcoming from the GEB, yet it called a strike of mammoth proportions against a "railroad king." The executive board did not alert Powderly or the GEB to its decision to strike; Powderly instead learned of the walkout on March 7 by telegram from a Missouri Pacific official and by reading about it in the newspaper. Though locals and districts regularly called strikes before informing the GEB, Powderly had agreed in September 1885 to arbitrate with Gould any trouble as a representative of the Knights; thus, the conflict placed him in an awkward position before the public. From his perspective, the decision of DA 101 to bypass him demonstrated the chief danger of the order's rapid growth—the disorder threatened by raw, hot-headed new members ready to exercise their power.[46] Nor did DA 101 possess the support of skilled trainmen. Joseph Buchanan, the

Knights activist from Denver, had predicted the consequences of this in a speech to Gould-system Knights leaders the previous summer, when Missouri Pacific Knights delegates had pushed for a sympathy strike with the Wabash men: "You know as well as I do that you cannot defeat a railway company if the trains continue to run; therefore you will attempt to stop the trains. The police, deputy United States marshals, deputy sheriffs, and constables will swarm in the yards and on the tracks.... You are husky fellows and full of fight, so I'll admit you can whip [them]. Then the militia of the various states through which the roads run will be called out.... Still guns are plentiful in your part of the country and most of you are pretty good shooters yourselves... Now what happens? The federal judges, under whom the roads are being operated, appeal to the President...and the regulars are sent to put down what has by this time become an armed revolution—rebellion, in fact."[47] For Craig Phelan, the fatal flaw of the Knights of Labor was its inability to rein in the inexperienced, rash recruits flooding the membership rolls in the mid-1880s. A beleaguered Powderly, Phelan argues, struggled to deal with an explosion of strikes called by local Knights, many of which were motivated more by "passion rather than reason."[48] Does "passion" sufficiently explain why Irons and other DA 101 Knights embarked on such a misadventure? Like most historical treatments of the strike, Phelan's interpretation centers on Powderly and Gould. His solid defense of Powderly's leadership is made at the expense of the strikers, whose motives and perceptions are only superficially explored. The actions of DA 101 require a fuller explanation.

One place to begin is with the 1885 confrontations, which had impressed on its members the power of mass action by railroaders, the ready generosity of fellow "producers," and the fact that, however well-intentioned, the intervention of outsiders—the national Knights and public officials—had in the end failed to change the terms and conditions of work on the Gould system. By early 1886, railroaders along the Southwest system lines could have pointed to the gains that the labor movement had made over even the previous year, especially among miners. Hundreds of Missouri miners, for example, had engaged in a total of twelve strikes in 1885, five of which were won and another four of which partly succeeded. Miners in Macoupin County and Peoria County, Illinois, waged a total of eight strikes, seven of which ended in victory.[49]

Certainly the misguided notion that right makes might is evident among Knights on the eve of the Southwest strike. "One word," a strike leader claimed on March 4, "is enough to call out the 9,000 knights who work for the Gould system and to bring to their assistance the same day 190,000 knights who do not work for the railroads, but who are our sworn brothers and who are within reach to help us." A frustrated Wabash Knight urged Powderly to call a general strike on the southwestern roads: "Don't think there is a brother on the western southern System Refuse to give us a Helping Hand and it would not Last over a week in all." Others appealed to principle alone. When in August 1885 Joseph Buchanan challenged the preparedness of Gould system delegates who sought to strike with the Wabash men, one delegate had cried, "We'll fight it out to the bitter end!"[50]

The material and spiritual help that railroaders had enjoyed in 1885 encouraged such unbounded optimism. Local labor organizations and hundreds of Houston and San Antonio railroad employees, for example, had pledged their cooperation. Most impressive by far was the offer of Knights of Labor among Union Pacific employees, who had sent Joseph Buchanan to the scene of the 1885 Gould strike to organize and to offer $30,000 in aid.[51] Not without some cause, strikers placed their confidence in "producers," and railroaders especially. The alternative of relying on the hard-pressed national Knights to approve funds would have delayed action for an open-ended period with no guarantee of aid, and to put off a walkout until a more auspicious time meant giving Gould managers the opportunity to further weaken the fragile cross-occupational and cross-racial alliance that the Knights had built over the previous year.

Probably for similar reasons, Irons gave the strike order without first informing the GEB of developments. Doing so risked considerable friction with the national leadership and wider public. However, alerting the GEB would have placed the fate of DA 101 in the hands of a national organization that had proved distant, overwhelmed, and unable to secure company compliance with the 1885 agreements. While more seasoned leaders might have better appreciated that, regardless of Gould system managers' dismal record, the long-term national credibility of the Knights of Labor depended on whether it upheld its end of the bargain, one can imagine how, with the September accord already in tatters due to management violations, this reasoning did not hold sway with Knights confronting the Gould system in the Southwest.

The Strike Begins

At 9:30 a.m. on March 6, a committee of shop employees arrived in the office of Leroy Bartlett, master mechanic at the St. Louis shops of Missouri Pacific, to inform him that, though they had no personal troubles with the company, they had orders to walk out at 10 o'clock. When the bell rang at 10:00 a.m., Bartlett went to the shops and "found the men all taking off their working clothes and getting ready to go out. They all formed in double file and marched out of the shop... In the space of half an hour, I suppose, they were all gone." When one engineer arrived in a De Soto shop to change engines, he found he "had nobody to attend to the engine but myself and the fireman. There was a crowd of men on the street, and I saw a great many men in the Knights of Labor hall." Similar scenes played out on March 6 in shops along the lines of the Gould system. In Sedalia, about 700 quit work, 340 in De Soto, 200 to 300 in St. Louis, and 300 in Little Rock. Two days later a Missouri newspaper headline read, "Traffic Throttled: The Gould System at the Mercy of the Knights of Labor."[52]

Participants in the March 1885 walkout had relied primarily upon moral suasion to stop engineers and firemen from running the trains. But in 1886, at numerous points on the Gould system, striking Knights immediately and in large numbers took possession of shops and roundhouses and proceeded to "kill" and disable locomotive engines as a means of stopping freight traffic, despite the calls of Knights leaders to "forebear from any violence whatsoever, or any injury to the company's property or act of lawlessness." Between March 6 and March 12, strikers took one or both of these actions at Atchison, Sedalia, Parsons, Denison, De Soto, Marshall, Whitesborough, Waco, Taylor, Big Springs, Palestine, Mineola, Texarkana, and Alvarado. Some did not sabotage equipment but "guarded" the shops. Knights in St. Louis, for example, held a meeting directly after the walkout, and a few hours later about twenty-five returned to take charge of the locomotives and roundhouse. They did not touch the engines, but, as a body, prevented any repair work on them in order to thwart the movement of trains.[53]

In taking these actions, strikers revealed some uncertainty as to whether skilled trainmen would support them. Otherwise they would not have risked the costs, in terms of both public opinion and the law, of escalating the conflict. Some cause existed for them to believe that engineers and firemen would back the strike and thus grind freight traffic to a halt—a key ingredient to any successful railroad strike. A number of brotherhood men also held membership in the Knights, and St. Louis engineers reportedly expected the leader of their brotherhood, Peter Arthur, to declare in favor of the strike. Strikers assured Terence Powderly that the engineers were initially in complete sympathy with them, but, even when trainmen quickly complied with requests to leave their posts, strikers took the extra step of climbing on board the trains and killing the engines. Their unwillingness to depend on the support of trainmen surely stemmed from a fear that the narrow trade unionism of the brotherhoods might ultimately prove a stronger draw to skilled men than the industrialism of the Knights. Also, some strikers apparently consulted engineers and firemen as a group only after the walkout had already commenced, which probably increased this concern. De Soto Knights, for example, did not meet with a committee of engineers in the city to discuss the strike until March 6, the day of the walkout.[54]

Beyond these strategic issues, the takeover of shops and machinery plainly expressed strikers' occupational identity and a sense of their ownership over the shops and the railroad generally. To kill or disable an engine required technical know-how, muscle, determination, and cooperation, those "manly" qualities skilled and semiskilled railroaders most associated with their work. A *Waco Daily Examiner* reporter documented one very public display: "A bold Knight . . . mounted the steps and stood in the cab. Opening the fire doors, he flung in a pocket of water on the fire, and kept it up by drawing water from the tender and throwing it in the fire doors . . . Soon a brother knight . . . came down, and shoving the throttle valve down against an upright pipe, he tied it fast there . . . and taking a hammer he struck the 'connecting link' which holds the hose together [and] runs water from the tender to the engine . . . Then the big fellow . . . disconnected some more links . . . [I]n about thirty minutes the engine was dead."[55] The practice of sabotaging engines was not always so exposed to reporters, but it was a key spectacle of the strike and to a large extent replaced the March 1885 ritual of crowds surrounding trains and appealing to and winning the active sympathy of trainmen. While the latter practice underlined the broad-based nature of the strikers' support and their dependence on that support, the former communicated strikers' identity as railroaders who held the power and the right to resume or halt freight traffic.

These actions and others also illustrate the distance that had grown between railroading Knights and large sections of the public over the previous year. In contrast again to the 1885 strike, the newspapers reported relatively few open, mass meetings. Although Knights held a "monster meeting" in Fort Worth and frequent public meetings in De Soto, more often large groups of strikers stood on street corners and outside of shops and yards, talked amongst themselves, and expressed suspicion of outsiders, even refusing to answer press questions about the company's treatment of them. In St. Louis, the yards of the Wabash, the Missouri Pacific, and Union Depot were all deserted "except by strikers who gather around in small groups and discuss the matter earnestly." More so than in 1885, strikers held numerous secret meetings in Knights of Labor halls, in St. Louis, De Soto, East St. Louis, and Denison.[56]

Cassity characterizes the mood of the strikers who congregated on the streets as nervous and tense. Certainly, many feared the presence of spies, and a number clearly distrusted newspaper reporters, as during the previous fall and spring various local assemblies had boycotted the *St. Louis Globe-Democrat*, *St. Louis Post-Dispatch*, and *Kansas City Journal*, charging these papers with anti-strike coverage and discrimination against unionists. In addition, some businessmen had at once expressed hostility to the walkout. In Palestine, merchants proposed boycotting the Knights rather than submitting to the order's call for a boycott of the T&P.[57] More ominous still was railroad officials' response to the walkout. On March 4, Governor Brown of the T&P refused the call of a Marshall citizens committee for arbitration, reserving the right of receivers to operate the railroad as they deemed "wise and prudent," and pledging to retain those men who had filled strikers' places even if the walkout's participants sought to return to work. On March 9, William Kerrigan of the Missouri Pacific notified strikers that, as they had "voluntary abandoned" their jobs, their names had "been stricken from the rolls" and that they must immediately leave the company's premises. On the following day, the railroad began advertising in the daily newspapers for "machinists, carpenters, car repairers, car cleaners, engine wipers, yardmen, switchmen, trackmen, and laborers." Then on March 10 the *St. Louis Post-Dispatch* warned that the company was "getting . . . in shape to make a lasting fight," as it had suspended about five thousand non-strikers, including clerks, telegraph operators, yard watchmen, and others idled by the walkout.[58]

Despite such foreboding signs, some optimism surfaced during the first week of the protest. On March 8 and 10 the press described "hopeful and firm" Knights in various towns in Texas, Kansas, and Missouri. This was likely not simply a show of confidence. Traffic in Missouri, Arkansas, Kansas, and Texas was reportedly immobilized by the walkout. Moreover, by March 13 no strikers in Marshall had answered the railroad's advertisements for new men, bridge hands had struck on the Missouri Pacific, and rumors were afoot that conductors, engineers, firemen, switchmen, and brakemen would join the Knights of Labor cause and that the strike might even spread to the more than sixteen thousand Knights working on railroads throughout the Southwest. Indeed, by March 8 the strike on the Southwest system had spread to trackmen, shopmen, and switchmen on the St. Louis Bridge and Tunnel Railroad, preventing the traffic of seventeen lines of railway over the bridge between East St. Louis and St. Louis.[59]

Strikers also had grounds to be encouraged by non-railroaders' initial response. Marshall citizens reportedly backed the walkout and expressed disgust with T&P officials, who many felt had disregarded the town's efforts to bring about a settlement. In De Soto, one Knight claimed, "We had large public meetings... All the ministers were there... and they all gave us every assurance that we had their entire sympathy." While the *Kansas City Journal* saw the walkout as unjustified, both the *Missouri Republican* and *St. Louis Post-Dispatch* urged railroads to settle the strikers' grievances. After receiving a $20 donation from employees of a shoe factory for the Knights' cause, the *Post-Dispatch* encouraged "every workingman" to take up a collection.[60]

More critically, if what railroad officials and several state military officers charged was true, then at numerous points—Pacific, De Soto, Atchison, Palestine, and Newport, for example—city officials and the men they deputized chose not to enforce the law because they were sympathetic to the strike. We should not take such claims at face value. In Palestine, for example, Kerrigan noted that "deputy sheriffs acted as spectators" when two hundred strikers killed an engine. One can assume that the sheer number of strikers involved in taking over company workhouses and equipment simply overwhelmed local law enforcement at some points. Regarding other towns, however, Kerrigan probably correctly argued that local authorities either tolerated these actions or identified with the Knights and hoped, like many Knights who opposed the use of violence, that they were capable of containing the situation. De Soto's mayor, for example, was a Knight, and he swore in strikers as special deputy marshals. When he and the other leading citizens, including the local master workman, met with state military officers, most were, according to one of the officers, Major Parks, "fiercely denunciatory of Jay Gould at the meeting" and resisted all talk of state military intervention. A similar situation prevailed at Pacific. If these small communities did indeed identify with strikers and attempt to shield them against the Gould system, then this would confirm historian Herbert Gutman's thesis that small towns tended to side with their working-class members in battles against large, invasive, exploitative corporations. Even if it were not the case that city officials tolerated workhouse takeovers and disabling of engines, their reticence to order the intervention of state troops gave strikers more room and time in which to act, and thus encouragement.[61]

For Cassity, the worried mood predominating among strikers demonstrates that its origins and meaning were "distant" to many railroaders, at least in Sedalia. He points to the variety of grievances that strikers cited before Oscar Kochtitzky, Missouri's labor commissioner, which included violations of the 1885 contract, a long-term worsening of conditions, Gould's monopolistic designs, and the troubles of bridgemen and trackmen, and concludes that "the cloudiness of the situation" indicates that "these strikers were honoring a commitment, not to a cause, but to an organization." Furthermore, Cassity argues, DA 101 leaders' conception of workers' power and organization as necessarily centralized violated rank-and-file Knights' commitment to local autonomy, as they quickly realized during the strike.[62] In these judgments he echoes Missouri Pacific officials such as Hoxie, who essentially argued in a March 6 circular to Missouri Pacific strikers that they had carelessly heeded the command of dictatorial leaders and betrayed their individual interests and identities.[63]

The proposition that the 1886 Southwest Strike was largely imposed upon Gould-system Knights also comes from another, more unexpected source. In his autobiography, *The Path I Trod*, Powderly detailed a story that Martin Irons had related to him privately. He had authorized a system-wide walkout against his will and the will of the rank and file. This story is well worth considering, since it is still repeated, probably because it is a sensational tale but also because it conforms to a popular, potent image of the West as a particularly volatile region, the history of which turns more on the brazen acts of individuals than larger social forces. Indeed, historians had once seen western working-class radicalism as a "response of pioneer individualists to frontier conditions." Recent interpretations of western mining have rejected this thesis, but the myth of the frontier lives on in Irons's story, in which the order to greatly expand a major railway strike comes as a consequence of the threats of a lone gunman.[64]

When the two met at a conference to discuss the strike on March 20, 1886, Irons related to Powderly that a few days after the strike had begun, he was given strong cause to suspect that the vote on the strike order had been dishonestly reported and so he had considered calling off the walkout. At a meeting of the executive board in St. Louis, a member invited him to his hotel room and forced him at gunpoint to sign a confirmation of the strike order. Then the man took turns with an accomplice shadowing Irons for four days and nights until, as Ruth Allen put it, "the strike had developed beyond the power of any individual to stop it." Irons withheld this information, she wrote, so as to avoid depriving strikers of their "support, confidence, and strength" and because the truth "would not save them from their tragic aftermath." Allen accepted the story as fact and speculated that the unnamed man was either a company hireling, or, she thought more likely, a railroader tired of compromise.[65]

Undoubtedly consolidation increased the distance between Gould-system Knights and their leaders, and a number of strikers followed the majority in obeying the order out of respect or fear, or a mix of the two. When the yardmaster of the Iron Mountain road asked some of the men he knew to return to work, they told him they could not, "on account of the Knights of Labor; that they had grievances over which they had no control." "It was not safe for any man to be out of their ranks," testified one bitter machine shop foreman, who had joined the Knights in September 1885 but withdrew shortly after the 1886 strike began.[66] The number of participants in the walkout who came to oppose the action and who sought to return to work multiplied as the walkout wore on and met with a series of grave obstacles.

Still, in all likelihood it was not the case that an aggressive minority within DA 101 forced a strike on fellow Knights or that Knights struck in a lockstep to the order of DA 101. First, Knights' response to the strike order between March 6 and 12 was a massive, active, determined illegal effort to stop the trains by taking possession of engines and the buildings that housed them. The large number of men who occupied the De Soto roundhouse on March 11 was not unusual. In Denison, two hundred Knights disabled engines on March 8, one hundred in Sedalia on March 10, and three hundred in Parsons on March 12. Though one can safely assume that a number did not attend their local assembly meetings, or simply followed their fellow Knights out, the strike vote was widely and immediately supported, suggesting that it was probably legitimate.[67] Second, it is implausible that anyone, even a board member, could have successfully intimidated Irons into remaining silent on the strike vote over the course of four days as he spoke with strikers on the streets, at meetings, and in the inner sanctum of their union halls. The story makes more sense as an attempt by Irons to diminish his role in what had become by March 20 a much more desperate effort. When Irons offered Powderly this explanation for ordering the strike, he also told him, Powderly recalled, that "defeat was sure and certain staring them in the face." He had reason to despair over the decision to order a walkout, a decision in which he had played a key role and one in which DA 101 had not included Powderly or the GEB. Personal tragedy may have also affected Irons's perspective on the strike at that time, as only about two weeks prior and in the midst of the conflict, his second wife had died in Sedalia of pneumonia.[68] Finally, neither strikers' diverse grievances nor their desire to heed the order of DA 101 necessarily suggests confusion or unthinking allegiance to the Knights of Labor as an institution. For many, recognition of the order represented a chief means of securing redress on the multiplicity of issues that affected them. As DA 101 executive board member M. H. Palmer noted before the committee, "I don't think it looks reasonable to suppose that a lot of men would strike and didn't know what they were striking for."[69]

The focus on self-organization led strikers to hold themselves at a distance from the non-working-class public and skilled workers. The "First Official Statement of Grievances of Gould's Employés," prepared by Irons, appeared on March 8, two days after the conflict had extended beyond the T&P and weeks after Hall's termination. Neither Irons nor any other executive board member testified that they had submitted railroaders' grievances to the press prior to this date. That DA 101 leaders waited so long to relate the key issues of the conflict to the public suggests more than poor organization. It illustrates again the reliance of the Gould system Knights self-organization rather than public intervention in resolving the "labor question."[70]

Two demands in particular reflected a desire for internal mechanisms for ensuring that managers did not abuse their power. In order to protect Knights from discrimination, DA 101 proposed that members accused of unsatisfactory workmanship be allowed to defend themselves before a board composed of "disinterested parties" chosen from both sides. A second demand involved establishing a system, which it outlined in detail, "for the government of the employ and wages of apprentices." These demands accord well with Irons's stated objective before the congressional committee in May 1886: "I wanted something that would be hung up in the hall or the shops so that we could do away with this continual making of little grievances that was so annoying... I wanted something substantial, and if an employé violated it I wanted him thrown out as quick as I would have the company redress a violation they made." Knights compared the DA 101 struggle to those made by engineers and firemen for recognition. Strikers in Atchison wrote to engineers and firemen: "Boys, we want to thrown off the YOKE of SERFDOM and be FREE men like yourselves."[71]

To the extent that DA 101 saw a role for the non-railroading community, the assumption seemed to be that the public would automatically sympathize with the Knights' cause, surely because of the anti-monopolist enthusiasm of many communities during the 1885 strikes. The "Official Statement of Grievances" begins, for example, by deriding a Missouri Pacific circular, presumably one authored by Hoxie on March 6. In it, Hoxie forcefully appealed to "every independent, free thinking co-laborer" to abandon the "arbitrary, useless, and uncalled-for" strike: "A few men whom you have voluntarily given power, are depriving many thousand of their collaborators of their accustomed wages, divesting this company of the capacity to pay its employés for their services, shutting up the avenues of traffic in four States, and preventing some 4,000,000 of people from obtaining their customary supplies and the necessities of life, because it is claimed that one employé of the car department of the Texas and Pacific Railway... a road over which this company has no control, has been discharged by the agents of the United States court." The statement of DA 101 dismissed rather than responded to Hoxie's argument: "We consider the circular too insignificant to reply to in detail." With much of the public startled by events, and DA 101 initially unwilling to make its case, railroad officials quickly dominated the terms of the debate.[72]

The trouble seemed to have been that Southwest system Knights did not fully comprehend the weakness in the pro-strike coalition in which they had participated during the previous year with their middle- and upper-class neighbors. Middle-class and business elements in Sedalia, Cassity has argued, came to see divergent meanings in the 1885 and 1886 conflicts. In the former case, widespread support among merchants had stemmed from "local pride" and "the untrammeled spirit of the competitive market." These ideals held that workers should earn enough to allow them to be self-sufficient contributors to their cities and towns, which should not be under the power of a "giant monopoly" backed by state militias. In 1886, the issues were not so simple as a wage cut but involved multiple charges, so that the "origins of the walkout" appeared "confused and obscure." Moreover, the decision to strike came not from a local body of workers but from DA 101, a centralized body encompassing the system as a whole and with Martin Irons at its head. The key principle of solidarity, which was absolutely central to union recognition and a sympathy strike, was alien and abhorrent to many non-unionists. DA 101's solution depended not on the intervention of a cross-class union of "the people," but on the collective strength of an industrial union to check the power of the Gould system.[73]

The Biracial Alliance

In 1941, an elderly white socialist named Patrick Cassidy wrote to Ruth Allen about his participation in the 1886 Gould system strike. In his letter, he mentioned that at the beginning of the conflict the Knights had taken over the railroad yards in Palestine, Texas, and had made the railway coaches their meeting place. Then he supplied one of the few surviving bits of evidence by a Knight on race relations and the strikes: "The two coaches we got for the whites and the one for the colored people. We had lots of fun going from one car to another... that lasted about three weeks. Then the company got out injunctions on us all to keep us from going on the railroad, so that kept us busy running... I believe we sent a colored Blacksmith from Palestine to represent us at the first K. of L. Convention in St. Louis in 1886, and we got credit for sending one of the best delegates at the convention."[74] Does Cassidy's recollection of interracial camaraderie reveal more about the "interests of the teller"—perhaps a unite-and-fight romanticism—than black-white interactions more than a half-century prior in a Texas town with deep roots in the Old South?[75] Two sources, also distant, confirm his memory of significant black involvement, but in contradictory ways. In June 1886, *John Swinton's Paper* described Palestine's black Knights as "among the most loyal" to the order. Yet, alongside this picture of enthusiastic black support stands the testimony of an anti-strike businessman, who described the same scene in Palestine as Cassidy but who intimated that hierarchy and separation more so than familiarity and cooperation characterized the order's cross-racial alliance. He testified that one coach "was full of negroes, from twenty-five to thirty of them...and in another coach, *in the other end of the yard* [my emphasis], there was [the Knights'] general headquarters, and they were claiming that they were protecting the company's property."[76]

What then was the nature of the Knights' cross-racial alliance on the Gould system in 1886? Why did near silence on the issue of black-white relations, instead of controversy over the specter of "social equality," greet Knights' efforts for most of the upheaval? Answers to these questions do not come easily, in part because accounts of both walkouts on the Gould system do not dwell on the issue of race. The strikes never devolved into "race strikes," nor did the railroads or the local press make much mention or use of race until late into the 1886 conflict. Before this point, much of what is documented was said in passing. This was so despite the fact that the racially inclusive Knights organized in an industry, a region, and an era in which racial strife, racial separation, and racial violence were endemic.

The Knights' attempt to attract the unskilled stemmed in part from the empathy that better-paid and more regularly employed Knights felt toward the unskilled. One striking blacksmith later testified, "When they would bring work in the shops we would often pass a word or so, 'How is times?' or something of that sort. In the winter time he told me how hard they were pushed and how their time was cut down and what they was making."[77] Beyond these more compassionate sentiments, in 1886 the reluctance of skilled trainmen to support the Knights made a cross-racial appeal to the largely black unskilled labor force strategically important. The Knights' list of demands therefore called for wage increases for all laborers, including section men, trackmen, and crossing-watchmen, and, because the unskilled faced intense labor competition, an end to the employment of convict and Chinese labor on the Gould system roads.[78]

In Marshall, Texas, at least, casting white and black participation in 1886 as a biracial alliance seems perverse. The East Texas town was located in a black-majority county that only recently had come under Democrats' control. The *Marshall Tri-Weekly Herald* embraced at once "Redemption," the Knights, and a murderously anti-black credo. The degree to which the *Herald*'s vision relied upon racial terror is revealed in its comments, published several weeks after it praised the Knights 1885 Fourth of July parade, on a lynching in nearby Elkhart of five black people, who, along with other black townspeople, were rounded up and threatened by a mob until one "confessed" to the brutal rape and murder of the young white wife of a local law official. A white witness to the mob's actions later described the scene: "A mob of two hundred or more men gathered and rounded up every negro in this section. They put the negroes in confinement in an old abandoned storehouse in Elkhart and guarded them vigilantly while others in the mob would take the negroes out, one at a time, in effort to scare the truth from them. Finally, after many unsuccessful attempts to fix the guilt, they drug a batch of them to the top of the hill (where the Elkhart high school now stands) and told them that they were going to hang them all in order to get the guilty ones." While Texas newspapers often sympathized with lynch mobs, the *Herald*'s warning was unusual in its venom and sweep: "The lonely grave by the roadside is a warning that colored people would do well to heed."[79] To be fair, the local paper did not necessarily represent the sentiments of white Knights in Marshall, but in this context, for black strikers, the line between coercion and cooperation was likely a thin one, as a Marshall Knights of Labor handbill intimates: "We have resolved to come to the rescue of our downtrodden brethren, known as unskilled laborers... We call upon all laborers, trackmen, engine wipers, coach cleaners, baggage and freight hands, and coal heavers, to lend us their aid... Trackmen, get clear out of sight of the track until we gain your victory."[80] Authored by an overwhelmingly skilled and semiskilled, white leadership and addressed to a racially mixed, unskilled workforce, it also instructs and subtly threatens.

As the key spectacles of the 1886 conflict indicate, race was central to white Knights' conception of their struggle all along the Gould roads, and this, along with the practice of racially segregating local assemblies, worked to mitigate the degree to which local communities saw the Knights' biracial alliance as a threat to the racial order. Little evidence exists of black participation in strikers' efforts to overpower trainmen who sought to take out freight engines and to take possession of shops and roundhouses, and no records have surfaced to suggest that black Knights helped to kill or disable locomotive engines as a means of stopping freight traffic.[81] The practice seemed to communicate white strikers' strong occupational and also racial identity, as killing or disabling an engine displayed technical know-how, muscle, determination, and cooperation, the same "manly" qualities that skilled and semiskilled white railroaders most associated with whiteness. In addition, the racially exclusive and public nature of much of the strikers' engine sabotage conveyed to the public white domination and authority, so that when black striker Wyatt Owens was arrested on trespassing charges, his white jailer did not see him as the source of the trouble; it was "those white son of bitches" he was after.[82] These actions of course represented the main means for strikers to exert their power and immobilize freight traffic, but they also at the same time demonstrated white control and authority, undercutting white apprehension about a biracial strike.

Despite the association between the major symbols of the strike and whiteness, black workers took part in significant numbers and in leading positions. Black strikers were arrested and jailed at Marshall, Palestine, Paris, and elsewhere in Texas. Although exceptional, a more vivid scene of black involvement emerges from a report on crowd action in Palestine that derailed an engine: "Engineer Jack Kimbrough knocked one of the colored strikers from the engine with a hammer, but was soon overpowered by numbers." Moreover, Patrick Cassidy's forty-five-year-old memory that black participation extended to leadership roles is corroborated by other examples. The receiver for the T&P, John Brown, met with one black and two white Knights from Denison on the eve of the strike to discuss grievances, and Dallas black leader and Knights supporter Melvin Wade spoke before a mass meeting of fifteen hundred people at the height of the conflict. At the statewide level, David Black served as an executive board member. He was a key negotiator for Galveston Knights who had launched a boycott and then a strike against the Mallory Company, and also spoke in Fort Worth on behalf of the Knights.[83]

In regard to C. Van Woodward's classic thesis that southern white workers swung ambivalently between exclusive and inclusive approaches to black workers, Leon Fink has observed that, in Richmond, Virginia, the fact that "black and white workers were not actively competing for the same jobs ... presented southern white labor leaders with a strategic choice.... In short, [they] need not have greeted blacks directly as competitors or as brothers." The situation was comparable for skilled shopmen and semiskilled trainmen. Whites filled these positions while blacks were virtually always regulated to unskilled work. Also, as in Richmond, the Knights in no way explicitly challenged the racial hierarchy at work. However, a greater percentage of whites labored at the bottom of the occupational ladder in Dallas than in Richmond, 40 percent as opposed to 20 percent.[84] Probably it was the need in 1886 to attract a base of unskilled workers, who experienced labor competition across racial lines, that explains why a further element binding black and white Knights proved so important: the demand to drive convict and Chinese labor from the Gould system roads.

Anti-Chinese and anti-convict-labor sentiment came in large part from the unskilled themselves, black and white. Strikers in numerous Texas towns, and trackmen at the January 1886 Knights state district assembly meeting, related that one of their major grievances was employment of "Chinamen" and convicts on the road.[85] At first glance, neither group worked on the railroads in large enough numbers to warrant strikers' attention. In 1886, only 293 convicts worked on Texas railroads, and the Gould system employed but a hundred or so Chinese in West Texas, far from the scene of the strikes.[86] However, strikers had some reason to fear that the seemingly all-powerful Jay Gould, whom Knights condemned as "the arch-monopolist of the world," might dramatically and suddenly multiply those numbers. Local newspaper reports fanned fears of economic competition. Railroaders perhaps recalled the use of Chinese labor to construct roads in West Texas in the early 1880s, and conjectured that the state might easily and quickly shift the majority of convicts from agriculture to railroad labor.[87] Finally, strikers likely sensed in the anti-Chinese cause a means to garner community sympathy and to unify an otherwise racially divided unskilled workforce.[88]

Both strikers and railroad managers appealed to the apparently widespread assumption that, at least in relation to Chinese workers, black and white workers shared a common citizenry. When the receivers for the Texas & Pacific defended the employment of Chinese workers in West Texas, one claimed he would prefer white and black labor because, in his words, "I am an American." The other insisted that Chinese workers were kept at "the lowest grade of labor" and that they were "not worked together with white men or with Negroes either."[89] Black Knights leader Melvin Wade hit upon a similar theme in his March 1886 speech before a gathering of hundreds of strikers and their supporters in Dallas. When asked why the Knights admitted black workers but not Chinese, he replied: "The Negro never came to this country of his own volition, the white man brought him here and it was only right that he should be cared for and given labor that he was a citizen of this country, but the Chinese never became citizens.... Negroes had more rights than the Chinese from the fact that they were brought here not of their own accord, while the Chinese came of their own accord, and that where as when a negro gets $5, he puts it into a lot... the Chinese would not give $15 for all the lots in America unless he could ship it back to China."[90] The aim of DA 101 to attract working men from a broad spectrum of railway occupations, from unskilled trackmen to semiskilled switchmen to skilled shop workers, was to an impressive extent realized. The *St. Louis Post-Dispatch* reported that most of those who walked out on March 6 were shopmen or machine shop employees and a number of switchmen. Switchmen and shopmen in De Soto, a railroad division superintendent testified, "joined together in one large body and marched out of the yards and up to the Knights of Labor hall, where they had a meeting and appointed a large number of guards, who took possession of the yards and shops." However, brakemen also joined the protest, as a St. Louis official related that "immediately after the strike [began], lots of [brakemen] went up in a body and joined" the order. In addition, one striker told the committee, trackmen also "all quit work at about the same time [March 6]... from Saint Louis to Kansas City, on the line of the Missouri Pacific Railroad... I understood that every foreman's gang hadn't a man on it."[91]

However, other aspects of the strike's first week or so augured badly for the Knights. Many railroaders did not belong to the Knights of Labor, and some who were members returned to work or never left. While a number of section men and trackmen struck, many others remained at work on the Missouri Pacific. Clashes between strikers and non-strikers began early on and were especially pronounced on the T&P, probably because the stakes involved in a strike against a railroad in receivership were much higher. At numerous places along the road in Texas, Knights combined takeovers of cars and workshops with threats against engineers, firemen, brakemen, and section men, in order to stop the movement of trains. These actions had stopped freight traffic by March 12, but less than a week later the U.S. marshal of the northern district of Texas had, under order from a U.S. district judge and with a force of deputy marshals, "dispersed all lawless men, put the road and its property... in the hands of agents of the receivers, set the freight trains moving, and put men to work in the shops."[92] At about the same time, federal courts took unprecedented legal actions against strikers on the Missouri Pacific.

Injunctions on the Missouri Pacific

Beginning on March 10, the Missouri Pacific placed notices on company property warning strikers to leave the shops and roundhouses. On March 13 the railroad's lawyers petitioned a St. Louis court for "an injunction against the interference with the traffic of the railway."[93] Two days later the railroad named as defendants 496 strikers, and on March 16 filed another suit in Palestine against 104 Knights who allegedly interfered with train movement and work in the shops. Many strikers in St. Louis and elsewhere ended their occupations of shops and roundhouses, and the company began to employ new men and some returning strikers.[94]

DA 101 could not have foreseen this turn of events, which dealt the walkout a mortal blow, because two major aspects of these legal difficulties were new. As matters stood until the 1886 "Great Southwest Strike," courts of equity had confined their issue of orders, or "writs of assistance," to workers who struck railroads in receivership. Injunctions were a separate type of court order meant to protect property generally in a time of crisis. With the 1886 Southwest Strike, judges implemented both types of orders on a vaster scale. State courts enjoined hundreds of striking employees from interfering, even peaceably, with solvent roads, and, in Texas, Judge Don A. Pardee held that a road's receivership status made any strike against it illegal.[95]

In some areas skilled trainmen continued to back the strike. The newspapers excitedly reported that when the Missouri Pacific attempted to move a freight train out of its St. Louis yards on March 11, "Engineer O'Neil was called from his post by the strikers and deserted his engine." An engineer, who had been unemployed since before Christmas, replaced O'Neil and took the train through a "threatening" crowd of men and boys, but not without the help of police and detectives, who manned the other parts of the train despite the "jeers and yells of the crowd." A second effort to run a train ended quickly when a "well-dressed young man" addressed the engineer and fireman. The strikers' "argumentary opposition," announced the *Post-Dispatch*, was "more forcible than blows" and "[might well] bring victory to the Knights of Labor."[96] The railroad's use of police and nonunion men to run trains drove engineers further into the strikers' camp. A BLE meeting in the city resolved to join the Knights' fight pending approval from BLE chief Peter Arthur. Until that time, they pledged to abandon their engines if requested to do so by the strikers. One Knight in a crowd that successfully called trainmen from their posts on March 13 said of the engineers, "Oh, I tell you they are with us."[97]

These scenes of cooperation between strikers and trainmen did not unfold everywhere. In Atchison, for example, the local Knights assembly sent barely concealed threats by letter to engineers, advising, "Do not undertake so risky a work" and "He that is not with us is against us." The experience of De Soto engineer M. Roberts, a representative of the BLE on the system, quickly embittered him and other engineers in the town toward the strikers. On the night of March 4, on his run from De Soto to St. Louis, he spied a man on the track throwing a switch: "The result was it ditched my engine and nine cars right in the face of a passenger train on the south bound track." The brakeman flagged the passenger train, preventing a collision. Roberts was unsure whether the Knights were responsible, but as a railroad man he considered the ditching of his engine a "cowardly low trick."[98]

When Roberts and other engineers met with Knights on March 10 in regard to the strike, he told them that "the company had lived up strictly to their contract and that we, as men, proposed to do the same thing." He advised the master workman to send the strikers back to work, arguing that the company would never treat with the Knights given the "impositions" the order had made on officials. Continuing the strike, Roberts told them, would "only injure the prospect of those men in De Soto that had little homes there and living comfortably." He then "tried to touch his finer feelings" on the question of violence. The members of the Knights committee denied that they would condone ditching engines or acts of violence, and promised him that De Soto's engines would remain unharmed. Two days later Roberts went to the town's raided roundhouse and found that, like the other engines, his engine's parts had been disconnected and "part of her . . . carried away." Upon his return from a trip to Sedalia, he found his wife "almost sick" because a committee had informed her that he was to be "roughly treated" for continuing to run his train. Roberts later told the committee, "They [the Knights] were all friends of mine. I told them I had nothing but my duty, and that while I sympathized with them personally, I couldn't uphold the work they were doing."[99] Roberts was clearly shaken by his experience and by the idea that railroad men especially would destroy engines or precipitate train wrecks. His story illustrates the ambivalence many engineers and firemen felt about a conflict that required them to choose between, on the one hand, men they considered friends and a cause they saw as reasonable, and, on the other hand, their "duty"—to railroading, security for their "little homes," the decisions of their brotherhoods, and the March 1885 contract that promised to guard them from labor competition.

Gould system Knights joined the 1886 walkout for reasons that were often particular to their work situations and managers, with a number, particularly shopmen, claiming no grievances at all. But the underlying cause of the strike involved the generalized fear that railroad officials meant to break their organization and to undermine and eventually abrogate the 1885 agreement, leaving them vulnerable to deteriorating conditions and wages. Their experiences in 1885 as well as those of Union Pacific railroaders in 1884 and Wabash men under receivership had impressed upon them the necessity of obtaining a permanent institutional voice on the railroads and of guarding carefully the gains they had made. Securing a voice on the railways for non-brotherhood men necessitated a biracial alliance. Black and white Knights found in the order's appeal to a "union of producers" a broad and elastic ideology that left room for a host of different interactions, goals, and strategies on the part of black and white members. White Knights' show of unambiguous white control rendered the Knights' cross-racial organizing unthreatening in most white onlookers' eyes for most of the conflict. Not race but the collapse of the walkout on the T&P, the developing fissures between the skilled and the less skilled and between strike supporters and opponents, the distance apparent at the conflict's outset between the public and DA 101, and particularly the unprecedented use of injunctions on the Missouri Pacific—these realities sealed the Knights' fate. Significant sections of the public, and many Knights themselves, increasingly turned against DA 101 and Irons in particular. In the weeks that followed, railroaders saw the gains of the previous year vanish and the Knights' organization on the Gould system reduced to shambles.

CHAPTER 7

Blaming Martin Irons

MARTIN IRONS DIED IN 1900 a disreputable, impoverished outcast in a small Texas town south of Waco. For the more renowned, longstanding labor leaders "Mother" Jones and Eugene Debs, he was not a pitiable, transitory figure; he was a martyr in the fight against forces of corporate tyranny. Historian Ruth Allen, who chronicled the "Great Southwest Strike," also saw him as a heroic if tragic figure—a selfless visionary who carried the burden of the strike's defeat with him for the rest of his life. Many of Irons's contemporaries, some of whom were pro-union, condemned him as either an aggressor or an egoist who had lured railroaders into a doomed clash with Gould. Knights in his home base of Sedalia, Missouri, ran him out of town following Gould's triumph. A congressional committee charged with investigating the causes and consequences of the walkout took up the arguments of railroad officials and much of the mainstream press in deeming him a "dangerous if not pernicious man." Numerous historians have echoed this negative judgment, casting Irons's role as either that of a reckless, "aggressive" autocrat or as a man in over his head, "so emotionally involved" that "he lost all perspective."[1]

For most of his critics, Irons epitomized the disastrous outcome of the walkout, especially what they saw as a foolish, desperate, costly bid to salvage the strike effort by pushing for its expansion. In the aftermath of the Knights' loss, the press dwelled disparagingly on the sordid details of his personal story, apparently as a means of explaining the social and cultural crisis that had grown out of the confrontation between Gould system Knights and their managers. The crisis was difficult to comprehend because, first, it lay bare the contradiction between the community ideal that had animated the 1885 confrontation with Gould and the overwhelming evidence of class tension exposed during the 1886 walkout. Second, it brought to the fore the ways in which Gould system Knights parted ways over the question of violence and over the degree to which they remained wedded to "free labor" ideology, the same ideology that federal courts relied on in enjoining strikers.

For Irons's part, his judgment to spread the strike eastward relied less on fact and more on faith. This move forced out into the open serious internal divisions among strikers, and, along with Irons's deep personal flaws, made him an easy scapegoat for both a lost labor struggle and the class tensions that struggle had made glaringly evident. Nevertheless, to view him as villain, fool, or hero divorces him from the context of the "Great Upheaval" and oversimplifies the choices available to Gould system strikers. It also obscures the fact that the Gould system strike was not entirely lost. In the end, the Knights' "union of producers" generated a biracial challenge to the anti-labor and fiercely anti-black political order in two states. Although the Knights' pragmatic motives and the larger context of racial violence and separation limited the extent to which the alliance disrupted racial hierarchies and identities, some of the relationships that black and white Knights developed fed directly into the larger history of populism. In this sense, too, Martin Irons's personal downward spiral serves as a poor metaphor for the "Great Southwest Strike."

Falling Apart

By late March, court orders had cleared strikers from the shops and workhouses, and controversy over the walkout had enveloped railroad communities and the ranks of skilled trainmen. In addition, several other key developments strained the relationships that Knights had built at work during the 1885 strike and boycott and within their assemblies. First and foremost, Peter M. Arthur, grand chief engineer of the Brotherhood of Locomotive Engineers, forbade members from supporting the Knights and ordered them back to work. Although F. P. Sargent of the Brotherhood of Locomotive Firemen was not as emphatic as Arthur, during a trip to St. Louis in mid-March he advised members to act cautiously. By March 25 one striking shopman in St. Louis, where trainmen had consistently deserted their engines prior to Arthur's order, bitterly told a reporter that the engineers' brotherhood had undermined the strike. Striking switchmen, firemen, brakemen, and shopmen, he said, "have no further use for them."[2]

THE STRIKE AT EAST ST. LOUIS—FIRING INTO THE CROWD.—Drawn by T. de Thulstrup.—[See Page 251.]

Picture published in *Harper's Weekly* to accompany an article about the situation at East St. Louis, April 17, 1886, p. 249.

On April 9, 1886, bloody clashes between a large crowd of strike supporters and a dozen deputies ended with six dead strikers, one deputy nearly beaten to death, and military suppression of widespread, often violent pro-strike sentiment in East St. Louis. A wave of sympathy strikes in East St. Louis and elsewhere had convinced Irons in late March to seek the strike's expansion, even as the Knights faced mounting legal, economic, and political obstacles. Harper's Weekly, *April 17, 1886.*

Second, with the tide turning against the walkout, Missouri Pacific vice president H. M. Hoxie brought to bear the immense power of the railroad system against the Knights, adamantly refusing to arbitrate with District Assembly 101 or the Knights' General Executive Board and announcing that the walkout had effectively terminated the employment of its participants. In reply to a March 15 letter from Irons that proposed a conference between a committee of DA 101 members and railroad company representatives, Hoxie replied the next day that no such meeting would repair the trouble, as the chief cause of the strike, the discharge of C. A. Hall, involved a road that was not under the Missouri Pacific's control and over which he "had no voice or authority." He went on to state that the strike had so badly affected business that few men were needed and any men rehired would have to be "acceptable" to the road's superintendents. To Terence Powderly's request for a meeting Hoxie responded that because the Knights had violated the September 1885 agreement by participating in "work stoppages without cause," he would only meet Powderly and other members of the GEB as citizens and not as employees' representatives.[3]

Third, after meeting with members of DA 101's executive board and Powderly, the governors of Kansas and Missouri requested that the Missouri Pacific abide by the March 1885 agreement in the interests of public welfare, even though, they concluded, "We are unable to find wherein the Missouri Pacific Railway Company has violated the terms and conditions of the agreement." The governors' conclusion that the 1886 strike was unjustified represented a major blow to the Knights. It apparently encouraged Hoxie, who restated that the Missouri Pacific would re-employ strikers as needed and then emphasized that it would consider only men who had not participated in or advised "destruction or injury of the company's property."[4]

By this time, the strike was disintegrating. At the same March 20 meeting in Kansas City at which Irons told Powderly his story about the forced strike order, Irons grieved over "how new men were deserting at various points, how new men were being brought in as strikebreakers every day, how the members of the railroad brotherhoods had not lived up to their promises not to operate trains with strikebreakers."[5] A number of strikers returned to work while others increasingly turned their energy to acts of sabotage and intimidation in order to stop the trains. One railroad superintendent witnessed "bruised heads and faces" on new men and returning strikers. Some who found employment in St. Louis slept and ate inside the shops rather than stay at boarding houses, because, as one superintendent testified, "They dare not go out . . . or . . . they would most assuredly get beaten . . . and badly used beyond question, which a number of them was." Men who tried to go home to their families in the southern part of St. Louis were "waylaid." In Denison and Atchison large groups of masked men overpowered guards and held them with drawn pistols as they killed both passenger and freight engines. Between March 16 and March 23, trainmen allegedly found in Alvarado a fire set on both ends of a bridge, a rail across the track outside of Little Rock, and sabotaged tracks at Irondale, Mineral Point, Jacksonville, Sedalia, and Parsons. On March 17 a missing spike in the track purportedly caused a passenger train to derail outside of Marshall.[6] Strikebreakers and strike opponents also received written and verbal warnings, some of which were friendly in tone and others of which threatened dire consequences, including expulsion from town or lynching, often illustrated with a sketch of a coffin or skull and crossbones. Friendly coffin notices warned of impending danger but offered some sympathetic appeal, such as, "From one who knows and wishes you well" or "Being a friend to you and not wishing you to get hurt."[7]

Contemporaries and historians have emphasized the conflict's violent character for understandable reasons; nonetheless, union violence during the walkout was not as endemic as supposed.[8] Overall, the Knights relied upon a range of tactics, most of which involved persuasion and community pressure. This is not immediately obvious, because the strike's opponents often conflated destruction or sabotage of property, the use of moral suasion, and crowd assemblies with violence. One foreman, for example, claimed that even the "appearance" of strikers around the shops "would naturally intimidate the men," so that even peaceable efforts to request that workers respect the strike were perceived as aggressive and dangerous.[9] Thus, anti-strike elements were responding to a general climate in which the line between peaceable and violent action appeared to blur. It was in this highly charged context that Knights leader George Bibb was arrested for contempt of court and placed under $1,500 bond for authoring a letter on behalf of his local assembly that merely informed strikebreaking members, without a hint of violence, that they faced expulsion from the order if they did not quit work.[10]

That said, the frequent confrontations between deputies and trainmen on the one hand and strikers on the other were rife with tension that might have easily escalated into violence. In St. Louis, for example, when the company sought to run a train out, the small force of twenty to thirty policemen could not keep up with the several hundred men who surrounded it and uncoupled its cars. The next day, between 100 and 150 police met with a crowd of several thousand men congregated on the tracks, around cars, in yards, and on bridges. As police roughly pushed the crowd back, some resisted; a fight broke out, and strikers threw stones from the bridge. After clearing the yard, the police purportedly found the caboose off track and an obstruction placed on the switch. As the train left the yards, men from the crowd ran alongside and attempted to uncouple moving cars, sometimes successfully. "Every day after that, for...about a week or more, the same or a larger number of policemen were furnished, and trains were taken out, about the same experience being had in each case."[11]

DA 101 blamed Hoxie for the rising tensions. Members of the executive board published a statement, "in justice to ourselves and the truth of history," on March 23. The statement began by denouncing the governors, who, they charged, had violated a promise to the board to turn over Hoxie's answer to the press before allowing them to "pass upon the terms of settlement." With the Missouri Pacific's disavowal of any association with the T&P in mind, it then condemned their "wink at gross violations of a sacred agreement in its plainly manifest spirit, because its technical letter gives an apparent advantage to a great corporation." "If Mr. Hoxie did not know that he was guilty of gross wrong and injustice," they asked, "why should he refuse to listen to our evidence and hear our appeal for redress?" The board answered, "Mr. Hoxie wanted trouble. He has provoked it...He is still inciting it, and making an innocent public pay the price of his perfidy. How long will the public consent for Gould and Hoxie and thus to rule or ruin?"[12]

Despite the executive board's appeal to local communities, a sense of doom overtook remaining strikers and their leaders. An address published March 26 by district assemblies 101, 93, and 17 to "Knights of Labor and Trades Assemblies throughout North America" admitted, "We have wearied the press and worn the types of the world in stating grievances, and demanding an opportunity to present them to Mr. Gould and his lieutenants." Recognizing the opposition that had emerged to the walkout among strikers, it again pointed to Gould, who it said "seeks to overawe and terrorize the weak and beget treason in our ranks." Its authors no longer looked to worldly courts, which "through the golden spectacles he places upon them...see but the rights of wealth." Instead, strikers must look to "that grander, higher court, that court whose verdict is final, as it is righteous." The authors of the address saw in the strike's dismal prospects not cause to abandon it but a true test of virtue or manhood. "The arch-monopolist of the world, Jay Gould, has thrown the challenge in our teeth, and bidden us come on to the conflict," it announced. The address called upon railroaders to protect "the sacred circle" of their homes from the "the bloated vampire of the body politic" who sought "to satiate his greed." However hopeless their struggle against him, however fortified Gould was "within the barricades of gold and courts," strikers were, they claimed, "clad in the armor of eternal right." Targeting those against them in the conflict—the "great corporations," the "terrorized merchants," and "the scabs," they drew firm battle lines: "Cowards to the rear, scabs to the enemy, and men to the front . . . Let us die when victory is assured to the generations behind us."[13]

Both strikers and those who returned or remained at work appealed to—and impugned—each other's manhood. One note to a re-employed "brother" from a local executive board stressed the Knights' fraternal ties: "We have not the railway company to fight, but the men in our own ranks who like you weaken and fall by the wayside . . . Remember the obligation you have taken at the alter."[14] Non-strikers, in turn, characterized strikers as poor providers for placing their jobs in jeopardy and as cowards for their covert attempts to stop freight traffic and for delivery of anonymous warnings. "They are not men enough to sign them," a De Soto engineer commented. Ex-Knight Nick O'Brien cast the Knights as thugs who "were not doing right . . . A man, because he has five or six hundred men at the back of him, wants to get another man out of his situation, and I don't believe in such business."[15]

The emergence of women and boys in crowd action late in the conflict underscored Knights' increasingly frantic claim that the railroad's policies assaulted not only railroaders but also their families. During its first two weeks, as in the 1885 strike, men alone appear to have engaged in both the public and clandestine attempts to stop freight traffic. Knights' union halls remained male spheres of activity throughout the conflict, but as the strike entered a period of crisis in late March, when trains began to move, women and boys joined the effort to block their path, employing certain tactics but not others. On March 25 in Pacific, for example, throngs of strikers "rushed out in full force" with each approaching train. The men threw a heavy oak plank across the tracks before one engine, climbed on board, and undertook to set the brake, while women and children threw stones at the deputies and men in the cars, "making it dangerous for them to stay there."[16] A similar scene unfolded at Parsons, where a large crowd gathered in the yards, blocked the engine, and warned trainmen to leave. When the railroad's attorney ordered the crowd to disperse, "strikers' wives bombarded him with eggs," causing the crowd to erupt in laughter. The women then convinced a number of guards to hand over their guns, from which they removed the shells.[17]

Public sympathy for the strike dissipated as incidents of violence, arson, and sabotage multiplied and as towns and cities struggled to contend with the shortages of fuel and coal as well as the disruption of business. In some towns, citizens voiced the fear that the railroad might move its shops elsewhere. Texas citizens held mass meetings in various towns, condemning the walkout, and Law and Order Leagues formed throughout the Southwest to protect strikebreakers and railroad property. On March 24 a meeting of St. Louis merchants issued a public statement demanding an end to "the strike now throttling the commerce of several States and checking the slowly returning prosperity of the whole country after three years of depression." The strikers, the meeting urged, must "resume work," "keep out of the way and cease intimidating others," or else expect citizens to call for the military intervention of the state and the national governments. At the same time, governors of Missouri, Kansas, Arkansas, and Texas proclaimed the strike against the public interest and appealed to "law-respecting citizens" to restore order.[18]

Gould himself contributed to the growing disarray in the strikers' ranks. On March 26, Powderly, at Irons's request, finally secured a meeting with Gould in New York. The meeting ended with Gould agreeing to arbitrate all "differences between the employees and the company, past or future" and to take back those strikers who had not participated in illegal acts; Powderly wired Irons, who called off the strike on March 29. Then, in a stunning turn of events, Gould denied that he meant to order Hoxie to arbitrate, reiterating that he had long ago delegated authority over the strike to Hoxie. Though Gould's most recent biographer called their meeting a "colossal misunderstanding" and explained that Gould frequently entrusted subordinates with control over his operations, this justification falls flat.[19] Why would Gould have met with Powderly at all if he had not intended to give the impression of his willingness to take command of the situation, which was completely within his power to do? Craig Phelan has observed, by the time of the New York meeting, "Gould, not Powderly or Martin Irons was in control of events." The T&P receivers refused to fire strikebreakers, as did Hoxie, who told national Knights leaders that the railroad would only need to rehire about half the strikers' numbers. The Missouri Pacific and Texas & Pacific railroads had for the most part resumed freight traffic by the end of March, but for Irons and others the conflict was far from over.[20]

East St. Louis

On March 26 one newspaper described the scene at several St. Louis railroad crossings, where only two days before a crowd of perhaps two thousand had tried and failed to stop the departure of a Missouri Pacific freight train manned by a bevy of policemen and an engineer. The special police at the shops carried double-barreled breechloaders, and police guarded the trains, the crossings, and the tracks. "There was," the reporter noted, "a silence and a lack of spirit in the crowd which had quite a saddening effect." Though fireman Dan Haley refused to take out his engine, that day three freight trains resumed operation with the help of authorities. The third passed a somber gathering of about three hundred people at one intersection. As it approached the Summit Avenue crossing, where "forty or fifty policemen had an easy time preserving order," the engine "put on steam and shot by the crowd." The men congregated about the tracks made but a "feeble effort at shouting," the paper commented. "The most feeling of the day was displayed by the women and girls who hissed and otherwise expressed their disgust besides shrieking 'scab' after the train crew."[21]

The following day, on March 27, 1886, one week after he had confided his disheartenment to Powderly, Irons pushed to expand the strike in order to save it. If the Missouri Pacific did not arbitrate, he threatened, the walkout might "extend overall the railroads in the country . . . and . . . to all Knights all over the country." Powderly charged that Irons had exceeded his authority, and Irons's critics cite this as evidence of either his hot-headedness or his lust for power. Certainly, his was an emotional decision that passed over the grave, now all-too-evident obstacles to the walkout that had developed in the preceding weeks. Irons must have felt demoralized and desperate. The relatively stable personal and public world that he had built for himself in Sedalia was falling apart. His wife was dead, federal courts had intervened on behalf of the railroads on an unprecedented scale, and Knights were returning to work, even stalwart local leaders such Daniel Millory, who was a grievance committee member, striker, and coauthor of a major pro-strike document. Also, the broader public sanction that railroaders had enjoyed in 1885 fragmented quickly in 1886 as reports of union violence, intimidation, arson, and sabotage multiplied and as towns and cities struggled to contend with the economic disruptions. The effort that Irons had so strongly identified with, personally and publicly, was hopeless without some new action.[22]

In the context of the "Great Upheaval" of 1886, when "a strike fever gripped the nation's workforce," events quickly transformed despair into hope. Over fourteen hundred strikes involving six hundred ten thousand workers shook U.S. society over the course of the year. According to one scholar, "Nothing like this had ever happened in America, or in Europe." For many unionists, history seemed to open up and hold out new possibilities. To borrow historian Herbert Gutman's formulation, "historical givens" became "contingencies." Doubtless, the speed and magnitude of events elsewhere helped to push DA 101 members to move to strike. Now, as Irons and others looked for deliverance from a doomed effort, news from East St. Louis appealed to their "messianic mood." Over 250 section men, trackmen, shopmen, and yardmen in that city had initiated a sympathy strike that was paralyzing traffic to St. Louis, and from East St. Louis all the way to Cincinnati and Louisville. One paper observed, "There is but one man switching on the bridge... When he quits the bridge will be closed to passenger traffic, as all the other men refuse to work while the strike continues." A national railway strike seemed possible to Knights who had seen the order undergo spectacular growth in membership over just the previous year, in large part by appealing to workers across lines of skill, race, ethnicity, region, religion, sex, and industry. More importantly, it was the national Knights' threat of expanding the August 1885 Wabash Railroad strike, which had also faced court orders and a divided public, to Knights on the Union Pacific, the rest of the Gould system, and "any other railroad" that had brought Gould to the table the preceding September, when he and Powderly had made their famous pact.[23]

Irons granted Powderly's point that he could not order strikes outside of his district, but, he rejoined, events in East St. Louis had "demonstrated" that a request by assemblies would "be the way" to produce them outside of the district.[24] For the most part, East St. Louis railroaders acted at the district assemblies' request. The St. Louis Knights called the walkout a sympathy strike, as did the county sheriff who helped to suppress it. The evidence indicates that most strikers in East St. Louis voluntarily left their posts and used persuasion as well as removal or destruction of equipment to enforce the walkout. One deputy sheriff admitted that strikers relied more upon their "overpowering numbers" to stop trains than physical violence. Tellingly, on April 2 a merchant advised the governor of Illinois that the "strong moral force... being exerted to prevent men who want to work from doing so" represented a great threat to business and that he should send state troops to quell the strike.[25]

Still, the decision to expand the walkout was imposed on a number of workers. The experience of the Chicago, Burlington & Quincy (CB&Q) yardmen is but one example. According to the superintendent, when a Knights committee visited the yards to alert workers to the strike, the men protested that they did not belong to the order and did not wish to participate. They quit work but returned almost to a man at the first opportunity. Strikers then visited the yards "almost every hour" and "used all manner of threats and intimidation" to enforce the strike. On April 7, 200 to 250 strike supporters, some armed, compelled the yardmen to stop work. Committees visited them nightly at their homes in order to prevent their return to the yards.[26]

Apparently, Knights and sympathetic non-railroaders committed to stopping traffic in East St. Louis devised a strategy for reducing their risk of arrest for violating court injunctions against interference with railway operation. Several railroad officials commented to the committee that the men who visited shops and yards were unknown to them. The vice president and general manager of the St. Louis, Alton, & Cairo Short Line, George W. Parker, offered this theory: "A great many more strikers would have been indicted but for the fact that they evidently elude this by a pre-concerted plan whereby the bulldozing business in a given yard was awarded to [men who were] strangers to the officials, and agents of that given road. For instance the striking employees of other and distant yards were assigned to duty in our yard; at least only strangers appeared in our yard to intimidate and abuse our men, and they could not be recognized or identified." Parker told the committee that he had no evidence for this beyond his observation that there was a "uniformity with which this rule was carried out, as the representatives of all the roads will doubtless testify, if you will ask them; on that point." Such a strategy would have made sense to Knights threatened with contempt of court for physically enforcing the strike.[27]

In a March 27 letter, railroad officials petitioned the mayor, the city council of East St. Louis, and the sheriff of St. Clair County to protect company property. The sheriff replied, "I am willing to take all necessary steps in my power" but "the freight yards in East Saint Louis are so extensive, and the combination to prevent the movement of freight trains so well organized and determined, I am satisfied that any efforts on my part would not enable you to move your freight trains." The city council and mayor gave the companies the same answer. Two days later, with traffic still at a halt, the railroads sent a committee to Governor Richard J. Oglesby of Illinois, who rebuffed the railroads' request for military protection and sent instead the state's adjutant general to survey the situation. After a crowd assaulted and severely injured a deputy on March 29, the sheriff telegraphed the governor: "There is an unlawful mob assembled in East St. Louis of fully one thousand men, which refuses to peacefully disperse when commanded by me...I had with me my regular deputies and all the specials I could get. I called the posse, but it was of the mob."[28]

That a large portion of the citizens of East St. Louis identified with the strikers and against the railroads made it virtually impossible for the sheriff to enlist help locally. On the day that the strike commenced, he attempted to obtain aid from the city police. Mayor Maurice Joyce, he said, had told him that he "had only a few men and those were resigning as fast as they could, so as not to be drawn into this trouble." The manager of the Louisville & Nashville Railroad later described the men whom the sheriff managed to secure as "untrained, undisciplined, unofficered, and a majority of them in sympathy with the strikers." When strikers beat one laborer, police placed him "in the station in order to protect him from further violence from the men that was beating him; that they could not arrest those men, that was understood, and that it was the best they could do."[29] After receiving several more wires for help, Governor Oglesby arrived in East St. Louis on March 31. He met with fifteen hundred Knights at Flanagan's Hall, called on them to respect the law, and instructed the sheriff to "exercise his powers to a fuller extent" and Mayor Joyce to appoint special policemen. The mayor protested, "I hadn't the money to pay them with," and, "[W]ho am I going to deputize that are not Knights of Labor in East St. Louis; the railroads don't want them."[30] The sheriff's attempts to procure volunteers met with repeated failure. As Mayor Joyce had warned, he was forced to revoke the commissions of the special policemen whom he had hired, because railroad officials complained that they were all Knights of Labor.[31]

The railroads in East St. Louis fought the strike with the same measures used on the west side of the river. On March 31 the grand jury of St. Clair County indicted fifty-three men on seven counts and set bail at $1000 on each count. Though the sheriff's threat to arrest those who failed to serve bond must have seemed a somewhat empty one, strikers faced new conditions within the week. On April 3 the railroads in East St. Louis announced their willingness to re-employ as needed, law-abiding strikers until April 5, after which the roads would accept new applicants. The railroads also offered five dollars per day plus board to "men of grit" who would agree to act as deputy sheriffs. The CB&Q ran trains with the help of thirty armed deputies who kept strikers out of the yards. The effect was mixed. The *St. Louis Post-Dispatch* reported on April 5 that a large crowd had looked on without interfering as three railroads sent trains out of the city.[32] Then on April 7 the agent of the Chicago & Alton railway recorded that about three hundred men had entered the yards and freight depot looking for strikebreakers. They found none, as managers had hidden the laborers in boxcars. Most of the remaining men had quit work, and managers were forced to house in the cars twenty men from outside the city.[33]

The manager of the Louisville & Nashville Railroad later commented that the Knights "became bolder and more determined" after the governor's visit. Certainly the governor's refusal to send militia must have encouraged strike supporters, and given the difficulty with which city and county police had enforced the law, his inaction no doubt represented an opening that the Knights used to exert pressure on railroads. This strategy worked for a time, but the weakness of local authority in East St. Louis ultimately deferred rather than prevented defeat, with tragic consequences for the strike and a number of its participants.[34]

At 10:00 A.M. on April 9, J. T. Harahan, manager of the Louisville & Nashville Railroad, found the sheriff and a deputy attempting to clear from the track what he called "a large mob, composed of strikers and others, congregated on what is known as the Broadway crossing" near Cahokia Creek. Harahan recalled: "They paid no heed to him, and only answered him with jeers.... Every time that we would attempt to do any switching at that point the mob would grow larger.... They stoned our switchmen and station agent, striking them and injuring them.... I saw among the strikers a number of revolvers that had been taken out of their concealment and exposed to view."[35] The sheriff later testified that, in response to his commands to disperse, members of the crowd had retorted that "they had heard that for the last two weeks; long enough; they were tired of it; I should go home... they were entitled to be on that public highway." Both the sheriff and Harahan left the crossing in the hands of a few deputies, and the sheriff wired the governor for militia. Though the day prior he had gained a posse of 150 men from Belleville, most of these had elected to stay home, because the governor had decided it best not to arm untrained men. At around 2:00 P.M. the railroad's special deputies joined their fellows at the crossing in protecting men readying a coal car in the yard. Altogether the deputies numbered about a dozen. The assembly, which included men, women, and children, swelled to around three hundred, and surrounded the train, shouting taunts at the brakemen.[36]

What happened next is ambiguous, but a confrontation quickly ensued in which some deputies fired their Winchester rifles into the throng, killing three men and one woman, injuring six others, and scattering the rest of the crowd in all directions. Furious citizens gave chase to one unarmed deputy. He was shot in the calf, and beaten and kicked nearly to death where he fell. Most of the deputies, along with the truck hands and clerks, ran in a panic for the large bridge connecting the city to St. Louis. Before the deputies escaped to the other side to turn themselves over to the authorities in St. Louis, Mayor Joyce and two other men attempted to arrest them. The deputies resisted capture, as they believed that the city's police could or would not protect them. As they broke free and ran across the bridge, or in the scuffle, a deputy shot and killed one of the pursuers, an unemployed shoemaker from St. Louis.[37]

Conflicting reports surfaced immediately. The deputies maintained that they had only sought to defend themselves from the "mob," which, they alleged, had stoned them and threatened them with pistols. This account, however, contradicts the testimony of numerous witnesses to the shooting, including that of a *St. Louis Post-Dispatch* reporter, who denied that rocks were thrown or shots fired. Many witnesses charged that the shooting was "entirely unprovoked," and several claimed that one of the deputies had yelled to the others, either as he fired or before he deliberately shot into the crowd, "The ball is open, give it to them," or some variation of this. One story had it that the crowd had begun to close in on the deputies just before the shooting began; others intimated that the deputies' arrest of a laborer had incited strikers and bystanders, touching off the bloody exchange.[38]

Certainly hostilities between crowds of strike supporters and the deputies in East St. Louis were building, a fact that lends credence to any of the above scenarios. April 8 saw at least two stand-offs. The Chicago & Alton force of armed deputy marshals blocked the efforts of strikers to access its freight houses and yards, while CB&Q men cleared an angry crowd from a levee by wielding their revolvers as clubs, and then, ominously, forming under orders a line parallel to the crowd. Besides these events, on the morning of April 9 both citizens and deputies likely had on their minds an episode that had occurred just six days prior outside of Fort Worth, where about half a dozen men had purportedly ambushed a group of deputy sheriffs manning a coal train. The ensuing battle had ended with four strike sympathizers and deputies severely wounded and one deputy killed.[39]

Five hundred state militia arrived in East St. Louis on the night of April 9. They found the Cairo Short Line's yards, boxcars, and oil room aflame. According to a reporter, "People living at a distance from . . . the conflagration imagined that the whole southern portion of the city was afire, and were greatly terrified." The fire department had only shortly before put out a blaze set in the Louisville & Nashville yards. Colonel R. M. Smith, who commanded the force, ordered his men to shift the trains to keep other cars from burning, but, as he recalled, "I discovered that they were still setting the cars on fire ahead of me, just about as fast as I could put the fire out." He gave the order to shoot incendiaries. The next morning when his men took their places as guards of railroad property, he observed "an antipathy existing against everybody that wanted to work, or tried to work, and also a very strong antipathy against the militia. . . . Wherever we went it seemed as though the children from two years old and up all had the same sentiments exactly about the matter."[40]

The presence of the militia allowed traffic to resume on the East. St. Louis roads, but only very slowly. According to a St. Louis paper, the railways found it "difficult to secure new men and next to hopeless to coax back the old ones." The general manager of the St. Louis Bridge & Tunnel Railroad told the congressional committee, "We had to hire help, had to pay extraordinarily for men to take the risk." That road also had trouble finding boardinghouses that would take the new men, because strikers had reportedly warned boardinghouse keepers that "they would board these men and keep these men only at the peril of their lives." None of the old men who were Knights returned to work at the Chicago & Alton. The railway boarded its new men out of town "to avoid intimidation and threats of personal violence." Although after the militia's arrival crowds no longer raided yards and freight-houses, men visited at night those who had returned to work.[41] Colonel Smith later commented, "I know it was not safe for a man to get out beyond the jurisdiction of his home or the jurisdiction of the militia, and if he went up Broadway and opened his mouth in such a way as to indicate that he wasn't in sympathy with the Knights of Labor, or that he had gone to work contrary to their orders the probability is that he would have got injured."[42]

Irons later testified that he had consistently counseled against the use of violence during the strike. He claimed to have advised the Knights to gain appointment as marshals to protect company property and to have sent circulars to warn Knights to refrain from damaging railroad property. He denied participating in a long list of violent incidents associated with the conflict, seeing an engine killed, or giving the order to destroy engines. Strikes, Irons conceded, have the "tendency... to induce men not to take the place of strikers" but rejected committee members' implication that strikers necessarily deserved blame for equipment sabotage, assaults against strikebreakers, and the breakup of trains.[43]

Presumably, Knights who denounced the use of force were sincere. In Irons's case, at least, the evidence suggests otherwise. The *Sedalia Bazoo* reported on March 12, for example, that he had obliquely warned, "If persuasion will not be effective in gaining the strikers' point, violence will not be used—at least not at present."[44] That statement received a good deal of attention from Irons's critics, who, like critics of labor historically, have tended to concentrate on union leaders' equivocal statements, especially "incendiary predictions," because such utterances were easily imagined to veil violent intent or the sanction of violence. We might dismiss the press's concern as hysteria at best or deliberate exploitation of public fears at worst, but, at a public meeting of strikers in East St. Louis on April 17, Irons reportedly urged: "Talk to the scabs and go to the houses and talk to their wives and make them quit. Do everything you possibly can to make them go out. Make them stop work and go out, and if they won't go out give them some pills... To hell with the Chinese; to hell with the scabs. We fought and won the Chinese fight, and we will win this fight."[45] That Knights leaders would have spoken so brazenly at a public meeting is questionable but not impossible. The walkout's widespread support in the city perhaps led Irons to let his guard down.

The source of the speech is A. F. Walsh, a paid railroad company spy. While it was in the railroad officials' interest to employ spies to concoct or exaggerate labor movement violence, another, more credible source confirms the spy's report. Colonel Smith gave essentially the same account of Irons's speech. Smith was a businesslike man, firmly committed to imposing economic and social order on the city, but he was also a keen observer whose interpretation of the strike allowed for nuance and complexity. His testimony regarding Irons's speech is nearly identical to Walsh's. However, in contrast to Walsh, Smith was careful to distinguish between the different positions of strikers. He pointed out to the committee that there were one or two men at the meeting who made "conciliatory'" remarks to the effect that they must "plead that their cause was just, as it was a fight of labor against capital." When the committee asked whether the Knights had prevented incendiaries from doing greater damage on April 9 than would have otherwise occurred, he answered evenhandedly, "I know in fact there is good men, of course, that belongs to the order, and that there are men that wouldn't set fire to nothing, but at the same time undoubtedly there was men connected with the fire that night."[46]

Smith's connection with and willingness to talk with strikers and to convey their sentiments to the committee offers us a rare glimpse of their inner fears and concerns. A large number of men with whom Smith spoke told him that "what they wanted was to have all of the [old] men to go to work," that "it was their fight for life or death," and that "if they didn't win this time... capital would crush them." He knew several of the "boys" personally. They were officers of the Knights of Labor in East St. Louis and had grown up in his town. They had told him, Smith reported, "that they were ordered out, and that they had gone out, and were going to stay out until the thing was settled." These men approached him daily about the likelihood of a settlement. "They said they were getting out of money," he related. "One or two of them were men of families."[47]

Smith's attempt to understand the motives of the strikers diverged sharply from the attitudes of East St. Louis railroad officials. In his testimony before the committee, C. M. Stanton, superintendent of the Ohio & Mississippi, made an effort to link the 1886 strike in East St. Louis not to the relationships that had developed between managers and railroaders over the previous decade but to the lawlessness of 1877. Like several other East St. Louis railroad officials, he believed that the city's government, with the sanction of its citizens, had conspired with strikers by deliberately neglecting to assist the railroads in enforcing the law. Stanton charged, "There is no difference in the social or local conditions of society in East Saint Louis—none now, different from what there has been for ten years. They are in thorough and hearty sympathy." He added, significantly, that in 1877 the city's mayor, chief of police, and one of its aldermen were, according to Stanton, "boss strikers" whom he had escorted to Springfield, where they were tried, sentenced, and jailed for violating federal law.[48]

Mayor Joyce vociferously denied Stanton's allegations, as did John Halloran, the city's chief of police. The city was unable to protect railroad property, not unwilling, Joyce contended. He pointed out, "East Saint Louis, with fifteen men, could not possibly give fifteen railroads, terminating in East Saint Louis, the police protection that they demanded. I find that Saint Louis, with a most excellent police force of 500 men, could not give even one road, the Missouri Pacific, the protection that they needed to operate their line." He readily admitted that he did not attempt to control the mobs of men who blocked railroad traffic: "I could not; they were mostly strangers to me... I had no power; I presume there is between two and three thousand men over there, all railroad men."[49]

That the mayor, citing the city's fuel shortages and factory shutdowns, had on April 1 quite publicly called upon the governor to send militia to restore order bolsters his claim that, whatever his sympathies, he had favored enforcing court orders against strikers. Nonetheless, in suggesting the depth of pro-strike feeling in East St. Louis, Stanton was perhaps right in emphasizing a connection between 1877 and 1886 in terms of the level of discontent, in the St. Louis area if not in Texas. When in mid-May the committee asked Colonel Smith to relate how matters stood in the city, he replied, "It hasn't changed a particle." Smith continued, "I think the ground work is all laid for [outrage and lawlessness] to commence at any time when the militia is withdrawn. I do not see that the militia being there has stopped intimidation in the matter at all, anything more than it has given the employer protection for the time being.... I am confident that if the troops were taken away... there would be trouble... I think it would naturally drift into that course."[50] The railroad companies agreed. On April 30 officials in East St. Louis unanimously protested the governor's order to gradually reduce troops in the city, a policy that they felt would leave them "again... abandoned to mob rule."[51]

Strikers' Views of Union Violence

While pro-strike sentiment ran deep in East St. Louis, among railroad workers and local citizens alike, the extent to which strike supporters there or elsewhere endorsed violent tactics is less clear. Take, for example, the case of George Bibb, a Knights leader in Marshall, Texas, who agreed with the committee's claim that a strike does not legitimately involve destruction of property, threats against strikebreakers, the imperilment of the traveling public or trainmen, or occupation of company property. "It simply means that the men shall be at liberty to walk out when they please?" asked one of the congressmen. "Yes, sir," Bibb responded, and then he acknowledged that a strike that conformed to these strictures in a context in which labor was plentiful would not "do much good."[52] Is Bibb's testimony a reflection, perhaps, not of his own convictions but of what he thought others wanted to hear in the aftermath of a disastrous walkout that by that point the mainstream press had condemned and even the national Knights leadership had pointedly and openly criticized? Or does his testimony signify a broader ambivalence toward the same "free labor" doctrine that many Gilded Age judges referenced in their court orders against strike activities—the belief that, while neither workers nor employers had the right to harm the public or community interest, the exercise of their freedom of contract was sacred?[53]

As with many things historical, the answer lies somewhere in the middle. Many Knights saw union violence or the threat of it as a legitimate response to the hazards on the southwestern railways, especially in the wake of state intervention that restored the business of railroads and also Gould's broken promise to arbitrate. The Knights relied upon a range of tactics, most of which involved persuasion and community pressure, but rank-and-file Knights as well as strike leaders divided over the question of violence, especially in regard to the treatment of strikebreakers. While judges met with fierce opposition on the Gould system to their "free labor" conviction that the right of workers and employers to contract at will was inviolable, a significant number of strikers, like Bibb, appear to have found this assumption compelling. The dissonance between those who saw the strike in absolute terms and those who felt caught between competing beliefs and commitments, to individualism and communalism, suggests, as one historian put it, that a "tension" existed "between the rights of workers (citizens) as individuals and as members of a collective (unions)."[54]

The congressional testimony on violence on this question is especially valuable, as strike supporters, its opponents, and observers of all kinds, appeared as witnesses and were pushed at various points under cross-examination to explain their ideas and to divulge details and background that newspapers rarely reported. That the committee's hearings occurred against a backdrop of the walkout's defeat as well as legal prosecutions of former strikers raises questions about the integrity of the testimony. Under these circumstances, one might point out, Knights would have been loath to discuss openly and honestly the walkout's most controversial tactics. Some strikers who were under indictment expressed a concern that their statements would be used against them in court or concern that naming fellow Knights would bring trouble down on the heads of those identified. However, several features of the hearings suggest that we need not endlessly second-guess strikers' testimony. Strikers and their supporters time and again spoke up frankly, differing with the committee on violence and other issues. Members of the audience, both pro- and anti-strike, frequently provided committee members with questions that they thought would advance their cause. Overall, the hearings were contentious rather than one-sided.[55]

The purpose here is not to enter into the debate over which side was more brutal or to make assumptions about who was responsible for specific acts.[56] Instead it is to gauge the level, forms, and discussions of violence during the strike in an effort to understand how various Knights thought about the use of force. Thus, in regard to the level of violence, two points should be made about the serious charge that Knights burned bridges and railway cars, and tampered with rails. First, it would be wrong to assume that each of these incidents was necessarily the work of strikers. One division superintendent estimated that eighty more fires occurred during the strike than in the preceding and subsequent months. While the larger context of a failing walkout and, for some, the desire for retribution might lend credence to railroad officials' charges of Knights' involvement, especially in East St. Louis, ultimately, we have no way of knowing who or what was responsible. Knights argued that the fires were a consequence of the railroads' negligence in maintaining the roads or conditions unrelated to the strike.[57] Two, while forced occupation of shops and yards and obstruction or disabling of trains were often accomplished by large crowd actions, only a small number need have known about or participated in the potentially deadly forms of sabotage and destruction of which DA 101 as a whole was accused.

Knights of Labor leaders claimed that they did not support violence, that the order pursued a peaceful strategy, that the charges of violence were overplayed, and that it could not always control its "black sheep."[58] At a meeting with other citizens in Fort Worth after the armed exchange between deputies and strike supporters, one Knight was emphatic: "If a man would have mentioned such a thing [ambushing deputies] there [in the union hall] he would have been kicked out of the house." Probably those who opposed violence did so for one or both of the reasons offered by one member of the order before the congressional committee: "I considered it wrong and unbecoming a Knight of Labor...and...it was something for the railroad company to get a hold on us for."[59] Indeed, many Knights made an effort to stay within the law, to avoid alienating public opinion, and to forgo physical confrontation. Various local assemblies offered to move freight from the railways to "places of storage, free of charge for labor" and to "perform any and all kinds of repairs necessary to secure the safety of passenger and mail trains." One Knights leader in Denison, Texas, helped the sheriff serve thirty to forty writs to members, who walked up to receive their papers when their names were called.[60]

Even as the trains began to move with the help of strikebreakers, deputies, and company guards, crowds of strikers and strike supporters often looked on rather than resisted. The absence of confrontation over the movement of trains did not last everywhere, and certainly these examples tell us little about the mood of the crowds—were its members sympathetic to the use of force in some form but simply too awed, stunned, and dispirited to act? Whatever the case, it took considerable time and provocation by armed guards and deputies to push Knights and their supporters to clash physically with authorities in Fort Worth and East St. Louis.[61]

While the strike was not the uprising that others have cast it as, neither was it the case that rogue individuals alone were responsible for the use or threat of force. Martin Irons and many Knights from both sides of the river evidently participated in or threatened violence. Furthermore, strike supporters' public pronouncements offered strikers interpretive room for an ideological rationale for violence. In St. Louis, a Catholic priest, C. F. O'Leary, claimed to speak on behalf of Knights who had "take[n] the law into their own hands." Though he had "counseled peace" during the walkout, he reprimanded the committee, "To tell people to bear grievances is moralizing." The "cause of the commotion" was "grievances and injustice and arbitrary power.... I would not have it said that I would allow a people ever [to] toil under the submission of slavery while they had hands and arms to use them."[62] Late in the conflict DA 101 and its ally district assemblies DA 17 and DA 93 addressed the "Workingmen of the World." It threw down the gauntlet: "Marshal yourselves upon the battlefield...Gould and his monopolies must go down or your children will be slaves." Here the use of force appears as a moral and strategic necessity. The issues are stark, immediate, and vital, and vengeance justified. Gould was "the giant fiend," the "money monarch," who was "dancing as he climbs over the grave of our order—over the ruin of our homes and the blight of our lives."[63]

Yet Bibb and others accepted the committee's stance that anything beyond moral suasion to prevent strikebreaking was illegitimate. Witnesses granted this even when committee members made the point that, in times of labor surplus, strikers who hoped to see their effort succeed must either prevent workers from taking their places or find some other means of combating the company. The case of Eugene Perry is instructive. A Sedalia striker convicted of disabling engines and trespassing, he abandoned the walkout after a train wreck, allegedly caused by strikers' tampering, injured four people.[64] Other Knights, especially early on, focused on taking possession of company property and disabling engines but usually stopped short of using direct physical force. These activities possibly represented a middle ground where strikers could preserve some commitment to individualism but still seek an effective, collective solution to their labor troubles on the Gould system. This tactic also in part rested on the idea among Knights that laborers do not merely own their labor in relation to their employers; they possess some personal connection to—even a sense of ownership of—their workplaces, tools, and the products of their work (in this case, the ability of the railroads to run freight). The sheriff of Little Rock, for example, told the committee that when he confronted a local Knights leader about the strikers' practice of taking railroad pins from yards and shops under their occupation, he denied that this was, as the sheriff termed it, "stealing." He told the sheriff, "These things would be returned; it was all where it could be got at."[65]

By the strike's waning days, in the wake of Gould's betrayal of his agreement with Powderly, the growing ability of the system to resume freight traffic, and especially the deaths of pro-strike men and women at the hands of railroad-paid deputies, feeling against the railroads and strikebreakers had hardened. In reference to the armed exchange outside of Fort Worth, the local paper reported, "There are hundreds of Knights of Labor in this city who do not appear to regret the occurrence of this day." One striker years later recalled that he and other young men in town had regarded the men who had clashed with the deputies as heroes.[66]

The deep divide over the issue of violence reflected in part the contradictions inherent in the "free labor" principle, which attempted to meld together two opposing commitments—community and individual rights. As long as the courts considered strikers' use of persuasion compatible with freedom of contract, and community pressure could be heavily brought to bear on strikebreakers, railroad companies and workers were more likely to turn to arbitration. This had been a longstanding practice since antebellum times.[67] But by the mid-1880s the courts increasingly saw even peaceable efforts to stem strikebreaking as a threat to freedom of contract, especially on roads like the T&P that were bankrupt and under the supervision of federal judges. The new reality was not entirely apparent during the 1885 walkout, because collective rights quickly prevailed without jeopardizing individual freedom on any large scale. With the agreement clearly an empty one for less-skilled railroaders, with trainmen and their unions dedicated to avoiding a sympathy strike, and with the rumors afoot of Gould's machinations to use bankruptcy as a bludgeon against labor unrest on his roads, a number of Knights came to reject the individualist side of "free labor" ideology and to embrace instead its collective aspects. While drawing a firm line between emotional and rational reasons for violence is difficult, some seemed to advocate violence as a strategy rather than simply falling into it out of frustration or as a desperate, visceral response to a failing strike. Others retained faith in a political or economic solution—a push for reform at the municipal and state levels and a reliance on the skill of striking shopmen, whose critical labor was not easily replaced.[68] These Knights did not see the necessity of using violence as the tactic of last resort.

In terms of strikers' occupational experiences, a tension also existed in railroad work between individualism and communalism. On the one hand, the hazards involved and the interdependence of much of the workforce encouraged collective identities, especially in the shops, where workers of varying skills labored under industrial conditions. The oppressive demands placed on workers by the Gould system's cost cutting and their growing inability to gain a hearing with the higher echelons of management bolstered collective solutions. Moreover, while the tendency of railroad workers to migrate frequently from job to job and town to town is often overstated, itinerancy among railroaders was not necessarily a barrier to a militant collective identity but instead under some circumstances fueled it. These circumstances involved just the sort of conditions prevalent by the mid-1880s in "newer towns," where "workers found the channels of promotion most congested and consequently perceived their opportunities in most jeopardy." On the other hand, identification with individual solutions continued to shape the world of work on the roads. Shelton Stromquist has observed that, while one group of railway workers became increasingly committed to labor protest with each lost strike, of which there were many, another group saw the consequences of defeat as a "personal calamity": their "sense of class loyalty was broken" and they "were prepared to reenter railroad employment under any conditions, even as scabs in the next strike." The older organization of railroad management, which placed a good deal of power in the hands of local managers, and which the Gould empire was fast replacing with more centralized forms of operation, also tended to strengthen one-on-one approaches to resolving labor conflict.[69] Finally, "boomer" railroaders' tactic of picking up stakes and moving to employment on another road or in another town represented a form of individualized labor protest.

"A Dangerous if not Pernicious Man"

Arguably, Powderly's opposition to expanding the strike eastward was a prudent position. Federal courts had by that point intervened on behalf of the railroads on an unprecedented scale, and Knights were returning to work.[70] However, while personal stress influenced Irons's thinking, as his story to Powderly in St. Louis indicates, Irons's strategy was not without merit. In the swirl of events in 1886, a year in which strike activity peaked, Irons gambled that he could revive the walkout by expanding its scope to Knights beyond the Gould system. Knights of Labor membership had risen dramatically over just the previous year, in large part by appealing to workers across lines of skill, race, ethnicity, region, religion, sex, and industry. Moreover, the national Knights of Labor had made the equally risky threat of expanding the August 1885 Wabash strike, which also faced court orders and dwindling support, to Knights on the Union Pacific, the rest of the Gould system, and "any other railroad." It was this bold move that had brought Gould to the table the preceding September, when he and Powderly had made their famous pact.[71]

In assigning responsibility for the 1886 strike, many contemporaries and historians focus on Irons. In their majority report, the congressional committee pointed neither to the "mob" nor to the Knights generally nor to

1877. Instead, it accepted the testimony of most Knights leaders that they had urged legal, peaceful methods, and acknowledged that "there were grievances that the laborers and workingmen of the road had just reason to complaint."[72] The crux of the problem, in the committee's estimation, was Martin Irons, "a dangerous if not pernicious man (but for whom . . . the strike would have been declared off at the request of Mr. Powderly, Grand Master Workman of the Knights of Labor)."[73] The press took a similar tack. A St. Louis paper, for instance, reported that Irons was plotting to impose his "more radical and aggressive principles" on the national leadership of the Knights, and praised Powderly's call for the education of new members of the Knights and his March 26 letter condemning strikes.[74]

Former strikers also took up the cry against Irons. On May 22 a mass meeting of Knights in Sedalia unanimously called for Irons's resignation from the district assembly's executive board and a committee forced him to leave town. The condemnation of Irons had been gathering outside of and within the Knights for some time. In late March, after Irons had attempted to expand the conflict, the *Sedalia Bazoo* reported that a "gentleman" from Rosedale, who allegedly had known Irons for nine years, characterized him as a "windbag," as "egotistical," and a "chronic kicker" who was "always finding fault" and "was ready for a strike at anytime, cause or no cause." The editor concluded that his followers were the "victims" of the "ambitions" and "wickedness" of their "drunken" leader. Irons, the paper went on, was "bitterly denounced by all parties here . . . The K of L had a five hours session this afternoon and decided to repudiate Irons and declare the strike off . . . They say they have no grievance against the company, and are only out at the tyrannical dictation of M. Irons."[75]

The charge that Irons was "a very cruel" parent and husband fit neatly into this framework for understanding the 1886 walkout. As the *New York Times* declared, "The story of his brutal life," demonstrated that "the strike was not inaugurated at the request of the best element in the Knights of Labor of the Southwest, but at the demand of the worst characters in the order." In a *Times* interview in May 1886, Mary Irons explained why when Irons left Richmond, Missouri, she and their five children did not go with him. Their son, Robert, had sought his arrest in Richmond, "charging him with assault to kill." Her stepmother, Amelia Brown, told reporters that the target of Irons's wrath was Mary. The couple never obtained a formal divorce. Irons sent Mary money, but, Mary informed the *Times*, it was "not enough to support me and my family." In the 1880 census she is listed as a widow, either a mistake on the part of the census official, a strategy by Mary to avoid the social disgrace of a failed marriage, or, one suspects, an indication of the intensity of her revulsion toward Martin.[76] In two letters, Irons's grandson, James R. Irons, confirmed Mary's characterization of her husband. "There is no doubt in my mind that Martin Irons did much good for the advancement of labor conditions. While he must have been sincere in that respect, he caused his own family much anxiety and grief by his neglect and abuse of them . . . I remember hearing my Father say one time that when his Father was sober a finer man never lived but when drinking he was selfish and unbearable. No doubt that was the chief cause for breaking up the family . . . I understand from my mother that my grandmother Mary Irons asked all her children that none of them ever name any offspring after Martin Irons. I have never heard any thing to indicate the contrary."[77] One may reasonably conjecture that Irons's stance on labor violence was in some way related to his own history of domestic violence. Research on domestic violence tells us that husbands who have engaged in moderate to severe violence against their wives or children are more predisposed to condone the use of violence generally and to engage in violence again. Also, the use of alcohol is more frequent with the worst of these abusers. Irons falls into this broad category. To what extent can we carry these findings back in time to the nineteenth century? Some cause exists to believe that we cannot. The use of psychohistory to explain the actions or thought process of historical actors is troubling on several counts. There is the piecemeal nature of historical evidence. We cannot, for example, ask Irons penetrating questions about his emotional state, and our knowledge of his personal life is quite limited. Also, psychological findings today may well be entirely anachronistic when applied to the past. As historian John Tosh has argued, "The structure of human personality over time is precisely what needs to be investigated, instead of being reduced to a formula." Even so, at the very least, Irons's "inner drives" are worth speculating about. Genetic influences and childhood experiences with brutality in the home are two major variables in the backgrounds of men who have used moderate to serious aggression against family members. While we have no idea whether Irons was genetically predisposed or whether he underwent such psychological hardship as a child, the former factor transcends historical context. Moreover, it seems overly rigid to throw out a psychological explanation altogether, to assume that, in the absence of clear documentation, Irons's private and public uses of force were entirely separate. As Tosh also points out, "The historian also requires imagination," which is distinct from "creative invention." A basic fact of historical interpretation is that "the past is never completely captured in the documents which it left behind. Again and again historians encounter gaps in the record which they can fill only by being so thoroughly exposed to the surviving sources that they have a 'feel' or instinct for what might have happened." The surviving evidence offers some interpretive room for suggesting that a connection existed between this particular person's private and public tendencies toward violence.[78]

Unquestionably, Irons's personal demons cannot explain the considerable violence associated with the 1886 strike. Instead, two features of the conflict brought the walkout to a crisis point and convinced a number of strikers that violence was justified: the use of strikebreakers and armed guards, precisely the employer strategies that most often encouraged violence during strikes throughout the late nineteenth and early twentieth centuries. Strikebreaking often elicited a strong reaction not only because it meant the loss of strikers' jobs but also because it punished with a permanent measure what strikers saw as a temporary measure and a legitimate form of protest, and it communicated the odious message that their work—however long or well they had performed their work—was easily replaced. The presence of armed guards offended for similar reasons. As one historian noted, "The very presence of the police or troops at a struck plant carried with it the implication that the strikers were lawbreakers," and company-paid guards were reputed for provoking violence as a form of job security.[79]

Furthermore, the long and infamous history of Pinkerton agents in labor disputes likely incited strikers' emotions. The Missouri Pacific seems to have employed the Furlong Detective Agency, not the Pinkerton Agency, but the latter's anti-labor reputation surely shaped the reception of the former. As the Pinkertons turned increasingly to guard service in the 1880s, intervening in seventy strikes between 1877 and 1892, popular revulsion toward the agency became endemic. The 1885 platform of the Knights of Labor demanded an end to the use of detectives in labor conflicts. By 1899 twenty-six states had enacted anti-Pinkerton legislation.[80] Company use of a private army of detectives and guards typified the Gould system's approach to the Knights in 1886, which was to insist absolutely that, as a private concern, it had the prerogative to run its business as its managers saw fit. In the railroad representatives' view, workers' protest did not legitimately go beyond the act of quitting work. One historian has captured well what was at stake: "The 1886 strike on the Gould system assumed an epic significance because it raised an essential question about American freedom: When a wage earner freely contracted with an employer, did the employee agree to sacrifice his liberty in return for compensation?"[81]

Ruth Allen was probably correct in surmising that the focus on Irons was a consequence of the public's need to "personify responsibility for the strike." As railroad officials' allusions to 1877 indicate, the 1886 strike raised the specter of class conflict and community fragmentation in a region that only one year earlier had championed class harmony, the use of moral suasion, and community unity. The only way to retain faith in the latter was to blame Irons. The Haymarket bombing in May 1886 made this leap all the easier, as the incident provoked a wave of anti-immigrant and anti-radical sentiment. Little reference was made to Irons's immigrant status in the public attacks on him. He had lived in the United States too long, and Scots did not appear as foreign to native-born Americans as the Germans, Bohemians, and Poles whom the press targeted in the wake of the bombing. Instead, the press quickly distinguished between "the great multitude of honest strikers" and "the lawless few." The *St. Louis Post-Dispatch* defended Gould system Knights: "There will be a few hoodlums in every large crowd. . . . but the law will deal with these, and American labor movements will instinctively work their way to some fair basis of adjustment by legal means and by methods which will seldom lead to even a momentary disorder which the ordinary police force cannot repress."[82] We need not sanction the pejorative term "hoodlums" to describe crowd members or disregard the sincerity of many Knights' call for peace in saying that this report flew in the face of fact. A sizeable number of strikers and their sympathizers engaged in violent or at least confrontational, illegal measures in attempting to enforce the walkout.

Notwithstanding the pronouncements that the mass of workers was conservative by nature, to his opponents Irons symbolized the danger of workers' power on the railroads, particularly the racially mixed, unskilled and semiskilled workers who participated in the walkout in large numbers. The post-strike embrace of Powderly as a force of reason and paragon of respectability betrayed the hollowness of the claim that Irons's great sin was his dictatorial actions and attitudes, for had Powderly ordered the strike this would have represented a far greater assumption of centralized control than Irons made. The trouble was that the 1886 strike tested workers and their communities in ways that the 1885 walkout had not. Rather than rely on a broad base of local and skilled trainmen's support, moral suasion, and the language of anti-monopoly, it raised disturbing questions about the proper balance of power between railroaders and their managers, the relationship between local institutions and regional or national bodies such as corporations or unions, the place of less-skilled railroaders and other workers within their communities, and the morality and efficacy of using violence to maintain strikes.

The viciousness of the post-strike press reports on Irons makes it impossible for the historian to separate fact from fiction. The *Sedalia Bazoo*, for example, described him as a "repulsive-looking, slab-sided, lantern jawed, blear-eyed figure in whose diminutive carcass there is concentrated so much low, cunning and unadulterated cussedness."[83] Irons reappeared in the news in 1891, when the story circulated that he had bought a farm in Thayer, Texas, married again, unsuccessfully sought a divorce, and wound up before the court on adultery charges for living with a neighbor's young daughter, who later left him.[84] Three years later Irons was again before the court, this time accused of assault with intent to rape a neighbor's seven-year-old daughter in Fort Worth, where he had opened a grocery story. The case was dismissed, as was Irons's suit for libel in which he held that the charges had been "concocted" by his "enemies."[85] His last days were spent in poverty and illness in the home of a fellow radical and outsider in Bruceville, Texas.[86]

Irons had little in his experience that recalled the stable, republican community that Mary "Mother" Jones found for a time or that Eugene Debs enjoyed in his youth. His frequent attempts at other occupations indicate that he rarely felt secure in his work as a machinist. Like Jones, Irons came of age as a transatlantic migrant and spent a good part of his life wandering, but the labor movement did not in the long run serve as his surrogate family, as it did for her.[87] Irons had a problem with alcohol, visited such terrible violence upon his family that they ended all ties with him, and saw his second wife grow ill and die during the 1886 walkout. The Gould system strikes must have given Irons's life new meaning and sense of purpose, which he probably was loath to give up. On a personal level, this helps to explain his initial effort to give the 1886 walkout careful, determined leadership, but with the walkout falling apart, he likely felt himself more and more the victim of forces beyond his control. Perhaps it also sheds additional light on why he committed unconditionally to the 1886 walkout, counseling violence even as courts handed down injunctions protecting the railroads, Powderly publicly chastised him for overstepping his authority, the press demonized him, and former strikers began returning to work.

Post-strike Biracialism

For the first full month of the 1886 Gould system strike, the main public criticisms levied against the Knights involved not race relations but strike tactics. As public hostility to the strike, and particularly Irons, grew, a flurry of reports surfaced that associated Knights with racial troubles. In late April, the *Texarkana Independent* warned, "Adventurers and meddlers are at work organizing some kind of secret societies amongst the colored men in the country." Texarkana whites reportedly feared that "half a dozen Negro assemblies of the Knights of Labor" in the area might "become the blind instruments of some bold Communist," in which case "their proverbial cunning and impenetrable superstition would render them an element far more dangerous in the estimation of law-abiding citizens than the white brotherhood of the Knights." Almost simultaneously, talk spread of Austin Knights allegedly organizing black cotton pickers along the Colorado River in order to "strengthen the hands of the strikers."[88] One might dismiss these charges as the paranoid and opportunistic projections of anti-labor elements. Events in Pulaski County, Arkansas, tell another story.

About two months after the official end of the 1886 railway strike, on a plantation outside of Little Rock, black men and women struck for a wage increase from seventy-five cents to a dollar a day, and for payment in cash rather than scrip. County sheriff Robert "Wat" Worthen and his posse moved in to arrest the alleged strike leader, Hugh Gill, at this home. Gill was shot in both arms for allegedly resisting arrest and brought with another strike leader to a plantation house, which was soon surrounded by about 250 armed black strikers. About one hundred had come from local Knights assemblies in the surrounding area. Deputy sheriff Ham Williams organized a group that engaged in a brief skirmish with strikers to aid Worthen, but Worthen's pledge to not take Gill and Larkin to Little Rock to stand trial defused the crisis. Once back in the city, Worthen reneged on his promise and called for reinforcements to put down what he claimed was a wider revolt by black laborers on area plantations. Reports of an impending race war followed. Although the strikers returned to work the next day and Gill was later tried and acquitted, "peace" did not "prevail," as the *Arkansas Gazette* declared. Within days a local planter discovered this note: "As you think it is Best for the Knights to keep off ov your Place... if you Don't want us to talk to hands you had Better turn them [off], if we take you in han it will Bee to Late for Wat Worthen to Come to help you and we wont Bee Long about it."[89]

The pro-Democrat *Arkansas Gazette* charged that white Knights had "told [the Tate plantation strikers] lies and tried to array them against the white citizens as a class." "Republican politics are at the bottom of the whole matter," it concluded. While vastly underestimating black Knights' leadership in the conflict, the paper rightly feared that a biracial labor coalition was in the making against the Democratic Party. The Tate plantation strike had attracted the aid of the city's Knights, a fact that Worthen recognized when he allowed two Little Rock Knights of Labor leaders to go to try to "control the colored men" at the Tate plantation, a black member reported only as "Merriman" and Don Tomson, the state assembly organizer. The two intervening Knights did seek to calm the waters, but Tomson clearly opposed Worthen's measures. Shortly thereafter he wrote in the Arkansas Knights organ that Worthen and his men had committed "outrages" at Tate "in the hope that the colored people, being organized, would resist, and that this would serve as a pretext to break up organization among them." At the same Little Rock meeting on the cotton pickers' strike, planter Colonel Anderson Mills rose to condemn the poor wages and scrip payment on Tate plantation, and Dr. F. M. Chrisman, whose son was a fireman, concurred. E. A. Fulton, a black speaker, then charged Democrats with stirring up the trouble at Tate for political reasons. In the September elections, Chrisman ran for county judge as a Republican candidate with the Knights' endorsement, as did pro-labor Republican Colonel Oliver. Oliver ran for county sheriff against Worthen, who had come to office in the wake of the state's "redemption" in 1875.[90]

The Pulaski County Republican Party made a concerted effort to appeal to Knights with a platform that easily could have been taken up across racial lines by both railroad and cotton plantation strikers. Democrats, it charged:

> have made judges of a few men and compelled us to depend upon their will for the tenure of their offices. They have sent officers to harass and disturb good, honest working people, and by bad laws

> and worse officers eaten up the substance of the people. They have without cause or shadow of law in time of peace kept standing armies as so called posse comitatus, and sent them out without the consent, even of our legislature. They have made the military independent of and superior to the civil power. They have sent armed troops among us and protected them by mock trials from punishment for assaults and attempted murders committed on the inhabitants of this state and county...They have sent armed men, without the shadow of law or authority, without even a warrant, into peaceable neighborhoods and performed acts of cruelty and perfidy.[91]

The condemnation of judges grew out of Gould system Knights' experience with injunctions and their efforts after the walkout's failure to push for a federal arbitration bill, but Sheriff Worthen and Deputy Sheriff Williams were the unstated targets of this platform, for it was they who had led the aggressive attack on the cotton picker's strike, and, two months earlier, the Gould railway system strike—delivering writs, taking out freight trains, and protecting strikebreakers and railroad property.[92]

Support for the pro-labor Republican slate was far from universal among either Knights or Republicans. Democrats charged Oliver with corruption, a theme that white Knight Jasper N. Ferguson also took up. "Though he [was] in earnest sympathy with the working classes," Ferguson gave a "stirring address" to the "working men of Pulaski County" to see that the election's central issue was "honesty or dishonesty" and not "personal grievances," presumably against Worthen and Williams. At the same time, some discontent existed among black Republicans. In June 1886, the *Arkansas Gazette* relayed that the *Sun*, "which speaks for a large number of colored Republicans of this county," had attacked the Republican party's white leadership for "taking all of the best paying and most honorable offices and the majority being placed on the tail and where worth, intelligence et al are equal."[93]

Nonetheless, some basis existed for the Democrats' fear of defeat in September 1886. The *Arkansas Democrat*'s shrill charges of corruption against Oliver, its mixture of threats and entreaties to black voters, and its oft-repeated plea, "Every Democrat to the polls" belied the editor's confident insistence that the county's comfortable white majority ensured a Democratic victory. In the end the ballot count gave Democrats a solid majority, but at least seven out of twenty-three townships and wards voted Republican.

Reports of election fraud raise the question as to whether Republicans had more support than the official tallies recorded. In Eastman Township, for example, Chrisman met with black voters about "not having access to the poll." A number wanted "to force their way in and see the vote counted."[94]

Despite defeat in Pulaski County, the Knights went on to play a key role in the populist movement in the state over the succeeding years. The Agricultural Wheel, which at an 1886 meeting with Knights had only begrudgingly agreed to accept blacks in "separate and distinct" assemblies, met with a staggering electoral defeat that convinced white members to expand the Wheel's appeal across racial and economic lines. In 1888 the state's farmer and labor movements formed the biracial Union Labor Party, which won considerable backing from disenchanted Republicans and Democrats statewide, and, in Pulaski County, 52 percent of the vote for the party's gubernatorial candidate and 60 percent for its congressional candidate, ex-railroad shopman Isaac McCracken. Democrats secured their victory in 1888 largely through fraud and violence, and in subsequent years by meeting some of farmers' demands and passing disfranchisement laws aimed at black voters, who had voted pro–Union Labor Party in significant numbers.[95]

Biracial political cooperation among farmers and laborers in various Texas locales tested the dominance of the Democratic Party. In Fort Worth in 1886, several Knights of Labor members won seats on the city council and two Democratic candidates lost the mayoral race to Dr. H. S. Broiles. Similar stories played out in Houston, San Antonio, and Austin. At the county level, the Farmers' Alliance candidates also surged into the political arena and took a number of offices in 1886 and throughout the 1880s.[96]

One well-documented, biracial, working-class challenge to the Democrats emerged in Dallas. In combination with a business element that hoped to reduce the class animosities exacerbated by the Southwest strikes, black and white workers supported local independent Winship C. "Bud" Connor in the 1887, 1889, and 1891 mayoral races. While Connor steadfastly voted Democrat at the state and national level, in Dallas he proclaimed himself free of partisan politics. His appeal to the city's laboring element was chiefly economic. Beyond his pro-labor and pro-Knights rhetoric, his administration's generous public spending on infrastructure and improvements created jobs for workers in the city. Wards that included the railroad yards and the warehouse districts were wells of pro-Connor sentiment. Indeed, in 1887, labor issues animated the election debate, with Connor and one opponent,

Ed Smith, wrangling over which candidate was truly the "workingman's" friend. Black Knights actively campaigned for both Smith and Connor, but by 1891, one prominent Dallas Democrat lamented, "The negroes, the Trafic [*sic*] men—gamblers & saloon men were practically solid for [Connor]."[97]

As in Arkansas, third-party gains prompted Democrats to intervene. The Texas legislature passed the Kimbrough Election Law, which required that disputed electors provide a witness who was a "well-known resident of the ward [to vouch] that he is a qualified voter at such election and in such ward." The policy disenfranchised many itinerant or newly settled laborers who made up much of Connor's coalition. In a large sample of votes challenged in Dallas's 1891 election, Alicia E. Rodriquez finds that most were cast by black citizens but that the "challenges also had a class dimension. The majority of the challenged men, black as well as white, whose occupations were listed in the city directory, were employed as laborers, porters, and in other unskilled or semiskilled jobs...They fit the profile of men supporting W. C. Connor's challenge to the Democratic party, and thus their race and class made them targets."[98]

The class dimensions of the Democrats' attack notwithstanding, the strength of black working-class activism in these post-strike independent political movements highlights the degree to which the Knights of Labor's cross-racial organizing was biracial rather than interracial. In terms of everyday interactions, racial separation and racial identity dominated. Pro-Connor black activists seem to have agitated among black voters, and, in both Pulaski County and Dallas, black Knights represented the most solid and aggressive block in the pro-labor party's ranks, suggesting the same spirit of political brokering that Leon Fink found among black Knights who backed a pro-labor ticket in Kansas City after the March 1886 strike. In both locales probably only a minority of white Knights left the Democratic Party to join the pro-labor ticket with black voters. During the railway strikes, too, black Knights apparently took responsibility for persuading or intimidating black strikebreakers to cease work. Biracialism in the Little Rock area and in Dallas weathered longer than in Richmond, where, Peter Rachleff argues, black and white Knights never inspired an interracial culture that could withstand the dominant parties' attempts to play upon racial fears and mistrust. It helped that neither city was the site of northern Knights' direct and dramatic challenge to southern segregation, as was Richmond. Even Fink's conclusion that Richmond Knights were "together but unequal" seems generous in regard to the race-conscious Gould system Knights and their post-strike coalitions.[99] The expedient motives for these alliances, along with the broader context of segregation in the railroad industry, in southern life, and in the Knights' own assemblies, curbed the extent to which those alliances encouraged equality and communalism among workers.

Given the power of racial hierarchies and ideas, any other outcome was unlikely. It is all the more extraordinary, then, that Knights in Arkansas and Texas exhibited some small measure of the "genuine fellowship" that Daniel Letwin discovered among Alabama miners. Beyond Patrick Cassidy's recollection of interracial comradeship in the railway yards of Palestine, a small but noteworthy distance developed between the racism espoused by some white supporters of biracialism and white Knights who remained within the fold of the Democratic Party. One can discern the former position in a report published in the Arkansas Knights organ, the *Industrial Liberator*, by Don Tomson, the white leader of the state assembly who had so resolutely defended Tate plantation strikers. While Tomson cast the order's role as an educator of "illiterate, ignorant, even superstitious" ex-slaves who were "entirely without culture" and "sadly lacking that independency characteristic of an American citizen," he departed from this uncomplicated language of white supremacy to emphasize that these traits had a historical rather than natural explanation: southern blacks were the victims of slavery, war, and the "adventurers, renegades and scoundrels" of the Reconstruction era...Thousands could be found among their ranks who were capable of exercising their power with the caution enjoined by the Order... [and benefiting] others, less fortunate of their race." He went on to salute Tate plantation strikers for remaining lawful, "even under such trying circumstances," and looked forward to the day when "colored men...with their white brothers" would "march onward in the army of progress and eventually raise themselves to that high and efficient standard of industrious and dignified citizenship that must be obtained before the masses can assert and maintain their right to the full product of their labor." Tomson's racial views brought together at once a fairly orthodox version of white paternalism and, paradoxically, a faith born of experience in black Knights' abilities. That ideological amalgam stood in stark contrast to the Democrats' creed, which, even when it sought black votes, allowed little to no room for black "producers" or citizens. White Knights who, along with the Farmers' Alliance, made their "fight in the Democratic party" of Dallas County typified the latter outlook. The county's Knights and Farmers' Alliance held a Fourth of July picnic in 1886 that stayed safely within the racial boundaries of "Redemption" politics. No allusions were made to black participation or leadership. Instead, to frequent applause and Confederate yells, Col. W. L. Crawford pledged that Dallas County Knights and Alliance members would "retake possession of the heritage that was given them by their patriotic ancestry... There was a time when the government of the United States protected the States and the people, and the people hardly knew that there was a federal government. Are you ready to bring back those good old times?"[100]

The nature of biracial working-class cooperation in Arkansas and Texas requires further study, as do the connections between black rural and railroad workers and between black Knights and black populists.[101] But clearly the spectacular defeat of the 1886 Gould system strike and its association with Irons's downfall has heretofore obscured the Knights' cooperation across racial lines, which, limited though it was, opened up political and cultural space for black activism and contributed to a larger wave of third-party politics.

Irons's ability to articulate widely felt grievances and a vision for counterbalancing managerial power with union power brought him to prominence as the chief leader of DA 101. In the end, it was his visibility as the major spokesperson of a bold strategy during a costly strike, his insistence on a class rather than cross-class community identity, his clear departure from the principle of freedom of contract in advocating force against strikebreakers, and his personal history which made him an easy scapegoat for labor troubles for which there was no easy solution. The trajectories of his private and public life, particularly his inclination toward violence, were possibly intertwined, but to see his strike leadership as merely a reflection of his inner troubles or as evidence of artlessness or egotism overlooks the larger circumstances in which Irons and other Gould system Knights worked, lived, and struck. The dwindling opportunities and daily tyrannies on the railways, the broad support that strikers had won in 1885, the failure of the 1885 agreements and the national Knights to ensure railroaders a meaningful voice, the fear of Gould's motivations and plans, and the heady context of the Great Upheaval propelled him, like thousands of other Knights, to take an independent path in backing the strike and, in the midst of the walkout's death throes, to desperately pin his hopes on the power of militant mass action.

Conclusion

"BOOMER" CHARLES BROWN retired from railroading to the industrial district of Los Angeles after an accident in the yards severed both his feet. He wrote his autobiography about his work life and ended melancholically: "I can see and hear the switch engines in the U.P. yards, switching and making up trains, and when a road engine comes down through the yards from the roundhouse with her bell ringing on her way to take out a train, the tones of that bell give me a thrill and a heartache.... because it brings back memories of the past when I was an able-bodied man booming around over the country working as a fireman, brakeman or switchman, first one place and then another... If things did not suit me one place I would bunch the job and take a little trip of a thousand miles or two across the country and get me another one." Brown remembered stopping his car in order to watch a train go by that was pulled by "the same engine" that he had "once fired for a time out of Needles on No. 8."[1] He watched it until "it pulled out of sight around a curve, for it was just like seeing an old friend that I had worked with years before."

The reminiscences of other boomer railroaders struck these same chords—their romantic relationship to the machine, the adventure of migration, the relative freedom and independence they possessed in picking up and finding a better situation. Yet any portrait of railroaders as rugged individualists and champions of the technological wonders of the age ignores the ties that they held to other railroaders and the frequency and intensity of boomers' collective approaches to improving safety, wages, hours, and work rules over the course of the late nineteenth and early twentieth centuries. In the nearly half-century of railway expansion and consolidation between 1877 and 1922, railroaders launched multiple strikes that extended over hundreds and sometimes thousands of miles of track, and attracted the active support of their neighbors, wives, children, and elected officials. In examining the pattern of nineteenth-century railroad labor protest, historian Shelton Stromquist has aptly called this period the "audacious era." It involved a different kind of daring than that exhibited by the "railroad king" Jay Gould or the lone, brave engineer at his post, but was elemental in giving voice, if not satisfaction, to the grievances, experiences, and contradictory values of the mass of railroad workers on vast stretches of road across the nation.[2]

The 1885–1886 Southwest system strikes were a turning point in the labor upheavals of the Gilded Age. First, they were part of a larger surge of activism in 1886 that was stirred by the promise of an eight-hour day and the "producer" ideal of the Knights of Labor. The sympathy strikes that railroaders engaged in on the Gould lines in 1886 were part of a rising tide of sympathy strikes on the railways and in other industries, so that the number of strikers who engaged in this strategy jumped from 11 percent in 1885 to 45 percent in 1894. The vast majority of railroaders nationwide engaged in sympathy strikes related to the Pullman boycott. Second, the legal measures taken against the 1886 strike were precedent-setting in that the courts issued injunctions to protect not only the T&P, which was in receivership, but also a solvent road, the Missouri Pacific, and judges held that even moral suasion constituted illegal interference with railway traffic. These decisions in part laid the basis for federal intervention in the Pullman conflict, as William Forbath explains: "By the eve of the Pullman Strike the main elements that composed the federal judicial role in that strike were also in place. Built up over sixteen years of judicial experience, they included: the enjoining of strikes and boycotts on non-receivership lines; the long experience of collaboration with railroad management and attorneys; the precedents for summoning troops over the heads and against the will of state authorities; the preference for summary proceedings over jury trials; and the transformation of the federal courtroom into "a kind of police court," in Judge Taft's words, "when railway workers went on strike."[3] Finally, that towns and cities in Texas, Arkansas, and Kansas were at the center of events in the labor contests of 1885–86 reminds us that this region was not only a land of cattle kingdoms and agriculture, and it was not a haven from the troubles wracking the East. The railroads brought to even predominantly rural areas of the region an industrial workforce, forcing local communities and their boomer railroaders to confront the problems of large-scale corporations, the "labor question," and industrial violence.

Southwest system railroaders, however much they spoke in terms of anti-monopoly, saw their world as rife with class tensions. Even skilled white railroaders perceived the condescension of their social "betters," despite the critical and recognized importance of their work to the nation's prosperity and expansion, and to passengers' safety. Boomers' sense of marginality grew during the 1880s, when western railroads' encouragement of labor competition and reduction in labor costs undermined the economic and social opportunities available to them and the cultural meanings they attached to their work. The March 1885 Wabash strike then represented at once a key shift in the relationships railroaders had to one another, particularly among skilled shopmen, the semiskilled, and unskilled, and a transformation in railroaders' sense of their place within their communities. They forged a cross-racial, cross-skill movement of "producers" that played a leading role in securing two historic agreements that year. When Knights waged a successful strike and boycott in the summer 1885 and laid down their tools in 1886, they assumed in both cases that the forces of anti-monopoly would follow their lead, as they had in the March 1885 confrontation with Gould, the chief nemesis of many a strike town, and that this support would bolster their collective power as railroad workers to block freight traffic.

Railroad officials, first, only partially fulfilled the 1885 agreements, and, second, announced that the Texas & Pacific receivership would not honor the 1885 compact, policies that convinced DA 101 to strike for the Knights' permanent presence on the railroads. It did so without the aid of the Knights' General Executive Board, which had its own preoccupations, and without the sanction of railroad communities, which, strikers likely assumed, would back them but with backing that would in the end be insufficient in the absence of a collective bargaining mechanism. The widespread, dramatic, and immediate response to the 1886 strike order suggests that the decision to walk out came from below, while the specific strategy of taking over shops and workhouses likely arose from tactical concerns but also railroaders' strong occupational identity and producers' ideology. The eventual disintegration of the 1886 strike was less the product of conflict within the Southwestern Knights than due to external forces, particularly in the form of injunctions. Defeat came when Gould system officials secured court orders and military aid against strikers, which drove them out of the shops, yards, and crossings, and convinced sympathetic engineers and firemen to remain at their engines.

In narrating events at the ground level, this book brings new evidence to bear on the question of the relationship between race and labor, an issue over which historians have long wrestled. Some historians have emphasized the strength of class feeling, and their critics, the overriding significance of race, or "whiteness," to the history of American workers. More recently, studies of New Orleans dockworkers and Alabama miners have pointed to the complexity and ambiguity of these relations, the "gradations" between the two extremes of race and class, and have eschewed the dichotomy altogether.[4] This study confirms the latter school's argument that the "the glass half-full/nine-tenths empty approach" to understanding working-class race relations, in abstracting social movements from their historical context, risks missing the degree to which biracialism opened up space for cross-racial activism and minimizing the power of employers and the state to limit a movement's strategies and aspirations.[5]

The focus on gradations and ambiguity at first glance seems ill suited to a history of race and labor on the railroads, where black laborers held considerably less power than on the waterfront of New Orleans or the mines of Alabama. However, boomer railroaders on the Gould system, who experienced their workplace as a bastion of racial exclusion and subordination, managed somehow to establish a connection across the racial divide. Cooperation was rooted in the promises and costs of railroading and some common notions of manhood and citizenship. White and black racial identities shaped these efforts in contradictory and likely explosive ways, with whites often understanding the alliance within the mythic framework of southern "Redemption" at the same time that blacks sought ways to reclaim the political leverage and relative autonomy that they had known under Reconstruction. Anti-eastern and anti-Gould sentiment held the coalition together during the strikes, backed up to varying degrees by the threat of racial violence. The Knights' biracial alliance proved uncontroversial during much of the strike; yet the relationships that it encouraged inspired political challenges to the Democratic Party in two states, challenges that fed into the larger stream of populist organizing. To a surprising extent, given the context, the story of the Gould system strikes confirms the complex nature of racial identities and suggests the unpredictable and potentially far-reaching outcomes of cross-racial organizing. Biracialism in this case brought a partial yet palpable shift in the allegiances of a significant number of white and black workers, away from the customary leadership and networks that had long divided them, and toward one another as participants in a cross-racial alliance.

Black and white strikers were free laborers who perceived their freedom slipping away on the western railways. In articulating the reasons for their discontent, they drew in part on older notions of "free labor" that valued economic liberty but in a context in which one could reasonably expect to rise, to know one's employer, to have time and energy to cultivate oneself as a citizen and as a human being, to seek resolution of grievances before an employer or, if need be, the community. They also sought to safeguard the power they still had by seeking the more modern instrument of collective bargaining and turning to Chinese and anti-convict labor sentiment as one means of carving out common ground for the Knights' coalition, particularly among the unskilled. The reduction of the meaning of "free labor" to simply freedom of contract in the minds of many Americans, especially judges, by the mid-1880s, and the resulting wave of injunctions against even peaceable forms of labor protest such as picketing, undermined the strength of workers' power on the railways to an unprecedented degree in 1886.

Railroaders were divided, sometimes within themselves, over how to react to these bewildering conditions. Some Knights responded with militant and even violent resistance to the new "free labor" principles that required them to restrict their dissent to simply quitting work and finding better work elsewhere. At railroad crossings there was a gut-level, crowd response to provocative circumstances, such as the departure of an engine and cars under railroad-hired police protection. At other points, violence was a conscious strategy employed against strikebreakers and armed guards in East St. Louis and deputies in Fort Worth, for example, and threatened against railroad officials, engineers, and firemen who attempted to operate trains. For a significant number of Knights, however, such actions troubled the individualist aspects of their ethos. They expressed discomfort with the subordination of individual choices to collective power, especially as the Knights' bold effort faltered. The commitment of these Knights to the strike was more conditional. In their minds, collective obligations had to be weighed, in some fashion that remained unclear, against individual goals and rights. Their ideas, the ambivalence evident in their ideas, could not help but be shaped by the society's dominant ideas about "free labor" and by their experiences with mutualism at work on the roads, both of which pulled at strikers' hearts and minds. The clash of ideas between Knights over postbellum "free labor" principles brings to mind historian Herbert Gutman's observation that "a central tension in all dependent groups over time has been between individualist (utilitarian) and collective (mutualist) ways of dealing with, and sometimes overcoming dependence and inequality."[6] It also tells us that while "labor republicanism" permits us a broad understanding of the belief system of the Southwest system strikers, its language was elastic and so concealed, until the strike was in crisis, the ways in which Knights' aspirations uncomfortably coexisted or clashed.

Robert Weir has commented, "Scale matters." The Knights faced mass industry in the mid-1880s, "and that alone explains a lot of the violence." Gould-system officials disregarded conservative attempts of the national Knights of Labor to arbitrate, and the many efforts by Gould system railroaders to gain redress of their grievances.[7] The inability of Gould system Knights to hold railway officials accountable to an older set of ideas about a just relationship between workers and employers shattered the unity that they had known during the strike the previous year and sent them on different paths in 1886. A violent course was very likely the chosen one for Martin Irons. He and other members of DA 101 attempted to expand the walkout by force in the face of enormous odds, an effort that testifies to their faith in the sympathy strike and the power of mass action. It also reveals the double-edged nature of community—its promise of solace and creative adaptation to wrenching changes, and its dangers: insular thinking, the repression of truths that do not serve or cement the whole, and a distorted perception of reality. The decision of Irons and others to expand the strike to East St. Louis and beyond relied not on an honest accounting of the strike's true condition in the wake of myriad assaults upon it but on an emotional identification with the previous year's victories and an apocalyptic view of the Great Upheaval's vast upsurge and of the role of their battle within what seemed to them a life-or-death struggle. Perhaps with the scenes of community unity in 1885 in mind, Irons and his compatriots in 1886 reached too far and depended too much on that transcendent moment that people experience when they feel themselves part of a whole. That said, to blame Irons, as many historians have done, or to cast the nature of rank-and-file Knights on the Southwest system as rash and aggressive is to go too far. It removes them from their historical context. The flux and turmoil of the Great Upheaval convinced many Americans that militant, mass, even violent action was the "hinge of history." As one writer has recently put it, "Who knows just what or where the hinge of history will turn out to be, or in which direction it will swing?"[8]

Notes

Introduction

The epigraph quotation from Powderley is from a draft of a letter sent to Jay Gould (Series A, Reel 47, Correspondence, General Master Workman, 1879–1893, Terence Vincent Powderly Papers, American Catholic History Research Center and University Archives, Catholic University of America, Washington, D.C. Cited hereafter as TVPP).

The epigraph quotation from the Knights of Labor committee is taken from the report of the United States House of Representatives, *Investigation of Labor Troubles in Missouri, Arkansas, Kansas, Texas, and Illinois*, 2 Parts, 1887, 49th Congress, 2nd Session, Report No. 4174, II, 317.

1. Terence Powderly to John W. Hayes, Letterbook copy, Apr. 14, 1886, Series A, Reel 47, Correspondence, General Master Workman, 1879–1893, TVPP; James Green, *Death in the Haymarket: A Story of Chicago, the First Labor Movement, and the Bombing That Divided Gilded Age America* (New York: Pantheon, 2006), 145; Nell Irvin Painter, *Standing at Armageddon: The United States 1877–1919* (New York: W. W. Norton, 1987), 40.

2. F. W. Taussig, "The South-Western Strike of 1886," *Quarterly Journal of Economics* 1, No. 2 (January 1887), 184. For a description of Taussig's contributions to the field of economics, see Howard S. Ellis, "Frank William Taussig, 1859–1940," *American Economic Review* 31, No. 1. (March 1941), 209–211.

3. Leon Fink, *Workingman's Democracy: The Knights of Labor and American Politics* (Urbana: University of Illinois Press, 1985), 112; Green, *Death in the Haymarket*, 149; William E. Forbath, *Law and the Shaping of the American Labor Movement* (Cambridge: Harvard University Press, 1991) 68, 73.

4. Fink, *Workingman's Democracy;* Kim Voss, *The Making of American Exceptionalism: The Knights of Labor and Class Formation in the Nineteenth Century* (Ithaca: Cornell University Press, 1993); Robert Weir, *Knights Unhorsed; Internal Conflict in a Gilded Age Social Movement* (Detroit: Wayne State University Press, 2000); Craig Phelan, *Grand Master Workman: Terence Powderly and the Knights of Labor* (Westport: Greenwood Press, 2000); David Stowell, *Streets, Railroads, and the Great Strike of* 1877 (Chicago: University of Chicago Press, 1999); Donald L. McMurry, *The Great Burlington Strike of 1888: A Case History in Labor Relations* (1956; reprint, Cambridge: Harvard University Press, 1973); Richard Schneirov, Shelton Stromquist, and Nick Salvatore, eds., *The Pullman Strike and the Crisis of the 1890s: Essays on Labor and Politics* (Urbana: University of Illinois Press, 1999); Colin J. Davis, *Power*

at Odds: The 1922 National Railroad Shopmen's Strike (Urbana: University of Illinois Press, 1997).

5. Ruth Allen, *The Great Southwest Strike* (Austin: University of Texas, Bureau of Research in the Social Sciences, 1942), 154–58. For a discussion of the distinction between myth and history, see Kevin Kenny, "The Molly Maguires in Popular Culture, *Journal of American Ethnic History* 14, no. 4 (Summer 1995), 27–46, and especially Roland Barthes, *Mythologies*, trans. Annette Lavers (1957; New York: Hill & Wang, 1972). More recently, "new western history" has rejected idealized conceptions of the West, although not without controversy. See, for example, Richard White, *"It's Your Misfortune and None of My Own": A New History of the American West* (Norman: University of Oklahoma Press, 1991) and Larry McMurtry, "Westward Ho Hum: What the New Historians Have Done to the Old West," *New Republic*, 9 October 1990, 32–38.

6. Two exceptions are Leon Fink's study of labor reform politics in Kansas City, Kansas, in *Workingman's Democracy*, 112–48, and Michael Cassity's essay on Sedalia, Missouri, in "Modernization and Social Crisis: The Knights of Labor and a Midwest Community, 1885–1886," *Journal of American History* 66, no. 1 (June 1979), 41–61.

7. Gerald N. Grob, *Workers and Utopia: A Study of Ideological Conflict in the American Labor Movement, 1865–1900* (Evanston: Northwestern University Press, 1961), 66–71; Norman J. Ware, *The Labor Movement in the United States, 1860–1895: A Study in Democracy* (New York: Vintage Books, 1964), 145–54. More recently, Craig Phelan has turned to this question in *Grand Master Workman*, 178–85. For Norman Ware, the strike represented yet another instance of the Knights' unrealistic effort to unite very different wage earners under the "producer" banner. "Restless" southwestern Knights had an "exaggerated faith in the invulnerability of the Order." He concludes that, "blinded by optimism" and led by the "aggressive" Irons, Gould system members looked for a reason to call the strike, a doomed effort Powderly should have ordered DA 101 to abandon early on. See Ware, *The Labor Movement in the United States, 1860–1895*, 147.

8. In his history of Sedalia, Missouri, a key strike town, Michael Cassity holds that local Knights quickly abandoned an effort called by a remote, even dictatorial regional body representing workers across the railway system. See "Modernization and Social Crisis: The Knights of Labor and a Midwest Community, 1885–1886," *Journal of American History* 66: 1 (June 1979), 41–61, and *Defending a Way of Life: An American Community in the Nineteenth Century* (Albany: State University of New York Press, 1989). The following supplies a good example of the dominant view of contemporaries in the wake of the walkout: Bureau of Labor Statistics and Inspection of Missouri, *The Official History of the Great Strike of 1886 on the Southwestern Railway System* (Jefferson City, Mo.: Tribune Printing Co., 1887), 7.

9. See the following major examples: Fink, *Workingmen's Democracy*; Paul Krause, *The Battle for Homestead: Politics, Culture, and Steel, 1880–1892* (Pittsburgh: University of Pittsburg Press, 1992); and Sean Wilentz, "Artisan Republican Festivals and the Rise of Class Conflict in New York City, 1788–1837," in Michael H. Frisch and Daniel J. Walkowitz, eds. *Working-Class America: Essays on Labor, Community, and American Society* (Urbana: University of Illinois Press, 1983), 37–77. Daniel T. Rodgers provides a penetrating analysis of historians' uses and abuses of the republican paradigm in "Republicanism: The Career of a Concept," *Journal of American History* 79, no. 1 (June 1992), 11–38.

10. The following characterization of Gould's role is typical: "He set about precipitating a conflict to rid himself of the nuisance of a feisty work force which, in the fevered climate of the upheaval, proved all too easy" (Phelan, *Grand Master Workman*, 187). More positive

portrayals of Gould can be found in Maury Klein, *The Life and Legend of Jay Gould* (Baltimore: Johns Hopkins University Press, 1986); H. Roger Grant, *"Follow the Flag": A History of the Wabash Railway Company* (DeKalb: Northern Illinois University Press, 2004); and Earle B. Young, *Tracks to the Sea: Galveston and Western Railroad Development, 1866–1900* (College Station: Texas A&M University Press, 1999).

11. Key titles on social movements in the region from the 1890s forward include Lawrence Goodwyn, *The Populist Moment: A Short History of the Agrarian Revolt in America* (New York: Oxford University Press, 1978); Gregg Cantrell, *Kenneth and John B. Rayner and the Limits of Southern Dissent* (Urbana: University of Illinois Press, 1993); George N. Green, "The Texas Labor Movement, 1870–1920," *Southwestern Historical Quarterly* 109, no. 4 (April 2006), 1–26; Clifford Farrington, *Biracial Unions on Galveston's Waterfront, 1865–1925* (Austin: Texas State Historical Association, 2007); Neil Foley, *The White Scourge: Mexicans, Blacks, and Poor Whites in Texas Cotton Culture* (Berkeley: University of California Press, 1999); and Michael R. Botson, *Labor, Civil Rights, and the Hughes Tool Company* (College Station: Texas A&M University Press, 2005). For works on Gilded Age Arkansas, Kansas, and Texas, see Fink's essay in *Workingman's Democracy*; Matthew Hild, "Labor, Third-Party Politics, and New South Democracy in Arkansas, 1884–1896," *Arkansas Historical Quarterly* 63 (Spring 2004), 24–43; Matthew Hild, *Greenbackers, Knights of Labor, and Populists: Farmer-Labor Insurgency in the Late Nineteenth-Century South* (Athens: University of Georgia Press, 2007); and Robert S. Shelton, " 'Which Ox Is in the Mire': Race and Class in the Galveston Longshoremen's Strike of 1898," *Southwestern Historical Quarterly*, 110, no. 2 (2006), 218–39.

12. E. P. Thompson, *The Making of the English Working Class* (New York: Vintage Books, 1966), 9. Historians debate how to define social history. I agree with Peter N. Stearns's view that social history illuminates, among other things, "popular belief systems" and the "interaction of mental attitudes and behavior." See Mark M. Smith, "Making Sense of Social History," *Journal of Social History* 37, no. 1, Special Issue (August 2003), 168.

13. The Knights' inclusive policy spawned massive and often brutal white resistance, within the order and without, in Georgia, South Carolina, Virginia, Louisiana, and elsewhere. The following explore this topic: Peter Rachleff, *Black Labor in Richmond, 1865–1890* (1984; reprint, Urbana: University of Illinois Press, 1989); John C. Rodrique, *Reconstruction in the Cane Fields: From Slavery to Free Labor in Louisiana's Sugar Parishes, 1862–1880* (Baton Rouge: Louisiana State University Press, 2001); Hild, "Labor, Third-Party Politics, and New South Democracy in Arkansas"; Melton A. McLaurin, *The Knights of Labor in the South* (Westport: Greenwood Press, 1978).

14. In answering these questions, this study enters the debate as to whether historians are wrong to emphasize the strength of class feeling rather than the overriding significance of "whiteness" to the history of American workers. Two important articles in this debate are Herbert Hill, "Myth-Making as Labor History: Herbert Gutman and the United Mine Workers of America," *International Journal of Politics, Culture and Society* 2, no. 2 (Winter 1988), 132–200, and Stephen Brier, "In Defense of Gutman: The Union's Case," *International Journal of Politics, Culture, and Society* 2, no. 3 (Spring 1989), 382–95. Eric Arnesen provides a valuable evaluation of this debate in "Up from Exclusion: Black and White Workers, Race, and the State of Labor History," *Reviews in American History* 26, no. 1 (March 1998), 146–74, and his own contribution with *Waterfront Workers of New Orleans; Race, Class, and Politics, 1863–1923* (Oxford University Press, New York, 1991). An example of the more recent trend, which represents the more middle position that this book also adopts, is Daniel Letwin, *The*

Challenge of Interracial Unionism: Alabama Coal Miners, 1878–1921 (Chapel Hill: University of North Carolina Press, 1998).

15. David Brody, "Free Labor, Law, and American Trade Unionism," in Stanley L. Engerman, ed. *Terms of Labor: Slavery, Serfdom, and Free Labor* (Stanford: Stanford University Press, 1999), 215–18 (quotation, 218). On the course of gradual emancipation in New York, for example, see Nell Irvin Painter, *Sojourner Truth: A Life, A Symbol* (New York: W. W. Norton, 1996), 20–23, 28, 32–36.

16. Eric Foner, *The Story of American Freedom* (New York: W. W. Norton, 1998), 63–66.

17. Foner, *The Story of American Freedom*, 58–63, 76; Leon Fink, "From Autonomy to Abundance: Changing Beliefs about the Free Labor System in Nineteenth-Century America," in *Terms of Labor: Slavery, Serfdom, and Free Labor*, 124.

18. Brody, "Free Labor, Law, and American Trade Unionism," 223 (quotation); Fink, "From Autonomy to Abundance," 126–30.

19. Brody, "Free Labor, Law, and American Trade Unionism," 213, 218–19, 223–26 (quotation, 223); David Grimsted, "Ante-bellum Labor: Violence, Strike, and Communal Arbitration," *Journal of Social History* 19, no. 1 (Autumn 1985), 14–15.

20. Brody, "Free Labor, Law, and American Trade Unionism," 228; Foner, *The Story of American Freedom*, 118–19.

21. Quoted in Brody, "Free Labor, Law, and American Trade Unionism," 233.

22. Forbath, *Law and the Shaping of the American Labor Movement*, 63–66 (quotations, 65, 66).

23. Forbath, *Law and the Shaping of the American Labor Movement*, 66–68. For an excellent analysis of the urban, cross-class crowd actions against the railways in 1877, see Stowell, *Streets, Railroads, and the Great Strike of* 1877.

24. Brody, "Free Labor, Law, and American Trade Unionism," 229–30; Forbath, *Law and the Shaping of the American Labor Movement*, 126 (quotation).

25. Brody, "Free Labor, Law, and American Trade Unionism," 228.

26. There is a longstanding debate over whether the "labor republicanism" of Knights and other labor activists represented a "viable labor culture" or a hopelessly contradictory collection of ideas that in the end echoed, more than countered, the economic individualism of the era. See the following spirited exchange: Leon Fink, "The New Labor History and the Powers of Historical Pessimism: Consensus, Hegemony, and the Case of the Knights of Labor," *Journal of American History* 75, no. 1 (June 1988), 115–36, and, in the same issue, Jackson Lears, "Power, Culture, and Memory," 137–40; John P. Diggins, "The Misuses of Gramsci," 141–45; and George Lipsitz, "The Struggle for Hegemony," 146–50. The history of the Knights on Gould's roads largely supports Fink's thesis that external pressures explain the Knights' defeat, but the point here is a less ambitious one. It is simply that the evidence on the strike confirms the conclusions of Melvyn Dubofsky, who posited that the "ethic of individualism" was and is a powerful one in American culture, not just among judges but also within working-class communities. See Melvyn Dubofsky, "The Federal Judiciary, Free Labor, and Equal Rights," in *The Pullman Strike and the Crisis of the 1890s: Essays on Labor and Politics*, ed. Richard Schneirov, Shelton Stromquist, Nick Salvatore (Urbana: University of Illinois Press, 1999), 166–68. For a competing view, see Forbath, *Law and the Shaping of the American Labor Movement*.

27. See, for example, "Freight Standing Still: No Change in the Situation of the Railroad Strikers," *New York Times*, March 14, 1885, 1; Editorial, *New York Times*, March 16, 1885, 4; "The Gould System Strike: Preparing for a Long and Bitter Struggle. Knights of Labor

Threaten to Paralyze Business in the Southwest—The Mallory Boycott Extended," *New York Times*, March 6, 1886, 5; "The Strike in the Southwest: Committeeman Bailey's System of Bookkeeping," *New York Times*, April 26, 1886, 5. Patricia Nelson Limerick makes the case for defining the West in historically specific terms in "The Case of the Premature Departure: The Trans-Mississippi West and American History Textbooks," *Journal of American History* 78, no. 4 (March 1992), 1380–94. In truth, however, Gilded Age Americans seem to have understood Kansas as part of the Middle West. See James R. Shortridge, "The Emergence of 'Middle West' as an American Regional Label," *Annals of the Association of American Geographers* 74, no. 2 (June 1984), 209–20.

Chapter 1

1. Maury Klein, *The Life and Legend of Jay Gould* (Baltimore: Johns Hopkins University Press, 1986), 296; Carl H. Moneyhon, *Arkansas and the New South*, 1874–1929 (Fayetteville: University of Arkansas Press, 1997), 26, 27; Earle B. Young, *Tracks to the Sea: Galveston and Western Railroad Development, 1866–1900* (College Station: Texas A&M University Press, 1999), 46; *The Routledge Historical Atlas of the American Railroad* (New York: Routledge, 1999), 40.

2. Shelton Stromquist, *A Generation of Boomers: The Pattern of Railroad Labor Conflict in Nineteenth-Century America* (Chicago: University of Illinois Press, 1987), 16–18; Eric Foner, *Reconstruction: America's Unfinished Revolution, 1863–1877* (New York: Harper & Row, 1988), 462–64; Alwyn Barr, *Reconstruction to Reform: Texas Politics, 1876–1906* (Austin: University of Texas Press, 1971), 14.

3. Foley, *The White Scourge*, 4; Barr, *Reconstruction to Reform*, 10, James Neal Primm, *Lion of the Valley, St. Louis, Missouri* (Boulder, Colo.: Pruett Publishing Company, 1981), 345; *St Louis Post-Dispatch*, July 13, 1883; Katharine T. Corbett and Howard S. Miller, *Saint Louis in the Gilded Age* (Saint Louis: Missouri Historical Society Press, 1993), 6; Roger Hunt, *"Follow the Flag": A History of the Wabash Railway Company* (DeKalb: Northern Illinois University Press, 2004), 41; V. V. Masterson, *The Katy Railroad and the Last Frontier* (Columbia: University of Missouri Press, 1988), 210; Leon Fink, *Workingman's Democracy: The Knights of Labor and American Politics* (Urbana: University of Illinois Press, 1983), 114–15.

4. David Meinig, *Imperial Texas: An Interpretive Essay in Cultural Geography* (Austin: University of Texas Press), 71–72.

5. Foley, *The White Scourge*, 28; Barr, *Reconstruction to Reform*, 11, 111.

6. Randolph B. Campbell, *A Southern Community in Crisis: Harrison County, Texas, 1850–1880* (Austin, Texas State Historical Association, 1983), 373–74; Foley, *The White Scourge*, 27; Young, *Tracks to the Sea*, 46.

7. Foner, *Reconstruction*, 395; Corbett and Miller, *Saint Louis in the Gilded Age*, 6–7; Primm, *Lion of the Valley*, 291–92.

8. Primm, *Lion of the Valley*, 291–93, 305–6; Corbitt and Miller, *Saint Louis in the Gilded Age*, 6, 9–10.

9. Meinig, *Imperial Texas*, 77; Barr, *Reconstruction to Reform*, 12–13, 15; Corbett and Miller, *Saint Louis in the Gilded Age*, 7–10; Moneyhon, *Arkansas and the New South*, 27–39; Campbell, *A Southern Community in Crisis*, 369. This reality stands in contrast to the portrait of the region offered by economist Ruth Allen in her history of the "Great Southwest Strike." Allen wanted to dispel popular images of "cattle empires, of cowboys, of cotton," and oil fields, but in doing so she overemphasized the role of corporations, holding that by the late

nineteenth century these forces had ensnared the Southwest in the web of the nation's market and industrial economy. Ruth Allen, *The Great Southwest Strike* (Austin: University of Texas at Austin Bureau of Research in the Social Sciences, 1942), 5, 9.

10. Darwin Payne, *Dallas: An Illustrated History* (Woodland Hills, Calif.: Windson Publications, 1982), 3, 70, 76–77, 81; Hazel, *Dallas Reconsidered*, 28–29, 31; *Immigrant's Guide to Texas Giving Descriptions of Counties, Towns, and Villages*, 1888, 210.

11. Corbett and Miller, *Saint Louis in the Gilded Age*, 7–10; Primm, *Lion of the Valley*, 345.

12. Stromquist, *Generation of Boomers*, 105–13, 143–45.

13. Texas Immigrant Aid and Supply Company, Denison, Texas, *Immigrant's Guide to Texas: Showing the Objects of the Texas Immigrant Aid and Supply Company: the Vast Extent of the State; the Variety and Productive Power of the Soil, the Diversity of its Products, the Remarkable Cheapness of its Lands, and how They may be Secured* (St. Louis, Mo.: C. F. Chamberlin & Co., 1872), 6, 31.

14. Stephen F. Smart, *Colorado Tourist and Illustrated Guide via the "Golden Belt Route": The Great Wheat and Corn Producing Region Extending from the Missouri River through Central Kansas and Colorado . . . to the Rocky Mountain Resorts* (Kansas City: Ramsey, Millet & Hudson, 1879), 47; *Immigrant's Guide to Texas: Giving Descriptions of Counties, Towns, and Villages with Valuable Historical and Statistical Information* (Dallas: Wilmans Bros., 1888), 26; F. E. Butterfield and C. M. Rundlett, *Directory of the City of Dallas for the Year 1875* (Dallas: Stone-Inge Books, 1979), 16; Texas Immigrant Aid and Supply Company, Denison, Texas, *Immigrant's Guide to Texas*, 1872, 3.

15. *Immigrant's Guide to Texas Giving Descriptions of Counties, Towns, and Villages*, 1888, 8, 12.

16. *Immigrant's Guide to Texas Giving Descriptions of Counties, Towns, and Villages*, 1888, 18.

17. *Immigrant's Guide to Texas Giving Descriptions of Counties, Towns, and Villages*, 1888, 4, 26; Texas Immigrant Aid and Supply Company, Denison, Texas, *Immigrant's Guide to Texas*, 1872, 6.

18. *American Sylvan Scenes*, 5–6, 8, 16; *Colorado Tourist and Illustrated Guide*, 66–72.

19. Texas Immigrant Aid and Supply Company, Denison, Texas, *Immigrant's Guide to Texas*, 1872, 23; *Immigrant's Guide to Texas: Giving Descriptions of Counties, Towns, and Villages*, 1888, 31.

20. *Colorado Tourist and Illustrated Guide*, 65; Texas Immigrant Aid and Supply Company, Denison, Texas, *Immigrant's Guide to Texas*, 1872, 31–32.

21. *Directory of the City of Dallas*, 1875, 7; Texas Immigrant Aid and Supply Company, Denison, *Immigrant's Guide to Texas*, 1872, 13.

22. Allen, *The Great Southwest Strike*, 20; Nell Irvin Painter, *The Exodusters: Black Migration to Kansas after Reconstruction* (New York: Alfred A. Knopf, 1977), 137; William Cohen, *At Freedom's Edge: Black Mobility and the Southern White Quest for Racial Control, 1861–1915* (Baton Rouge: Louisiana State University Press, 1991), 249–51, 257.

23. Painter, *Exodusters*, 147–49; Cohen, *At Freedom's Edge*, 169–71.

24. Quoted in Painter, *Exodusters*, 215.

25. Quoted in Painter, *Exodusters*, 67.

26. Painter, *Exodusters*, 159.

27. Cohen, *At Freedom's Edge*, 176–79.

28. Charlton H. Tandy Papers, 1868–1967, Collection 135, Western Historical Manuscripts Collection, University of Missouri at St. Louis.

29. "Exodusters" in Kansas Bureau of Labor and Industrial Statistics, *First Annual Report of the Bureau of Labor and Industrial Statistics* (Topeka: Kansas Publishing House, 1886), 248–49.

30. My analysis here owes a debt to Trevor Rossen, "Building a New South: The Crisis of Labor in Harrison County, Texas, 1878–1886," undergraduate research paper, University of Texas at Austin (in the author's possession).

31. *Marshall Tri-Weekly Herald*, June 20, 1885.

32. "Exodusters" in Kansas Bureau of Labor and Industrial Statistics, *First Annual Report of the Bureau of Labor and Industrial Statistics* (Topeka: Kansas Publishing House, 1886), 248–57.

33. Primm, *Lion of the Valley*, 328, 357; David T. Burbank, *Reign of the Rabble: The Saint Louis General Strike of* 1877 (1966), 4.

34. Corbett and Miller, *Saint Louis in the Gilded Age*, 21–23, 86; Primm, *Lion of the Valley*, 71.

35. Corbett and Miller, *Saint Louis in the Gilded Age*, 11; *The Third Annual Report of the Bureau of Labor Statistics of the State of Missouri* (Jefferson City, 1882*); The Fourth Annual Report of the Bureau of Labor Statistics of the State of Missouri* (Jefferson City, 1883).

36. Stromquist, *Generation of Boomers*, 9, 16–17.

37. Stromquist, *Generation of Boomers*, 16–19, 144.

38. Ayers, *Southern Crossing*, 10–12; Foner, *Reconstruction*, 392–94.

39. Leon F. Litwack, *Trouble in Mind: Black Southerners in the Age of Jim Crow* (New York: Knopf, 1998) 130, 132.

40. Foner, *Reconstruction*, 461, 468; Klein, *The Life and Legend of Jay Gould*, 296; Stromquist, *Generation of Boomers*, 15.

41. Klein, *The Life and Legend of Jay Gould*, 3–4, 232, 240, 317; Nell Irvin Painter, *Standing at Armageddon: The United States, 1877–1919* (New York: W. W. Norton), 33–34.

42. Klein, *The Life and Legend of Jay Gould*, 265, 304; Painter, *Standing at Armageddon*, 34.

43. Barr, *Reconstruction to Reform*, 112; Painter, *Standing at Armageddon*, 34; Klein, *The Life and Legend of Jay Gould*, 249, 265, 305. Gould controlled the Texas & Pacific, but the western division, which extended from Fort Worth west to El Paso, fared poorly in the mid-1880s. See Klein, 350.

44. Barr, *Reconstruction to Reform*, 112.

45. United States House of Representatives, Select Committee on Existing Labor Troubles, *Investigation of Labor Troubles in Missouri, Arkansas, Kansas, Texas, and Illinois.* 49th Congress. 2nd session. Washington, D. C.: GPO, 1887, 567.

46. Painter, *Standing at Armageddon*, 34; Klein, *The Life and Legend of Jay Gould*, 308.

47. Foner, *Reconstruction*, 478–80.

48. Foner, *Reconstruction*, 513–15; Melvyn Dubofsky, *The State and Labor in Modern America* (Chapel Hill: University of North Carolina Press, 1994), 19.

49. Primm, *Lion of the Valley*, 326–27; Philip S. Foner, *The Great Labor Uprising of* 1877 (New York: Monad Press, 1977), 8–9; Eugene E. Leach, "Chaining the Tiger: The Mob Stigma and the Working Class, 1863–1894," *Labor History* 35 (Spring 1994), 202–3.

50. Foner, *The Great Labor Uprising*, 9, 157, 170–2, 176, 187; Primm, *Lion of the Valley*, 326–31; *Galveston Daily News*, July 26, 1877; David Roediger, "Not Only the Ruling Classes to Overcome, but Also the So-called Mob: Class, Skill, and Community in the St. Louis General Strike of 1877," *Journal of Social History* 19 (Winter 1985), 213, 221.

51. Foner, *The Great Labor Uprising*, 40–41, 60–61, 192–93, 204, 234–235, 282; Painter, *Standing at Armageddon*, 17.

52. David O. Stowell, *Streets, Railroads, and the Great Strike of 1877* (Chicago: University of Chicago Press, 1999); Roediger, "Not Only the Ruling Classes to Overcome," 213.

53. Leach, "Chaining the Tiger," 201–9; St. Louis papers' quotations and analysis from Roediger, "Not Only the Ruling Classes to Overcome," 214–15. Roediger finds that serious divisions existed between strike leaders and rank and filers in St. Louis. The leadership called off street parades and mass meetings, he argues, due to its better material circumstances, stronger identification with trade unions, "rootedness," and fear of losing control of the crowds in terms of racial makeup, use of symbols, tactics, and targets. See Roediger, "Not Only the Ruling Classes to Overcome" 224–26.

54. Leach, "Chaining the Tiger" 201–7; Foner, *The Great Labor Uprising*, 51–52, 191–92.

55. Foner, *The Great Labor Uprising*, 210.

56. Foner, *The Great Labor Uprising*, 205–6, 213; Roediger, "Not Only the Ruling Classes to Overcome," 227.

57. Foner, *The Great Labor Uprising*, 209, 212–14. Joshua Brown argues that *Frank Leslie's Illustrated Newspaper* was ultimately forced to come to terms with the mass character of its readership and to abandon its deeply hostile portrayal of strikes and the unemployed. *Leslie's* response stands in contrast then to the pattern of images found elsewhere by Eugene Leach in the post-strike press of an almost bestial working class. Joshua Brown, "The Great Uprising and the Pictorial Order in Gilded Age America," in David O. Stowell, ed., *The Great Strikes of* 1877 (Urbana: University of Illinois Press, 2008), 15–54.

58. Leach, "Chaining the Tiger," 207.

59. Leach, "Chaining the Tiger," 207–9.

60. Leach, "Chaining the Tiger," 207–9; Fink, *Workingmen's Democracy*, xii, 13; Painter, *Standing at Armageddon*, 31.

61. Eric Foner, *The Story of American Freedom* (New York: W. W. Norton, 1998), 115–28.

62. Ayers, *Southern Crossing*, 82, 112–14; Painter, *Standing at Armageddon*, 60–61.

63. Ayers, *Southern Crossing*, 112.

64. *Barr, Reconstruction to Reform*, 45–52 (quotation, 46); Foner, *The Great Labor Uprising*, 204, 217, 219–27; Fink, *Workingmen's Democracy*, 225.

65. Ayers, *Southern Crossing*, 83; Barr, *Reconstruction to Reform*, 22–23, 44–46, 115, chapter 6.

66. Barr, *Reconstruction to Reform*, 113–14.

67. Barr, *Reconstruction to Reform*, 114; Klein, *The Life and Legend of Jay Gould*, 160; 113–14; *Fort Worth Gazette*, February 18, 1882; *Dallas Morning News*, October 3, 1885.

68. *St. Louis Post-Dispatch*, September 5, 1882.

69. *St. Louis Post-Dispatch*, September 23, 1884.

70. *St. Louis Post-Dispatch*, July 19, 25, 1883.

71. "Exodusters" in *First Annual Report of the Bureau of Labor and Industrial Statistics*, 249–55; Lawrence Goodwyn, *The Populist Moment: A Short History of the Agrarian Revolt in America* (New York: Oxford University Press US, 1978), 121.

72. Alwyn Barr, *Black Texans: A History of African-Americans in Texas,* 1528–1995 (Norman: University of Oklahoma Press, 1996), 71–73; Ayers, *Southern Crossings*, 82; Barr, *Reconstruction to Reform*, 44–61, 64, 71.

73. Fon Louise, Gordon, *Caste and Class: The Black Experience in Arkansas, 1880–1920* (Athens: University of Georgia Press, 1995), 4; "Exodusters" in *First Annual Report of the*

Bureau of Labor and Industrial Statistics, 249–55; *Proceedings of the Convention of Colored Men Held in Edwards Opera House, Parsons, Kansas, Apr. 27–28, 1882* (Parsons: W. B. Avery, 1882), 2, 4–5.

Chapter 2

1. Thomas Townsend Taber, comp., *Location of Historical Materials Concerning the Railroads in the State of Texas* and *Guide to Railroad Historical Resources, United States and Canada* (Muncy, Penn.: T. T. Taber III, 1993).

2. Edward J. M. Rhoads, "The Chinese in Texas," *Southwestern Historical Quarterly* 81, no. 1 (July 1977) and Matthew J. Mancini, *One Dies, Get Another: Convict Leasing in the American South, 1866–1928* (Columbia: University of South Carolina Press, 1996); U.S. Department of the Interior, Census Office, Tenth Census of the United States, 1880, Marshall and Texarkana, Texas; David Montejano, *Anglos and Mexicans in the Making of Texas, 1836–1986* (Austin: University of Texas Press, 1987), 91; Jeffrey Marcos Garcilazo, "Traqueros: Mexican Railroad Workers in the United States, 1870–1920," (PhD diss., University of Utah, 1995), 48–59; Emilio Zamora, *The World of the Mexican Worker in Texas* (College Station: Texas A&M University Press, 1993); Robert Oppenheimer, "Acculturation or Assimilation: Mexican Immigrants to Kansas, 1900 to World War II," *Western Historical Quarterly* 16 (October 1985), 432–44. The Atchison, Topeka, and Santa Fe hired large numbers of Mexicans, Pueblos, Navahos, and Mohaves for track work in the 1880s, but in New Mexico. See James H. Ducker, *Men of the Steel Rails* (Lincoln: University of Nebraska Press, 1983), 27–28.

3. See Gunther Peck, *Reinventing Free Labor: Padrones and Immigrant Workers in the North American West, 1880–1930* (Cambridge: Cambridge University Press, 2000), 117–57.

4. Stephen Thernstrom and other social historians have accumulated a good deal of quantitative evidence supporting the idea that geographic mobility hinders the development of feelings of class solidarity. Shelton Stromquist convincingly challenges this hypothesis in *A Generation of Boomers: The Pattern of Railroad Labor Conflict in Nineteenth-Century America* (Chicago: University of Illinois Press, 1987), 188–228. He argues that it was in the "newer, more homogeneous railroad towns that the social solidarity characteristic of worker communities was most likely to be developed" (227).

5. Stromquist, *A Generation of Boomers*, 104–15.

6. Paul Michel Taillon, "Culture, Politics, and the Making of the Railroad Brotherhoods, 1863–1916," (PhD diss., University of Wisconsin at Madison, 1997), 58; B. B. Adams, "The Every-Day Life of Railroad Men," in T. C. Clarke, *The American Railway* (New York: Charles Scribner's Sons, 1889), 409–10, 420.

7. Taillon, "Culture, Politics, and the Making of the Railroad Brotherhoods," 56–57; Adams, "The Every-Day Live of Railroad Men," 403.

8. Stromquist, *A Generation of Boomers*, 109–11.

9. Taillon, "Culture, Politics, and the Making of the Railroad Brotherhoods," 57–58.

10. Charles Brown and H. Roger Grant, *Brownie the Boomer: The Life of Charles P. Brown, an American Railroader* (DeKalb: Northern Illinois University Press, 1991), 48.

11. Taillon, "Culture, Politics, and the Making of the Railroad Brotherhoods," 59; Stromquist, *A Generation of Boomers*, 105.

12. Adams, "The Every-Day Life of Railroad Men," 420; Stromquist, *A Generation of Boomers*, 105, 110–11.

13. David Montgomery, *The Fall of the House of Labor: The Workplace, the State, and American Labor Activism, 1865–1925* (Cambridge: Cambridge University Press, 1987), 180; Stromquist, *A Generation of Boomers*, 106, 112–13.

14. Stromquist, *A Generation of Boomers*, 106–7.

15. Taillon, "Culture, Politics, and the Making of the Railroad Brotherhoods," 61–63, 101; Ducker, *Men of the Steel Rails*, 16–19, 21–22.

16. Licht, *Working for the Railroad*, 135–36; *St. Louis Post-Dispatch*, March 13, 1882, May 29, 1884; H. Roger Grant, *"Follow the Flag": A History of the Wabash Railway Company* (DeKalb: Northern Illinois University Press, 2004), 25–26.

17. Licht, *Working for the Railroad*, 142.

18. Ducker, *Men of the Steel Rails*, 6–7; Chauncey Del French, *Railroadman* (Norwood, Mass.: Macmillan, 1938), 61, 27, 80.

19. J. J. Thomas, *Fifty Years on the Rail* (New York: Knickerbocker Press, 1912), 39–41.

20. Mark Aldrich, *Death Rode the Rails: American Railroad Accidents and Safety, 1828–1965* (Baltimore: Johns Hopkins University Press, 2006), 103–4; *First Annual Report of the Bureau of Labor and Industrial Statistics* (Topeka: Kansas Publishing House, 1886), 261–66; Brown and Grant, *Brownie the Boomer*, 6, 215. Aldrich explains that American railroads were "more dangerous to operate than were British lines," because American railways ran much more freight than passenger cars and coupled cars with links and pins rather than by hook and chain.

21. *St. Louis Post-Dispatch*, May 24, 1884; Aldrich, *Death Rode the* Rails, 104–6.

22. Ducker, *Men of the Steel Rails*, 9; French, *Railroadman*, 15–22; *Missouri Republican*, March 2, 1885.

23. Aldrich, *Death Rode the Rails*, 159–61; United States House of Representatives, *Investigation of Labor Troubles in Missouri, Arkansas, Kansas, Texas, and Illinois*, 2 Parts, 1887, 49th Congress, 2nd Session, Report No. 4174, 1: 228–29 (quotation), 278, 288.

24. Aldrich, *Death Rode the Rails*, 161; *Fort Worth Gazette*, February 10, 1882. In contrast, European railroad companies of this period offered employees medical insurance or pension benefits. See Licht, *Working for the Railroads*, 147.

25. Ducker, *Men of the Steel Rails*, 134–38; French, *Railroadman*, 194–95.

26. *St. Louis Post-Dispatch*, September 23, 1884.

27. Robert E. Weir, *Beyond Labor's Veil: The Culture of the Knights of Labor* (University Park: Pennsylvania State University Press, 1996), 169.

28. Paul Michel Taillon, "'What We Want is Good, Sober Men': Masculinity, Respectability, and Temperance in the Railroad Brotherhoods, c. 1870–1910," *Journal of Social History* 36, no. 2 (2002), 320–22; Ducker, *Men of the Steel Rails*, 33.

29. Taillon, "'What We Want is Good, Sober Men,'" 321; French, *Railroadman*, 159.

30. Taillon "Culture, Politics, and the Making of the Railroad Brotherhoods," 74–75; Charles B. George, *Forty Years on the Rail: Reminiscences of a Veteran Conductor*, 3rd ed. (Chicago: Donelley & Sons, 1887), 164–65. Examples of stories that sentimentalized danger include: "The Fate of a Brave Engineer" in *Locomotive Engineer's Monthly Journal* 18, no. 10 (October 1884), 608, and "Death on the Track" in *Locomotive Engineer's Monthly Journal* 19, no. 2 (February 1885), 99–100.

31. Taillon, "Culture, Politics, and the Making of the Railroad Brotherhoods," 73; French, *Railroadman*, 2; Untitled, 3D179, Folder 3, undated, John Avery Lomax Family Papers, Center for American History, University of Texas at Austin.

32. Adams, "The Every-Day Life of Railroad Men," 401–2.

33. *St. Louis Post-Dispatch*, July 28, 1883; Adams, "The Every-Day Life of Railroad Men," 401–2.

34. George P. Rawick, *The American Slave: A Composite Autobiography*, Supplement, Series 2, 10 vols. (Westport: Greenwood Press, 1979), vol. 3: Texas Narratives (Part 1), 495; French, *Railroadman*, 21.

35. French, *Railroadman*, 21–22.

36. French, *Railroadman*, 50–52; Ducker, *Men of the Steel Rails*, 54.

37. "The Wreck on the C. & O." in John A. Lomax and Alan Lomax, *American Ballads and Folk Songs* (1934; Mineola, N.Y.: Dover Publications, 1994), 31–34.

38. Peck, *Reinventing Free Labor*, 135–36.

39. Paul Michel Taillon, "'To Make Men out of Crude Material': Work Culture, Manhood, and Unionism in the Railroad Running Trades, c. 1870–1900" in *Boys and Their Toys? Masculinity, Technology, and Class in America*, Roger Horowitz, ed. (New York: Routledge, 2001), 38–39; Horace Herr quoted in B. A. Botkin and Alvin Harlow, *A Treasury of Railroad Folklore* (New York: Crown Publishers, 1953), 312.

40. Charles Maier, "The Realization of My Boyhood Dream," Box 2E302, Folder 2, 1–5, Labor Movement in Texas Collection, Center for American History, University of Texas at Austin (hereafter cited as LMTC).

41. French, *Railroadman*, 2–3; George, *Forty Years on the Rail*, 19–25; Thomas, *Fifty Years on the Rail*, 10–13.

42. Ducker, *Men of the Steel Rails*, 57; Stromquist, *A Generation of Boomers*, 194, 196; George, *Forty Years on the Rail*, 26; French, *Railroadman*, 9–11.

43. Rawick, *The American Slave*, Supplement 2, Series 2, 1979, Vol. 3, 821–23.

44. Edward L. Ayers, *The Promise of the New South: Life After Reconstruction* (New York: Oxford University Press, 1992), 13.

45. Rawick, *The American Slave*, Supplement 2, Series 2, 1979, Vol. 3, 852; Arnesen, *Brotherhoods of Color: Black Railroad Workers and the Struggle for Equality* (Cambridge: Harvard University Press, 2001), 24.

46. *St. Louis Post-Dispatch*, July 19, 1883; Ayers, *The Promise of the New South*, 150, 151.

47. Lesley Poling-Kempes, *The Harvey Girls: Women Who Opened the West* (New York: Paragon House, 1991), xiii.

48. Tenth Census of the United States, 1880, for Marshall, Texas; Ducker, *Men of the Steel Rails*, 13–14, 65–68.

49. Tenth Census of the United States, 1880, for Marshall, Texas. These numbers include laborers only when the census specified that a laborer worked for the railroad.

50. Taillon, "'What We Want is Good, Sober Men,'" 321–22; French, *Railroadman*, 11–12.

51. Ducker, *Men of the Steel Rails*, 6; Rawick, *The American Slave*, Supplement 2, Series 2, 1979, Vol. 3, 354.

52. *St. Louis Post Dispatch*, September 15, 1884.

53. Taillon, "Culture, Politics, and the Making of the Railroad Brotherhoods," 87; French, *Railroadman*, 11–12.

54. Thomas, *Fifty Years on the Rail*, 11–12, 15, 40, 49.

55. George P. Rawick, *The American Slave*, Supplement 2, Series 2, 1979, Vol. 3, 821–23. See the following for examples: *Switchmen's Journal* 1 (October 1886), 263, 267, 268, 274; *Locomotive Firemen's Magazine* 10 (February 1886), 90; *Railroad Brakeman's Journal* 3 (March 1886), 5.

56. Tenth Census of the United States, 1880, for Marshall, Texas; Stromquist, *Generation of Boomers*, 196–97.

57. Victor S. Clark, "Employment Conditions in Road and Yard Service," Report of the Eight Hour Commission (Washington, D.C.: 1918); Stromquist, *Generation of Boomers*, xiii, 100–1 (quotations).

58. Stromquist, *Generation of Boomers*, 101, 195.

59. French, *Railroadman*, 81–82.

60. Ducker, *Men of the Steel Rails*, 56–57; James Michael Brodie, *Created Equal: The Lives and Ideas of Black American Innovators* (New York: William Morrow, 1993), 61.

61. *Railroad Brakemen's Journal* 3, no. 1 (March 1886), 37–41; Fulton, *Sam Hobart, the Locomotive Engineer*, 36.

62. Maier, "The Realization of My Boyhood Dream," LMTC, Box 2E302, Folder 2, 3–4.

63. Rawick, *The American Slave*, Supplement 2, Series 2, 1979, Vol. 3, 354; Vol. 10, 4305; Vol. 7, 2665; *St. Louis Post-Dispatch*, February 10, 1882.

64. Fulton, *Sam Hobart, the Locomotive Engineer*, 48–52.

65. Leon F. Litwack, *Been in the Storm so Long: The Aftermath of Slavery* (New York: Vintage Books, 1979), 244–45.

66. *The Promise of the New South*, 68–69; Ada M. Holland and C. C. White, *No Quittin' Sense* (Austin: University of Texas Press, 1969), 5.

67. *Switchman's Journal*, May 1886, 4–6.

68. Ayers, *The Promise of the New South*, 68–69.

69. *Locomotive Engineer's Monthly Magazine* 20, no. 5 (May 1886), 309; "Railroad Songs," 3D179, Folder 4, undated, John Avery Lomax Family Papers, Center for American History, University of Texas at Austin.

70. Quoted in Ayers, *The Promise of the New South*, 24.

71. Peck, *Reinventing Free Labor*, 141.

72. Holland and White, *No Quittin' Sense*, 86–88.

73. *Railroad Brakemen's Journal* 3, no. 1 (March 1886), 5.

74. *St. Louis Post-Dispatch*, March 13, 1882; *Fort Worth Gazette*, February 9, 17, 18, 1882.

75. *Railroad Brakemen's Journal* 3, no. 1 (March 1886), 5; *Railroad Brakemen's Journal* 4, no. 4 (April 1887), 156. Poem quoted in Aldrich, *Death Rode the Rails*, 74.

76. *Locomotive Engineer's Monthly Journal* 18, no. 5 (May 1885), 153–54, 279; *Locomotive Firemen's Magazine* 10, no. 2 (February 1886), 70.

77. *Fort Worth Gazette*, February 25, 1882; *St. Louis Post-Dispatch*, September 25, 1884.

78. Stromquist, *Generation of Boomers*, 192; Brown and Hunt, *Brownie the Boomer*, 35, 63 (quotation), 90–95, 124, 133–34, 145–46, 210. My conception of class comes from E. P. Thompson: "Class happens when some men, as a result of common experiences (inherited or shared), feel and articulate the identity of their interests as between themselves, and as against other men whose interests are different from (and usually opposed to) theirs. The class experience is largely determined by the productive relations into which men are born—or enter involuntarily." E. P. Thompson, *The Making of the English Working Class* (New York: Vintage Books, 1966), 9.

Chapter 3

1. George P. Rawick, *The American Slave: A Composite Autobiography*, Supplement, Series 2, 10 vols. (Westport: Greenwood Press, 1979), Vol. 3: Texas Narratives (Part 2), 489, 492–94.

2. Eric Arnesen, *Brotherhoods of Color: Black Railroad Workers and the Struggle for Equality* (Cambridge: Harvard University Press, 2001), 6 (quotation); *Directory of the City of Dallas,*

1886 (Galveston, Morrison & Fourmy, 1886); Eliot Albert Sholes, *Shole's Directory of the City of Little Rock and Argenta, 1883–1884* (Little Rock: Mitchell & Bettis, 1883); Rawick, *The American Slave*, Supplement 2, Series 2, 1979, 2965–66; Alton King Briggs, "The Archeology of 1882 Labor Camps on the Southern Pacific Railroad, Val Verde County, Texas" (master's thesis, University of Texas at Austin, 1974), 31, 33–34.

3. U.S. Department of the Interior, Census Office, Tenth Census of the United States, 1880, Marshall and Texarkana, Texas. Kevin Kenny has asked this question in regard to the American Irish in *The American Irish: A History* (Essex, UK: Pearson Education Limited, 2000), 69–70.

4. Here "free laborers" (and "free labor") refer to workers who were uninhibited by long-term contracts or the power of the state to compel them to work. The term "free labor" describes their actual status, while the phrase "free labor ideology" pertains to the set of ideas that, by the late nineteenth century, exalted the economic freedom of employers and employees to strike bargains with one another, untrammeled by the intervention of the state or collective bodies such as unions.

5. Walter Licht, *Working for the Railroad: The Organization of Work in the Nineteenth Century* (Princeton: Princeton University Press, 1983), 239–43; Nick Salvatore, *Eugene V. Debs: Citizen and Socialist* (Urbana: University of Illinois Press, 1984), 37–38, 47–49; Donald L. McMurry, *The Great Burlington Strike of 1888: A Case History in Labor Relations* (1956; New York: Russell & Russell, 1973), 30–37.

6. Shelton Stromquist, *A Generation of Boomers: The Pattern of Railroad Labor Conflict in Nineteenth-Century America* (Chicago: University of Illinois Press, 1987), 55.

7. *Locomotive Firemen's Magazine*, January 1886, 8–9; Paul Michel Taillon, "Culture, Politics, and the Making of the Railroad Brotherhoods, 1863–1916" (PhD diss., University of Wisconsin at Madison, 1997), 392.

8. Stromquist, *Generation of Boomers*, 108–9.

9. Stromquist, *Generation of Boomers*, 58–59.

10. Salvatore, *Eugene V. Debs*, 23–24.

11. Taillon, "Culture, Politics, and the Making of the Railroad Brotherhoods," 138–39, 159; French, *Railroadman* (Norwood, Mass.: MacMillan Company, 1938), 134.

12. Taillon, "Culture, Politics, and the Making of the Railroad Brotherhoods," 158.

13. Taillon, "Culture, Politics, and the Making of the Railroad Brotherhoods," 76–77.

14. George N. Green, "Lone Star Labor," unpublished manuscript, 10–19.

15. *Locomotive Engineer's Monthly Magazine* 19, no. 3 (March 1885), 155; Stromquist, *Generation of Boomers*, 107–8; Taillon, "Culture, Politics, and the Making of the Railroad Brotherhoods," 390–91.

16. Licht, *Working for the Railroad*, 267; Donald L. McMurry, "Federation of the Railroad Brotherhoods, 1889–1894," *Industrial and Labor Relations Review* 7, no. 1 (1953), p. 74; *Switchmen's Journal* 1, no. 1 (May 1886), 2–3. For a listing of the towns and cities hosting lodges of the Switchmen's Mutual Aid Association and the Brotherhood of Railroad Brakemen, see any 1885 or 1886 issue of these unions' journals.

17. Kansas Bureau of Labor and Industrial Statistics, *First Annual Report of the Bureau of Labor and Industrial Statistics* (Topeka: Kansas Publishing House, 1886), 91–92; Stromquist, *Generation of Boomers*, 50, 54.

18. Stromquist, *Generation of Boomers*, 50–54; 125–26. For a case study of the pre-1877 roots of industrial unionism in one railroad town, see Shelton Stromquist, "'Our Rights as Workingmen": Class Traditions and Collective Action in a Nineteenth-Century Railroad

Town, Hornellsville, N.Y., 1869–82," in David O. Stowell, ed., *The Great Strikes of* 1877 (Urbana: University of Illinois Press, 2008), 55–75.

19. Taillon, "Culture, Politics, and the Making of the Railroad Brotherhoods," 79–80; Stromquist, *Generation of Boomers*, 110.

20. Engineers and conductors came into conflict in part because both represented the top authority figures on the trains. Taillon, "Culture, Politics, and the Making of the Railroad Brotherhoods," 80–82. The following offers a discussion of gender ideologies as a "field within which or by means of which power is articulated": Joan Wallach Scott, *Gender and the Politics of History* (New York: Columbia University Press, 1988), 44–46, 139–63.

21. French, *Railroadman*, 82–85; Ducker, *Men of the Steel Rails*, 53.

22. Eric Arnesen, "'Like Banquo's Ghost: It Will Not Down': The Race Question and the American Railroad Brotherhoods, 1880–1920," *American Historical Review* 99, no. 5, 1613–17 (quotation, 1615).

23. Arnesen, "'Like Banquo's Ghost, It Will Not Down,'" 1612–13.

24. See "Frontier Reminiscences" in the *Locomotive Fireman's Magazine; Silver City Chronicle* quoted in Jeffrey Marcos Garcilazo, "'Traqueros': 'Mexican Railroad Workers in the United States" (PhD diss., University of California, Santa Barbara, 1995), 25.

25. Fulton, *Sam Hobart, the Locomotive Engineer*, 98–99.

26. Fulton, *Sam Hobart, the Locomotive Engineer*, 101; Taillon, "Culture, Politics, and the Making of the Railroad Brotherhoods," 93.

27. Arnesen, "'Like Banquo's Ghost, It Will Not Down,'" 1614; Thomas, *Fifty Years on the Rail*, 47; David Roediger termed these psychological benefits "the wages of whiteness" in David R. Roediger, *The Wages of Whiteness: Race and the Making of the American Working Class* (New York: Verso, 1991).

28. Taillon, "Culture, Politics, and the Making of the Railroad Brotherhoods," 78; Arnesen, *Brotherhoods of Color*, 16–17.

29. Katharine T. Corbett and Howard S. Miller, *Saint Louis in the Gilded Age* (St. Louis: Missouri Historical Society Press, 1993), 61.

30. U.S. Census 1880 for Marshall and Texarkana, Texas; *Directory of the City of Dallas*, 1886; *Shole's Directory of the City of Little Rock and Argenta, 1883–4*; United States House of Representatives, *Investigation of Labor Troubles in Missouri, Arkansas, Kansas, Texas, and Illinois*, 2 Parts, 1887, 49th Congress, 2nd Session, Report No. 4174, 2: 122; Arnesen, *Brotherhoods of Color*, 24–25; Daniel Letwin, *The Challenge of Interracial Unionism: Alabama Coal Miners*, 1878–1921 (Chapel Hill: University of North Carolina Press, 1998), 77–78.

31. Licht, *Working for the Railroad*, 222–225; Arnesen, *Brotherhoods of Color*, 6–9; Garcilazo, "Traqueros: Mexican Railroad Workers in the United States," 52–54.

32. U.S. Census 1880 for Marshall and Texarkana, Texas; *Directory of the City of Dallas*, 1886; *Shole's Director of the City of Little Rock and Argenta, 1883–4;* Rawick, *The American Slave*, Supplement 2, Series 2, 1979, Vol. 8: Texas Narratives (Part 7), 2965–66; Briggs, "The Archeology of 1882 Labor Camps," 31, 33–34.

33. Licht, *Working for the Railroad*, 223; U.S. Census 1880 for Marshall and Texarkana, Texas; Martin Irons, "My Experiences in the Labor Movement," *Lippincott's Monthly Magazine* 37 (June 1886), 625–27; Mary Irons interview, *New York Times*, May 10, 1886. *Investigation of Labor Troubles*, II, 436–37.

34. See French, *Railroadman*.

35. Kenneth W. Porter, "Negro Labor in the Western Cattle Industry," *Labor History* 10, no. 3 (Summer 1969), 346–74.

36. Arnesen, *Brotherhoods of Color*, 6; Kenny, *The American Irish*, 125, 157.

37. French, *Railroadman*, 3–5; U.S. Census 1880 for Marshall and Texarkana, Texas; *Investigation of Labor Troubles*, 1: 452–53; David R. Walker, *Penology for Profit: A History of the Texas Prison System, 1867–1912* (College Station, TX: Texas A&M University Press, 1988), 60.

38. George P. Rawick, *The American Slave: A Composite Autobiography*, Supplement, Series 2, Vol. 1 and *The American Slave: A Composite Autobiography*, Supplement, Series 1, 12 Vols. (Westport: Greenwood Press, 1977), Vol. 2. Interviews conducted in Missouri, Kansas, and Arkansas did not yield evidence on black railroaders.

39. Rawick, *The American Slave*, Supplement 2, Series 2, 1979, Vol. 10: Texas Narratives (Part 9), 4213; Vol. 3, 852; Vol. 5, 1620.

40. Rawick, *The American Slave*, Supplement 2, Series 2, 1979, Vol. 7: Texas Narratives (Part 6), 2456; Vol. 10, 4235; *Proceedings of the Convention of Colored Men Held in Edwards Opera House, Parsons, Kansas, Apr. 27–28, 1882* (Parsons: W. B. Avery, 1882), 2.

41. Rawick, *The American Slave*, Supplement 2, Series 2, 1979, Vol. 3: Texas Narratives (Part 1), 148–49, 719–20.

42. Eric Foner, *Reconstruction: America's Unfinished Revolution, 1863–1877* (New York: Harper & Row, 1988), 400–1.

43. Edward L. Ayers, *The Promise of the New South: Life After Reconstruction* (New York: Oxford University Press, 1992), 68.

44. Susan Curtis, *Dancing to a Black Man's Tune: The Life of Scott Joplin* (Columbia: University of Missouri Press, 1994), 34–35, 40–41.

45. Ayers, *The Promise of the New South*, 68–69; Curtis, *Dancing to a Black Man's Tune*, 34–35.

46. Leon Litwack, *Been in the Storm So Long: The Aftermath of Slavery* (New York: Random House, 1979), 87–93, 96–97, 102–3, 267–74.

47. George Rawick, *The American Slave*, Supplement 2, Series 2, 1979, Vol. 3: Texas Narratives (Part 2), 489, 492–94; Robin G. Kelley, "We Are Not What We Seem": Rethinking Black Working-Class Opposition in the Jim Crow South," *Journal of American History* 80, no. 1. (June 1993), 75–112; Arnesen, "'Like Banquo's Ghost, It Will Not Down,'" 1612, 1613; Scott Reynolds Nelson has unearthed evidence of the real John Henry in *John Henry: The Untold Story of an American Legend* (New York: Oxford University Press, 2006).

48. *Arkansas Weekly Mansion*, June 30, July 28, August 4, August 18, September 1, and October 6, 1883; *Arkansas Weekly Mansion*, August 4, October 6, 1883; *Benevolent Banner*, June 18, August 27, 1887; Fon Louise Gordon, *Caste and Class: The Black Experience in Arkansas, 1880–1920* (Athens: University of Georgia Press, 1995), 4.

49. Gordon, *Caste and Class*, 4.

50. *Benevolent Banner*, August 27, 1887; *Arkansas Weekly Mansion*, October 6, 1883; *Kansas Herald*, February 13, 1880; *Colored Patriot*, April 27, 1882.

51. Gunther Peck, *Reinventing Free Labor: Padrones and Immigrant Workers in the North American West, 1880–1930* (Cambridge: Cambridge University Press, 2000), 50–51. Where whites were able to enforce labor control laws, freedom was largely nominal for black laborers. However, in the main, black southerners were able to move about in search of work with a fair degree of freedom when jobs were available. See William Cohen, *At Freedom's Edge: Black Mobility and the Southern White Quest for Racial Control, 1861–1915* (Baton Rouge: Louisiana State University Press, 1991).

52. Edward J. M. Rhoads, "The Chinese in Texas," *Southwestern Historical Quarterly* 81, no. 1 (July 1977), 2, 5–8; Garcilazo, "Traqueros: Mexican Railroad Workers in the United States," 52.

53. Peck, *Reinventing Free Labor*, 51–52; Quoted in Stephen E. Ambrose, *Nothing Like It in the World: The Men Who Built the Transcontinental Railroad, 1863–1869* (New York: Simon & Schuster, 2000), 241. Peck does not compare contract labor to colonial-era indentured servitude as I do here.

54. Quoted in Rhoads, "The Chinese in Texas," 10.

55. Peck, *Reinventing Free Labor*, 50–52.

56. Rhoads, "The Chinese in Texas," 11–13.

57. Rhoads, "The Chinese in Texas," 3, 7, 14–15; Judy Yung, *Chinese Women of America: A Pictorial History* (Seattle: University of Washington Press, 1986), 118.

58. Rhoads, "The Chinese in Texas," 2–3, 13; Briggs, "The Archeology of 1882 Labor Camps," 198.

59. Briggs, "The Archeology of 1882 Labor Camps," 34, 198.

60. Rhoads, "The Chinese in Texas," 5; Briggs, "The Archeology of 1882 Labor Camps," 27.

61. Rhoads, "The Chinese in Texas," 10; *Texas Permiam Historical Annual* 13 (December 1973), 38; *Fort Worth Gazette*, February 8, 1882; *Austin-American Statesman*, December 4, 1885, Box 2E189, Labor Movement in Texas Collection, Center for American History, University of Texas at Austin.

62. Rhoads, "The Chinese in Texas," 4; Ambrose, *Nothing Like It in the World*, 241.

63. Maury Klein, *The Life and Legend of Jay Gould* (Baltimore: Johns Hopkins University Press, 1986), 151–52; Rhoads, "The Chinese in Texas," 15–16; *Galveston Daily News*, July 31, August 1, 1877.

64. Rhoads, "The Chinese in Texas," 1–2, 7.

65. See Alexander Saxton, *The Indispensable Enemy: Labor and the Anti-Chinese Movement in California* (Berkeley: University of California Press, 1971).

66. Rhoads, "The Chinese in Texas," 15. See Stuart Creighton Miller, *The Unwelcome Immigrant: The American Image of the Chinese, 1785–1882* (Berkeley: University of California Press, 1969).

67. Ambrose, *Nothing Like It in the World*, 150.

68. Ambrose, *Nothing Like It in the World*, 150–51.

69. Rhoads, "The Chinese in Texas," 12; Ambrose, *Nothing Like It in the World*, 151.

70. Peck, *Reinventing Free Labor*, 130, 227–28.

71. Peck, *Reinventing Free Labor*, 166. For similar newspaper reports, see *Missouri Republican*, March 5, 1885, and *Marshall Tri-Weekly Herald*, July 21, 1885. Peck observed, "Transience . . . was almost always a marker of non-whiteness in the West in 1900. The best illustration of this was the ambiguous racial status of 'hoboes,' transient men known in any other context as white, Anglo-Saxon Protestants."

72. Quoted Ayers, *The Promise of the New South*, 22.

73. Ayers, *The Promise of the New South*, 156–57.

74. *Investigation of Labor Troubles*, 1: 378–379; Matthew J. Mancini, *One Dies, Get Another: Convict Leasing in the American South, 1866–1928* (Columbia: University of South Carolina Press, 1996), 125, 175; Walker, *Penology for Profit*, 57.

75. Mancini, *One Dies, Get Another*, 117–18, 120, 122, 175, 179.

76. Mancini, *One Dies, Get Another*, 177–78; Walker, *Penology for Profit*, 64.

77. Mancini, *One Dies, Get Another*, 122, 172–74, 177.

78. Mancini, *One Dies, Get Another*, 117, 121–22, 172–73, 177; Walker, *Penology for Profit*, 60–61, 64.

79. *Missouri Republican*, March 4, 1886; Peck, *Reinventing Free Labor*, 8–9. I take the question "How free is free?" from Litwack, *Been in the Storm So Long*.

80. Quoted in Mancini, *One Dies, Get Another*, 22–23.

Chapter 4

1. Shelton Stromquist, A *Generation of Boomers: The Pattern of Railroad Labor Conflict in Nineteenth Century America* (Chicago: University of Illinois Press, 1987), 11–14; Paul Michel Taillon, "Culture, Politics, and the Making of the Railroad Brotherhoods, 1863–1916," (PhD diss., University of Wisconsin at Madison, 1997), 378.

2. Bradley Hansen, "The People's Welfare and the Origins of Corporate Reorganization: The Wabash Receivership Reconsidered," *Business History Review* 74, no. 3 (2000), 377–79, 385–89.

3. Stromquist, *Generation of Boomers*, 101, 120–23.

4. Stromquist, *Generation of Boomers*, 114, 120–26.

5. James H. Ducker, *Men of the Steel Rails: Workers on the Atchison, Topeka & Santa Fe Railroad, 1869–1900* (Lincoln: University of Nebraska Press, 1983), 13–17, 42 (quotation); Stromquist, *Generation of Boomers*, 58, 116–17, 124–25, 132–33.

6. Stromquist, *Generation of Boomers*, 102, 125–26.

7. Maury Klein, *The Life and Legend of Jay Gould* (Baltimore: Johns Hopkins University Press, 1986), 340–42, 346.

8. Klein, *The Life and Legend of Jay Gould*, 340–41, 348–50.

9. The term "frontier of labor scarcity" is taken from Stromquist, *Generation of Boomers*, 100–1, 127, 268–69.

10. Ruth Allen, *The Great Southwest Strike* (Austin: University of Texas, Bureau of Research in the Social Sciences, 1942) 30; *Missouri Republican*, March 11, 1885.

11. United States House of Representatives, *Investigation of Labor Troubles in Missouri, Arkansas, Kansas, Texas, and Illinois*, 2 Parts, 1887, 49th Congress, 2nd Session, Report No. 4174, 1: 155–56, 159, 161, 177, 227–28, 444, 445, 447; Bureau of Labor Statistics and Inspection of Missouri, *The Official History of the Great Strike of* 1886 *on the Southwestern Railway System* (Jefferson City, Mo.: Tribune Printing Company, 1887), 23–24, 444–45, 450, 460, 478–79, 484–87. Other examples of the use of indirect management strategies to press down wages on the Southwest system can be found in chapter 6. While railroad companies often contracted shop work to outside establishments as a way to cut costs, this does not appear to have been a major strategy of the Missouri Pacific during the mid-1880s. According to one leader of the 1886 strike, the Missouri Pacific contracted work to a Parsons foundry, which led to underemployment in Parsons shops, but this was the only instance of contracted work that strikers and their sympathizers cited. See *Investigation of Labor Troubles*, 1: 435.

12. *Locomotive Engineer's Monthly Magazine* 19, no. 5 (May 1885), 276.

13. 3D179, Folder 3, undated, John Avery Lomax Family Papers, Center for American History, University of Texas at Austin.

14. *Investigation of Labor Troubles*, 1: 466.

15. *Investigation of Labor Troubles*, 1: 486–87; Ducker, *Men of the Steel Rails*, 19.

16. Charles Maier, "The Realization of My Boyhood Dream," Box 2E302, Folder 2, pp. 7, 15, Labor Movement in Texas Collection, Center for American History, University of Texas at Austin (hereafter cited as LMTC). Although Maier recorded these recollections fifty years after the fact, his memory was apparently quite good. The 1886 testimony of railroad superintendent William Kerrigan concerning mob actions at Parsons, Kansas, during the 1886 Southwest Strike for the most part corroborates the detailed description given to Ruth Allen by Maier half a century later. Compare *Investigation of Labor Troubles*, 1: 370–71, and Maier's "Realization of My Boyhood Dream," Box 2E302, Folder 2, p. 25, LMTC.

17. Maier, "The Realization of My Boyhood Dream," Box 2E302, Folder 2, pp. 11, 13–15, LMTC.

18. Taillon, "Culture, Politics, and the Making of the Railroad Brotherhoods," 95–96, 99, 100.

19. Chauncey Del French, *Railroadman* (Norwood, Mass.: Macmillan Company, 1938), 15; Nick Salvatore, *Eugene V. Debs: Citizen and Socialist* (Chicago: University of Illinois Press, 1982), 20.

20. Taillon, "Culture Politics, and the Making of the Railroad Brotherhoods," 93–94; *Fourth Biennial Report of the Bureau of Labor Statistics of Illinois, 1886* (Springfield: H. W. Rokker, 1886).

21. Edward L. Ayers, *The Promise of the New South: Life after Reconstruction* (New York: Oxford University Press, 1992), 69; "Exodusters" in Kansas Bureau of Labor and Industrial Statistics, *First Annual Report of the Bureau of Labor and Industrial Statistics* (Topeka: Kansas Publishing House, 1886), 204–215, 251.

22. *St. Louis Post-Dispatch*, July 13, 1883; September 25, 1884.

23. Stromquist, *Generation of Boomers*, 231–33.

24. Karen Orren, *Belated Feudalism: Labor, the Law, and Liberal Development in the United States* (Cambridge: Cambridge University Press, 1991), 176–79.

25. *Investigation of Labor Troubles*, 1: 474, 2: 256–57, 263, 291; Paul V. Black, "Experiment in Bureaucratic Centralization: Employee Blacklisting on the Burlington Railroad, 1877–1892," *Business History Review* 51, no. 4. (1977), 447; Richard Schneirov, Shelton Stromquist, and Nick Salvatore, eds., *The Pullman Strike and the Crisis of the* 1890*s: Essays on Labor and Politics* (Urbana: University of Illinois Press, 1999), 25; David L. Lightner, *Labor on the Illinois Central Railroad, 1852–1900: The Evolution of an Industrial Environment* (New York: Arno Press, 1977), 252.

26. Norman Ware, *The Labor Movement in the United States, 1860–1890: A Study in Democracy* (New York: Vintage Books, 1964), 128–31.

27. Joseph Buchanan, *The Story of a Labor Agitator* (New York: Outlook, 1903), 71–72, 75–78.

28. Buchanan, *The Story of a Labor Agitator*, 80–99; Stromquist, *Generation of Boomers*, 68.

29. Michael Cassity, "Modernization and Social Crisis: The Knights of Labor and a Midwest Community, 1885–1886," *Journal of American History* 66, no. 1 (March 1979), 44; *Missouri Republican*, March 6, 7, 8, 1885; *St. Louis Post-Dispatch*, March 7, 1885.

30. Edwin James Forsythe, "The Gould Strikes and Missouri Newspaper Opinion" (master's thesis, University of Missouri, 1949), 13; Jerry Wayne Chandler, "The Knights of Labor and the Southwestern Strikes" (master's thesis, Florida State University, 1970), 26; *St. Louis Post-Dispatch*, March 10, 1885; *Missouri Republican*, March 9, 1885; Buchanan, *The Story of a Labor Agitator*, 143.

31. *Investigation of Labor Troubles*, 1: ii; Chandler, "The Knights of Labor and the Southwestern Strikes," 23–24; *St. Louis Post-Dispatch*, March 7, 1885; *Galveston Daily News*, March 3, 6, 1885; Maier, "The Realization of My Boyhood Dream," Box 2E302, Folder 2, pp. 8–9, LMTC.

32. *St. Louis Post-Dispatch*, March 7, 1885; *Missouri Republican*, March 11, 1885; Klein, *The Life and Legend of Jay Gould*, 340; *Investigation of Labor Troubles*, 1: ii.

33. *Marshall Tri-Weekly Herald*, March 3, 1885; *St Louis Globe-Democrat*, March 10, 1885.

34. *Missouri Republican*, March 11, 1885.

35. *Marshall Tri-Weekly Herald*, March 7, 1885; *Missouri Republican*, March 11, 1885.

36. *Galveston Daily News*, February 27, 28, 1885.

37. *Galveston Daily News*, February 28, March 6, 1885; *Investigation of Labor Troubles*, 1: ii. Missouri Pacific shopmen in Palestine, Texas, struck a few days earlier, on March 5, 1885 (*Galveston Daily News*, March 6, 1885).

38. Cassity, "Modernization and Social Crisis," 44.

39. Michael Cassity, *Defending a Way of Life: An American Community in the Nineteenth Century* (Albany: State University of New York Press, 1989), 128–29; Cassity, "Modernization and Social Crisis," 44; Ware, *The Labor Movement in the United States*, 136. For a brief overview of the Ancient Order of United Workingmen, see Mary Ann Clawson, *Constructing Brotherhood: Class, Gender, and Fraternalism* (Princeton: Princeton University Press, 1989), 140–44.

40. *Marshall Tri-Weekly Herald*, March 3, 5, 1885; *Galveston Daily News*, March 2, 3, 6, 1885; *Missouri Republican*, March 6, 1885.

41. Buchanan, *The Story of a Labor Agitator*, 158–59; *Missouri Republican*, March 6, 1885.

42. Cassity, "Modernization and Social Crisis," 45, 47; *Marshall Tri-Weekly Herald*, March 3, 1885; *Missouri Republican*, March 8, 10, 1885. On March 7, 1885, the *Dallas Daily Herald* reported that coal-chute men were "without pay," "voluntarily" loading passenger engines, and taking care to not obstruct mail or express trains, all policies that helped them to keep the "sympathy of the people."

43. Cassity, "Modernization and Social Crisis," 45–46; *Investigation of Labor Troubles*, 1: iii.

44. *Galveston Daily News*, March 6; *Labor Enquirer*, March 14; Cassity, "Modernization and Social Crisis," 46; *Missouri Republican*, March 16, 1885.

45. *Investigation of Labor Troubles*, 1: iii.

46. *Missouri Republican*, March 11, 1885; *Locomotive Engineer's Monthly Magazine* 19, no. 5 (May 1885), 276.

47. Chandler, "The Knights of Labor and the Southwestern Strikes," 30; *St. Louis Globe-Democrat*, March 9, 1885; *Missouri Republican*, March 7, 1885.

48. Buchanan, *The Story of a Labor Agitator*, 142.

49. Chandler, "The Knights of Labor and the Southwestern Strikes," 26.

50. *St. Louis Globe-Democrat*, March 10, 1885; *Missouri Republican*, March 10, 11, 1885; *Labor Enquirer*, March 21, 1885.

51. Buchanan, *The Story of a Labor Agitator*, 144–48; *Labor Enquirer*, March 21, 1885.

52. *Missouri Republican*, March 7, 1885; *Marshall Tri-Weekly Herald*, March 5, 1885; Cassity, "Modernization and Social Crisis," 45–46.

53. *Missouri Republican*, March 12, 1885; *Galveston Daily News*, March 2, 1885; *Marshall Tri-Weekly Herald*, March 12, 1885.

54. *Investigation of Labor Troubles*, 1: iii; *Missouri Republican*, March 8, 11, 1885.

55. *Missouri Republican*, March 10, 11, 13, 1885

56. *Missouri Republican*, March 8, 9, 11, 14, 1885.

57. *Marshall Tri-Weekly Herald*, March 5, 1885; *Missouri Republican*, March 10, 1885.

58. *Missouri Republican*, March 9, 10, 12, 1885; *Marshall Tri-Weekly Herald*, March 9, 1885; Cassity, "Modernization and Social Crisis," 47; Maier, "The Realization of My Boyhood Dream," Box 2E302, Folder 2, pp. 8–9, LMTC.

59. Cassity, *Defending a Way of Life*, 108.

60. *St. Louis Globe-Democrat*, March 9, 1885; Forsythe, "The Gould Strikes and Missouri Newspaper Opinion," 45–47.

61. *Marshall Tri-Weekly Herald*, February 2, 21, 1885; *Missouri Republican*, February 17, 1885.

62. In *Defending a Way of Life: An American Community in the Nineteenth Century*, and "Modernization and Social Crisis: The Knights of Labor and a Midwest Community, 1885–1886," Michael J. Cassity relies upon this explanation and also the argument that Sedalia's citizens resented the railroad's and state's violations of local authority. See Cassity, *Defending a Way of Life*, 97–114.

63. *Missouri Republican*, March 8, 10, 11, 1885; *Dallas Daily Herald*, March 11, 1885; *St. Louis Republican*, March 7; *Marshall Tri-Weekly Herald*, March 7, 1885.

64. Cassity, *Defending a Way of Life*, 108; *Investigation of Labor Troubles*, 1: iii. Similarly, Denison officials could not arrest strikers, though some had entered the yard and locked up the engines, because no one would testify against them. See *Labor Enquirer*, March 14, 1885.

65. *Missouri Republican*, March 11, 1885.

66. Cassity, "Modernization and Social Crisis," 45.

67. *St. Louis Globe-Democrat*, March 10, 1885; *Labor Enquirer*, March 14, 1885.

68. *Marshall Tri-Weekly Herald*, March 7, 1885; *Missouri Republican*, March 10, 1885; *Labor Enquirer*, March 21, 1885. Judge Kelso is probably David Kelso, who testified before the congressional committee in Parsons in 1886. See *Investigation of Labor Troubles*, 1: 29.

69. *Missouri Republican*, March 12, 14, 1885.

70. *Galveston Daily News*, March 6, 1885; Forsythe, "The Gould Strikes and Missouri Newspaper Opinion," 103–4.

71. A number of secret meetings were held between February 26 and March 6, 1885. Wabash men in Springfield and Moberly assembled in secret, as did railroad workers in Sedalia on March 6 and Parsons strikers on March 10. See *Galveston Daily News*, February 28, 1885; Forsythe, "The Gould Strikes and Missouri Newspaper Opinion," 103–4; Cassity, "Modernization and Social Crisis," 44; and *Missouri Republican*, March 5, 10, 1885. Strikers, "neatly dressed," organized, and "entirely sober," apparently led the mass meetings in Sedalia. See *Missouri Republican*, March 13, 1885.

72. *Missouri Republican*, March 7, 9, 1885; *Dallas Daily Herald*, March 11, 1885.

73. *Missouri Republican*, March. 11, 1885; *Labor Enquirer*, March 14, 1885.

74. *Missouri Republican*, March 11, 1885.

75. *Missouri Republican*, March 16, 1885.

76. *Missouri Republican*, March 16, 1885.

77. *Missouri Republican*, March 10, 1885; *Dallas Daily Herald*, March 11, 1885. No calls were made upon troops in Texas but Gov. Martin used state militia against strikers in Kansas. See *Report of the Adjutant General*, December 1886, and Forsythe, "The Gould Strikes and Missouri Newspaper Opinion," 50.

78. *Missouri Republican*, March 10, 1885; Cassity, *Defending a Way of Life*, 109.

79. Cassity, *Defending a Way of Life*, 109; *Missouri Republican*, March 12, 1885; Jamison quoted in Forsythe, "The Gould Strikes and Missouri Newspaper Opinion," 18; *Investigation of Labor Troubles*, 1: iii.

80. *Labor Enquirer*, March 14, 1885; Chandler, "The Knights of Labor and the Southwestern Strikes," 26.

81. *Investigation of Labor Troubles*, 1: iv; *Missouri Republican*, March 12, 16, 17, 1885; Forsythe, "The Gould Strikes and Missouri Newspaper Opinion," 17; *Marshall Tri-Weekly Herald*, March 17, 1885.

82. *Missouri Republican*, March 16, 1885; *Locomotive Engineer's Monthly Journal* 19, no. 5 (May 1885), 275–76; Stromquist, *Generation of Boomers*, 133.

Chapter 5

1. Edward Ayers, *Southern Crossing: A History of the American South, 1877–1906* (New York: Oxford University Press, 1995), 83; Ruth Allen, *The Great Southwest Strike* (Austin: University of Texas, Bureau of Research in the Social Sciences, 1942), 25; Jonathan Garlock, *Guide to the Local Assemblies of the Knights of Labor* (Westport: Greenwood Press, 1982), 86–89, 130–31, 138–39, 148–49, 240–59, 491–507.

2. Charles Maier to Ruth Allen, November 18, 1939, and "The Realization of My Boyhood Dream," 9–10, Box 2E302, Folder 2, Labor Movement in Texas Collection, Center for American History, University of Texas at Austin (cited hereafter as LMTC); Michael Cassity, "Modernization and Social Crisis: The Knights of Labor and a Midwest Community, 1885–1886," *Journal of American History* 66, no. 1 (March 1979), 48; W. H. Blackshaw to Terence Powderly, November 9, 1885, Incoming Correspondence, Reel 11, Terence Vincent Powderly Papers, American Catholic History Research Center and University Archives, Catholic University, Washington (cited hereafter as TVPP); George Downs to Terence Powderly, November 11, 1885, Reel 11, Incoming Correspondence, TVPP; Letter to Terence Powderly, December 19, 1885, Reel 12, Incoming Correspondence, TVPP; P. A. McMeany to Terence Powderly, June 27, 1885, Incoming Correspondence, Reel 10, TVPP.

3. "Proceedings of the State Convention of the Knights of Labor," Fort Worth, Texas, July 20–22, 1885 (Austin, Tex.: N. P. Houx, 1885), pp. 3, 9, Reel 66, TVPP; Garlock, *Guide to the Local Assemblies of the Knights of Labor*, 491–507.

4. For references to these presses, see *Journal of United Labor*, August 25, December 25, 1885; *Labor Enquirer*, March 21; and "Proceedings of the State Convention of the Knights of Labor," Fort Worth, Texas, July 20–22, 1885 (Austin, TX: N.P. Houx, 1885), pp. 3, 9, Reel 66, TVPP; Illinois, Bureau of Labor Statistics of Illinois, *Fourth Biennial Report of the Bureau of Labor Statistics of Illinois*, 1886 (Springfield: H. W. Rokker, 1886), 191.

5. *Marshall Tri-Weekly Herald*, June 30, July 7, 1885.

6. Garlock, *Guide to the Local Assemblies of the Knights of Labor*, 86–89, 130–31, 138–39, 148–49, 240–59, 491–507; Craig Phelan, *Grand Master Workman: Terence Powderly and the Knights of Labor* (Westport: Greenwood Press, 2000), 158 (quotation); *Fourth Biennial Report of the Bureau of Labor Statistics of Illinois*, 1886, 190. Garlock notes that a "mixed" assembly may have included an assembly in which members from one trade represented a minority, because the Knights employed the "rule of ten." This said that a mixed assembly was one that "lacked ten members in any one occupation or else included more than ten members

in each of at least two trades." The dates given for the formation of local assemblies between 1880 and 1886 are more reliable. See Garlock, xviii, xxiii.

7. Garlock, *Guide to the Local Assemblies of the Knights of Labor*, 86–89, 130–31, 138–39, 148–49, 240–59, 491–507.

8. Garlock, *Guide to the Local Assemblies of the Knights of Labor*, xxi–xxii. One historian has speculated that due to the dangers of organizing, blacks often masked their locals as fraternal orders with names such as "Franklin," "Washington," or "Protective." See Robert Weir, *Beyond Labor's Veil: The Culture of the Knights of Labor* (University Park: Pennsylvania University Press, 1996), 49–51.

9. Garlock, *Guide to the Local Assemblies of the Knights of Labor*, 139, 246, 247, 249, 251, 255, 491–95; Maier, "Realization of My Boyhood Dream," 10, Box 2E302, Folder 2, LMTC.

10. *Marshall Tri-Weekly Herald*, March 5, 1885; *Missouri Republican*, March 7, 12, 1885.

11. Maier, "Realization of My Boyhood Dream," 10, Box 2E302, Folder 2, LMTC; *Missouri Republican*, March 12, 17, 1885.

12. Leon Fink, *Workingmen's Democracy: The Knights of Labor and American Politics* (Urbana: University of Illinois Press, 1983), 14; Nick Salvatore, *Eugene V. Debs: Citizen and Socialist* (Chicago: University of Illinois Press, 1982), 58–59; Shelton Stromquist, *A Generation of Boomers: The Pattern of Railroad Labor Conflict in Nineteenth Century America* (Chicago: University of Illinois Press, 1987), 64–65; Executive Board, Knights Local Assembly #2932 of Ellis, Kansas, "A Plea for Federation," 1885, Reel 10, TVPP.

13. Stromquist, *A Generation of Boomers*, 64–65; United States House of Representatives, *Investigation of Labor Troubles in Missouri, Arkansas, Kansas, Texas, and Illinois*, 2 Parts, 1887, 49th Congress, 2nd Session, Report No. 4174, I, 434–88.

14. Fink, *Workingmen's Democracy*, 6–7.

15. *St. Louis Globe-Democrat*, March 10, 1885; *Journal of United Labor*, June 25, 1885.

16. Fink, *Workingmen's Democracy*, 12; Foner, *Reconstruction*, 479.

17. J. B. Sawyer to Terence Powderly, November 1885, 11, Incoming Correspondence, TVPP.

18. *Marshall Tri-Weekly Herald*, July 7, 1885.

19. *Marshall Tri-Weekly Herald*, March 28, 1885.

20. Clifford Farrington, *Biracial Unions on Galveston's Waterfront, 1865–1925* (Austin: Texas State Historical Association, 2007), 59–62, 67–72.

21. Philip S. Foner and Ronald L. Lewis, eds., *The Black Worker: A Documentary History from Colonial Times to the Present, Vol. III, The Black Worker During the Era of the Knights of Labor* (Philadelphia: Temple University Press, 1978), 72, 242–43.

22. Two excellent sources on the Richmond convention are Fink's *Workingmen's Democracy* and Peter Rachleff's *Black Labor in the South* (Philadelphia: Temple University Press, 1984).

23. Foner, *The Black Worker*, 243, 252–53; Terence Powderly to Day Frayer Tomson of Hot Springs, Arkansas, January 28, 1886, Outgoing Correspondence, Reel 47, pp. 18–19, TVPP.

24. Eric Arnesen, "Following the Color Line of Labor: Black Workers and the Labor Movement Before 1930," *Radical History Review* (Winter 1993), 68; D. Smith to Terence Powderly, November 15, 1885, Reel 11, Incoming Correspondence, TVPP.

25. "Proceedings of the State Convention of the Knights of Labor," Fort Worth, Texas, July 20–22, 27; 1885, Foner, *The Black Worker*, 104, 256–59; *Journal of United Labor*, April 10, 1885.

26. Ayers, *Promise of the New South*, 273–74. Biracialism among Alabama coal miners took on a similarly sectional tone in that they made a distinction between regional and northern capital. See Letwin, *The Challenge of Interracial Unionism*, 75. The sectional theme also surfaced in the Memphis, Louisville, and Nashville newspapers during the 1877 strike, which "took the opportunities presented by widespread violence across the North in July 1877 to proclaim the superiority and righteousness of their own region." A series of labor protests in all three cities undermined the presses' claim that southern labor was content and pliant, however. See Steven J. Hoffman, "Looking North: A Mid-South Perspective on the Great Strike," in David O. Stowell, *Streets, Railroads, and the Great Strike of 1877* (Chicago: University of Chicago Press, 1999), 105–35.

27. *Dallas Daily Herald*, March 14, 1885.

28. Alwyn Barr, *Black Texans: A History of African Americans in Texas, 1528–1995* (Norman: University of Oklahoma Press, 1996), 72–73; Gerald T. Hanson and Carl H. Moneyhon, *Historical Atlas of Arkansas* (Norman: University of Oklahoma Press, 1989), 135.

29. Eric Arnesen makes this point regarding black participation in pre–Congress of Industrial Organizations trade unions in "Following the Color Line of Labor," 69–70.

30. Foner, *The Black Worker*, 52, 104, 105; Melton Alonza McLaurin, *The Knights of Labor in the South* (Westport: Greenwood Press, 1978), 138–40; Foner, *Reconstruction*, 479.

31. Clawson, *Constructing Brotherhood: Class, Gender, and Fraternalism* (Princeton: Princeton University Press, 1989), 123, 131–35; Weir, *Beyond Labor's Veil*, 49–51; Foner, *The Black Worker*, 104, 256–59; Peter Rachleff, *Black Labor in Richmond, 1865–1890* (Urbana: University of Illinois Press, 1989), 24–33.

32. Foner, *The Black Worker: Vol. 3*, 72, 242–43, 252–53.

33. "An Address," Reel 10, TVPP; *Investigation of Labor Troubles*, I, 378, 553; *Marshall Tri-Weekly Herald*, March 3, 1885 (quotation).

34. Clawson, *Constructing Brotherhood*, 195, 200; Fink, *Workingmen's Democracy*, 12–13; Susan Levine, *Labor's True Woman: Carpet Weavers, Industrialization, and Labor Reform in the Gilded Age* (Philadelphia: Temple University Press, 1984), 10; Phelan, *Grand Master Workman*, 156.

35. *Austin American Statesmen*, October 31, 1885, Box 2E189, LMTC; *Journal of United Labor*, June 25, 1885; Cassity, "Modernization and Social Crisis," 52. Both Clawson and Fink understandably view the Knights as a fraternal order notwithstanding its female membership. See Clawson, *Constructing Brotherhood*, 4–6.

36. *Missouri Republican*, February 20, March 2, 4, 1885; *Labor Enquirer*, March 28, 1885.

37. Clawson, *Constructing Brotherhood*, 185; *Missouri Republican*, March 3, 4, 1885; *Labor Enquirer*, March 14, 1885.

38. Weir, *Beyond Labor's Veil*, 52–54; Clawson, *Constructing Brotherhood*, 124; *Journal of United Labor*, October 25, 1885.

39. *St. Louis Post-Dispatch*, March 7, 10, 1885; Philip S. Foner, *The Great Labor Uprising of 1877* (New York: Monad Press, 1977), 154–55.

40. "An Address," Reel 10, TVPP, *Investigation of Labor Troubles*, I, 414 (first quotation), 421, 536–37 (second quotation).

41. Jerry Wayne Chandler, "The Knights of Labor and the Southwestern Strike" (master's thesis, Florida State University, 1970), 43; Phelan, *Grand Master Workman*, 43, 158; "Strikers' Handbill" in Allen, *The Great Southwest Strike* (first quotation), 31; Capital Assembly to Terence Powderly, June 17, 1885, Incoming Correspondence, Reel 10, TVPP (second quotation).

42. Phelan, *Grand Master Workman*, 158; Terence Powderly to J. T. Brown, June 21, 1885, Outgoing Correspondence, Reel 47, TVPP; Allen, *The Great Southwest Strike*, 30.

43. Terence Powderly to J. T. Brown, June 21, 1885, Outgoing Correspondence, Reel 47, TVPP.

44. Terence Powderly to George P. Shedd, June 25, 1885, Outgoing Correspondence, Reel 47, TVPP.

45. L. A. #2455 to Terence Powderly, July 20, 1885, Incoming Correspondence, Reel 10, TVPP.

46. Phelan, *Grand Master Workman*, 159.

47. Edwin James Forsythe, "The Gould Strikes and Missouri Newspaper Opinion" (master's thesis: University of Missouri, 1949), 53; Allen, *The Great Southwest Strike*, 33; telegram to Terence Powderly, July 16, 1885, Incoming Correspondence, Reel 10, TVPP; Phelan, *Grand Master Workman*, 159.

48. "An Address," Incoming Correspondence, Reel 10, TVPP; Phelan, *Grand Master Workman*, 159.

49. "An Address," Incoming Correspondence, Reel 10, TVPP.

50. *Investigation of Labor Troubles*, I, v; Phelan, *Grand Master Workman*, 160.

51. *Investigation of Labor Troubles*, I, vi; John R. Commons et al., *History of Labour in the United States*, vol. 2 (New York: Macmillan, 1918), 369.

52. *Investigation of Labor Troubles*, I, vi; Phelan, *Grand Master Workman*, 160; Chandler, "The Knights of Labor and the Southwestern Strike," 46–47; Joseph Buchanan, *Story of a Labor Agitator* (New York: Outlook, 1903), 219–28.

53. Chandler, "The Knights of Labor and the Southwestern Strike," 49; Buchanan, *Story of a Labor Agitator*, 216, 218; Phelan, *Grand Master Workman*, 160; O. R. Lakey to Terence Powderly, August 22, 1885, Incoming Correspondence, Reel 10, TVPP.

54. Chandler, "The Knights of Labor and the Southwestern Strike," 50–51; *Investigation of Labor Troubles*, I, vi–vii.

55. Forsythe, "The Gould Strikes and Missouri Newspaper Opinion," 24; Terence Powderly to Jay Gould, August 29, 1885, Outgoing Correspondence, Reel 10, TVPP.

56. Allen *The Great Southwest Strike*, 33; *Investigation of Labor Troubles*, I, x.

57. Phelan, *Grand Master Workman*, 161; Weir, *Beyond Labor's Veil*, 11–12.

58. R. G. Gruellick to Terence Powderly, September 17, 1885, and Letter to Terence Powderly, September 23, 1885, Incoming Correspondence, Reel 10, TVPP; Allen, *The Great Southwest Strike*, 25.

59. *Dallas Morning News*, October 4, 1885.

60. Terence Powderly to Dan Frazier Tomson, January 28, 1886, pp. 18–19, Letterpress Book, Vol. 15, Jan. 22, 1886–Sept. 24, 1886, Outgoing Correspondence, Reel 47, TVPP (first quotation); Phelan, *Grand Master Workman*, 161 (second quotation), 172–75.

61. M. Griffiths to Terence Powderly, October 28, 1885, Incoming Correspondence, Reel 10, TVPP. I found relatively little hostility to Powderly among participants in the 1886 Southwest Strike.

62. Allen, *The Great Southwest Strike*, 25; *Investigation of Labor Troubles*, I, 437, 481; *Investigation of Labor Troubles*, II, 202, 437, 457; Cassity, "Modernization and Social Crisis," 48.

63. Cassity, "Modernization and Social Crisis," 48; *Investigation of Labor Troubles*, I, 250–52. Cassity contends that Drew was in a "position of only limited authority" but was "expected to speak from a broad mandate." Therefore, in heeding his instructions, "the

railroad company had essentially created a centralized worker bargaining agency and imposed it on the workers." While the company's action may have been a factor in legitimizing workers' leadership, Cassity overstates the situation considerably by underestimating the larger trend toward consolidation among discontented railroaders.

64. Forsythe, "The Gould Strikes and Missouri Newspaper Opinion," 57, 59.

65. *Lippincott's Magazine* 38 (June 1886), 618–27.

Chapter 6

1. Ruth Allen, *The Great Southwest Strike* (Austin: University of Texas, Bureau of Research in the Social Sciences, 1942), 9–10, 56–61, 137; Craig Phelan, *Grand Master Workman: Terence Powderly and the Knights of Labor* (Westport: Greenwood Press, 2000), 179, 183.

2. Dundee Old Parish Registers and Dundee Street Directories, 1818–1861, Dundee Library and Information Services, Local History Centre, Dundee, UK.

3. Louise Miskell, Christopher A. Whatley, and Bob Harris, eds., *Victorian Dundee, Image and Realities* (East Lothian, Scotland: Tuckwell Press, 2000), 3, 38–39, 49.

4. United States House of Representatives, *Investigation of Labor Troubles in Missouri, Arkansas, Kansas, Texas, and Illinois*, 2 Parts, 1887, 49th Congress, 2nd Session, Report No. 4174, II, 436.

5. No record of Irons's father-in-law has surfaced. The only information on his brother-in-law, with whom Martin also worked, is that his first name was John and that he and Martin went into the restaurant business together in Cincinnati. One John Brown lived in the town of Richmond in Ray County, Missouri, in 1880. He hailed from Scotland and was old enough (fifty-seven) to have been Mary's brother, but there the trail on the Brown family ends. U.S. Department of the Interior, Census Office, Tenth Census of the United States, 1880, manuscripts via Heritage Quest Online, http://persi.heritagequestonline.com/hqoweb/library/do/census/search/basic, *New York Times*, May 10, 1886; *Investigation of Labor Troubles*, II, 437.

6. The advertisements can be found in the 1875 and 1876 issues of the local Richmond newspapers in the Ray County Library, Richmond, Missouri.

7. E. T. Behrens, "Dedication to Martin Irons," September 1907, Box 2E302, Folder 13, Labor Movement in Texas Collection, Center for American History, University of Texas at Austin (cited hereafter as LMTC).

8. *Investigation of Labor Troubles*, II, 437. The local was #3476.

9. Allen, *Great Southwest Strike*, 25; *Investigation of Labor Troubles*, II, 202, 437, 457; Knights of Labor, *By-Laws of District Assembly No. 101* (Sedalia, Missouri, 1886).

10. *Lippincott's Magazine*, June 1886; *Investigation of Labor Troubles*, II, 435, 467.

11. *Investigation of Labor Troubles*, II, 440–41.

12. Letter from Moberly, Missouri, to Terence Powderly, September 23, 1885, and Jay Gould to Terence Powderly, October 11, 1885, Incoming Correspondence, Reel 10, Terence Vincent Powderly Papers (cited hereafter as TVPP).

13. Knight of Local #3841 to Terence Powderly, Nov. 3, 1885, Incoming Correspondence, Reel 10, TVPP.

14. Railroad officials disputed a number of grievances before the congressional committee (*Investigation of Labor Troubles*, I, 365–69, for example), but did not address the specific issues outlined here.

15. *Investigation of Labor Troubles*, I, 378, 434–35, 448, 466–67.

16. *Investigation of Labor Troubles*, I, 553.

17. *Investigation of Labor Troubles*, I, 218–19, 225–26, 378–79, 434–35, 444–45, 448, 450–451, 478–79, 485–86, 553–56.

18. *Investigation of Labor Troubles*, I, 479 (first quotation), 480–81 (second quotation).

19. *Investigation of Labor Troubles*, I, 217, 220 (first quotation), 449 (second quotation).

20. *Investigation of Labor Troubles*, I, 434–35, 444, 445, 447, 448, 464, 474.

21. *Investigation of Labor Troubles*, I, 220 (first quotation), 221 (second quotation).

22. *Investigation of Labor Troubles*, I, 561 (first quotation), 445 (second quotation).

23. See, for instance, testimony taken in Texas: *Investigation of Labor Troubles*, II, 116–17, 123–24, 131, 134–35, 138, 232, 257, 414.

24. *Investigation of Labor Troubles*, I, 452–53.

25. *Investigation of Labor Troubles*, I, 468–69 (quotation), II, 445.

26. James A. Ward, *The Railroads and the Character of America, 1820–1887* (Knoxville: University of Tennessee Press, 1986), 154–55; *Investigation of Labor Troubles*, I, 455 (first quotation), II, 445 (second quotation).

27. *Investigation of Labor Troubles*, I, 455, 463, 559.

28. *Investigation of Labor Troubles*, I, 334–336.

29. *Investigation of Labor Troubles*, I, 434–35, 438; II, 258–59, 439. The executive board of the Knights of Labor in this case was a precursor to the executive board that Southwest system employees formed a little over a month later in September 1885 (see *Investigation of Labor Troubles*, I, 434).

30. *Investigation of Labor Troubles*, I, 434–35.

31. *Investigation of Labor Troubles*, I, 378, 553.

32. Allen, *The Great Southwest Strike*, 45–46; *Investigation of Labor Troubles*, I, xi, 444, 481. DA 101 delegate John Delay testified that about three thousand members voted in favor of the propositions at a time when membership stood at between thirty-five hundred and five thousand.

33. *Investigation of Labor Troubles*, I, 482 (first quotation); *St. Louis Post-Dispatch*, March 11, 1886 (second quotation).

34. *Investigation of Labor Troubles*, II, 438, 440 (quotation); Michael J. Cassity, "Modernization and Social Crisis: The Knights of Labor and a Midwest Community, 1885–1886," *Journal of American History* 66: 1 (March 1979), 60.

35. *Investigation of Labor Troubles*, I, 302, 397.

36. *Investigation of Labor Troubles*, I, 397.

37. *Investigation of Labor Troubles*, II, 172, 173, 180.

38. *St. Louis Post-Dispatch*, January 30, 1886.

39. E. T. Behrens to Ruth Allen, Box 2E302, Folder 11, LMTC; *Investigation of Labor Troubles*, I, 337, 440 (2nd quotation), II, 439–41.

40. *Investigation of Labor Troubles*, I, 337, 439–41. Sheldon did go to Marshall but only briefly met with Irons.

41. Allen, *The Great Southwest Strike*, 50; *Investigation of Labor Troubles*, II, 176, 441, 445. A striker and friend of Martin Irons later wrote that the vote in favor of the executive board's proposition was nearly unanimous. See E. T. Behrens to Ruth Allen, July 27, 1940, Box 2E302, Folder 11, LMTC.

42. *Investigation of Labor Troubles*, I, 332, 333, 334 (quotation); *Missouri Republican*, March 4, 1886; Allen, *The Great Southwest Strike*, 49.

43. *Investigation of Labor Troubles*, I, 332 (second quotation), II, 441 (first quotation); *St. Louis Post-Dispatch*, March 8, 1886.

44. James Green, *Death in the Haymarket: A Story of Chicago, the First Labor Movement, and the Bombing That Divided Gilded Age America* (Pantheon, 2006), 149–50.

45. *Investigation of Labor Troubles*, I, 332, II, 441 (quotation); *St. Louis Post-Dispatch*, March 5, 6, 1886.

46. Phelan, *Grand Master Workman*, 178–83; Terence Powderly, *The Path I Trod*, Harry J. Carman et al., eds. (New York: Columbia University Press, 1940), 119.

47. Joseph Buchanan, *Story of a Labor Agitator* (New York: Outlook Co., 1903), 224–25.

48. Phelan, *Grand Master Workman*, 184. A similar interpretation can be found in Ware, *The Labor Movement in the United States*, 145–54.

49. Illinois Bureau of Labor, *Statistics of Illinois, Fourth Biennial Report of the Bureau of Labor Statistics of Illinois, 1886* (Springfield: H. W. Rokker, 1886), 396–98; Missouri Bureau of Labor Statistics, *Ninth Annual Report of the Bureau of Labor Statistics of the State of Missouri* (Jefferson City: Office of Bureau of Labor Statistics and Inspection, 1887), 274–77.

50. *Missouri Republican*, March 4, 1886 (first quotation); Letter from Moberly, Missouri, to Powderly, September 23, 1885, Incoming Correspondence, TVVP (second quotation); Buchanan, *Story of a Labor Agitator*, 223 (third quotation).

51. Phelan, *Grand Master Workman*, 179; Chandler, "The Knights of Labor and the Southwestern Strikes," 30; *St. Louis Globe-Democrat*, March 9, 1885; *Missouri Republican*, March 7, 1885; Buchanan, *The Story of a Labor Agitator*, 142.

52. *Investigation of Labor Troubles*, I, 394, 421; *St. Louis Post-Dispatch*, March 6, 8, 1886.

53. *Investigation of Labor Troubles*, I, 371–78, 393–94, 560 (quotation); *Missouri Republican*, March 5, 1886; *St. Louis Post-Dispatch*, March 8, 1886.

54. *St. Louis Post-Dispatch*, March 14, 1886; Shelton Stromquist, *Generation of Boomers: The Pattern of Railroad Labor Conflict in Nineteenth Century America* (Chicago: University of Illinois Press, 1987), 56; Cassity, "Modernization and Social Crisis," 55.

55. *Waco Daily Examiner*, March 9, 1886, quoted in Allen, *The Great Southwest Strike*, 73.

56. *St. Louis Post-Dispatch*, March 6, 8, 10, 1886; Cassity, "Modernization and Social," 55; *Investigation of Labor Troubles*, I, 392, 522–23.

57. *Missouri Republican*, March 11, 1886; *Investigation of Labor Troubles*, I, 185–89; *Journal of United Labor*, April 25, 1885; "Notice to Workingmen" by St. Louis Knights of Labor and Trades Unions, November 29, 1885, Reel 11, TVPP; *St. Louis Post-Dispatch*, March 5, 1886.

58. *Investigation of Labor Troubles*, I, 343, II, 178; *St. Louis Post-Dispatch*, March 10, 1886.

59. *St. Louis Post-Dispatch*, March 8, 10, 1886; *Investigation of Labor Troubles*, I, 499.

60. Edwin James Forsythe, "The Gould Strikes and Missouri Newspaper Opinion," (master's thesis, University of Missouri, 1949), 65–66; *St. Louis Post-Dispatch*, March 6, 10, 11, 12, 1886; *Investigation of Labor Troubles*, I, 441, 522–23.

61. *Investigation of Labor Troubles*, I, 316–17, 330, 372–73, 404; Herbert G. Gutman, "Workers Search for Power: Labor in the Gilded Age," in *Power and Culture: Essays on the American Working Class*, ed. Ira Berlin (New York: New Press, 1987), 70–92.

62. Cassity, "Modernization and Social Crisis," 54, 60.

63. *Investigation of Labor Troubles*, I, 334–36, 342–43.

64. The debate over the role of the frontier in inspiring western-based radicalism among workers has centered on the history of the Industrial Workers of the World. John R. Commons emphasized the ways that the West shaped the labor movement in *History of*

Labour in the United States (New York: Macmillan, 1918–35). For histories that look beyond region to other causal factors, see Melvyn Dubofsky, *We Shall Be All: A History of the Industrial Workers of the World* (1969; reprint ed., Urbana: University of Illinois Press, 1988); Elizabeth Jamison, *All That Glitters: Class, Conflict, and Community in Cripple Creek* (Urbana: University of Illinois Press, 1998); and David Brundage, *The Making of Western Labor Radicalism: Denver's Organized Workers, 1878–1905* (Urbana: University of Illinois Press, 1994).

65. Terence Powderly, *The Path I Trod*, Harry J. Carman et al., eds. (New York: Columbia University Press, 1940), 120–23; Allen, *The Great Southwest Strike*, 56–61. Supporting evidence that the story was not concocted after the fact by Powderly himself can be found in a letter from Terence Powderly to Martin Irons, March 25, 1886, typed copy in Box 2e302, folder 4, LMTC.

66. *Investigation of Labor Troubles*, I, 402 (first quotation), 415–16 (second quotation).

67. *Investigation of Labor Troubles*, I, 339, 370, 371.

68. *New Orleans Times-Democrat*, March 12, 1886, typed copy in Box 3E302, Folder 9, LMTC.

69. *Investigation of Labor Troubles*, I, 438.

70. *St. Louis Post-Dispatch*, March 8, 11, 1886.

71. *St. Louis Post-Dispatch*, March 11, 18, 1886; *Investigation of Labor Troubles*, I, 200; II, 449–50.

72. *Investigation of Labor Troubles*, I, 342–43, 378–79; *St. Louis Post-Dispatch*, March 12, 1886.

73. Michael Cassity, *Defending a Way of Life: An American Community in the Nineteenth Century* (Albany: State University of New York Press, 1989), 110–11, 136–37.

74. Patrick Cassidy to Ruth Allen, February 5, 1941, Box 2E303, LMTC.

75. Quoted in Allesandro Portelli, *The Death of Luigi Trastulli and Other Stories: Form and Meaning in Oral History* (New York: State University of New York Press, 1991), 2.

76. *Investigation of Labor Troubles* II, 75; *John Swinton's Paper*, June 13, 1886. I found no black delegates representing Palestine in the records of the Knights' *1885–1890* General Assembly meetings. Knights of Labor, *Record of Proceedings of the General Assembly of the Knights of Labor* (Reading, PA: The Assembly, 1886) and *Proceedings of the General Assembly of the Knights of Labor of America*, 1887–1913 (Minneapolis, MN: The Assembly). Cassidy may have meant a regional meeting, but I could not locate a record of this.

77. *Investigation of Labor Troubles*, I, 467.

78. *Dallas Daily Herald*, March 14, 1885; *Investigation of Labor Troubles*, I, 378–79.

79. Randolph B. Campbell, *A Southern Community in Crisis: Harrison County, Texas, 1850–1880* (Austin: Texas State Historical Association, 1983); *Marshall Tri-Weekly Herald*, June 25, 1885; Isaac T. Davis, "Interview of Pioneer by Isaac T. Davis, Elkhart, Texas," *American Life Histories: Manuscripts from the Federal Writers' Project, 1936–1940*, http://memory.loc.gov/ammem (accessed Nov. 2005). The 1930s-era interview with Davis repeated many of the details reported in the Marshall paper's 1885 description of the incident.

80. *Fort Worth Gazette*, March 4, 1886.

81. *Investigation of Labor Troubles*, II, 301; *Waco Daily Examiner*, March 26, 1886, and *Austin Statesman*, April 27, 1886, typed copies in Box 2E 303, LMTC; Ruth Allen, *The Great Southwest Strike*, 87.

82. *Investigation of Labor Troubles*, II, 115–17.

83. *Investigation of Labor Troubles*, II, 182; *Dallas Morning News*, March 23, 1886; *Galveston Daily News*, March 5, 9, 12, 13, 27 (quotation), 31, April 1, 10, 27, 1886.

84. Fink, *Workingmen's Democracy*, 150, 171 (quotation).

85. *Fort Worth Gazette*, March 4, 1886; *Galveston Daily News*, March 5, 10, 25, 1886; *Investigation of Labor Troubles*, I, 378–79; II, 104, 159, 165, 206; "Proceedings of First Annual Session at Galveston, District Assembly No. 78," January 1886, pp. 52–53, Reel 66, TVPP.

86. L. L. Foster, *Forgotten Texas Census: First Annual Report of the Agricultural Bureau of the Department of Agriculture, Insurance, Statistics, and History, 1887–88*, ed. Barbara J. Rozek (Austin: Texas State Historical Association, 2001), 290; Edward J. M. Rhoads, "The Chinese in Texas," *Southwestern Historical Quarterly* 81, no. 1 (July 1977), 2, 5–8; *Investigation of Labor Troubles*, II, 206.

87. *St. Louis Globe-Democrat*, March 26, 1886; *Arkansas Gazette*, September 5, 1885; Foster, *Forgotten Texas Census*, 290. While the 1882 Chinese Exclusion Act slowed Chinese immigration to a trickle, the belief that the law was inadequate was widespread. See Erika Lee, *At America's Gates: Chinese Immigration During the Exclusion Era, 1882–1943* (Chapel Hill: University of North Carolina, 2003), 44.

88. Rhoads, "The Chinese in Texas," 10 (quotation); Briggs, *The Archeology of 1882 Labor Camps on the Southern Pacific Railroad*, 34, 198. Similarly, political expediency drove support for the 1882 Exclusion Act among eastern workers. Andrew Gyory, *Closing the Gate: Race, Politics, and the Chinese Exclusion Act* (Chapel Hill: University of North Carolina Press, 1998), 222, 228–29.

89. *Investigation of Labor Troubles*, II, 183–84, 206.

90. *Dallas Morning News*, March 23, 1886.

91. *St. Louis Post-Dispatch*, March 6, 1886; *Investigation of Labor Troubles*, I, 401 (second quotation), 407 (first quotation), 449 (third quotation).

92. *Investigation of Labor Troubles*, I, 343, 438–39, II, 218–19.

93. *Investigation of Labor Troubles*, I, 344, 392.

94. *St. Louis Post-Dispatch*, March 15, 1886; *Labor Enquirer*, March 20, 1886.

95. Donald L. McMurray, "The Legal Ancestry of the Pullman Strike Injunctions," *Industrial and Labor Relations Review* 14, no. 2 (January 1961), 237–39.

96. *St. Louis Post-Dispatch*, March 12, 13, 15, 1886.

97. *Missouri Republican*, March 13, 1886.

98. *Investigation of Labor Troubles*, I, 424–25, 614–15.

99. *Investigation of Labor Troubles*, I, 424–25.

Chapter 7

1. Elliot J. Gorn, *Mother Jones: The Most Dangerous Woman in America* (New York, 2001), 167; Eugene Debs, "Martin Irons, Martyr," December 9, 1900," in *Debs: His Life, Writings, and Speeches* (Girard, Kan., 1908), 273–75; Ruth Allen, *The Great Southwest Strike* (Austin, University of Texas, Bureau of Research in the Social Sciences 1942), 9–10, 56–61, 137; United States House of Representatives, *Investigation of Labor Troubles in Missouri, Arkansas, Kansas, Texas, and Illinois*, 2 Parts, 49th Congress, 2nd session, report. 4174 (Washington, 1887), I, xiii, xiv (first quotation); 622–25, II, 476–77; Michael J. Cassity, "Modernization and Social Crisis: The Knights of Labor and a Midwest

Community, 1885–1886," *Journal of American History* 66 (June 1979): 54, 60; Norman J. Ware, *The Labor Movement in the United States, 1860–1895: A Study in Democracy* (New York, 1964), 100, 147 (second quotation), 181; Craig Phelan, *Grand Master Workman: Terence Powderly and the Knights of Labor* (Westport: Greenwood Press, 2000), 178–83 (third quotation, 180).

2. *St. Louis Post-Dispatch*, March 15, 25, 1886. Eugene Debs, a Brotherhood of Locomotive Firemen leader who edited the *Firemen's Magazine* at this time, was more equivocal in his pronouncements on the strike. See Nick Salvatore, *Eugene V. Debs, Citizen and Socialist* (Urbana: University of Illinois Press, 1984), 69.

3. *Investigation of Labor Troubles* I, 345–47.

4. *Investigation of Labor Troubles*, I, 349–50.

5. Terence Powderly, *The Path I Trod: The Autobiography of Terence V. Powderly*, Harry J. Carman, ed. (New York: Columbia University Press, 1940), 123.

6. *Investigation of Labor Troubles*, I, 371, 372, 375, 376, 392–94; *Labor Enquirer*, March 20, 1886; Bureau of Labor Statistics and Inspection of Missouri, *Official History of the Great Strike of 1886 on the Southwestern Railway System* (Jefferson City: Tribune Printing Co., 1887), 51.

7. *Investigation of Labor Troubles*, II, 152, 383, 387–88. See "This is Your Box" sketch on p. 383.

8. *Investigation of Labor Troubles*, I, 505; Allen, *The Great Southwest Strike*, 155; Michael J. Cassity, *Defending a Way of Life: An American Community in the Nineteenth Century* (Albany, NY: State University of New York Press, 1989), 142.

9. *Investigation of Labor Troubles*, II, 104, 292.

10. *Investigation of Labor Troubles*, II, 305, 348.

11. *Investigation of Labor Troubles*, I, 307–8.

12. *Investigation of Labor Troubles*, I, 350–51.

13. *St. Louis Globe-Democrat*, March 26, 1886.

14. *Investigation of Labor Troubles*, I, 617.

15. *Investigation of Labor Troubles*, I, 400, 415–18, 428. I see little evidence in the Gould-system labor conflict to support Stephen H. Norwood's contention, in *Strikebreaking and Intimidation: Mercenaries and Masculinity in Twentieth-Century America* (Chapel Hill: University of North Carolina Press, 2002), that the strikebreaker represented to the press and public "a new soldier of fortune" who put on "conspicuous display... the more primitive and virile behavior that society increasingly valued in men because of its anxiety about 'overcivilization' and 'overrefinement.'" However, Norwood's focus is the professional strike-breaking business, which flourished during the twentieth century, not the Gilded Age.

16. *Investigation of Labor Troubles*, I, 388.

17. Charles Maier, "The Realization of My Boyhood Dream," pp. 24–26, Box 2E302, Folder 2, Labor Movement in Texas Collection, Center for American History, University of Texas at Austin (hereafter cited as LMTC).

18. *Official History of the Great Strike of 1886*, 51–62; *Investigation of Labor Troubles*, I, 407, 423; Cassity, "Modernization and Social Crisis: 56.

19. Maury Klein, *The Life and Legend of Jay Gould* (Baltimore: Johns Hopkins University Press, 1986), 361–62.

20. Phelan, *Grand Master Workman*, 183; *Official History of the Great Strike of 1886*, 75; *Investigation of Labor Troubles*, I, 361; *Galveston Daily News*, April 2, 1886.

21. *St. Louis Post-Dispatch*, March 24, 26, 1886.

22. *New Orleans Times-Democrat*, March 12, 1886, typed copy in Box 3E302, Folder 9, LMTC; *Investigation of Labor Troubles*, 316, 318–19, 407, 423; *Official History of the Great Strike of 1886*, 51–63; Cassity, "Modernization and Social Crisis," 56.

23. *St. Louis Globe-Democrat*, March 27, 1886; *Investigation of Labor Troubles*, I, vi, 494, 503, 504; John R. Commons, et al., *History of Labour in the United States*, vol. 2 (New York: Macmillan, 1918), 35, 369; James Green, *Death in the Haymarket: A Story of Chicago, the First Labor Movement, and the Bombing That Divided Gilded Age America* (Pantheon, 2006), 145; Herbert G. Gutman, *Power and Culture: Essays on the American Working Class*, Ira Berlin, ed. (New York: New Press, 1987), 346; Leon Fink, *Workingman's Democracy: The Knights of Labor and American Politics* (Urbana: University of Illinois Press, 1985), 226.

24. *St. Louis Globe-Democrat*, March 27, 1886; *Investigation of Labor Troubles*, I, 494, 503, 504.

25. *St. Louis Globe-Democrat*, March 27, 1886; *St. Louis Post-Dispatch*, April 1, 5, 1886; *Investigation of Labor Troubles*, I, 496, 500, 526, 534, 545.

26. *St. Louis Post-Dispatch*, April 13, 1886; *Investigation of Labor Troubles*, I, 488–89, 490, 492.

27. *Investigation of Labor Troubles*, I, 492, 498 (quotations), 525, 544.

28. *Investigation of Labor Troubles*, I, 494 (first quotation), 495 (second quotation), 508 (third quotation).

29. *Investigation of Labor Troubles*, I, 496, (third quotation), 531 (second quotation), 550 (first quotation).

30. *Investigation of Labor Troubles*, I, 496, 564 (third and fourth quotations); *St. Louis Post-Dispatch*, April 1, 1886 (first and second quotations).

31. *Investigation of Labor Troubles*, I, 510 (quotation), 564.

32. *Investigation of Labor Troubles*, I, 489, 497, 512; *St. Louis Post-Dispatch*, April 5, 1886; *Official History of the Great Strike of 1886 on the Southwestern Railway System* (Jefferson City: Tribune Printing Co., 1887), 101 (quotation).

33. *Investigation of Labor Troubles*, I, 511, 533.

34. *Investigation of Labor Troubles*, I, 530.

35. *Investigation of Labor Troubles*, I, 528–29.

36. *Investigation of Labor Troubles*, I, 549–50 (quotation), 530; *St. Louis Post-Dispatch*, April 9, 10, 1886.

37. *Investigation of Labor Troubles*, I, 511, 569–72, 575–84; *St. Louis Post-Dispatch*, April 10, 11, 12, 1886.

38. *Investigation of Labor Troubles*, I, 487; *Official History of the Great Strike of 1886*, 102–3; *St. Louis Post-Dispatch*, April 9 (first quotation), 10, 12 (second quotation), 1886.

39. *Investigation of Labor Troubles*, I, 490, 511, 533; Allen, *The Great Southwest Strike*, 79–80.

40. *St. Louis Post-Dispatch*, April 10, 1886 (first quotation); *Investigation of Labor Troubles*, I, 538 (second quotation).

41. *St. Louis Post-Dispatch*, April 13, 1886 (first quotation); *Investigation of Labor Troubles*, I, 501 (second and third quotations), 523, 529, 530, 533, 534.

42. *Investigation of Labor Troubles*, I, 541.

43. *Investigation of Labor Troubles*, II, 456–57.

44. *Investigation of Labor Troubles*, I, 536–37; quoted in Cassity, *Defending a Way of Life*, 142.

45. Rhodri Jeffreys-Jones, *Violence and Reform in American History* (Franklin Watts, 1978), 45; *Investigation of Labor Troubles*, I, 538–40.

46. *Investigation of Labor Troubles*, I, 540.

47. *Investigation of Labor Troubles*, I, 538–39.

48. *Investigation of Labor Troubles*, I, 493, 494, 503, 505 (quotations), 534.

49. *Investigation of Labor Troubles*, I, 562 (third and fourth quotations), 567 (first quotation). Colonel Smith largely confirmed Joyce on this point. See *Investigation of Labor Troubles*, I, 538–39.

50. *St. Louis Post-Dispatch*, April 1, 1886; *Investigation of Labor Troubles*, I, 539.

51. *Investigation of Labor Troubles*, I, 514.

52. *Investigation of Labor Troubles*, II, 345–46.

53. Melvin Dubofsky, "The Federal Judiciary, Free Labor, and Equal Rights," in *The Pullman Strike and the Crisis of the 1890s: Essays on Labor and Politics*, ed. Richard Schneirov, Shelton Stromquist, Nick Salvatore (Urbana: University of Illinois Press, 1999), 166–68. For a competing view of the relationship between the law and the labor movement, see William Forbath, *Law and the Shaping of the American Labor Movement* (Cambridge: Harvard University Press, 1989).

54. Dubofsky, "The Federal Judiciary, Free Labor, and Equal Rights," 166–68. This thesis grew out of my reading of a chapter on informers in James Sidbury, *Ploughshares into Swords: Race, Rebellion, and Identity in Gabriel's Virginia, 1730–1810* (Cambridge: Cambridge University Press, 1997), 95–117.

55. See, for instance, *Investigation of Labor Troubles*, II, 92, 108, 185, 318, 322.

56. For a discussion of the pitfalls of these approaches to the issue of labor violence, see Elizabeth Jameson, *All That Glitters: Class, Conflict, and Community in Cripple Creek* (Urbana: University of Illinois Press), 233–34.

57. *Investigation of Labor Troubles*, I, 341–43, 384; Kevin Kenny, *Making Sense of the Molly Maguires* (New York: Oxford University Press, 1998), 8–9, describes retributive justice as "a form of collective violence designed to redress violations against a particular understanding of what was socially right and wrong."

58. *Investigation of Labor Troubles*, I, 109.

59. *Fort Worth Gazette*, April 7, 1886.

60. *Investigation of Labor Troubles*, II, 84, 94, 115.

61. *Waco Daily Examiner*, March 27, 30, April 1, 2, 4, 6, 1886; *Fort Worth Gazette*, April 6, 1886.

62. *Investigation of Labor Troubles*, I, 470–71.

63. *St. Louis Globe-Democrat*, March 26, 1886; *Marshall Tri-Weekly Herald*, April 9, 1886.

64. *Investigation of Labor Troubles*, II, 259–60, 352, 406, 408–10; Cassity, *Defending a Way of Life*, 142–43.

65. *Investigation of Labor Troubles*, II, 393.

66. *Investigation of Labor Troubles*, II, 324–28; *Waco Daily Examiner*, April 4, 1886; R. N. Parmley to Ben L. Owens, Mar. 18, 1939, Box 2E301, Folder 7, LMTC. "Killing" an engine involves taking the water out before extinguishing the fire, which burns the engine up beyond repair. One may disable an engine quite easily by removing its set screws (*Investigation of Labor Troubles*, II, 371, 381).

67. David Grimsted, "Antebellum Labor: Violence, Strike and Communal Arbitration," *Journal of Social History* 19, no. 1 (Autumn 1985), 5–28.

68. *Investigation of Labor Troubles*, II, 408.

69. Shelton Stromquist, *Generation of Boomers: The Pattern of Railroad Labor Conflict in Nineteenth-Century America* (Chicago: University of Illinois Press, 1987), 194–97, 224, 227; Walter Licht, *Working For The Railroad* (Princeton: Princeton University Press, 1983). For an overview of the longstanding debate over the relationship between transience and militancy, see Gunther Peck, *Reinventing Free Labor: Padrones and Immigrant Workers in the North American West, 1880–1930* (Cambridge: Cambridge University Press, 2000), 204–6.

70. *Investigation of Labor Troubles*, I, 316, 318–19.

71. *Investigation of Labor Troubles*, I, vi; John R. Commons, et al., *History of Labour in the United States*, vol. 2 (New York: Macmillan, 1918), 369.

72. *Investigation of Labor Troubles*, I, xvi (first quotation), xxiii (second quotation), xxv.

73. *Investigation of Labor Troubles*, I, xiv (second quotation), xxv (first quotation).

74. *Investigation of Labor Troubles*, I, xiii, xiv; 622–25, II, 476–77; *St. Louis Post-Dispatch*, May 10, 1886.

75. *Sedalia Bazoo*, March 27, May 21, 22, 1886, Box 2E302, Folder 10, LMTC.

76. Mary Irons interview, *New York Times*, May 10, 1886; Interview with Mrs. Amelia Brown, May 13, 1886, *Sedalia Bazoo*, Box 2E302, Folder 10, LMTC; U.S Department of the Interior, Census Office, Tenth Census of the United States, 1880; Steven Ruggles, "The Rise of Divorce and Separation in the United States, 1880–1990," *Demography* 34, no. 4 (November 1997), 456.

77. Martin's domestic abuse may have extended to his children. The grandson disclosed to Allen that Irons was arrested in Richmond because he "got rough" with his son (probably Robert). James R. Irons to Ruth Allen, June 27 and October 18, 1937, Box 2E302, Folder 8, LMTC.

78. John Tosh, *The Pursuit of History* (London: Pearson Education Limited, 2002), 158–59, 276, 277. Psychologists have recently developed a typology of male batterers. A "family-only" batterer is more likely to use low levels of violence against family members, to feel remorse, and to be alcohol- and drug-free. They are "the least likely to engage in violence outside the home or to have related legal problems." "Dysphoric/borderline" and "Generally violent/antisocial batterers" are distinguished mainly by the severity of their abuse. They (the latter group more than the former) are more likely to use alcohol or drugs and to "engage in...extrafamilial aggression." See Amy Holtzworth-Munroe and Gregory L. Stuart, "Typologies of Male Batterers: Three Subtypes and the Differences Among Them," *Psychological Bulletin* 116, no. 3 (1994), 476–98. More recent research on batterer typologies has confirmed these findings and has also suggested that these subgroups tend to continue to differ over time. See Amy Holtzworth-Munroe and Jeffrey C. Meehan, "Partner Violence and Men: A Focus on the Male Perpetrator," in William Pinsof and Jay Lebow, eds., *Family Psychology: The Art of the Science* (New York: Oxford University Press, 2005), 169–89, and "Do Subtypes of Maritally Violent Men Continue to Differ Over Time?" *Journal of Counseling and Clinical Psychology* 71, no. 4 (2003), 728–40.

79. H. M. Gitelman, "Perspectives on American Industrial Violence," *Business History Review* 47, no. 1 (Spring 1973), 1–23 (quotation, 17).

80. Robert Michael Smith, *From Blackjacks to Briefcases: A History of Commercialized Strikebreaking and Unionbusting in the United States* (Athens: Ohio University Press, 2003), 7–14; Frank Morn, *Eye That Never Sleeps: A History of the Pinkerton National Detective Agency*

(Bloomington: Indiana University Press, 1982), 95–101; Thomas Furlong, *Fifty Years a Detective* (St. Louis: C. E. Barnett, 1912). The Furlong Secret Service Company later went on to become a major source of intelligence for Porfirio Díaz's regime in Mexico on revolutionary exiles, including Francisco Madero and the magonistas. See William Dirk Raat, "The Diplomacy of Suppression: Los Revoltosos, Mexico, and the United States, 1906–1911," *Hispanic American Historical Review*, 56, No. 4 (Nov. 1976), 544–47. Raat and Smith note that the term "Pinkerton" was often used generically to describe any company-paid guard or detective.

81. Green, *Death in the Haymarket*, 149–50.

82. Allen, *The Great Southwest Strike*, 101; Eugene E. Leach, "Chaining the Tiger: The Mob Stigma and the Working Class, 1863–1894," *Labor History* 35 (Spring 1994), 208–11; *St. Louis Post-Dispatch*, May 6, 11, 1886.

83. *Sedalia Bazoo*, April 21, 1886, in Box 2E302, Folder 5, LMTC.

84. *Jefferson City Daily Tribune*, December 17, 1891, in Box 2E302, Folder 9, LMTC.

85. *Fort Worth Gazette*, October 1, 1894, August 9, 1895, typed copies in Box 2E302, folder 5, LMTC.

86. *Fort Worth Gazette*, October 1, 1894, August 9, 1895, typed copies in Box 2E302, folder 5, LMTC.

87. Gorn, *Mother Jones*, 34–41; Nick Salvatore, "Eugene V. Debs: From Trade Unionist to Socialist," in Melvyn Dubofsky and Warren Van Tine (eds.), *Labor Leaders in America* (Urbana: University of Illinois Press), 89–110.

88. *Texarkana Independent*, April 19, 21, 1886; *Louisville Commercial*, April 21, 1886; *Galveston Daily News*, April 6, 1886.

89. *Arkansas Democrat*, July 6, 8, 1886; *Dallas Morning News*, July 6, 1886; *Arkansas Gazette*, July 7, 10, 1886; William Warren Rogers, "Negro Knights of Labor in Arkansas: A Case Study of the 'Miscellaneous' Strike," *Labor History* 10, no. 3 (Summer 1969), 498–505.

90. *Arkansas Gazette*, July 6, 8, August 31, September 5, 10, 1886; *Tenth Census of the United States*, 1880, for Little Rock, Arkansas; Carl H. Moneyhon, *Arkansas and the New South, 1874–1929* (Fayetteville: University of Arkansas Press, 1997), 3; *Journal of United Labor*, September 25, 1886.

91. *Arkansas Gazette*, September 1, 1886.

92. *Arkansas Democrat*, March 11, 18, April 9, 1886; Matthew Hild, "Labor, Third-Party Politics, and New South Democracy in Arkansas, 1884–1896," *Arkansas Historical Quarterly* 63 (Spring 2004), 31.

93. *Arkansas Gazette*, June 22, August 29, 31, September 7, 1886.

94. *Arkansas Democrat*, August 25, 1886; *Arkansas Gazette*, September 7, 8, 10, 1886; *Daily Texarkana Independent*, September 14, 1886.

95. *Arkansas Gazette*, August 29, 31, September 8, 1886; Moneyhon, *Arkansas and the New South, 1874–1929*, 82, 85–86, 90–91; Hild, "Labor, Third-Party Politics, and New South Democracy in Arkansas," 28, 30, 34, 36, 38; Hanson and Moneyhon, *Historical Atlas of Arkansas*, 135. The Knights represented one of many protest organizations in which black agrarians participated. The networks that emerged from these efforts laid the basis for black populism. See Omar H. Ali, "Black Populism in the New South, 1886–1898" (PhD diss., Columbia University, 2003). Matthew Hild emphasizes the close relationship between the Knights and agrarianism in Texas, Arkansas, and other southern states. He argues that the "Great Southwest Strike" played a pivotal role in galvanizing farmers and workers to cooperate, eventually under the banner of populism. See Matthew Hild, *Greenbackers, Knights of*

Labor, and Populists: Farmer-Labor Insurgency in the Late Nineteenth-Century South (Athens: University of Georgia Press, 2007).

96. George N. Green, "Lone Star Labor," unpublished manuscript, 71–110; Hild, *Greenbackers, Knights of Labor, and Populists*, 84–88; Alwyn Barr, *Reconstruction to Reform: Texas Politics, 1876–1906* (Austin: University of Texas Press, 1971), 98–110; Lawrence Goodwyn, *Democratic Promise: The Populist Moment in America* (New York: Oxford University Press, 1976), 62–63.

97. Alicia E. Rodriquez, "Disfranchisement in Dallas: The Democratic Party and the Suppression of Independent Political Challenges in Dallas, Texas, 1891–1894," *Southwestern Historical Quarterly* 108, no. 1 (July 2004), 46, 52, 63; and "Urban Populism: Challenges to Democratic Party Control in Dallas, Texas: 1887–1900" (PhD diss., University of California, Santa Barbara, 1998), 57; *Dallas Morning News*, April 2, 6, 1887.

98. Rodriquez, "Disfranchisement in Dallas," 50–51.

99. *Dallas Morning News*, April 6, July 5, 1886; *Arkansas Gazette*, August 31, 1886; Rachleff, *Black Labor in Richmond*, 200–1; Fink, *Workingmen's Democracy*, 121, 129, 142; Rodriquez, "Urban Populism," 64–66.

100. Daniel Letwin, *The Challenge of Interracial Unionism: Alabama Coal Miners, 1878–1921* (Chapel Hill: University of North Carolina Press, 1998), 6–7; *Journal of United Labor*, September 25, 1886, 2178; *Dallas Morning News*, July 5, 1886. The following inspired my analysis of the nuances of Tomson's racial views: Gunther Peck, "White Slavery and Whiteness: A Transnational View of the Sources of Working-Class Radicalism and Racism," *Labor: Studies in Working-Class History of the Americas* 1, no. 2 (Summer 2004), 41–63.

101. Joe William Trotter Jr. recommends such a course in "African-American Workers: New Directions in US Labor Historiography," *Labor History* 35 (Fall 1994), 495–523.

Conclusion

1. Charles Brown and H. Roger Grant, *Brownie the Boomer: The Life of Charles P. Brown, an American Railroader* (DeKalb: Northern Illinois University Press, 1991), 219–20.

2. Shelton Stromquist, *A Generation of Boomers: The Pattern of Railroad Labor Conflict in Nineteenth-Century America* (Chicago: University of Illinois Press, 1987), 21.

3. Shelton Stromquist, *Reinventing "The People": The Progressive Movement, the Class Problem, and the Origins of Modern Liberalism* (Urbana: University of Illinois Press, 2006), 18; William E. Forbath, *Law and the Shaping of the American Labor Movement* (Cambridge: Harvard University Press, 1991), 73.

4. Two important articles in this debate are Herbert Hill, "Myth-Making as Labor History: Herbert Gutman and the United Mine Workers of America," *International Journal of Politics, Culture and Society* 2, no. 2 (Winter 1988), 132–200, and Stephen Brier, "In Defense of Gutman: The Union's Case," *International Journal of Politics, Culture, and Society* 3, no. 2 (Winter 1989), 382–95. Eric Arnesen provides an excellent evaluation of this debate in "Up from Exclusion: Black and White Workers, Race, and the State of Labor History," *Reviews in American History* 26, no. 1 (March 1998), 146–74. Examples of the more recent trend are Daniel Letwin, *The Challenge of Interracial Unionism: Alabama Coal Miners, 1878–1921* (Chapel Hill: University of North Carolina Press, 1998) and Eric Arnesen, *Waterfront Workers of New Orleans: Race, Class, and Politics, 1863–1923* (Oxford University Press, New York, 1991).

5. Eric Arnesen, "'Like Banquo's Ghost, It Will Not Down,' The Race Question and the American Railroad Brotherhoods," *American Historical Review* 99, no. 5 (December 1994), 1603; Arnesen, "Up From Exclusion," 146–74.

6. Herbert Gutman, *Power & Culture: Essays on the American Working-Class* (New York: Pantheon Books, 1987), 327.

7. Robert Weir, October 17, 2002, H-Labor Discussion Network, Subject: "Violence and Taking Sides with Capital against Labor."

8. Ian Frazier, "Invaders: Destroying Baghdad," *New Yorker*, April 25, 2005.

Bibliography

Manuscripts

Charlton H. Tandy Papers, 1868–1967. Western Historical Manuscripts Collection, University of Missouri at St. Louis.

John Avery Lomax Family Papers. Center for American History, University of Texas at Austin, Austin, Texas.

Labor Movement in Texas Collection. Center for American History, University of Texas at Austin, Austin, Texas.

"Newspaper Clippings from the St. Louis Republican . . . on the Strikes on the Missouri Pacific Railway, Mar. 7, 1885–May 30, 1886." Center for American History, University of Texas at Austin, Austin, Texas.

Terence Vincent Powderly Papers. Catholic University of America, Washington, D.C.

Government Publications

Kansas. Bureau of Labor and Industrial Statistics. *First Annual Report of the Bureau of Labor and Industrial Statistics.* Topeka: Kansas Publishing House, 1886.

Illinois. Bureau of Labor Statistics of Illinois. *Fourth Biennial Report of the Bureau of Labor Statistics of Illinois, 1886.* Springfield: H. W. Rokker, 1886.

Missouri. Bureau of Labor Statistics and Inspection. *Third Annual Report of the Bureau of Labor Statistics of the State of Missouri.* Jefferson City: Office of Bureau of Labor Statistics and Inspection, 1882.

———. *Fourth Annual Report of the Bureau of Labor Statistics of the State of Missouri.* Jefferson City: Office of Bureau of Labor Statistics and Inspection, 1883.

———. *Ninth Annual Report of the Bureau of Labor Statistics of the State of Missouri.* Jefferson City: Office of Bureau of Labor Statistics and Inspection, 1887.

———. *Official History of the Great Strike of* 1886 *on the Southwestern Railway System.* Jefferson City: Tribune Printing Company, 1887.

U.S. Congress. House. Select Committee on Existing Labor Troubles. *Investigation of Labor Troubles in Missouri, Arkansas, Kansas, Texas, and Illinois.* 2 pts. 49th Congress, 2nd Session, Report No. 4174. Washington, D.C.: Government Printing Office, 1887.

U.S. Department of the Interior. Census Office. *Tenth Census of the United States. Population.* Washington, D.C.: Government Printing Office, 1880.

Trade Union Periodicals

Locomotive Engineer's Monthly Journal
Locomotive Firemen's Magazine
Railroad Brakeman's Journal
Switchmen's Journal

Newspapers

Arkansas Democrat
Arkansas Weekly Mansion, 1883
Benevolent Banner, 1887
Colored Patriot, 1882
Daily Texarkana Independent, 1886
Dallas Daily Herald, 1885
Dallas Mercury, 1885–1886
Fort Worth Gazette, 1882, 1885
Galveston Daily News, 1885–1886
Kansas Herald, 1880
Journal of United Labor, 1884–1886
Labor Enquirer, 1885–1886
Marshall Tri-Weekly Herald, 1885–1886
Missouri Republican, 1885–1886

St. Louis Globe-Democrat, 1885–1886
St. Louis Post-Dispatch, 1883–1886
St. Louis Republican, 1885–1886

City Directories

Directory of the City of Dallas. Galveston: Morrison & Fourmy, 1886.

Butterfield, F. E., and C. M. Rundlett. *Directory of the City of Dallas . . . for the Year 1875.* 1875. Reprint, Dallas: Stone-Inge Books, 1979.

Sholes, Albert Elliot. *Shole's Directory of the City of Little Rock and Argenta, 1883–4.* Little Rock: Mitchell & Bettis, 1883.

Books and Articles—Primary Sources

Adams, B. B. "The Every-Day Life of Railroad Men." In *The American Railway*, by T. C. Clarke. New York: Charles Scribner's Sons, 1889.

American Sylvan Scenes in Winter-Summer Lands along the Lines of the Missouri Pacific Railway. St. Louis: Missouri Pacific Railway, 1888.

Botkin B. A., and Alvin Harlow. *A Treasury of Railroad Folklore.* New York: Crown Publishers, 1953.

Brown, Charles and Roger Hunt. *Brownie the Boomer: The Life of Charles P. Brown, An American Railroader.* Urbana: Northern Illinois University Press, 1991.

Buchanan, Joseph. *The Story of a Labor Agitator.* New York: Outlook Co., 1903.

Foster, L. L. *Forgotten Texas Census: First Annual Report of the Agricultural Bureau of the Department of Agriculture, Insurance, Statistics, and History, 1887–88.* Edited by Barbara J. Rozek. Austin: Texas State Historical Association, 2001.

French, Chauncey Del. *Railroadman.* Norwood, Mass.: Macmillan Company, 1938.

Fulton, Justin D. *Sam Hobart, Locomotive Engineer: A Workingman's Solution of the Labor Problem.* New York: Funk & Wagnalls, 1883.

Furlong, Thomas. *Fifty Years a Detective.* St. Louis: C. E. Barnett, 1912.

George, Charles B. *Forty Years on the Rail: Reminiscences of a Veteran Conductor.* 3rd ed. Chicago: Donelley & Sons, 1887.

Holland Ada M., and C. C. White. *No Quittin' Sense.* Austin: University of Texas Press, 1969.

Immigrant's Guide to Texas: Giving Descriptions of Counties, Towns, and Villages with Valuable Historical and Statistical Information. Dallas: Wilmans Bros., 1888.

Irons, Martin. "My Experience in the Labor Movement." *Lippincott's Magazine* 38 (June 1886): 618–27.

Powderly, Terence. *The Path I Trod: The Autobiography of Terence V. Powderly.* Edited by Harry J. Carman. New York: Columbia University Press, 1940.

Proceedings of the Convention of Colored Men Held in Edwards Opera House, Parsons, Kansas, Apr. 27–28, 1882. Parsons, Kan.: W. B. Avery, 1882.

Rawick, George P., ed. *The American Slave: A Composite Autobiography.* 39 vols. Westport: Greenwood Press, 1972–1979.

Smart, Stephen F. *Colorado Tourist and Illustrated Guide via the Golden Belt Route: The Great Wheat and Corn Producing Region Extending from the Missouri River...to the Rocky Mountain Resorts.* Kansas City: Ramsey, Millet & Hudson, 1879.

Taussig, F. W. "The South-Western Strike of 1886." *Quarterly Journal of Economics* 1, no. 2 (January 1887): 184–222.

Texas Immigrant Aid and Supply Company, Denison, Texas. *Immigrant's Guide to Texas: Showing the Objects of the Texas Immigrant Aid and Supply Company.* St. Louis: C. F. Chamberlin & Co., 1872.

Thomas, J. J. *Fifty Years on the Rail.* New York: Knickerbocker Press, 1912.

Books and Articles—Secondary Sources

Aldrich, Mark. *Death Rode the Rails: American Railroad Accidents and Safety,* 1828–1965. Baltimore: Johns Hopkins University Press, 2006.

Allen, Ruth. *The Great Southwest Strike.* Austin: University of Texas, Bureau of Research in the Social Sciences, 1942.

Ambrose, Stephen E. *Nothing Like It in the World: The Men Who Built the Transcontinental Railroad, 1863–1869.* New York: Simon & Schuster, 2000.

Arnesen, Eric. "'Like Banquo's Ghost, It Will Not Down': The Race Question and the American Railroad Brotherhoods, 1880–1920." *American Historical Review* 99 (December 1994): 1601–33.

———. "Up from Exclusion: Black and White Workers, Race, and the State of Labor History." *Reviews in American History* 26, no. 1 (March 1998): 146–74.

———. *Brotherhoods of Color: Black Railroad Workers and the Struggle for Equality.* Cambridge: Harvard University Press, 2001.

Ayers, Edward L. *The Promise of the New South: Life After Reconstruction.* New York: Oxford University Press, 1992.

———. *Southern Crossing: A History of the American South.* New York: Oxford University Press, 1995.

Baron, Ava. "Gender and Labor History: Learning from the Past, Looking to the Future." In *Work Engendered: Toward a New History of American Labor.* Edited by Ava Baron. Ithaca: Cornell University Press, 1991.

Barr, Alwyn. *Black Texans: A History of African-Americans in Texas, 1528–1995.* Norman: University of Oklahoma Press, 1996.

———. *Reconstruction to Reform: Texas Politics, 1876–1906.* Austin: University of Texas Press, 1971.

Brier, Stephen. "In Defense of Gutman: The Union's Case," *International Journal of Politics, Culture, and Society* 3, no. 2 (Winter 1989): 382–95.

Brodie, James Michael. *Created Equal: The Lives and Ideas of Black American Innovators.* New York: William Morrow, 1993.

Brundage, David. *The Making of Western Labor Radicalism: Denver's Organized Workers, 1878–1905.* Urbana: University of Illinois Press, 1994.

Burbank, David T. *Reign of the Rabble: The Saint Louis General Strike of 1877.* New York: A. M. Kelley, 1966.

Campbell, Randolph B. *A Southern Community in Crisis: Harrison County, Texas, 1850–1880.* Austin: Texas State Historical Association, 1983.

Cassity, Michael. *Defending a Way of Life: An American Community in the Nineteenth Century.* Albany: State University of New York Press, 1989.

———. "Modernization and Social Crisis: The Knights of Labor and a Midwest Community, 1885–1886." *Journal of American History* 66 (June 1979): 41–61.

Clawson, Mary Ann. *Constructing Brotherhood: Class, Gender, and Fraternalism.* Princeton: Princeton University Press, 1989.

Cohen, William. *At Freedom's Edge: Black Mobility and the Southern White Quest for Racial Control, 1861–1915.* Baton Rouge: Louisiana State University Press, 1991.

Commons, John R., David J. Saposs, Helen L. Sumner, E. B. Mittelman, H. E. Hoagland, John B. Andrews, and Selig Perlman. *History of Labour in the United States.* 4 vols. New York: Macmillan, 1918–35.

Corbett, Katharine T., and Howard S. Miller. *Saint Louis in the Gilded Age.* St. Louis: Missouri Historical Society Press, 1993.

Curtis, Susan. *Dancing to a Black Man's Tune: The Life of Scott Joplin.* Columbia: University of Missouri Press, 1994.

Dubofsky, Melvyn *We Shall Be All: A History of the Industrial Workers of the World.* 1969. Urbana: University of Illinois Press, 1988.

Ducker, James H. *Men of the Steel Rails: Workers on the Atchison, Topeka & Santa Fe Railroad, 1869–1900.* Lincoln: University of Nebraska Press, 1983.

Fink, Leon. *Workingmen's Democracy: The Knights of Labor and American Politics.* Urbana: University of Illinois Press, 1983.

Foley, Neil. *The White Scourge: Mexicans, Blacks, and Whites in Texas Cotton Culture.* Berkeley: University of California Press, 1997.

Forbath, William. *Law and the Shaping of the American Labor Movement.* Cambridge: Harvard University Press, 1989.

Foner, Eric. *Reconstruction: America's Unfinished Revolution, 1863–1877.* New York: Harper & Row, 1988.

———. *The Story of American Freedom.* New York: W. W. Norton, 1998.

Foner, Philip S. *The Great Labor Uprising of* 1877. New York: Monad Press, 1977.

Foner, Philip S., and Ronald L. Lewis, eds. *The Black Worker: A Documentary History from Colonial Times to the Present.* Vol. 3, *The Black Worker During the Era of the Knights of Labor.* Philadelphia: Temple University Press, 1978.

Franklin, John Hope. *Reconstruction After the Civil War.* Chicago: University of Chicago Press, 1961.

Garlock, Jonathan. *Guide to the Local Assemblies of the Knights of Labor.* Westport: Greenwood Press, 1982.

Goodwyn, Lawrence. *The Populist Moment: A Short History of the Agrarian Revolt in America.* New York: Oxford University Press, 1978.

Gordon, Fon Louise. *Caste and Class: The Black Experience in Arkansas,* 1880–1920. Athens: University of Georgia Press, 1995.

Gorn, Elliot. *Mother Jones: The Most Dangerous Woman in America.* New York: Hill and Wang, 2001.

Grant, H. Roger. *"Follow the Flag": A History of the Wabash Railway Company.* DeKalb: Northern Illinois University Press, 2004.

Green, James. *Death in the Haymarket: A Story of Chicago, the First Labor Movement, and the Bombing That Divided Gilded Age America.* New York: Pantheon, 2006.

Grimsted, David. "Ante-bellum Labor: Violence, Strike, and Communal Arbitration." *Journal of Social History* 19, no. 1 (Autumn 1985): 5–28.

Grob, Gerald N. *Workers and Utopia: A Study of Ideological Conflict in the American Labor Movement, 1865–1900.* Chicago: Quadrangle Paperbacks, 1961.

Gutman, Herbert G. *Power and Culture: Essays on the American Working Class.* Edited by Ira Berlin. New York: New Press, 1987.

Gyory, Andrew. *Closing the Gate: Race, Politics, and the Chinese Exclusion Act.* Chapel Hill: University of North Carolina Press, 1998.

Hansen, Bradley. "The People's Welfare and the Origins of Corporate Reorganization: The Wabash Receivership Reconsidered." *Business History Review* 74, no. 3 (Winter 2000): 377–405.

Hazel, Michael V., ed. *Dallas Reconsidered: Essays in Local History.* Dallas: Three Forks Press, 1995.

Higbie, Frank Tobias. *Indispensable Outcasts: Hobo Workers and Community in the American Midwest, 1880–1930.* Urbana: University of Illinois Press, 2003.

Hild, Matthew. *Greenbackers, Knights of Labor, and Populists: Farmer-Labor Insurgency in the Late Nineteenth-Century South.* Athens: University of Georgia Press, 2007.

———. "Labor, Third-Party Politics, and New South Democracy in Arkansas, 1884–1896." *Arkansas Historical Quarterly* 63 (Spring 2004): 24–43.

———. "Organizing Across the Color Line: The Knights of Labor and Black Recruitment Efforts in Small-Town Georgia." *Georgia Historical Quarterly* 81 (Summer 1997): 287–310.

Hill, Herbert. "Myth-Making as Labor History: Herbert Gutman and the United Mine Workers of America." *International Journal of Politics, Culture and Society* 2, no. 2 (Winter 1988): 132–200.

Jamison, Elizabeth. *All That Glitters: Class, Conflict, and Community in Cripple Creek.* Urbana: University of Illinois Press, 1998.

Jeffreys-Jones, Rhodri. *Violence and Reform in American History.* New York: Franklin Watts, 1978.

Kelley, Robin G. "'We Are Not What We Seem': Rethinking Black Working-Class Opposition in the Jim Crow South." *Journal of American History* 80, no. 1 (June 1993): 75–112.

Kenny, Kevin. *The American Irish: A History.* Essex: Pearson Education Limited, 2000.

———. *Making Sense of the Molly Maguires.* New York: Oxford University Press, 1998.

Klein, Maury. *The Life and Legend of Jay Gould.* Baltimore: Johns Hopkins University Press, 1986.

Leach, Eugene E. "Chaining the Tiger: The Mob Stigma and the Working Class, 1863–1894." *Labor History* 35 (Spring 1994): 187–215.

Letwin, Daniel. *The Challenge of Interracial Unionism: Alabama Coal Miners, 1878–1921.* Chapel Hill: University of North Carolina Press, 1998.

Levine, Lawrence. *Black Culture and Black Consciousness: Afro-American Folk Thought from Slavery to Freedom.* New York: Oxford University Press, 1977.

Levine, Susan. *Labor's True Woman: Carpet Weavers, Industrialization, and Labor Reform in the Gilded Age.* Philadelphia: Temple University Press, 1984.

Licht, Walter. *Working for the Railroad.* Princeton: Princeton University Press, 1983.

Lightner, David L. *Labor on the Illinois Central Railroad, 1852–1900: The Evolution of an Industrial Environment.* New York: Arno Press, 1977.

Litwack, Leon F. *Been in the Storm So Long: The Aftermath of Slavery.* New York: Vintage Books, 1980.

———. *Trouble in Mind: Black Southerners in the Age of Jim Crow.* New York: Knopf, 1998.

Lomax, John A., and Alan Lomax, *American Ballads and Folk Songs.* 1934. Reprint, Mineola, NY: Dover Publications, 1994.

Mancini, Matthew J. *One Dies, Get Another: Convict Leasing in the American South, 1866–1928.* Columbia: University of South Carolina Press, 1996.

Masterson, V. V. *The Katy Railroad and the Last Frontier.* Columbia: University of Missouri Press, 1988.

McLaurin, Melton. *The Knights of Labor in the South.* Westport: Greenwood Press, 1978.

McMurry, Donald L. "Federation of the Railroad Brotherhoods, 1889–1894." *Industrial and Labor Relations Review* 7, no. 1 (October 1953): 73–92.

———. *The Great Burlington Strike of 1888: A Case History in Labor Relations.* 1956; New York: Russell & Russell, 1973.

———. "The Legal Ancestry of the Pullman Strike Injunctions," *Industrial and Labor Relations Review* 14, no. 2 (January 1961): 235–56.

Meinig, David W. *Imperial Texas: An Interpretive Essay in Cultural Geography.* Austin: University of Texas Press, 1975.

Miskell, Louise, Christopher A. Whatley, and Bob Harris, eds. *Victorian Dundee: Image and Realities.* East Lothian, Scotland: Tuckwell Press, 2000.

Moneyhon, Carl H. *Arkansas and the New South, 1874–1929.* Fayetteville: University of Arkansas Press, 1997.

Morn, Frank. *Eye That Never Sleeps: A History of the Pinkerton National Detective Agency.* Bloomington: Indiana University Press, 1982.

Norwood, Stephen H. *Strikebreaking and Intimidation: Mercenaries and Masculinity in Twentieth-Century America.* Chapel Hill: University of North Carolina Press, 2002.

Orren, Karen. *Belated Feudalism: Labor, the Law, and Liberal Development in the United States.* Cambridge: Cambridge University Press, 1991.

Painter, Nell Irvin. *The Exodusters: Black Migration to Kansas after Reconstruction.* New York: Alfred A. Knopf, 1977.

———. *Standing at Armageddon: The United States, 1877–1919.* New York: W. W. Norton, 1987.

Payne, Darwin. *Dallas: An Illustrated History.* Woodland Hills, Cal.: Windson Publications, 1982.

Peck, Gunther. *Reinventing Free Labor: Padrones and Immigrant Workers in the North American West, 1880–1930.* Cambridge: Cambridge University Press, 2000.

———. "White Slavery and Whiteness: A Transnational View of the Sources of Working-Class Radicalism and Racism." *Labor: Studies in Working-Class History of the Americas* 1, no. 2 (Summer 2004): 41–63.

Phelan, Craig. *Grand Master Workman: Terence Powderly and the Knights of Labor.* Westport: Greenwood Press, 2000.

Poling-Kempes, Lesley. *The Harvey Girls: Women Who Opened the West.* New York: Paragon House, 1991.

Porter, Kenneth W. "Negro Labor in the Western Cattle Industry." *Labor History* 10 (Summer 1969): 346–74.

Porterfield, Nolan. *The Last Cavalier: The Life and Times of John A. Lomax, 1867–1948.* Urbana: University of Illinois Press, 1996.

Primm, James Neal. *Lion of the Valley, St. Louis, Missouri.* Boulder: Pruett Publishing Co., 1981.

Rachleff, Peter. *Black Labor in the South.* Philadelphia: Temple University Press, 1984.

Rhoads, Edward J. M. "The Chinese in Texas." *Southwestern Historical Quarterly* 81 (July 1977): 1–36.

Rodriquez, Alicia E. "Disfranchisement in Dallas: The Democratic Party and the Suppression of Independent Political Challenges in Dallas, Texas, 1891–1894," *Southwestern Historical Quarterly* 108, no. 1 (July 2004): 43–64.

Roediger, David. "Not Only the Ruling Classes to Overcome, But Also the So-called Mob: Class, Skill, and Community in the St. Louis General Strike of 1877." *Journal of Social History* 19 (Winter 1985): 213–40.

———. *The Wages of Whiteness: Race and the Making of the American Working Class.* New York: Verso, 1991.

Rogers, William Warren. "Negro Knights of Labor in Arkansas: A Case Study of the 'Miscellaneous' Strike." *Labor History* 10, no. 3 (Summer 1969): 498–505.

Salvatore, Nick. *Eugene V. Debs: Citizen and Socialist.* Chicago: University of Illinois Press, 1982.

Saxton, Alexander. *The Indispensable Enemy: Labor and the Anti-Chinese Movement in California.* Berkeley: University of California Press, 1971.

Schneirov, Richard, Shelton Stromquist, and Nick Salvatore, eds. *The Pullman Strike and the Crisis of the 1890s: Essays on Labor and Politics.* Urbana: University of Illinois Press, 1999.

Scott, Joan Wallach. *Gender and the Politics of History.* New York: Columbia University Press, 1988.

Sidbury, James. *Ploughshares into Swords: Race, Rebellion, and Identity in Gabriel's Virginia, 1730–1810.* New York: Cambridge University Press, 1997.

Smallwood, James. *Time of Hope, Time of Despair: Black Texans During Reconstruction.* New York: Kennikat Press, 1981.

Smith, Mark M. "Making Sense of Social History." *Journal of Social History* 37, no. 1, Special Issue (Autumn 2003): 165–86.

Smith, Robert Michael. *From Blackjacks to Briefcases: A History of Commercialized Strikebreaking and Unionbusting in the United States.* Athens: Ohio University Press, 2003.

Stowell, David O., ed. *The Great Strikes of 1877.* Urbana: University of Illinois Press, 2008.

———. *Streets, Railroads, and the Great Strike of 1877.* Chicago: University of Chicago Press, 1999.

Stromquist, Shelton. *A Generation of Boomers: The Pattern of Railroad Labor Conflict in Nineteenth-Century America.* Chicago: University of Illinois Press, 1987.

Taber, Thomas Townshend, comp. *Location of Historical Materials Concerning the Railroads in the State of Texas and Guide to Railroad Historical Resources, United States and Canada.* Muncy, Penn.: T. T. Taber III, 1993.

Taillon, Paul Michel. "'To Make Men out of Crude Material': Work Culture, Manhood, and Unionism in the Railroad Running Trades, c. 1870–1900." *In Boys and Their Toys? Masculinity, Technology, and Class in America.* Edited by Roger Horowitz. New York: Routledge, 2001.

———. "'What We Want is Good, Sober Men': Masculinity, Respectability, and Temperance in the Railroad Brotherhoods, c. 1870–1910." *Journal of Social History* 36, no. 2 (2002): 319–38.

Tosh, John. *The Pursuit of History.* London: Pearson Education Limited, 2002.

Trotter, Joe William Jr. "African-American Workers: New Directions in US Labor Historiography." *Labor History* 35 (Fall 1994): 495–523.

Walker, David R. *Penology for Profit: A History of the Texas Prison System, 1867–1912.* College Station: Texas A&M University Press, 1988.

Ward, James A. *The Railroads and the Character of America,* 1820–1887. Knoxville: University of Tennessee Press, 1986.

Ware, Norman. *The Labor Movement in the United States, 1860–1890: A Study in Democracy.* New York: Vintage Books, 1964.

Way, Peter. *Common Labour: Workers and the Digging of North American Canals, 1780–1860.* New York: Cambridge University Press, 1993.

Weir, Robert E. *Beyond Labor's Veil: The Culture of the Knights of Labor.* University Park: Pennsylvania State University Press, 1996.

Williams, Brett. *John Henry: A Bio-Bibliography.* Westport: Greenwood Press, 1983.

Young, Earle B. *Tracks to the Sea: Galveston and Western Railroad Development, 1866–1900.* College Station: Texas A&M University Press, 1999.

Yung, Judy. *Chinese Women of America: A Pictorial History.* Seattle: University of Washington Press, 1986.

Zamora, Emilio. *The World of the Mexican Worker in Texas.* College Station: Texas A&M University Press, 1993.

Dissertations and Unpublished Papers

Briggs, Alton King. "The Archeology of 1882 Labor Camps on the Southern Pacific Railroad, Val Verde County, Texas." Master's thesis, University of Texas at Austin, 1974.

Chandler, Jerry Wayne. "The Knights of Labor and the Southwestern Strikes." Master's thesis, Florida State University, 1970.

Farrington, Cliff. "The Galveston Waterfront and Organized Labor, 1866–1900." Master's thesis, University of Texas at Austin, 1997.

Forsythe, Edwin James. "The Gould Strikes and Missouri Newspaper Opinion." Master's thesis, University of Missouri, 1949.

Garcilazo, Jeffrey Marcos. "Traqueros: Mexican Railroad Workers in the United States, 1870–1920." PhD diss., University of Utah, 1995.

Rodriquez, Alicia E. "Urban Populism: Challenges to Democratic Party Control in Dallas, Texas: 1887–1900." PhD diss., University of California, Santa Barbara, 1998.

Rossen, Trevor. "Building a New South: The Crisis of Labor in Harrison County, Texas, 1878–1886." Undergraduate research paper, University of Texas at Austin. Photocopy.

Taillon, Paul Michel. "Culture, Politics, and the Making of the Railroad Brotherhoods, 1863–1916." PhD diss., University of Wisconsin at Madison, 1997.

Index

ISBN-13: 978-1-60344-170-4
ISBN-10: 1-60344-170-0